Public Relations and Social The

Public Relations and Social Theory broadens the theoretical scope of public relations through its application of the works of prominent social theorists to the study of public relations. The volume focuses on the work of key social theorists, including Jürgen Habermas, Niklas Luhmann, Michel Foucault, Ulrich Beck, Pierre Bourdieu, Anthony Giddens, Robert Putnam, Erving Goffman, Peter L. Berger, Gayatri Chakravorty Spivak, Bruno Latour, Leon Mayhew, Dorothy Smith and Max Weber. Unique in its approach, the collection demonstrates how the theories of these scholars come to bear on the understanding of public relations as a social activity. Understanding public relations in its societal context entails a focus on such concepts as trust, legitimacy, understanding, and reflection, as well as on issues of power, behavior, and language.

Each chapter is devoted to an individual theorist, providing an overview of that theorist's key concepts and contributions, and exploring how these concepts can be applied to public relations as a practice. Each chapter also includes a box giving a short and concise presentation of the theorist, along with recommendation of key works and secondary literature.

Overall, this volume will enhance understanding of theories and their applications in public relations, expanding the breadth and depth of the theoretic foundations of public relations. It will be of great interest to scholars and graduate students in public relations and strategic communication.

Communication Series
Jennings Bryant/Dolf Zillmann, General Editors

Selected Titles in Public Relations (James Grunig, Advisory Editor) include:

Strategic Public Relations Management
Planning and Managing Effective Communication Programs, Second Edition
Austin/Pinkleton

Gaining Influence in Public Relations
The Role of Resistance in Practice
Berger/Reber

Public Relations Theory II
Botan/Hazleton

Manager's Guide to Excellence in Public Relations and Communication Management
Dozier/Grunig/Grunig

Crisis Communications
A Casebook Approach, Third Edition
Fearn-Banks

Excellence in Public Relations and Communication Management
Grunig

Applied Public Relations
Cases in Stakeholder Management
Lamb/McKee

The Crisis Manager
Facing Risk and Responsibility
Lerbinger

The Future of Excellence in Public Relations and Communication Management
Challenges for the Next Generation
Toth

Public Relations and Social Theory

Key Figures and Concepts

Edited by

Øyvind Ihlen
Betteke van Ruler
Magnus Fredriksson

Routledge
Taylor & Francis Group

NEW YORK AND LONDON

First published 2009
by Routledge
711 Third Avenue, New York, NY 10017

Simultaneously published in the UK
by Routledge
2 Park Square, Milton Park, Abingdon, Oxon OX14 4RN

Routledge is an imprint of the Taylor & Francis Group, an informa business

© 2009 Taylor & Francis

Typeset in Baskerville and Gill Sans by EvS Communication Networx, Inc.

Library of Congress Cataloging in Publication Data
Public Relations and Social Theory / [edited] by Øyvind Ihlen, Magnus Fredriksson, and Betteke van Ruler.
p. cm. — (Communication series)
1. Public relations—Evaluation. 2. Public relations—Research. 3. Social sciences—Philosophy. 4. Social scientists. I. Ihlen, Øyvind. II. Ruler, Betteke van, 1948– III. Fredriksson, Magnus.
HM1221.S63 2009
659.201—dc22
2008031606

ISBN10 HB: 0-415-99785-2
ISBN10 PB: 0-415-99786-0
ISBN10 EB: 0-203-88323-3

ISBN13 HB: 978-0-415-99785-0
ISBN13 PB: 978-0-415-99786-7
ISBN13 EB: 978-0-203-88323-5

Contents

Preface   vii

1 Introduction: Applying Social Theory to Public Relations   1
   ØYVIND IHLEN AND BETTEKE VAN RULER

2 On Beck: Risk and Subpolitics in Reflexive Modernity   21
   MAGNUS FREDRIKSSON

3 On Berger: A Social Constructionist Perspective on Public
   Relations and Crisis Communication   43
   MATS HEIDE

4 On Bourdieu: Public Relations in Field Struggles   62
   ØYVIND IHLEN

5 On Foucault: A Toolbox for Public Relations   83
   JUDY MOTION AND SHIRLEY LEITCH

6 On Giddens: Interpreting Public Relations through Anthony
   Giddens's Structuration and Late Modernity Theory   103
   JESPER FALKHEIMER

7 On Goffman: Researching Relations with Erving Goffman as
   Pathfinder   119
   CATRIN JOHANSSON

8 On Habermas: Understanding and Public Relations   141
   ROLAND BURKART

9   On Latour: Actor-Network-Theory (ANT) and Public
    Relations   166
    PIET VERHOEVEN

10 On Luhmann: Contingency, Risk, Trust, and Reflection   187
    SUSANNE HOLMSTRÖM

11 On Mayhew: The Demonization of Soft Power and the
    Validation of the New Citizen   212
    RICHARD C. STANTON

12 On Putnam: Bowling Together—Applying Putnam's Theories
    of Community and Social Capital to Public Relations   231
    VILMA LUOMA-AHO

13 On Feminist Theory of Public Relations: An Example from
    Dorothy E. Smith   252
    LANA F. RAKOW AND DIANA IULIA NASTASIA

14 On Spivak: Theorizing Resistance—Applying Gayatri
    Chakravorty Spivak in Public Relations   278
    MOHAN JYOTI DUTTA

15 On Weber: Legitimacy and Legitimation in Public Relations   301
    ARILD WÆRAAS

16 Conclusions on the Domain, Context, Concepts, Issues, and
    Empirical Avenues of Public Relations   323
    ØYVIND IHLEN AND PIET VERHOEVEN

17 Commentary: Linking Sociology with Public Relations—
    Some Critical Reflections in Reflexive Times   341
    GÜNTER BENTELE AND STEFAN WEHMEIER

    Contributors   363
    Index   369

Preface

Øyvind Ihlen, Betteke van Ruler, Magnus Fredriksson

The idea for this edited volume originated with Magnus Fredriksson in 2003. At that time, we felt rather unhappy with the development of theory within the field of public relations. Or to be more specific, we felt that the instrumental bias in public relations was too limiting. So long as public relations is a powerful source of influence in society, why are there so few attempts to study this social activity in its own right? At a meeting between Scandinavian public relations scholars, we began to discuss how many of us were using different social theorists in our work and how it would be fun to pull our experience together and offer it to colleagues and students. Our original idea was that an edited volume would be set against the backdrop of the peculiar social democratic tradition of Scandinavia. Observant readers will also note how Scandinavian scholars are well represented amongst the contributors. Soon, however, it dawned on us that the project would benefit from engaging with scholars from other regions as well. We are very pleased that the list of contributors now represents scholars working in a wide range of countries: Austria, Australia, Denmark, Finland, Germany, the Netherlands, Norway, Sweden, and the United States.

The social theorists that are presented and discussed throughout the book were chosen based on a very simple principle: If a public relations scholar has used a particular social theorist, let's hear about it! We have looked high and low for contributors, and issued several invitations. We are happy to say that most of these were accepted and nearly all solicited manuscripts survived three anonymous reviews. Hence, the book you are reading contains chapters on theorists whose work belongs to various categories of such fields as functionalism, postmodernism, constructionism, social constructionism, poststructuralism, feminism, or postcolonialism. Some of the theorists are classical sociologists, whereas others belong in the broader category of social theory. Some are deceased; some are still very much with us. Some are frequently cited within public relations studies, others may be new to public relations scholars.

The project made progress when several of us were involved in preparing a successful preconference on "Prominent Social Theorists and Their Significance for Public Relations," at the 56th Annual Conference of the International Communication Association, June 2006, in Dresden, Germany. One result of this conference was the invitation to edit a special issue of *Public Relations Review* that was published in Fall 2007. This issue contains shorter versions of some of the chapters in the present book. At this time Betteke van Ruler also joined the editorial team.

We as editors would like to extend a big thank you to all the contributors for their input and patience. Some of the authors prepared their first drafts as far back as 2005. We also want to thank Pete Smudde, Carl Botan, and Krishnamurthy Sriramesh for help along the way, as well as James E. Grunig and the two anonymous project reviewers for their very generous remarks and useful comments. Special thanks are also due to senior editor Linda Bathgate for believing in the project and making it a Routledge publication.

Chapter 1

Introduction

Applying Social Theory to Public Relations[1]

Øyvind Ihlen and Betteke van Ruler

Abstract

Public relations is often studied from a managerial, instrumental perspective. However, to understand its role in building trust or creating mistrust and in developing—or destroying—a company's license to operate, public relations also needs to be studied as a social phenomenon. With this book, we attempt to broaden the theoretical scope of public relations studies by applying the work of a group of prominent social theorists. What can be culled from the perspectives of these scholars? We suggest that insights can be garnered for public relations studies at the macro-, meso-, and microlevels. In other words, social theory can help us to make sense of public relations at the societal, organizational, and individual levels. This introductory chapter locates our project in the scientific landscape of social theory and sociology.

Contemporary everyday life is influenced by increased complexity, rapid change, globalization, and the deconstruction of social structures. As a result, corporations and other organizations today have a greater need to build relationships with their stakeholders and to communicate with them about their aims and behavior. In this interaction, it becomes essential to offer answers to such questions as "Who are we?" "What are our goals?" and "How should we act to reach our goals?" This not only gives public relations new frames of reference, but also gives it a much more prominent position in the management of organizations. Corporations increasingly tend to see public relations as a senior management function, and a wider range of organizations have started to utilize public relations. The public relations consultancy industry is indeed thriving.

With this boost in the prominence of public relations, we argue that its practice needs to be understood in relationship to societal (macro), organizational (meso), and individual (micro) properties. Emerging from this, we also argue that there is a need to integrate social theory and sociology (we often use the terms interchangeably, although the former may be said to be a broader term) as dimensions of public relations research. We intend to apply social theory, which can be understood as the "effective effort by communities of scholars to make sense of their social world" (Baran & Davis, 2000, p. 4).

In this introduction, we first discuss the necessity of making the methodological (in its widest sense) roots of research explicit and then argue for pluralistic studies of public relations and against intellectual isolationism. We then briefly discuss the current schools of thought in public relations research and argue that a focus on the societal level has largely been neglected. After this, we take a brief look at how public relations has been described in social theory and then provide a general overview of the way in which public relations scholars have used it. A short discussion of some of the concepts that permeate many of the approaches in this book follows, and we collectively set these concepts apart from many of the prevailing theories in the field. The chapter ends with a presentation of the structure of the book.

How Public Relations Works

The purpose of research is to build theories to solve the problems that researchers face in a particular domain (Littlejohn, 1995). The core questions for every public relations researcher are how does public relations work and what does it do in, to, and for organizations, publics, or the public arena, in other words, society as a whole. The answers to these questions depend on the methodologies that the researcher uses. Here, methodologies are understood as a combination of deontological principles, schools of theoretical thought, and accompanying methods. Behind this combination stands the "personal biography of the researcher: he or she approaches the world with a set of ideas, a framework (theory, ontology) that specifies a set of questions (epistemology, analysis)" (Denzin & Lincoln, 2000, pp. 18–19). In addition, the use of methodologies is influenced by social factors, such as the attitudes that prevail in the research collective and among those financing the research.

Whether they are predefined by a particular Weltanschauung or constructed by the researcher's peer group (Sallot, Lyon, Acosta-Alzuru, & Jones, 2003), several scholars have pointed out that our understandings of phenomena are built on certain underlying philosophical assumptions. Although public relations can be seen as a scientific discipline in its own right, with specialized journals, professional and scholarly associations, and a network of collaborative relationships (Botan & Taylor, 2004), every public relations researcher has his or her own deontological background and disciplinary roots. These provide particular perspectives. Consequently, a researcher's methodological roots heavily influence his or her perspective on what public relations is, how it works, and how it should be researched. This is why it is important to make these roots explicit. We do not believe that it is possible to rid oneself of philosophical assumptions and become an "objective" researcher. At most, we can hope to reflect openly about the norms and structures that influence us, check for alternative explanations, allow for additional explanatory factors, and be careful not to overstate our research findings.

This book provides an overview of how public relations scholars use social theorists to develop research questions about how public relations works and, consequently, construct typical socially oriented public relations approaches. Contrary to most public relations approaches, a socially oriented view is not oriented toward management problems, but rather toward the relationship that public relations has with the societies in which it is produced and with the social systems it coproduces. However, we argue that sociological approaches to public relations can also give meaning to practices at the mesolevel of organizations and the microlevel of individual practitioners. Thus, many of the contributors to this book also point to some of the practical implications of the theoretical insights on offer.

Perspectives on Public Relations

It is obvious that public relations theory can be and, in fact, is rooted in a number of disciplinary fields, such as mass communications, interpersonal/speech communications, (social) psychology, economics, and sociology, and in different schools of thought, such as functionalism, constructivism, feminism, Marxism, or cultural theories. Some may see this as a curse because they may believe that it can lead to confusion about the nature of public relations or what it can be. Ledingham (2003), for example, prefers one general theory of public relations—relationship management theory—and sees this as an appropriate framework for its study, teaching, and practice. He locates his approach in the fields of management and interpersonal communication theory.

Despite such calls to produce one general theory of public relations, there seems to be growing interest among public relations scholars for differentiation in methodology (in the wider sense of the word). Over the past few years, the major U.S. journals in the field, the *Journal of Public Relations Research* and *Public Relations Review*, have published a growing number of articles with alternative methodological approaches. The *Journal of Public Relations Research* also produced a special issue on alternative paradigms in public relations (2005), with the somewhat unfortunate title of "Public Relations from the Margins." If one adopts a multiparadigmatic perspective, then one cannot defend the existence of one mainstream and several marginal approaches. In such a view, there are only more suitable and less suitable approaches. We would like to challenge our readers to review the chapters of this book to determine the suitability for public relations of the concepts presented. You may look for commonalities or differences between the perspectives suggested and existing public relations theories, and you are bound to find both. We agree with McKie (2001), who criticized the discipline for its intellectual isolation. This is why we prefer to see the multiparadigmatic approach as a blessing. It provides a rich source of ideas and insights into an elusive area of organizational and social life. As Stacks (2002) notes: "[I]t is wrong to believe that one methodology is better than the other. Each methodology has advantages and disadvantages" (p. 5). We also believe that it can be seen as a sign of maturity for a discipline to contain different, comparative schools of thought and to rest on different theoretical foundations (i.e., Botan & Hazelton Jr., 2006). As Szmatka and Lovaglia (1997) stated, a broad range of paradigms and research methods contributes to the growth of a knowledge field.

Methodologies in Use

As an area of systematic scholarly inquiry, public relations is a relative newcomer. When Grunig and Hickson (1976) took stock of the academic research on public relations, they concluded that there was little theory to be found. A similar conclusion was reached by Mary Ann Ferguson in 1984 (as cited in Sallot et al., 2003). Sallot et al. (2003) duplicated her research and found that public relations has become a much richer field theoretically than it was in its early days. Botan and Taylor (2004) came to the same conclusion:

> Over the last 20 years public relations has evolved into a major area of applied communication based in research of significant quantity and quality. Public relations has become much more than just a corporate communication practice. Rather, it is a theoretically grounded and research based area that has the potential to unify a variety of applied communication areas. (p. 659)

Botan and Hazleton (2006) state in their book *Public Relations Theory II* that "a leading body of work has developed around Symmetry/Excellence Theory, which has probably done more to develop public relations theory and scholarship than any other single school of thought" (p. 6). Earlier, Botan and Taylor (2004) argued that the most striking trend in public relations has been the movement from a functionalist to a cocreational perspective, focusing on publics as cocreators of meaning and emphasizing the building of relationships with all publics. According to Toth (1992), the scholarly field of public relations can be divided into rhetorical, critical and systems approaches. Van Ruler and Verčič (2005) claimed that most public relations theory can be placed under the headings of two axes, one defined by communication approaches and the other by organizational and management approaches. They also identified four models of public relations—informational, persuasive, relational, and discursive—that are rooted in information processing theory/functionalistic mass communication theory, social psychology, interpersonal communication and consensus building theory, and speech communication and rhetoric, respectively.

As to whether there are one or more prevailing schools of thought in use, Vasquez and Taylor (2000) stated: "Many different definitions of public relations have been offered, but it is generally accepted that public relations is strategic communication between an organization and its publics" (p. 324). Indeed, contemporary public relations theories mainly focus on management/the organization as one actor in the public relations process and the publics/target groups/stakeholders/contributors as the other actors. There are some exceptions. Dozier and Lauzen (2000) argued that public relations should not be obedient to management, but should take a more distant stance. Their basic point was that scholarship should not be too tightly linked to the social institution it studies because this leads to a loss of or a preoccupation with only one perspective. We argue that the instrumental and administrative approaches that currently prevail must be supplemented with societal approaches that expose what public relations is in society today, rather than only what it should be at the organizational level. Such a "warts and all" approach ultimately questions the role of public relations and the sometimes uncritical presentation found in many textbooks that public relations is an ever-evolving and positive social force (Duffy, 2000).

Stanley Deetz (2001) has written about the so-called dissensus-oriented approaches in organizational communication that do not have as one of their chief aims the construction of better practice. Dissensus approaches try to disrupt the prevailing discourse and provide either "forums for and modes of discussion to aid in the building of more open consensus" or "show the partiality (the incompletion and one-sidedness) of reality and the hidden points of resistance and complexity" (Deetz, 2001, pp. 26–31). Such a pluralistic perspective attempts to address issues of partiality and power, instead of being linked to the social institution it studies through a conflation of normative and descriptive perspectives.

A nonmanagerial perspective was also the basis for Olasky's alternative exposition of U.S. public relations history, especially in his differentiation between "public" and "private" relations. Referring to the sociologist Habermas, Olasky (1989) claimed that public relations practitioners and academics should approach organizations from a "public" perspective because they are concerned with phenomena of reflectivity (of organizational behavior) and societal legitimacy.

Most public relations theorists, however, are concerned with the relationship between an organization and its publics and not so much with the problem of how an organization relates itself to the public arena and to society at large. Many of the prominent theories in the field have been developed from (social-) psychological, systems, or rhetorical perspectives of communication management, and most perceive a relationship between organizations (management) and certain individuals or groups of individuals. In most of these approaches, the societal level is rather overlooked. Consequently, they are insufficient to cope with societal issues or the societal legitimation of organizations. In most sociological approaches, legitimacy is neither a moral nor an ethical deontological principle, but rather it is related to the empirical issue of what is good and justifiable for (the members of) society: "The legitimacy of an organization is a measure of the extent to which the public and the public sphere at a given time and place find the organization sensible and morally justifiable" (Nielsen, 2001, p. 19). This is why sociological approaches to public relations provide many more empirical than normative theories.

Public Relations in Social Theory

Media sociologists have focused on the relationship between organizations as sources and the media (e.g., Cottle, 2003; Davis, 2002; Schlesinger, 1990). Issues of power and resources and the ability to gain favorable media coverage have been the important focus of such research (see the chapter on Bourdieu in this volume). However, media relations are but one part of public relations, and public relations as a practice has received remarkably scant attention in the field of social theory and sociology. Exceptions do of course exist, among which are Boorstin (1962/1992), Habermas (1989), and Mayhew (1997).

With his landmark book *The Image: A Guide to Pseudo-Events in America*, Daniel J. Boorstin (1962/1992) coined the term *pseudoevent* to describe events that only exist to create publicity. Boorstin saw the flourishing of such events as marking a shift in American culture: everything was now staged, "packaged," and scripted for publicity. Looking at the practice of Edward L. Bernays, Boorstin described how a hotel gained publicity by staging a jubilee celebration, rather than making changes to its "product" as such. The question had changed from "is this correct," to "does this have news value"? The images or illusions created by such pseudoevents often bear no relationship to reality. For Boorstin, it was exactly this "menace of unreality" that threatened contemporary society. In other words, Boorstin probably wrote one of the first critical academic accounts of the influence of public relations in society.

The German thinker Jürgen Habermas also paid some attention to public relations, although perhaps mostly in passing. Habermas is probably best known for his theory of "the public sphere" (see the chapter on Habermas in this volume). In brief, the public sphere constitutes that societal arena in which citizens convene and discuss social problems freely. This public sphere forms a new basis for authority, with a consensus rooted in open-ended, rational, and critical argumentation and debate (Habermas, 1962/1989). In his highly acclaimed book *The Structural Transformation of the Public Sphere*, which was originally published in German in 1962, Habermas denounced public relations for undermining the critical public sphere by cultivating a consensus that is not based on rationality or good arguments, but rather on the ability to portray oneself as having the public interest in mind while hiding one's real business intentions:

> [Public relations] mobilizes for the firm or branch or for an entire system a quasi-political credit, a respect of the kind one displays toward public authority. The resulting consensus, of course, does not seriously have much in common with the final unanimity wrought by a time-consuming process of mutual enlightenment, for the "general interest" on the basis of which alone a rational agreement between publicly competing opinions could freely be reached has disappeared precisely to the extent that the [public relations practitioner's] self-presentations of privileged private interests have adopted it for themselves…. For the criteria of rationality are completely lacking in a consensus created by sophisticated opinion-molding services under the aegis of a sham public interest. (Habermas, 1962/1989, pp. 193–195)

The public sphere that is encouraged by public relations is one in which the public is supposed to fulfill its role by applauding decisions, rather than voicing critiques or engaging in discussion. This public sphere is unfolding in *front* of the audience, rather than *among* it, and it has become impossible to separate what serves private interests from what serves the public interest. Habermas's accusation is that the goal of the public sphere is no longer debate, but rather the furthering of special interests.

Apparently, however, he has changed his view somewhat since the original publication of the aforementioned book. Bentele and Wehmeier (2007) have commented that: "As far as we can see, Habermas revised his originally highly critical point of view concerning public relations and understands—to mention one example—lobbyists in their societal function parallel to politicians or actors of the civil society" (p. 295).

Other social theorists, however, have taken up Habermas's critique, most notably perhaps Leon Mayhew (1997). Mayhew too argued that professional communicators such as public relations practitioners are dominating the public sphere, that they have a grasp of what people believe and want and how they can be manipulated. What is described as "public opinion" is increasingly the result of marketing research that allows professional communicators to push the right buttons. This is what he has called *The New Public* in a book of the same name (see chapter 11, this volume).

The negative picture of public relations painted by these theorists has not stopped public relations scholars from attempting to use social theory. A few have aimed to extend these criticisms, but many have also attempted to improve practice with the help of insights from social theory.

Social Theory in Public Relations

This book is certainly not the first attempt to bring social theories to bear upon public relations. Sociological approaches seem to be relatively frequently used in such countries as Germany, Denmark, and New Zealand, and some U.S. academics have also applied or extended the framework or concepts of social theory. In Britain, such scholars as L'Etang and Pieczka have written from the perspective of the sociology of professions (L'Etang, 2004; Pieczka, 2000, 2002; Pieczka & L'Etang, 2001), but also from critical theory (L'Etang & Pieczka, 1996, 2006). Their publication of *Critical Perspectives in Public Relations* in 1996 marked a watershed for non-instrumental-oriented studies of public relations. The 1992 collection *Rhetorical and Critical Perspectives on Public Relations* also contained essays with a critical bent (Toth & Heath, 1992). Others too have been interested in the related dimension of power (e.g., Berger, 2005; Cottle, 2003; Courtright & Smudde, 2007; Edwards, 2006; Plowman, 1998; Weaver, Motion, & Roper, 2006).

Scholars have used a range of perspectives from social theory, for instance, postmodernism (e.g., Holtzhausen, 2000, 2002; Holtzhausen & Voto, 2002; McKie & Munshi, 2007; Mickey, 1997); feminism (e.g., Aldoory, 1998; L. A. Grunig & Hon, 2001; O'Neil, 2003; Toth, 2001); constructivism (e.g., Merten, 2004); communitarianism (e.g., Hallahan, 2004; Kruckeberg & Starck, 1988; Leeper, 2001; Starck & Kruckeberg, 2001); cultural theory (e.g., Banks, 1995; Leichty, 2003; Leichty & Warner, 2001); critical theory (e.g., Moffitt, 1992); postcolonial theory (e.g., Dutta-Bergman, 2005; McKie & Munshi, 2007; Munshi & Kurian, 2005); and structuration theory (e.g., Durham, 2005).

The theorist who has probably received the most attention is Habermas, in particular his work on the public sphere, but also his discussion of discourse ethics (e.g., Burkart, 2004; Jensen, 2001; Leeper, 1996; Maier, 2005; Meisenbach, 2005; Olasky, 1989; Pearson, 1989a, 1989b, 1990). However, public relations scholars have also been accused of misusing Habermas's work because the strategic intention of public relations puts it at odds with the ideals of communicative action, of yielding to a better argument that serves the public interest (Benson, 2008; Mayhew, 1997; Holmström, 1997). Furthermore, it is often argued that the way in which public relations is actually practiced is a far cry from the Habermasian ideals put forward in textbooks on public relations (Moloney, 2000, 2005).

The work of Niklas Luhmann has also been popular among public relations academics in the German-speaking world and in Denmark (e.g., Geist, 2001; Holmström, 1997, 2004; Merten, 2004; Ronneberger & Rühl, 1992). Public relations activities have also been analyzed using Foucault's discourse theory (e.g., Livesey, 2002; Motion, 1997; Motion & Weaver, 2005) and Bourdieu's field theory (e.g., Edwards, 2006, 2007; Ihlen, 2004, 2005).

The present volume takes stock of several of these perspectives and approaches to the study of public relations and, in the process, deals with such themes and keywords as reflexivity, legitimacy, power, resources, actor/agency, agent/system, reflectiveness, late modernity, inequality, subalterness, and social capital, to mention but a few. Of particular importance are the concepts of publics, the public, and the public sphere, which we dwell on briefly in the following section to clarify the aim of this book.

Publics, Public, and the Public Sphere

The German communications scholar Kückelhaus (1998) described three approaches to public relations: product-oriented, marketing-oriented, and societally (sociologically) oriented. As van Ruler (2004) pointed out, product orientation can be likened to a one-way emission model of public relations (called "the publicity model" by J. E. Grunig & Hunt, 1984), whereas a marketing orientation can be equated with Grunig's asymmetrical two-way model (J. E. Grunig, 2001). However, the societal perspective cannot be equated with Grunig's other model, the two-way symmetrical model, because this perspective uses the society as a whole as a unit of analysis and considers its social structure and institutions to be the basis and outcome of public relations. This implies that the main interest is not the corporation or organization itself, but rather its place in society as a whole (i.e., in the social structure). In this respect, society is seen from the perspective of what in German is called

Öffentlichkeit ("in public"). *Öffentlichkeit* does not mean "the public" as in publics or audiences, but rather "publicly," as in "what is potentially known to and can be debated by all" (Hollander, 1988, p. 88) and "public sphere," which can be defined as "a space for communication, which in principle is available to all." Certain rules apply in this communication space, which is characterized by certain structures (Raupp, 2004). *Öffentlichkeit* is an outcome, and therefore it is a quality of the public communication system in the society (Ronneberger & Rühl, 1992). Journalism, advertising, and public relations all play a role in developing or destroying the quality of this public communication system. Consequently, the public sphere cannot be seen as the aggregation of individual views (see Price, 1992), but rather as having a dynamic of its own and thus creating a symbolic reality. The moment an organization brings out a certain message, it produces a certain component of the public sphere by presenting meaning and constructing frames in the public debate. Although we agree with Grunig that public relations should not be thought of only as communication and that it also has something to do with the *behavior* of organizations (J. E. Grunig, 1993), we concur that the creation of meaning is a crucial activity of organizations.

The Concept of Meaning

An essential aspect of a sociological perspective on public relations is its concern with issues and values that are publicly relevant and publicly debated, in other words, issues that relate to the "public sphere," as Jensen (2000) argues. Also, in most sociological approaches to public relations, the public sphere is seen as a social construction of mankind. Ihlen (2004), for example, combines the rhetorical approach with the sociological approach and shows the way in which public relations constitutes the struggle of actors in a public battlefield of meanings, thereby contributing to "the" public meaning, or, in other words, to social reality. In these sociological approaches, public relations serves the same kind of (democratic or antidemocratic) function as journalism does; both contribute to the free or controlled flow of information and its meanings and to the development of the public sphere in size ("How many people are involved in public life?"), level ("What is the level at which we discuss public matters?"), and quality ("What are the frames used in the debates?"). This echoes what Carey (1975) called a cultural approach to communication (communication produces cultural identity). In many European countries, theory building in public relations is closely related to journalism, not only because its practitioners deal with journalists and influence media content, but also because of their overlapping functions in society.

In the premodern societal setting, values and norms were concrete and fundamental, even if their truths were not necessarily taken for granted (Zijderveld, 2000). They were institutionally fixed and closed to reflection and relativization. In the modern world, society is institutionally pluralistic, humanly individualistic, and culturally generalized; that is, the situation is reversed, and this allows for the empirical foundation of a constructionist view of society. Although constructionism is rooted in continental European sociology, it is certainly not a typical European perspective. It was John Dewey in 1916 who argued that society is not only maintained by communication, but also constituted by it (cited in Kückelhaus, 1998). The basic premise of a sociologically constructivist approach to public relations is that human beings reflect the other to themselves and social reality in a dynamic process (Bentele, 1997). Hence, constructing social reality is a shared process of meaning construction (Bentele & Rühl, 1993). In this view, reflective interpretation and the conceptualization of meaning are at the forefront in a constant process of de- and reconstruction (Nistelrooij, 2000); they are a "reflection." Krippendorf (1994), a constructionist communication scientist, discussed the "recursiveness" of communication: it is an ongoing social process of the de- and reconstruction of interpretations. This is why Faulstieg (1992) and other constructionist public relations scholars state that public relations is not so much interaction between human beings, but rather societal action.

Van Ruler and Verčič (2005) proposed viewing a sociologically oriented approach to public relations not so much as an alternative but as a macroview, one that is additional to the meso(management-oriented) and micro(people-oriented) views. Public relations as an academic discipline needs an understanding of how the public relations function works and how it is influenced by and influences social structures. Such research endeavors have an obvious and legitimate role in themselves, and they cannot rest merely upon the obligation to point to ideal practices before or after criticizing current practices. It is time to gain a better grasp of how public relations works in society. Along the way, knowledge that has implications for practice, that is, for public relations at the meso- and microlevels, may also be gained.

Structure of the Book

Each of the following chapters contains an overview and a presentation of a chosen theorist's key concepts, followed by a discussion of how the insights of these concepts can be applied to public relations theory. Most of the chapters also point to the relevance for public relations practice in one way or another, although they vary in the extent to which they address this. Some of the contributors propose elaborate models using insights from "their" theorist as raw material, whereas others mainly point out and briefly illustrate the potential that certain of "their" theorist's concepts have for public relations. Some stick closely to the sources; others use these mainly as a springboard for their own thoughts. We encourage our readers to consult the boxes in each chapter that present short biographies of the presented theorists and pointers to their major works and the secondary literature, where available.

Rather than attempt to impose or construct a hierarchy of importance or popularity, we opted to put the chapters in alphabetical order. Thus, the volume begins with a chapter on Ulrich Beck written by Magnus Fredriksson (of the University of Gothenburg). Fredriksson uses Beck's work to point to the centrality of responsibility in current discourses and to the way in which public relations is seen to (re)present organizations or loosely coupled networks and to serve up arguments for their outlooks and negotiate their responsibilities, but also to manipulate facts to serve their interests.

Next, Mats Heide (Lund University, Helsingborg) draws on the work of Peter L. Berger to discuss crisis and public relations. Heide argues that the social constructionism advocated by Berger and his colleague Thomas Luckmann helps us to remember that crisis is not necessarily an "objective" phenomenon that hits an organization.

In chapter 4, Øyvind Ihlen (University of Oslo) suggests that the work of Pierre Bourdieu is useful to the study of the power struggle that organizations engage in with the help of public relations. This, it is argued, affords public relations research with a much more realistic view, based on a conflict model, than is on offer in the many normative theories of the field.

This interest in the study of power can also be seen in the chapter on Michel Foucault that follows. Judy Motion and Shirley Leitch (both from the University of Wollongong) discuss how Foucauldian theory can help public relations theory move toward an understanding of public relations as a discourse practice with effects on power.

In chapter 6, Jesper Falkheimer (Lund University, Helsingborg) presents the work of Anthony Giddens and uses it as a lens to show how public relations has developed in a sociohistorical context. Falkheimer contends that a Giddens perspective might constitute a "third way public relations perspective": one that lies between managerial, functionalistic, and prescriptive traditions and between critical and interpretative approaches.

Catrin Johansson (Mid-Sweden University) treats us to the work of another classic theorist, Erving Goffman. Johansson argues that Goffman helps us to understand how communication at the interpersonal level has important implications for public relations. Goffman was also the first sociologist to discuss framing, a concept that has become extremely popular within media studies and that has begun to make inroads into public relations. Other relevant Goffman concepts include impression management, footing, and face, which are also explored in this chapter.

In chapter 8, Roland Burkart (Vienna University) applies and extends the work of Jürgen Habermas in relation to the concept of *understanding* as it is found in Habermas's work. Burkart presents a model for communication that addresses validity claims that are related to truth, trustworthiness, and legitimacy. Burkart maintains that all public relations practitioners should take these issues into account in their planning and communication in the four specific phases suggested by his model.

Chapter 9 is devoted to the French thinker Bruno Latour. Piet Verhoeven (University of Amsterdam) argues that Latour's so-called actor-network theory could be useful in analyzing how public relations practitioners conduct their work and how they play a role in the collective by constructing reality and shared definitions of the world.

Using Niklas Luhmann's systems perspective, Susanne Holmström (Roskilde University) points to the way in which public relations has helped organizations to move toward a so-called reflective paradigm, in which the organization realizes that its worldview and rationale is but one among many.

In chapter 11, Richard Stanton (University of Sydney) scrutinizes the writing of Leon Mayhew. Despite Mayhew's negative view of public relations, Stanton points to the way in which certain of Mayhew's ideas could in fact serve to build an ethical public relations practice, for instance, through mechanisms that help redeem the rhetorical tokens of influence.

Vilma Luoma-aho (University of Jyväskylä) shows how the writings of Robert Putnam have relevance to public relations through the concept of social capital. Putnam's insistence on the importance of maintaining a sense of community and his emphasis on the way in which social networks have long-term benefits can be transferred to public relations.

Partly in keeping with the spirit of this particular theoretical approach, and partly to remedy the fact that a long list of male theorists dominates this book, chapter 13 addresses a theoretical stream, namely feminist theory, as well as the work of an individual theorist. After an overview of work in this area, Lana F. Rakow and Diana Nastasia (both from the University of North Dakota) proceed to a discussion of the work of Dorothy Smith. They posit that feminist studies of public relations have been concerned with the lives of women in public relations rather than with public relations in the lives of women.

Although Western male theorists dominate the book, Mohan Jyoti Dutta (Purdue University) introduces Gayatri Chakravorty Spivak and discusses the work of this important postcolonial theorist on public relations. Using Spivak as a springboard, Dutta argues that the knowledge structures of public relations must be seen in relation to the politics of representation, power, and materiality. He points to the possibility that public relations can commit itself to emancipatory goals through an interrogation of the communicative practices that connect transnational corporations, nation states, and global structures.

In chapter 15, Arild Wæraas (University of Tromsø) uses the work of classic sociological theorist Max Weber to discuss the processes of legitimacy and legitimation and how they are important for public relations. Wæraas claims that these processes are at the very heart of what public relations is all about.

The book is then rounded off with conclusions drawn by Øyvind Ihlen (University of Oslo) and Piet Verhoeven (University of Amsterdam), who bring together the insights offered by the book's contributors. They present five conclusions that pertain to what can be seen as the domain of public relations studies, the context in which public relations ought to be studied, and the concepts, issues, and empirical avenues that follow from the two first conclusions.

The book concludes with a commentary in which Günter Bentele (University of Leipzig) and Stefan Wehmeier (University of Greifswald) take its contributors to task for their treatment of the social theorists presented. Bentele and Wehmeier call for public relations theorists to draw on the theories presented, and also to look further at concepts that have not been treated in this volume, to model public relations as a social system in society.

For practitioners, this book is meant to help them take a step back and reflect on their practice beyond day-to-day strategizing. For scholars, our hope is that these chapters can serve as inspiration. We hope they will take up some of the theories on offer, either by adopting the suggestions of our contributors or by adapting and modifying the insights presented. In the vast theoretical landscape that is social theory, there are also plenty of other theorists to choose from, and the potential for a second, expanded volume of this book is great. Nothing would please us more.

Note

1. A previous version of this chapter was published as: How public relations works: Theoretical roots and public relations perspectives, in *Public Relations Review, 33*(3), 2007.

References

Aldoory, L. (1998). The language of leadership for female public relations professionals. *Journal of Public Relations Research, 10*(2), 73–101.

Banks, S. (1995). *Multicultural public relations: A social-interpretive approach.* Thousand Oaks, CA: Sage.

Baran, S. J., & Davis, D. K. (2000). *Mass communication theory: Foundations, ferment, and future.* Belmont, CA: Wadsworth.

Benson, R. D. (2008, May). *Public relations in the public sphere: Habermas, Bourdieu, and the question of power.* Paper presented at the 58th Annual Conference of the International Communication Association, Montreal, Canada.

Bentele, G. (1997). Public relations and reality: A contribution to a theory of public relations. In D. Moss, T. MacManus, & D. Vercic (Eds.), *Public relations research: An international perspective* (pp. 89–109). London: International Thomson Business Press.

Bentele, G., & Rühl, M. (Eds.). (1993). *Theorien oeffentlicher Kommunikation* [Theories of public communication]. München, Germany: Ölschläger.

Bentele, G., & Wehmeier, S. (2007). Applying sociology to public relations: A commentary. *Public Relations Review, 33*(3), 294–300.

Berger, B. K. (2005). Power over, power with, and power to relations: Critical reflections on public relations, the dominant coalition, and activism. *Journal of Public Relations Research, 17*(1), 5–28.

Boorstin, D. J. (1992). *The image: A guide to pseudo-events in America.* New York: Vintage Books. (Originally published in 1962)

Botan, C. H., & Hazelton, V., Jr. (Eds.). (2006). *Public relations theory II.* Hillsdale, NJ: Erlbaum.

Botan, C. H., & Taylor, M. (2004). Public relations: State of the field. *Journal of Communication, 54*(4), 645–661.

Burkart, R. (2004). Consensus-oriented public relations (COPR): A concept for planning and evaluation of public relations. In B. van Ruler & D. Verčič (Eds.), *Public relations and communication management in Europe: A nation-by-nation introduction to public relations theory and practice* (pp. 459–465). Berlin: Walter de Gruyter.

Carey, J. W. (1975). A cultural approach to communication. *Journal of Communication, 2*(1), 1–22.

Cottle, S. (Ed.). (2003). *News, public relations and power.* London: Sage.

Courtright, J. L., & Smudde, P. M. (Eds.). (2007). *Power and public relations.* Cresskill, NJ: Hampton.

Davis, A. (2002). *Public relations democracy: Public relations, politics and the mass media in Britain.* Manchester, UK: Manchester University Press.

Deetz, S. A. (2001). Conceptual foundations. In F. M. Jablin & L. L. Putnam (Eds.), *The new handbook of organizational communication: Advances in theory, research, and methods* (pp. 3–46). Thousand Oaks, CA: Sage.

Denzin, N. K., & Lincoln, Y. S. (2000). The discipline and practice of qualitative research. In N. K. Denzin & Y. S. Lincoln (Eds.), *Handbook of qualitative research* (pp. 1–29). Thousand Oaks, CA: Sage.

Dozier, D. M., & Lauzen, M. M. (2000). Liberating the intellectual domain from the practice: Public relations, activism, and the role of the scholar. *Journal of Public Relations Research, 12*(1), 3–22.

Duffy, M. E. (2000). There's no two-way symmetrical about it: A postmodern examination of public relations textbooks. *Critical Studies in Mass Communication, 17*(3), 294–315.

Durham, F. D. (2005). Public relations as structuration: A prescriptive critique of the Starlink global food contamination case. *Journal of Public Relations Research, 17*(1), 29–47.

Dutta-Bergman, M. J. (2005). Civil society and public relations: Not so civil after all. *Journal of Public Relations Research, 17*(3), 267–289.

Edwards, L. (2006). Rethinking power in public relations. *Public Relations Review, 32*(3), 229–231.

Edwards, L. (2007). *Exploring power in public relations: A Bourdieusian perspective* Unpublished doctoral dissertation. Leeds Metropolitan University, Leeds, UK.

Faulstieg, W. (1992). *Oeffentlichkeitsarbeit. Grundwissen: Kritische Einführung in Problemfelder* [Public relations. Basics: Critical introduction to problems]. Bardowick, Germany: Wissenschaftlicher Verlag.

Geist, U. (2001). Om paradokser, usandsynligheder og tillid—en præsentation af Luhmanns teori om sociale systemer [The paradoxes unlikely entirely and confidence—an introduction to the theory Luhmanns of the social systems]. In M. Femø Nielsen (Ed.), *Profil og offentlighed: Public relations for viderekomne* [Profile and publicity—public relations for the advanced] (pp. 301–334). Frederiksberg, Denmark.

Grunig, J. E. (1993). Image and substance: From symbolic to behavioral relationships. *Public Relations Review, 19*(2), 121–139.

Grunig, J. E. (2001). Two-way symmetrical public relations: Past, present, and future. In R. L. Heath (Ed.), *Handbook of public relations* (pp. 11–30). Thousand Oaks, CA: Sage.

Grunig, J. E., & Hickson, R. H. (1976). An evaluation of academic research in public relations. *Public Relations Review, 2*(2), 31–43.

Grunig, J. E., & Hunt, T. (1984). *Managing public relations.* New York: Holt, Rinehart & Winston.

Grunig, L. A., & Hon, L. C. (2001). *Women in public relations: How gender influences practice.* New York: Guilford.

Habermas, J. (1989). *The structural transformation of the public sphere: An inquiry into a category of bourgeois society* (T. Burger, Trans.). Cambridge, MA: MIT Press.

Hallahan, K. (2004). "Community" as a foundation for public relations theory and practice. *Communication Yearbook, 28*(1), 233–279.

Hollander, E. (1988). *Lokale communicatie en locale openbaarheid: Openbaarheid als communicatiewetenschappelijk concept* [Local communication and local public sphere: Public sphere as communication scientific concept]. Nijmegen, the Netherlands: Katholieke Universiteit Nijmegen.

Holmström, S. (1997). The inter-subjective and the social systemic public relations paradigms. *Journal of Communication Management, 2*(1), 24–39.

Holmström, S. (2004). *Grænser for ansvar: Den sensitive virksomhet i det refleksive samfund* [Limits for responsibility: The sensitive business in the reflective society]. Unpublished doctoral dissertation no. 41/2003, Roskilde Universitetscenter, Roskilde, Denmark.

Holtzhausen, D. R. (2000). Postmodern values in public relations. *Journal of Public Relations Research, 12*(1), 93–114.

Holtzhausen, D. R. (2002). Towards a postmodern research agenda for public relations. *Public Relations Review, 28,* 251–264.

Holtzhausen, D. R., & Voto, R. (2002). Resistance from the margins: The postmodern public relations practitioner as organizational activist. *Journal of Public Relations Research, 14*(1), 57–84.

Ihlen, Ø. (2004). *Rhetoric and resources in public relations strategies: A rhetorical and sociological analysis of two conflicts over energy and the environment* (Doctoral dissertation). Oslo, Norway: Unipub forlag.

Ihlen, Ø. (2005). The power of social capital: Adapting Bourdieu to the study of public relations. *Public Relations Review, 31*(4), 492–496.

Ihlen, Ø., & van Ruler, B. (2007). How public relations works: Theoretical roots and public relations perspectives. *Public Relations Review, 33*(3), 243–248.

Jensen, I. (2000, July). *Public relations and the public sphere in the future.* Paper presented at the 7th International Public Relations Research Symposium, Bled, Slovenia.

Jensen, I. (2001). Public relations and emerging functions of the public sphere: An analytical framework. *Journal of Communication Management, 6*(2), 133–147.

Moffitt, M. A. (Ed.). (2005). Public relations from the margins [Special issue]. *Journal of Public Relations Research, 17*(1).

Krippendorf, K. (1994). A recursive theory of communication. In D. Crowley & D. Mitchell (Eds.), *Communication theory today* (pp. 78–104). Cambridge, UK: Polity Press.

Kruckeberg, D., & Starck, K. (1988). *Public relations and community.* Westport, CT: Praeger.

Kückelhaus, A. (1998). *Public relations: Die Konstruktion von Wirklichkeit: Kommunikationstheoretische Annäherungen an ein neuzeitliches Phänomen* [Public relations: The construction of reality: Communication scientific perspectives into a current phenomenon]. Opladen, Germany: Westdeutscher Verlag.

Ledingham, J. A. (2003). Explicating relationships management as a general theory of public relations. *Journal of Public Relations Research, 15*(2), 181–198.

Leeper, R. V. (1996). Moral objectivity, Jürgen Habermas' discourse ethics and public relations. *Public Relations Review, 22,* 133–150.

Leeper, R. V. (2001). In search of a metatheory for public relations: An argument for communitarianism. In R. L. Heath (Ed.), *Handbook of public relations* (pp. 93–104). Thousand Oaks, CA: Sage.

Leichty, G. (2003). The cultural tribes of public relations. *Journal of Public Relations Research, 15*(4), 277–304.

Leichty, G., & Warner, E. (2001). Cultural topoi: Implications for public relations. In R. L. Heath (Ed.), *Handbook of public relations* (pp. 61–74). Thousand Oaks, CA: Sage.

L'Etang, J. (2004). *Public relations in Britain: A history of professional practice in the twentieth century.* Mahwah, NJ: Erlbaum.

L'Etang, J., & Pieczka, M. (Eds.). (1996). *Critical perspectives in public relations.* London: International Thomson Business Press.

L'Etang, J., & Pieczka, M. (Eds.). (2006). *Public relations: Critical debates and contemporary practice*. Mahwah, NJ: Erlbaum.

Littlejohn, S. W. (1995). *Theories of human communication* (5th ed.). Belmont, CA: Wadsworth.

Livesey, S. M. (2002). The discourse of the middle ground: Citizen Shell commits to sustainable development. *Management Communication Quarterly, 15*(3), 313–349.

Maier, C. T. (2005). Weathering the storm: Hauser's vernacular voices, public relations and the Roman Catholic Church's sexual abuse scandal. *Public Relations Review, 31*(2), 219–227.

Mayhew, L. H. (1997). *The new public: Professional communication and the means of social influence*. Cambridge, UK: Cambridge University Press.

McKie, D. (2001). Updating public relations: "New science," research paradigms and uneven developments. In R. L. Heath (Ed.), *Handbook of public relations* (pp. 75–92). Thousand Oaks, CA: Sage.

McKie, D., & Munshi, D. (2007). *Reconfiguring public relations: Ecology, equity and enterprise*. New York: Routledge.

Meisenbach, R. J. (2005). Habermas' discourse ethics and principle of universalization as a moral framework for organizational communication. *Management Communication Quarterly, 20*(1), 39–62.

Merten, K. (2004). A constructivistic approach to public relations. In B. v. Ruler & D. Verčič (Eds.), *Public relations and communication management in Europe: A nation-by-nation introduction to public relations theory and practice* (pp. 45–54). Berlin: Walter de Gruyter.

Mickey, T. J. (1997). A postmodern view of public relations: Sign and reality. *Public Relations Review, 23*(3), 271–284.

Moffitt, M. A. (1992). Bringing critical theory and ethical considerations to definitions of a "public." *Public Relations Review, 18*(1), 17–29.

Moloney, K. (2000). *Rethinking public relations: The spin and the substance*. London: Routledge.

Moloney, K. (2005). Trust and public relations: Center and edge. *Public Relations Review, 31*(4), 550–555.

Motion, J. (1997). Technologising the self—An art of public relations. *Australian Journal of Communication, 24*(2), 1–16.

Motion, J., & Weaver, C. K. (2005). A discourse perspective for critical public relations research: Life sciences network and the battle for truth. *Journal of Public Relations Research, 17*(1), 49–67.

Munshi, D., & Kurian, P. (2005). Imperializing spin cycles: A postcolonial look at public relations, greenwashing, and the separation of publics. *Public Relations Review, 31*(4), 513–520.

Nielsen, J. M. (2001). *The legitimacy concept and its potentialities: A theoretical reconstruction with relevance to public relations*. Roskilde University Center, Roskilde, Denmark. Unpublished manuscript .

Nistelrooij, A. v. (2000). *Collectief organiseren: Een sociaal-constructionistisch onderzoek naar het werken met grote groepen* [Collective organizing: A social-constructionistic research project into large scale group work]. Utrecht, the Netherlands: Lemma.

Olasky, M. N. (1989). The aborted debate within public relations: An approach through Kuhn's paradigm. *Public Relations Research Annual, 1*, 87–95.

O'Neil, J. (2003). An analysis of the relationships among structure, influence, and gender: Helping to build a feminist theory of public relations. *Journal of Public Relations Research, 15*(2), 151–180.

Pearson, R. (1989a). Beyond ethical relativism in public relations: Coorientation, rules, and the idea of communication symmetry. In J. E. Grunig & L. A. Grunig (Eds.), *Public relations research annual* (Vol. 2, pp. 67–86). Hillsdale, NJ: Erlbaum.

Pearson, R. (1989b). Business ethics as communication ethics: Public relations practice and the idea of dialogue. In C. H. Botan & V. Hazelton Jr. (Eds.), *Public relations theory* (pp. 111–131). Hillsdale, NJ: Erlbaum.

Pearson, R. (1990). Ethical values or strategic values? The two faces of systems theory in public relations. In L. A. Grunig & J. E. Grunig (Eds.), *Public Relations Research Annual* (Vol. 2, pp. 219–234). Hillsdale, NJ: Erlbaum.

Pieczka, M. (2000). Objectives and evaluation in public relations work: What do they tell us about expertise and professionalism? *Journal of Public Relations Research, 12*(3), 211–233.

Pieczka, M. (2002). Public relations expertise deconstructed. *Media, Culture & Society, 24*(3), 301–323.

Pieczka, M., & L'Etang, J. (2001). Public relations and the question of professionalism. In R. L. Heath (Ed.), *Handbook of public relations* (pp. 223–235). Thousand Oaks, CA: Sage.

Plowman, K. D. (1998). Power in conflict for public relations. *Journal of Public Relations Research, 10*(4), 237–261.

Price, V. (1992). *Public opinion.* Newbury Park, CA: Sage.

Raupp, J. (2004). The public sphere as central concept of public relations. In B. van Ruler & D. Verčič (Eds.), *Public relations and communication management in Europe: A nation-by-nation introduction to public relations theory and practice* (pp. 309–316). Berlin: Walter de Gruyter.

Ronneberger, F., & Rühl, M. (1992). *Theorie der public relations: Ein entwurf* [Public relations theory: An outline]. Opladen, Germany: Westdeutscher Verlag.

Sallot, L. M., Lyon, L. J., Acosta-Alzuru, C., & Jones, K. O. (2003). From aardvark to zebra: A new millennium analysis of theory development in public relations academic journals. *Journal of Public Relations Research, 15*(1), 27–90.

Schlesinger, P. (1990). Rethinking the sociology of journalism: Source strategies and the limits of media-centrism. In M. Ferguson (Ed.), *Public communication: The new imperatives: Future directions for media research* (pp. 61–83). London: Sage.

Stacks, D. W. (2002). *Primer of public relations research.* New York: Guilford.

Starck, K., & Kruckeberg, D. (2001). Public relations and community: A reconstructed theory revisited. In R. L. Heath (Ed.), *Handbook of public relations* (pp. 133–146). Thousand Oaks, CA: Sage.

Szmatka, J., & Lovaglia, M. J. (1997). The significance of method. *Sociological Perspectives, 39*(3), 393–415.

Toth, E. L. (1992). The case for pluralistic studies of public relations: Rhetorical, critical, and systems perspectives. In E. L. Toth & R. L. Heath (Eds.),

Rhetorical and critical approaches to public relations (pp. 3–16). Hillsdale, NJ: Erlbaum.

Toth, E. L. (2001). How feminist theory advanced the practice of public relations. In R. L. Heath (Ed.), *Handbook of public relations* (pp. 237–246). Thousand Oaks, CA: Sage.

Toth, E. L., & Heath, R. L. (Eds.). (1992). *Rhetorical and critical approaches to public relations*. Hillsdale, NJ: Erlbaum.

van Ruler, B. (2004). The communication grid: An introduction of a model of four communication strategies. *Public Relations Review, 30*(2), 123–143.

van Ruler, B., & Verčič, D. (2005). Reflective communication management: Future ways for public relations research. In P. J. Kalbfleisch (Ed.), *Communication yearbook* (Vol. 29, pp. 239–274). Mahwah, NJ: Erlbaum.

Vasquez, G. M., & Taylor, M. (2000). Public relations: An emerging social science enters the new millennium. In W. B. Gudykunst (Ed.), *Communication yearbook* (Vol. 24, pp. 319–342). Thousand Oaks, CA: Sage.

Weaver, K., Motion, J., & Roper, J. (2006). From propaganda to discourse (and back again): Truth, power, the public interest and public relations. In J. L'Etang & M. Pieczka (Eds.), *Public relations: Critical debates and contemporary practice* (pp. 7–21). Mahwah, NJ: Erlbaum.

Zijderveld, A. C. (2000). *The institutional imperative: The interface of institutions and networks*. Amsterdam: Amsterdam University Press.

Chapter 2

On Beck

Risk and Subpolitics in Reflexive Modernity

Magnus Fredriksson

Abstract

By turning to the work of the German sociologist Ulrich Beck and his concepts of reflexive modernity, risk society, and subpolitics we get a better understanding of the preconditions for public relations as it is practiced in formal organizations. It is a description of how the transformation of modernity constructs uncertainties about the interpretations of the world and how this advances the use of communication as a strategic means. But it is also a presentation on how public relations is used by social movements—formed as loosely coupled networks—to raise claims of responsibility when trying to achieve political ends outside traditional political institutions.

As an agent for an organization's communication, public relations is used for a wide variety of purposes, one of which has become increasingly influential: the *(re)presentation* of the organization, its goals, and its self-understanding, often within the discourses of *responsibility*. Historically these discourses have been well defined by their arenas (e.g., business/politics), participants (e.g., customers/citizens), and principles (e.g., return on investment/quality of government), which has served to limit debate to specific events or phenomena. However, as a consequence of structural transformation and the dissolution of social boundaries, the discourses of responsibility have become dominated by multiplicity, uncertainty, and ambivalence.

In the words of the German sociologist Ulrich Beck, this transformation represents the transition of modernity into *reflexive modernity*. According to Beck, modernity, driven by rationality and a search for technological and economic development, created incalculable *risks*. In reflexive modernity social life is arranged in relationship to these risks and Beck describes reflexive modernity as a time when we see the emerging contours of a *risk society* leading to new forms of political participation. The institutional arenas of politics are not replaced but they are questioned and conquered in the realm of *subpolitics*. This is a form of political participation without ideological reference, where modernity's separation of economics and politics is reconciled, with the nonpolitical becoming political and politics becoming nonpolitics, with responsibility as one of several key issues.

As a result, responsibility has become one of the dominating discourses in the public debate, with corporate social responsibility as one of several examples. But as much as it is a debate about specific events or phenomena, it is a debate about responsibility in itself. When ideology, belief, and culture lose power as signposts, the ideas and boundaries of responsibility become unclear, and because positions and doctrines have undergone fundamental changes, the debate becomes as much a debate about responsibility in itself.

The aim of this chapter is to present how the concepts of Beck could be used to get a wider understanding of the preconditions for public relations as it is practiced in organizations. How risks and subpolitics constitute uncertainties about the interpretations of the world and how this advances the use of communication as a strategic means. But it is also a presentation on how public relations is used by social movements—formed as loosely coupled networks—to raise claims of responsibility when trying to achieve political ends outside traditional political institutions.

Reflexive Modernization—When "Or" Becomes "And"

In the introduction to *Die Erfindung des Politischen,* Beck (1993, Eng. Trans. 1997, Swe. Trans. 1995) refers to Wassily Kandinsky's essay "Und." Here the distinction between "or" and "and" is pointed out as the difference between the 19th and 20th century. In the words of Beck, it becomes the distinction between modernity and reflexive modernity. As Beck says, "then"—modernity—is a time of unequivocal and predictable specialization.

It is an era that has created clear separations between social institutions—such as the one between the private and the public—with the nation-state as an example of a constituent unit. Economics, politics, and culture are defined by territorial boundaries, and individual actions are performed predominantly in relationship to collectives.

Modernity is also a period when full employment is declared as a political ambition and where the welfare state functions as a defender of the well-being of the citizens in relation to emergencies and risks. Work is the base for status, consumption, social security, and overall it is the grounds for civic participation. As a consequence, the ideal of full employment permeates all political as well as social activities and it is a value built on rationality, instrumental control, specialization, and differential functionality.

"Now"—reflexive modernity—is a time of *and* where multiplicity, uncertainty, and ambivalence are dominating principles. It is a time where a variety of principles of rationalization and a wide variety of values arise, constructing an infinite number of positions. The question of organizations' *raison d'être* becomes an essential part of society's discourses and often there are situations where boundaries "become not boundaries so much as a variety of attempts to draw boundaries" (Beck, Bonss, & Christoph, 2003, p. 19). To a high degree it is a question answered in the realm of responsibility. "Who are we?" is answered by the answer in the question, "What do we do and how do we take responsibility for that?"

Reflexive Modernization: A Radicalization of Modernity not a Postmodernity

Reflexive modernization succeeds modernity but Beck dissociates himself from the concept of a postmodernity as suggested by Lyotard (1979), Baudrillard (1994), and others. Beck, in line with Giddens (1990), does not describe modernity's transformation as a start that contrasts with an end, but rather as a transformation where the qualities of an epoch are rationalized by its own processes.

Reflexive modernization is a challenge to modernity and its principal formations; it is a radicalization of itself, its structures, actions, and self-conceptualizations, but it is not a replacement. It is a secondary effect of the everyday practice of modernity and as such it is not a process governed by political reformation, political replacement, or revolution.

Beck's presentation of reflexive modernity is extensive and it rests on several conceptualizations, but in my view there are two aspects more vital than others if we want to get a fuller understanding of public relations: (1) the self-confrontation of modernity's self-produced and manufactured *risks*, and (2) the deinstitutionalization of political practice taking form as *subpolitics*.

Risk Society—When Modernity Meets Its Own Side Effects

Beck (1986) is probably best known for his seminal work *Risikogesellschaft: Auf dem Weg in einen andere Moderne* (Eng. Trans. 1992, Swe. Trans. 1998b). The book became a bestseller when it was published in Germany 1986. The book sold more than 60,000 copies in the first five years, and according to Beck himself this should be seen as a confirmation of the *anthropological* shock many experienced during that period as a result of the Chernobyl disaster the same year. By the term *anthropological* he means a shock that was all embracing in the sense that it overcame time, space, and social differentiations.

In *Risk Society* risks have become a structural factor of society, organizing social life, science, the economy, and politics. But in contrast to class—one of the dominating structuring principles of industrial society—risk-consciousness *creates* the existence, whereas class-consciousness springs *from* the existence.

Risk society is a concept used by Beck to describe a society where the production and distribution of prosperity is interlinked with the production and distribution of risks. Risk society is a society to come, we are not there yet but the managing of risk, and threats of risk, are central themes for individuals, organizations, and institutions in our time. By this Beck doesn't imply that risk did not occur in earlier periods. Risks have been present in all eras, but their proportions, scope, and range in time and space has been immensely extended. *Then*, risks often emerged from work (on-the-job casualties, working oneself "to death") they were local, personal, often direct, visible, and caused by deficiency (e.g., the lack of hygiene). *Now*, risks come from the sources of life (food, air, water), they are global, all embracing, vague in their contours, invisible, and caused by zealotry.

The consequences of contemporary risks turning into catastrophes, as happened with the explosion of the nuclear reactor at Chernobyl, are unlimited. They transcend geographical and political borders but also spatial dimensions. There are children still unborn who will suffer from the radiation that the Chernobyl explosion spread worldwide and its end results. As in the case of Chernobyl, present risks are to a great extent the result of human actions. They are the side-effects of industrialization, the consequences of technological, scientific, and economic development and our urge to satisfy material needs and create surplus. The side-effects of these activities have been known for a long period Beck argues, but they have been ignored as the discourse of industrial society created an order of precedence where risks were subordinated to expansion as well as to the creation of welfare.

Beck is very clear in his description of industrial development and the creation of opulence as two intertwined courses of event. Risks and possibilities are two sides of the same coin. If you search and strive for development you will automatically be confronted by risk.

Subpolitics—The Deinstitutionalization of Politics

In the wake of an emerging risk society and in the realm of an escalating individualization, the politicization of areas that were nonpolitical in earlier periods could be seen as a reaction to the shortcomings of formal politics. Subpolitics is the concept used by Beck to describe the transformation and expansion of politics in reflexive modernity. In modernity, politics is centralized to political institutions, formal structures, and citizenship. It is a practice performed by citoyens in contrast to the nonpolitical practices performed by the bourgeoisie. The two roles were related to two distinctive spheres (the political-administrative sphere and the techno-economic sphere) a diversion based on the differentiation between social development (e.g., the building of a welfare state) and economic and technical progress. As citoyens we are expected to discuss and criticize, and by these means make legitimate political decisions based on what's good for all; and as members of the bourgeoisie we are expected to maximize our own returns. The latter does not need legitimacy because individual (technological and economic) development also means collective (social) development: "Progress replaced acclamation" (Beck, 1998a, p. 307).

In reflexive modernity the ground for political legitimacy is questioned as the side effects (risks) of modernity become clear. It is to a high degree a question of responsibility in a situation where the systems of institutional politics and the welfare state can't offer the security searched for. But it is more than a change in sphere, subpolitics is also politics in relation to other areas. Whereas institutionalized politics often focused on administrative matters, laws, regulations, and the need for legitimization, subpolitics is about the structure of living conditions.

The nonpolitical becomes political *and* the political becomes nonpolitical as subpolitics override institutional politics as an arena for debate and policy formation. In many aspects it is a praxis questioning the division of responsibility in society and it brings to the fore the relationship between corporations, the state, and other formal and informal collectives as well as individual standpoints. What responsibilities do the institutional politics have in a society where individuals direct their demands directly toward corporations and other institutional actors? And to what extent do these actors have to take these demands into account?

The starting point for Beck's writing on subpolitics is his critique of the assumption of a decline in political participation in western democracies—a thesis represented by Robert Putnam (2000; also see chapter 12 in this volume) and others. According to Beck (1995): these scholars search for politics "at the wrong places, with false concepts, at incorrect floors, on the wrong pages in the newspapers" (p. 139). Beck calls traditional definitions of political participation into question and he argues for a wider understanding of the notion. In his view politics cannot be limited to formal actors (the state, the parliament, and political parties), formal activities (voting in elections, membership in political organizations and acclamation), or formal structures (formal organizations, hierarchies, and executive leadership). There is a need for a wider understanding of politics with an opening for issues traditionally defined as *nonpolitical* (consumption, genetics) other organizational forms (network based structures, other occasional constellations and others), and actors (professions, campaign based social movements, corporations).

In many ways subpolitics could be described as a form of political participation in response to the demise of ideological structures. In line with Giddens (1990), Castells (1997) and others feel subpolitics could be seen as a form of individual lifestyle politics, a concept coined by Lance Bennet (2004).[1] It is used to describe how political considerations to a larger extent are made in relationship to individual considerations rather than ideological ones. As we have learned from Beck, the structures of modernity (class, family, gender) become less important in the reflexive modernity. When there is a lack of an alternative to capitalism the individual creates her own political worldview based on her own life experiences, lifestyle, values, and the narratives that reproduce them. This could be soap operas, news, and other cultural forms but also advertising brands and other forms of corporate expression. The individual searches for new forms to express her political commitment and often it is a striving for activities that are less time consuming, less bureaucratic, with room for more individual ideas and moldable structures. As such it is political activities with strong self-interest where politics works as an agent in the search for meaning and substance. To save the world becomes an aspect of a life with content.

To a high degree this form of political participation is based on communication at a point when the formal structures of organizations, politics, and actions become obsolete. It is a form of political participation practiced by individuals as well as collectives and it is a form of political participation performed by formal organizations as well as loosely composed networks.

The Critique

The work of Beck is extensive, creative, and relevant for our understanding of everyday life as well as the function of the political and economic systems. As a scholar he is productive, he elaborates on a large number of concepts, and his work encompasses both the individual's situation in society as well as the properties of the nation-states in the global arena. In many ways it is an impressive effort.

However, there are critical voices pointing toward weaknesses in his work and one aspect many return to is the lack of empirical evidence for his conclusions (Dingwall, 1999; Lupton & Tulloch, 2001, 2002; Wilkinson 2001). In his own work Beck tends to be niggardly with references to empirical results that support his conclusions and those references that are included are often from German studies. In others' work that uses Beck as a starting point, it seems hard to find empirical evidence for the conclusions presented in his work: People still seem to be shaped by the structures of modernity (class, family, work) and the risks of the risk society seem to be less present than expected (Lupton & Tulloch, 2001, 2002).

Another point of criticism is the importance Beck gives to risks as an autonomous force for the development of society. Here he is criticized for his blindness toward other forces and some also propose that the properties of risk haven't changed as dramatically as Beck suggests. Earlier we had plague and syphilis, today it is BSE (Mad cow disease) and bird flu (Elliot, 2002; Latour, 2003; Turner, 1994).

These descriptions return in relation to several of the concepts used by Beck (risk, individualization, among others) and some suggest that his drive for a general theory makes him blind to counterevidence, conflicting developments, and contradictions in the developments he describe.

The criticism is relevant and it asks several important questions about Beck's work. However, I don't think these questions disqualify the work as a whole and I consider that the advantages that derive from Beck's work overcome the disadvantages. My main argument is the style of reading. If one reads Beck literally, the critique is devastating because it shows counterarguments for several of Beck's conclusions. But a reading that takes its departure in an understanding of Beck's work as a *perspective* rather as an *empirical analysis*, shows how the work can give major insights. Such a reading would underline the importance of the structural rather than the individual, multiplicity rather than singularity, and the social rather than the economic. From this reading we can get relevant insights not offered by other theorists into the everyday life of individuals and the functioning of institutions. From my point of view, this is a highly significant argument.

Public Relations—A Practice of Modernity

Public relations is in many respects a practice of modernity and as such an exercise with strong connections to capitalism, mass consumption, and media development. It was born in the wake of industrialization and it can be seen as an integral part of the modernization of work, family relations, communities, and tradition, with the division of the private and the public as one dominating principle (Cutlip, Center, & Broom, 2000; Ewen, 1986; Mayhew, 1997).[2]

The genesis of public relations is perhaps further interlinked with the development of organizations as social entities. In modernity, merchants established corporate bodies to extend their economic and political freedom of action. In time the entities became totally decoupled from their owners following the construction of limited companies and the expansion of specialized production, management, and bureaucratization (Beck, 1998a). Communication then becomes a central aspect of the supervision of production and the (re)presentation of corporations. To be able to achieve predictability, attract investors, insure legitimacy, and separate the mass produced products from others, the aim of communication becomes the construction of a prepossessing appearance.

From a European perspective this is a picture which needs to be supplemented with a description of the central position the welfare state has had and its influence on the development of public relations. When the state becomes the surety of people's well-being there is a need for instruments conducive to the efficiency of the bureaucracy, the distribution of subsidies, and the management of tax enforcement. Public relations is one of the tools among others that are used to achieve stability and efficiency, as well as enlightenment and education. But it is also a tool used to secure legitimacy for an idea in conflict with other voices. Because even if the welfare state is omnipresent, it takes different forms and its existence isn't the result of consensus, but rather it is an institutional form that is highly questionable on ideological grounds (Beck, 1998a, 1998b).[3]

The Maturation of Public Relations in Reflexive Modernity

Modernity could be described as the cradle of public relations while reflexive modernity has caused it to mature and develop into an established practice. It functions by using a multiplicity of instruments, techniques, and strategies that are also used by a wide variety of organizations with different aims and goals. It is in the radicalization of modernity that the practice of public relations becomes a managerial tool in line with others, and it is here that the symbolic constructions become of equal significance to instrumental means.

The intensified interest for communications is a result of numerous transformations, but in the light of Beck (1995, 1998a, 1998b) one could point toward:

- The increasing threats to organizational operations caused by actual risks or the fear caused by assumed risks.
- The implosion of modernity's dualism, as is the case with the division between the private and the public sphere.
- The individualization of opinions and values often expressed in the realm of subpolitics.

Altogether these structural transformations change the positions and conditions for corporate as well as governmental bodies with an increasing need to legitimate their existence, their structures, their products and services, and their means of production. As the interactions between the actors to a large extent are mediated there is an increased need for a coherent and valued presentation.

It is very much a question of responsibilities and how these should be divided between different institutions and across the actors operating within their frames. Who are those actors that are responsible for the risks of reflexive modernity? How should we deal with them? What happens if a risk develops into a crisis? The answers to these questions aren't fixed and it is therefore necessary for different types of organizations to allocate resources for representation and negotiations: in other words, public relations. Here public relations could be seen as a function not only of organizational expressivity but also as a striving to reduce uncertainty and complexity in the interpretation of society. These aspects are intensified by the fact that our conceptions of the future to a decreasing extent can be based on earlier experiences. The integration of opinions, values, and ideas creates a situation where different rationalities meet, which contributes to increasing complexity and a considerably larger number of possible scenarios about the future.

It is here, in Beck's descriptions of the turmoil of rationalities and the multiplicity of boundaries that one can see how his work can help us understand the drivers and functions of public relations. We will find a perspective that focuses on public relations as a means used by corporate bodies to deal with the demands of responsibility and the aftermath of modernity, with legitimacy and trust as two core elements. But it is also a perspective that describes public relations as a tool used by loosely coupled networks to put these pretentions on accountability into question. It is not made in the frame of institutional politics, but rather it is performed in the realm of subpolitics. A divergence of interests comes to life in different scenarios but they are at their most conspicuous in *risk conflicts*. In short a type of conflict where different actors seek to gain discursive control over our perceptions on risks and their consequences, now and in the future (Beck & Willms, 2004).

Risk Conflicts—A Search for Discursive Control

Reflexive modernity is to a large extent a society organized around risks. But even though they are present in many social interactions, the risks of reflexive modernization are unspecific, universal, and unpredictable. According to Beck (1998a), we must initially understand risk as arguments with a need to be interpreted before they can be visible to or perceptible by the human senses. The definitions of risk to a high degree have great economic and political impact. Risks have extensive consequences and the acceptance of a phenomenon as a risk necessarily rearranges much of the social infrastructure. The universal denial of risk from institutional actors (corporations as well as the science establishment and others) has to be understood in relationship to the costs, monetary as well as political, that an acceptance of risk will bring. For a single actor the acceptance of risk could mean bankruptcy; for institutions the acceptance of risk could mean demands for fundamental changes that might create economic, political, and social turbulence, and in the process raise questions about the foundations of our society's way of life.

This creates a situation where there is often a clash between different discourses, frequently in terms of a conflict between laypeople and experts. According to Beck, risks cannot be limited to the language of science and engineering because they formulate questions about human existence and as such involve questions of morality, philosophy, and culture. Risks put forward ethical, political, and cultural aspects in domains where scientific, economic, and technical aspects have dominated, and as a result, the monopoly of knowledge held by the latter is questioned by the former. The debate on nuclear power is one example used by Beck (1998a, 1992) to show how the use of probability calculus is confronted by the (public) understanding of risks, whereby the likelihood of one misfortune is one misfortune too many.

Earlier, when risks that often emerged from work were local and personal, these kinds of risk conflicts were neutralized by a system of allocation. According to Beck, the state acted as a guarantor, thereby providing legitimacy to the system, because it was the patron of the nation-state's citizens. The state also functioned as the judge in conflicts between different interests. It was a system where conflicts were disarmed and where causalities were given a standard equivalent in the frame of the welfare state (e.g., the loss of an arm was compensated with a given sum of money). In the modernization of modernity, the grand narrative of social progress loses force as the construction of the welfare state comes to an end. The social transformation coincides with the emergence of the side effects of industrial society's technological development and the delegitimization of that development which follows. According to Beck (1998a, 1992; Beck & Willms, 2004), the political system loses its authority as patron and judge, and there is intensification in risk conflicts.

It is here that public relations becomes of vital importance because it contributes to and influences the interpretations made by different actors. In this context Beck (1998a) himself makes explicit comments on the use of advertising and other forms of "controlled" communication. He also emphasizes the significance of the mass media as a forum for the construction as well as the reconstruction of risks. It is in the mass media (in the broadest sense) that many of the risk conflicts take place.

A risk conflict in reflexive modernity follows a rather general pattern (Beck, 1998a; Beck & Willms, 2004). It starts with a media scenario where the risk is described as creating anxiety among the public. The political, and corporate, reaction is denial, an act based on instrumental rationality and the invalidation of anxiety, rather than probability as the foundation for the description of risks. If there isn't a clear line of causality there are no openings for acceptance. The kind of "erroneous" interpretations made by laypeople are often defined as an information problem. The implication is that if the public had the same knowledge as the scientists (and were rational) they would be calm. The solution: to disseminate more developed calculations and to use public relations to depreciate the public's "irrational fears." Often these contributions have unforeseen consequences, and as the effects of and the writings about the risk increase; and the frustration and anger also increase among those affected. The next step is the formation of a social movement with political aims. The intentions aren't necessarily to change the *politics* behind the risk, but rather the goal could as well be to change the *corporation* that is behind the risk.

Mediatization—A Driver for Public Relations

According to Beck the importance of symbolic means are amplified by the fact that most of the experiences we make are mediatized. In reflexive modernity the function of the mass media is vital when people create their frames of reference. In general terms this could be described as a concept pointing toward how individuals use mediatized representations as a frame of reference in consumption, political positioning, and the valuation of life (Jansson, 2001). It is not a concept used by Beck, but in my opinion it is a concept that makes it easier to understand how mass media and other symbolic means are integrated in reflexive modernity, and it also gives clarity to the rather disparate descriptions of mass media and communication in Beck's work.[4]

Mediatization as a general concept points toward mass media as a cultural form with genre conventions, journalistic routines, and forms of presentation that replace tradition and religion and work as a map giving guidance in an imaginary community partly with cultural overtones (the nation-state, language). As the media institutions themselves meet the consequences of individualization and commercialization as well as globalization—one effect being a considerable increase in supply—there is a development toward communities being gathered around interests, values, and opinions and breaking with traditional frames of reference. Here the importance of visual representations increases and the communities become expressive networks bounded by brands, symbols, artifacts, and other imagery (Kellner, 1995).

In more specific terms, mediatization points toward the increasing power of the mass media as an arena and gatekeeper (Asp, 1986). Here mediatization helps us understand how and why corporations, politicians, and others adapt to the logic of mass media in their work. When news, TV shows, and websites become the central tools that enable people to navigate in their everyday life they also become the mediators between organizations and their stakeholders. This leads to a media adoption in the choice of strategies and maneuvers. Politicians choose not to present a bill or choose to change the content and presentation, because it can't be adapted to the media agenda as it stands. The board of a corporation chooses a specific candidate as managing director because he or she has a profile in line with the mediatized stereotype. The logics of the mass media become the dominating principles in understanding society and what can be said and how it can be said. It is therefore one of the more important forces when corporations and other institutional actors are navigating in society (Asp, 1986; Beck, 1998a, 1992; Thompson, 1995).

From a public relations perspective, the search for media attention and the avoidance of scrutiny are by no means new phenomena: they have been central to the practice of public relations from the outset. But due to the structural changes of reflexive modernity, mass media are given a much more central position than was once the case in business, politics, and social life. It means that increasing numbers of considerations are made in relationship to the logistics of the mass media. This is also due to the fact that as they have become political, corporations have lost their ability to hide behind the state (Beck, 1998a). Today, many corporations offer services and goods that were once produced and delivered by the state (electricity, telephone) followed by a number of private solutions (retirement annuity, private health insurance) to secure benefits for people in case of accidents and changed life conditions (illness, unemployment). Corporations act in the realm of institutional politics as well as subpolitics and they are seen as one of many special interests in the political arena. In line with the journalistic ideal of being the watchdog of society, corporations will ultimately receive the same scrutiny as other political actors (Beck, 1998a).

From a corporate perspective the implosion in roles and forms of judgment, and the expectations that follow, create rhetorical difficulties because demands are awakened in the remainder of the population for a political discourse in which humanity and public interest are the dominating principles—in sharp contrast with the ideals of efficiency, productivity, and self-interest that dominate the economic discourse (Beck, 1998a). Other areas show the same pattern of implosion as laypeople contradict the statements of scientific experts and nature becomes culture. The differing rationales lead to different principles of reasoning but also different claims of knowledge. The result is a myriad of boundaries and difficulties that construct end solutions. There is no one answer to the problem of global warming, but there is instead a continuing debate about it, which includes a multitude of voices.

To be able to achieve a balance between the different rationales of economics, politics, and ethics and present a trustworthy identity, corporations search for identification with frames that will provide acceptance among primary groups. Employees are used as ambassadors for a collective *We* in the articulation of opinions, values, and positions often formulated in a rhetoric heavily weighted by symbols and iconographic representations. It is a strategy striving for individual identification where the use of imagery inspires contradictory interpretations without creating conflicts because individuals and groups can make their own interpretations independent of each other. It is when the interpretations are explicit that they come into question. Further, it is a rhetoric embedded in value-based management where the use of communication is essential. The aim with corporate communications is still promotion, to ensure (institutional) political acceptance, but it is also to determine the demands put forward by other interests, negotiate on the content, and as such public relations functions as an agent for organizations' self-reflexivity.

The integration of heterogeneous discourses could largely be described as an attempt to reduce risks. The revelation of irregularities presents substantial threats to the existence of a business when reputation and intangible assets become essential in the economic valuation of corporations. From a corporate perspective one central target group is the investors and other actors in the marketplace that are striving for economic returns; that is, the weighing of calculated risk in relationship to the expected dividend. Traditionally these calculations have been made in a frame of analysis of competition, product development, and other aspects of market positions. In reflexive modernity such calculations have to include a wider variety of subject areas because the risks related to corporate activities can't be limited to economic matters. Environmental risks, cultural clashes, religion, terrorism, and international conflicts are areas which have to be included in a thorough analysis. Also essential are conflicts of ideas and threats toward immaterial values. Increasingly, more of a corporation's assets become bound to competence, ideas, and reputation

In such a complex context *re*-action isn't sufficient; the organizations have to be proactive. It is necessary to communicate risk-awareness in relation to societal factors; acting according to the laws of the market isn't sufficient if a corporation is to be a potential object of investment in a heterogeneous climate of opinions.

Public Relations as a Tool of Subpolitics

In many ways the discussion of public relations from an organizational perspective based on the work of Beck follows the same patterns as that offered by the work of Giddens (1990), Luhmann (1993), and many others. The idea of a turn in society and the escalation, amplification, and radicalization of structural changes leads to an intensification in the reflexivity over our living conditions. Here public relations becomes an agent for the self-reflexive process of organizations, with responsibility and identity as central themes.

However, if one wants to make full use of Beck's work, there is a need for a second perspective, one that turns away from formal organizations and formal strategies, a perspective that focuses on public relations as a practice used by social networks with social change as a core idea. Often these public relations activities are planned in line with the idea of managerial public relations work, but the creative dimension is often salient with the use of irony and unconventional presentations as distinct features. One well-known example is the network of Adbusters, formed in the late 1980s. The formation of social movements is central in the understanding of these lines of development as well and the increasing importance of rhetorical and symbolic means within the scope of subpolitics (Beck, 1998a, 1998b; also see Demetrious, 2006; Jones, 2002).

The breeding ground for this kind of subpolitical network shows a wide variety of properties, but risks and the idea of responsibility are essential. In the realm of globalization the reach for institutional politics is limited, and the searchlight therefore aims at those who are presumed to have the resources, insight, and means to change the forms of production and distribution on global markets. Often this is argued to be the multinational corporations or trading organizations such as the World Trade Organization (WTO), and therefore the activities of these corporations and organizations are scrutinized and questioned. The presentation from the networks often returns to the idea of responsibility but it is not a search for support of the network in itself. The idea is not to present a responsible organization. These informal networks are often transitory and anonymous so far as the larger public is concerned, and their position is fundamentally based on the causes they promote (environmental issues, human rights etc.). The main idea is rather to question the claims of accountability and deconstruct the fundamentals of legitimacy that corporations and others put forward in support of their existence and activities.

Subpolitics is practiced in many different ways, but communication is essential, and in the words of Micheletti, Føllesdal, and Stolle (2003) it could be described as an expression for a change in attitude toward corporations and an expansion of information technology as a means of political participation. One example of subpolitics where communication has become essential is *political consumption*, the use of the principles and resources of markets to gain political influence. Political consumption is the support ("buycotts") and boycotts of producers and products and investments using the same logic. The goals differ but often the aim is described as a striving for control on a global market without political or legal control (Bennet, 2004; Boström, Føllesdal, Klintman, Micheletti, & Sørensen, 2005; Andersen, Tobiasen, & Tobiasen, 2001; Micheletti, 2003; Stolle, Hooghe, & Micheletti, 2005).

The point of entry here, with explicit reference to the work of Beck, is the importance of symbolic strategies as a complement or replacement of instrumental actions in the realm of subpolitics. What we can see is an increasing use of communication campaigns as the organizational foundation for political participation. These campaigns, unlike institutional politics, are often permanent and collect people from a variety of social areas as well as people with different orientations and objectives (Bennet, 2004).

One example offered by Lance Bennet (2004) is the campaign against Microsoft, which collected actors from many countries (the campaign was global), and actors with clearly different political orientations (progressive as well as conservative) as well as actors with clearly different mandates (hackers, corporations, NGOs, the EU Commission, etc.). Even if there are antagonisms in other areas, the informal structures open for new liaisons and single issues could become the mobilizing force and organizational structure for political participation. The opening for such liaisons is the organic form of network structure and the absence of ideological grounds. The point of union is rather an interest in the issue as an isolated phenomenon coupled with self-expression. In relationship to the latter, the part taken in a campaign offers an opportunity for identity construction, for individuals as well as collectives, and the possibility of a wider self-understanding in relationship to other actors. It is a practice used by individuals to secure their own well-being as well as the well-being of others.

The use of communication as a dominant means in the practice of subpolitics is a result of several entities, one of which is the spatial properties of political participation on a global level. The transformations of reflexive modernity have a global reach and many of the questions raised by the increasing number of risks are global as well. At the same time, institutional politics is limited to nation-states with agreements as the only available tools for coordination in international politics. To be able to reach political goals and to construct the infrastructure for political participation it is essential to overcome these shortcomings. This could be offered by organized communication using the infrastructure of already existing networks such as the Internet (Bennet, 2003, 2004; Micheletti, 2003).

The use of communication could also be seen as a way to level the resources between different interests. The main targets for many campaigns, for example, are multinational corporations, so there are clear differences in availability of economic resources between the targets and those who are targeting them; but by using the logic of the mass media (e.g., the David against Goliath syndrome) these differences can be less significant than might be supposed. Here one could also see how the use of creativity and unconventional ideas could bring advantages to networks. As described by Deetz (1992) and others, the organizational structures of large organizations often make it difficult if not impossible to respond to specific situations with sufficient flexibility.

Another aspect of this is the fact that an activity (such as a boycott) is highly dependent on the number of participants, their persistence, and their commitment. With a lack of dedication there is always a risk of failure. In such cases better communication could open up a given situation for effective action because it doesn't necessarily ask for essential changes in behavior or values among the participants. Among those who have internalized the use of a product in their everyday life, a boycott implies putting an immediate stop to the use of the product in question, and therefore it could be difficult to engage those people in an instrumental campaign to boycott that product (Friedman, 2003).

The use of communication could also be seen as a response to the strategies used by corporations to claim accountability in their search for legitimacy. Often this is made within the frame of the particular brand where a constructed concept becomes the de facto spokesperson. Brands have become an essential frame of reference in the interactions between people, in the construction of lifestyles (individualization), as well as in the interactions between corporations (Cheney, 1992). Corporate symbols have become a commodity. Here it is fruitful to point toward the platform that brands could form for communication campaigns. Well-known brands are often easily identified and therefore the critique of brands is a shortcut to public exposure and media coverage. It is also a shortcut to people uninterested in institutional politics, using the brands, their affiliates, or competitors as a platform for political discourse. In line with this, the networks try to hold brands hostage in such circumstances as logo campaigns, petitions, and culture jams.

The preference for these sorts of strategies is also a result of the difficulties connected to the identification of the corporations behind the brands. Many corporations choose to use a brand strategy in their self-presentation, making it hard to identify the corporation (Olins, 1989, 2000). In addition, there is the cross-ownership of corporations, which creates a lack of transparency that makes it difficult to affiliate single products with different corporate actors. Lastly, corporations often have a wide variety of brands, making it difficult to create a well-defined focus for a boycott. A communication campaign offers a chance to direct attention toward a corporation because it is concerned with the brand and that in itself makes the corporation behind the brand visible to the public (Bennet, 2004).

Communication as the Organizational Structure

For a majority of the movements described here, the Internet fills a central structural function. In traditional organizations the use of information technology is subordinated to organizational structure. Internet, Intranet, and e-mail are tools used to develop and maintain already existing formations and processes. Here the Internet has *become* the organizational structure as it expands the possibilities of global interactions as well as the construction of networks.

The Internet is also the dominating tool used to gain access to traditional mass media. Often actors participating in social movements are separated from commercial news media by the principles of news selection. But by the increasing use of the Internet as a resource among journalists, the campaign of a rather small network can reach the front pages of national news papers as well as the headlines on national television. By disseminating information on websites, blogs, and forums, social movements have a direct connection to journalists in conventional media.

Here it could also be pointed out that political consumption in many situations is made easier by the increasing (global) information exchange because it also means transparency about corporate practice. It becomes easier therefore to disseminate information about production conditions and other aspects of vital importance for the consumer. Furthermore, globalization means decreasing costs for the practice of political consumption, the distribution and sale of products that fulfill the demands put forward by political consumers are made easier (Scammell, 2000).

A second aspect of the technological development is the changing character of Internet use. What we can see is a differentiation in the use and an expansion of alternative resources. As more people tend to use the Internet as a primary resource there is an increasing use of sources beyond the websites of conventional mass media. In this line of thought one could see alternatives to traditional forms of communication, such as demonstrations and other forms of public intervention. These are means that are often marred by complications. The images of protesters in clashes with police and other officials (a common occurrence) do not have an identical impact on the different elements of the audience, such as the public or corporations. Rather, there is dissociation from those events rather than identification with them. It is also clear that the threat from protests and other forms of instrumental actions is viewed differently by the participants than it is by those in power. By the use of communication campaigns these clashes can be avoided and the recurring question of the movement's responsibilities can be avoided.

Conclusion

So far as I am concerned, Beck's theories offer a relevant and coherent description of the preconditions for interactions between social actors—individuals, organizations, as well as loosely coupled networks. I particularly find the theory of reflexive modernity relevant for a macroanalysis of public relations as a function of organizational reflexivity in a dialectic relationship to norms and values. Here Beck's work points toward the importance of symbolic means and it raises questions about the use of public relations to construct and reconstruct opinion and ideas. One of the central advantages is his ability to integrate economic, political, as well as social and cultural aspects in his theories. Often these are dealt with separately, in a manner that reduces our ability to understand the prerequisites, intentions, and consequences of public relations.

This integration gives us a better understanding of the preconditions of public relations because it points toward the importance that "responsibility" is given in reflexive modernity. The answers to the claims for responsibility aren't fixed, and here public relations could be seen as a function not only for organizational expressivity, but as a function that strives for the reduction of uncertainty and complexity in the interpretation of society.

For practitioners his work points toward the need for a reflexive approach. Here the word *reflexive* is more to the point than *reflection*—thinking about oneself—the word *reflexive* brings to the fore the need for self-understanding as well as self-confrontation. This applies to the practice of public relations in itself—public relations practitioners have to understand their role in the organization as it is seen by internal as well as external actors—as well as the activities of the organization for which it is used.

For scholars there are two main arguments for using Beck's theories in public relations research: (1) the theory of reflexive modernity may enhance our understanding of public relations as an evolving practice in sociohistorical terms, and (2) the theory challenges the ideas of "organizations" and "management" as the starting point for an analysis of public relations. Beck's work enhances the holistic understanding of how public relations is used in different contexts by different actors with different means. It is crucial to understand this, and by turning to Beck it is possible to develop a more dynamic and open ended understanding of public relations.

Notes

1. Also see Andersen and Tobiasen (2001) for a direct comparison between the concepts used by Beck and Giddens.
2. For a fuller account of perspectives used to describe the history of public relations see Pearson (1992).
3. This doesn't mean that it takes the same form in all regions. See the contributions in Pierson and Castles (2000) for a discussion on the different faces of the welfare state in Europe.
4. For a more detailed presentation and discussion on Beck's work and how his theories deal with mass media, see Cottle (1998).

References

Andersen, G., Tobiasen, J., & Tobiasen, M. (2001). *Politisk forbrug og politiske forbrugere* [Political cosumption and political consumers]. Arhus: Aarhus Universitetsforlag.

Asp, K. (1986). *Mäktiga massmedier: Studier i politisk opinionsbildning* [Powerfull media. Studies of the formation of political opinions]. Stockholm: Akademilitteratur.

Baudrillard, J. (1994). *Simulacra and simulation.* Ann Arbor, MA: University of Michigan Press.

Beck, U. (1986). *Risikogesellschaft: Auf dem Weg in einen andere Moderne.* Frankfurt am Main: Suhrkamp.

Beck, U. (1992). *Risk society: Towards a new modernity.* London: Sage. (Original work published 1984)

Beck, U. (1993). Die Erfindung des Politischen. Zu einer Theorie reflexiver Modernisierung. Frankfurt am Main: Suhrkamp.

Beck, U. (1995). *Att uppfinna det politiska. Bidrag till en teori om reflexiv modernisering* [The reinvention of politics: Rethinking modernity in the global social order]. Gothenburg: Daidalos.

Beck, U. (1997). *The reinvention of politics: Rethinking modernity in the global social order.* Cambridge, UK: Polity Press.

Beck, U. (1998a). *Risksamhället: På väg mot en annan modernitet* [Risk society: Towards a new modernity]. Gothenburg: Daidalos.

Beck, U. (1998b). *Vad innebär globaiseringen? Missuppfattningar och möjliga politiska svar* [What is globalization?]. Gothenburg, Sweden: Daidalos.

Beck, U. (2000a). *What is globalization?* Malden, MA: Polity Press.

Beck, U. (2000b). *The brave new world of work.* Cambridge, MA: Polity Press.

Beck, U., Bonss, E., & Christoph, L. (2003). The theory of reflexive modernization: problematic, hypotheses and research programme. *Theory, Culture & Society, 20*(2) 1–33.

Beck, U., & Willms, J. (2004). *Conversations with Ulrich Beck*. Cambridge, UK: Polity Press.

Bennet, W. L. (2003). Communicating global activism: Strengths and vulnerabilities of networked politics. *Information, Communication & Society, 6*(2) 143–168.

Bennet, W. L. (2004). Branded political communication: Lifestyle politics, logo campaigns, and the rise of global citizenship. In M. Micheletti, A. Føllesdal, & D. Stolle (Eds.), *Politics, products, and markets: Exploring political consumerism past and present* (pp. 101–126). Edison, NJ: Transaction Books.

Boström, M., Føllesdal, A., Klintman, M., Micheletti, M., & Sørensen, M. P. (2005). Studying political consumerism. In M. Boström, A. Føllesdal, M. Klintman, M. Micheletti, & M. P. Sørensen (Eds.), *Political consumerism: Its motivations, power and conditions in the Nordic Countries and elsewhere* (pp. 9-24). Proceedings from the 2nd International Seminar on Political Consumerism, Oslo August 26-29, 2004, TemaNord 2005:517 Copenhagen: Nordisk Ministerråd. Retrieved 2008-09-18 from <http://www.norden.org/pub/velfaerd/konsument/sk/TN2005517.pdf>

Castells, M. (1997). *The power of identity: The information age: Economy, society and culture* (Vol. 2). Oxford, UK: Blackwell.

Cheney, G. (1992). The corporate person (re)presents itself. In E. L. Toth & R. L. Heath (Eds.), *Rhetorical and critical approaches to public relations* (pp. 165–183). Hillsdale, NJ: Erlbaum.

Cottle, S. (1998). Ulrich Beck, "risk society" and the media: A catastrophic view? *European Journal of Communication, 13*(1), 5–32.

Cutlip, S. M., Center, A. H., & Broom, G. M. (2000). *Effective public relations* (8th ed.). Upper Saddle River, NJ: Prentice-Hall.

Deetz, S. A. (1992). *Democracy in an age of corporate colonization: Developments in communication and the politics of everyday life.* Albany, NY: State University of New York Press.

Demetrious, K. (2006). Active voices. In J. L'Etang & M. Pieczka (Eds.), *Public relations: Critical debates and contemporary practice* (pp. 93-110). London: Erlbaum.

Dingwall, R. (1999). "Risk society": The cult of theory and the millennium? *Social Policy & Administration, 33*(4), 474–491.

Elliott, A. (2002). Beck's sociology of risk: A critical assessment. *Sociology, 36*(2), 293–315.

Ewen, S. (1996). *PR! A social history of spin.* New York: Basic Books.

Friedman, M. (2003). Marketplace, media, and moral considerations. In M. Micheletti, A. Follesdal, & D. Stolle (Eds.), *Politics, products, and markets: Exploring political consumerism past and present* (pp. 45–62). New Brunswick, NJ: Transaction.

Giddens, A. (1990). *The consequences of modernity.* Cambridge, UK: Polity.

Graham, K., & Josh, G. (2002). Promotionalism and subpolitics: Nike and its labor critics. *Management Communication Quarterly, 15*(4), 541–570.

Jansson, A. (2001). *Image culture: Media, consumption and everyday life in reflexive modernity.* Gothenburg, Sweden: Department of Journalism and Mass Communication, University of Gothenburg.

Jones, R. (2002). Challenges to the notion of publics in public relations: Implications of the risk society for the discipline. *Public Relations Review, 28*(1), 49–62.

Kellner, D. (1995). *Media culture: Cultural studies, identity and politics between the modern and the postmodern.* New York: McGraw-Hill.

Latour, B. (2003). Is re-modernisation occurring—and if so, how to prove it? A commentary on Ulrich Beck. *Theory, Culture and Society, 20*(2), 35–48.

Lupton, D., & Tulloch, J. (2001). Border crossings: Narratives of movement, "home" and risk. *Sociological Research Online, 5*(4). Retrieved 2008-09-18 from http://www.socresonline.org.uk/5/lupton.html

Lupton, D., & Tulloch, J. (2002). Risk is part of your life: Risk epistemologies among a group of Australians. *Sociology, 36*(2), 317–334.

Luhmann, N. (1993) *Risk: A sociological theory.* New York: de Gruyter.

Lyotard, J. F. (1979). *The postmodern condition: A report on knowledge.* Minneapolis, MN: University of Minnesota Press.

Mayhew, L. H. (1997). *The new public: Professional communication and the means of social influence.* Cambridge, UK: Cambridge University Press.

Micheletti, M. (2003). *Political virtue and shopping: Individuals consumerism and collective action.* New York: Palgrave Macmillan.

Micheletti, M., Føllesdal, A., & Stolle, D. (2003). Introduction. In M. Micheletti, A. Føllesdal, & D. Stolle (Eds.), *Politics, products, and markets: Exploring political consumerism past and present* (pp. 3–20). New Brunswick, NJ: Transaction.

Olins, W. (1989). *Corporate identity.* Boston, MA: Harvard Business School Press.

Olins, W. (2000). How brands are taking over the corporation. In M. Schultz, M. J. Hatch, & M. Holten Larsen (Eds.), *The expressive organization* (pp. 51–65). Oxford: Oxford University Press.

Pearson, R. (1992). Perspectives on public relations history. In E. L. Toth & R. L. Heath (Eds.), *Rhetorical and critical approaches to public relations* (pp. 111–130). Hillsdale, NJ: Erlbaum.

Pierson, C., & Castles, F. G. (Eds.). (2000). *The welfare state reader.* Cambridge, UK: Polity Press.

Putnam, R. D. (2000). *Bowling alone: The collapse and revival of American community.* New York: Simon & Schuster.

Scammell, M. (2000). The internet and civic engagement: The age of the citizen-consumer. *Political Communication, 17,* 351–355.

Stolle, D., Hooghe, M., & Micheletti, M. (2005). Politics in the supermarket: Political consumerism as a form of political participation. *International Political Science Review, 26*(3), 245–269.

Thompson, J. B. (1995). *The media and modernity: A social theory of the media.* Cambridge, UK: Polity Press.

Turner, B. S. (1994). *Orientalism, postmodernism, and globalism.* London: Routledge.

Wilkinson, I. (2001). Social theories of risk perception: At once indispensable and insufficient. *Current Sociology, 49*(1), 1–22.

Life and Work of Ulrich Beck

Ulrich Beck is a professor at the Institut für Soziologie at Ludwig-Maximilians-Universität in Munich, Germany. He was born in 1944 and after studies in sociology, philosophy, psychology, and political science he defended a doctoral dissertation in philosophy in 1972. He was a professor at the universities of Münster (1979–1981) and Bamberg (1981–1992) before he became a professor in Munich in 1992.

He has worked with several prominent sociologists, among others Anthony Giddens, while Beck was the British Journal of Sociology Professor at the London School of Economics. Beck is chief editor of *Soziale Welt* and he was a member of the Future Commission of the German Government. At the present time he is director of the research center Reflexive Modernization, established in 1999 by the German Research Foundation (DFG). It is a partnership between research groups in Munich and Augsburg.

As a scholar and teacher Beck concentrates on modernization theory, environmental sociology, the transformation of work, and social inequalities. Best known is his book *Risikogesellschaft: Auf dem Weg in einen andere Moderne* [*Risk Society: Towards a New Modernity*]. The book became a bestseller when it was published 1984, and it has sold more than 60,000 copies. He has written more than 25 books which have been translated into more than 25 languages. He has also authored or coauthored more than 100 scientific articles and his work is to be found in a wide range of nonacademic publications.

Ulrich Beck is married to Elisabeth Beck-Gernsheim, with whom he has coauthored *The Normal Chaos of Love* (1995) and *Individualization* (2002), among others.

Link to his website at the Ludwig-Maximilians-Universität: http://www.ls2.soziologie.uni-muenchen.de/personen/professoren/beck_ulrich/index.html (in German).

Chapter 3

On Berger

A Social Constructionist Perspective on Public Relations and Crisis Communication

Mats Heide

Abstract

Together with his colleague Thomas Luckmann, Berger introduced a social constructionist perspective to social science. Berger is interested in social interactions and how these interactions gradually produce a common social reality. In this chapter, I discuss how this perspective has bearing upon crisis communication as a subdiscipline of public relations. It is pointed out how crises are social constructions produced by the organizational member's perception and sense-making processes. Furthermore, crisis communication is not isolated to the postcrisis phase that primarily has interested scholars. Crisis is often a result of poor communication between organizations and its publics, and consequently more focus should be put on the precrisis phase and on building and maintaining long-lasting relationships. In sum, communication between an organization and its publics is a sense-making process where the social reality is constructed.

In this chapter I would like to propose a social constructionist perspective on crisis communication with inspiration from the American sociologist Peter L. Berger. My choice of Berger is related to his great influence on the epistemological movement of social constructionism. His well-known book *The Social Construction of Reality* (1966) is the first that has the term *social construction* in the title. Berger wrote this book together with the German sociologist Thomas Luckmann, and they are commonly regarded as a radar pair. I have chosen to focus on Berger because the reasoning in *The Social Construction of Reality* is developed from the thoughts in Berger's first book *Invitation to Sociology* (1963). Berger has published more books and articles than Luckmann. One of Berger's more important contributions to research is his focus on people's everyday reality, which is permeated both by social relations and material objects, and his emphasis on interpersonal social interactions in the social construction of reality. Furthermore, he has taught us to question and problematize things that we would otherwise take for granted, and has thereby enabled us to look through the eyes of society and its institutions. In sum, Berger's work is a good starting point for advancing a social constructionist perspective on crisis communication.

As remarked elsewhere (see Introduction, this volume), public relations as a research field seems to be stuck in a traditional epistemology, and there is a clear need for new perspectives and epistemologies in order to develop public relations theory. These characteristics are certainly also valid for the subfield of *crisis communication*. An exception to the rule is Heath's texts on public relations and crisis communication from a rhetorical perspective (e.g., Heath, 1993; Heath & Millar, 2004). In this chapter I will focus on crisis communication, and discuss it from a social constructionist perspective, or more precisely from a Peter Bergerian point of view.

On Crisis Communication

Scholars such as Beck (1992) and Giddens (1991) (see chapters 2 and 6, this volume) claim that we, as a consequence of late modernity, live in a risk society. We are all aware of the risk society, not at least through mass media's, more or less daily, reports on new risks, such as the Asian bird flu or various organizational crises. Perhaps the best known international organizational crisis during the last few years was the bankruptcy of the American energy company Enron in late 2001. Enron was one of the world's leading electricity companies with claimed revenues of $101 billion in 2000. Tragically, the founder of the company, Kenneth Lay, died in the beginning of June 2006 two months before his sentence—presumably life imprisonment—could be announced. As a consequence of the risk society and media's intensive focusing on crisis, crisis communication has received a lot of attention from PR-scholars and has become an emerging field in public relations (Grunig, Grunig, & Dozier, 2002). Since the late 1990s, there has been a constant flow of new articles and books on this subject. In fact, crisis communication is the core of public relations with direct connections to the historical development of the field; "damage control" set off the public relations industry (Ewen, 1996). Public relations is primarily used and shows its value when organizations face crisis situations.

A common feature in the greater part of the literature on crisis communication is the perception of a crisis as a result of some external threats in the surrounding environment. Thus, a crisis is normally understood as an objective and a "real" thing "out there," which hits and affects an organization at full strength. As a consequence, an organization is supposed to react to the objective crisis and immediately act in order to revert to an imagined state of equilibrium. Another common feature is the multiplicity of detailed guidelines and best practices, which are developed from practitioners' experiences (Seeger, Sellnow, & Ulmer, 2001). An additional characteristic of the field is the tendency to exclusively focus on postcrisis communication.

Obviously, crisis communication is a rather traditional field, where system theory is predominant. The open system theory emphasizes that an organization is dependent on its environment, and that interdependence comes from a mutual need. In order to survive, it is assumed that an organization continually has to adapt to changes in the environment. Many texts on crisis communication (e.g. Fearn-Banks, 2002; Zoch & Duhe, 1997) are grounded in a modernist epistemology. A problem is that there is seldom a focus on more theoretical perspectives and questions (Gilpin & Murphy, 2006). In other words, in this field there is an urgent need for theoretical development in order to get alternative and better understanding of the complex phenomenon of organizational crisis communication.

On Berger's Thinking

Peter L. Berger has written several books on sociological theory, sociology of religion, and Third World development. For most of us, his name is chiefly connected to one of his first books, *The Social Construction of Reality: A Treatise in the Sociology of Knowledge*, which I mentioned earlier. This book was first published in the United States in 1966 and has revolutionized the epistemology of social theory with its questioning of the traditional essentialism that has historically dominated the social sciences. Essentialism is the belief that the categorical structure of reality is determined by transhistorical essences that are independent of individual awareness. The relationship between society and the individual is often at the center of Berger's analysis. According to Berger, because society is constantly producing individuals, new human concepts or inventions will gradually become a part of our reality. Berger emphasizes that language is important in the production of social structures, which are formed by social processes. This focus on language and the weight of social interaction processes characterizes the thinking in social constructionism (Shotter & Gergen, 1994). In other words, both society and individuals exist within the language. Berger's thinking has, although implicitly, a communicative focus, especially when it comes to the construction of reality as a social process.

Berger regards sociology as having as its focus an understanding of contemporary society as a large complex of human relationships. The goal of sociology, according to Berger, is to uncover the different levels of meaning hidden from the consciousness of everyday life—to "see through" and "look behind," and to receive a better understanding of what goes on in a particular context in terms of social interaction. Hence, Berger claims that sociology has a particular perspective on explaining social life.

As mentioned, Berger's thinking can be placed within the epistemology of social constructionism. He states that people's worldviews are already a given in a society's language. There is little doubt that language "controls" individuals' relationship to reality. Language is a social phenomenon developed throughout the history of mankind, and it is not chosen by ourselves but "forced" upon us during our initial socialization. Berger (1963) maintains that: "[s]ociety predefines for us that fundamental symbolic apparatus with which we grasp the world, order our experience and interpret our own existence" (p. 117). Language also provides us with values, logic, and information from which we can appropriate knowledge. People's socialized worldviews are understood as natural and self-evident, or "taken for granted" as the Austrian sociologist Alfred Schütz puts it. Thus, reality is socially constructed, a view which stands in opposition to the traditional and widespread Durkheimian view of society as an objective facticity, where people are at different places in the social system.

A Human Perspective on Sociology

In *Invitation to Sociology: A Humanistic Perspective*, Berger (1963) presents the sociological perspective as a "form of consciousness" organized around four motifs (or themes). According to Berger, things are not what they seem; reality has many layers of meaning. The hallmark of sociological consciousness is its ability to try to understand reality from several, and often competing, systems of interpretation. In order to achieve this consciousness, Berger proposes a guide that consists of his four motifs. The first motif is the *debunking motif*, which is an ambition to unmask a situation and try to see through the facades of social structures. The roots of this motif are methodological and are reached by (1) being interested in other answers or goals than the generally accepted answers or official goals of human actions; (2) being conscious of the different levels of meaning in human events of which people often are not aware; and (3) being suspicious of official interpretations by authorities such as leaders of organizations. Berger also links ideology to the debunking motif.

The *unrespectability motif* is the second theme. Berger states that modern society is divided into two sectors: The respectable sector, which encompasses the middle class, dominates the definition of social reality. The unrespectable sector is everything else outside what is considered as respectable by the middle class. One of the most distinguishing features of the two sectors is language, which also is the most reliable identification tag. Berger's unrespectability motif means that scholars ought to look at and try to understand reality from several different perspectives, not only from that of persons with conventional middle class occupations but also from the point of view of the taxi driver, the dancer, the professional boxer, or the jazz musician. Consequently, this is a kind of underdog perspective.

The *relativization motif* is Berger's third theme, and it stresses the importance of seeing the value of the varied ways of understanding the world. This motif highlights the significance of not understanding the world as something given or natural. Thus, different cultures with diverse values and beliefs can provide other and new ways to understanding the world. In the modern world, sociology represents the consciousness of a world in which values have been radically relativized. In contrast to the traditional mind, the modern mind is mobile, spends time with others differently located from itself, and can easily consider changing professions or locations. Accordingly, the modern identity is uncertain and ever unstable. The relativization motif promotes an appreciation of the ways in which different meaning systems can provide a more total interpretation and understanding of reality.

Fourth and last is the *cosmopolitan motif*, which implies openness to the world and to other ways of thinking and acting, an attitude that is often the case with people who live in urban areas. Berger (1963) claims that: "his mind...is at home wherever there are other men [sic] who think. We would submit that sociological consciousness is marked by the same kind of cosmopolitanism" (p. 53). In brief, Berger maintains that sociologists ought to have an open mind and be interested in other cultures and eager to understand new horizons of human meaning.

An important concept that Peter Berger discusses in *Invitation to Sociology* is institution, which he defines as a distinctive complex of social actions that regulate and rule people's behavior in different situations. Examples of institutions are money, language, time, size and weight law, class, marriage, and organized religion. To understand an institution we first have to recognize the historical process in which it was produced. Institutions make people think and behave in certain ways that society finds desirable. In other words, institutions provide procedures that control human behavior in a patterned way. When institutions work, people perceive the procedures of institutions as the one and only ones to follow. There is a control aspect to all institutions, which control human behavior by predefining patterns of behavior. The control mechanism is thereby indirect as it directs people's way of thinking and acting. Through continuous socialization processes, people in a society are taught by such entities as family, friends, school, religion, mass media, work organization, or advertising, and learn the accepted procedures and ways of thinking, and incorporate behavior that enables them to be accepted as normal citizens. Berger claims that institutional imperatives work almost as instincts; mainly we have at most two different choices, which are predefined a priori. Society and its institutions are an objective facticity that cannot be denied. We live in society and everything we do or think is in some way coerced by the patterns of different institutions. If we obey and follow the rules of institutions, we are awarded, and if we do not, we are sanctioned; for example, through isolation from our fellow citizen, through being made the objects of ridicule, or through restrictions on our liberty. Sanctions can be produced and executed by the law, but most often they are produced and executed by the moral pressures of society.

People's Reality

The Social Construction of Reality (Berger & Luckmann, 1966) offers a theoretical explanation of how the social world is structured and functions. The authors attempt to answer the following questions: "How do subjective meanings become objective 'things'?" "How do human actors construct the world so that their products come to appear as things?" and "Why does the social world seem real to people?" The main theme throughout the book concerns the division of "structure" and "action," which Berger and Luckmann consider as dialectical rather than as two separate entities. The authors propose that the world we live in is constructed by a multiplicity of social arrangements and practices.

The book is one of the most important sources of inspiration to the epistemology of social constructionism, which since the late 1990s has become enormously popular among scholars in the social sciences. The book is rooted in phenomenology, and especially in Alfred Schütz's work and his attempt to understand the taken-for-granted world that people in a society share with their fellows.

According to Berger and Luckmann, the social world is a creation of human beings and they in turn are also the creation of their social world. This means that people together construct the human environment, which in turn affects people (cf. Giddens and his concept of "duality of structure"). A solitary human being exists at the animal level, and cannot develop, Berger and Luckmann claim. However, people are social animals. When people interact a social structure will evolve that establishes order and stability. Accordingly, a social order is not provided by nature or copied from any biological data, but develops through human activity and interaction. Social order is a product of human beings, and, as Berger and Luckmann emphasize, is an ongoing, never-ending process.

In the book three important concepts are presented: *externalization, objectivation,* and *internalization.* The environment in which humans act is complex and ever changing; it is never still and stable. To live under these conditions people need some minimal structure, and consequently they provide their own stable environment. When people repeatedly and frequently engage in an activity, a pattern eventually develops. The activity then takes less effort to be reproduced and becomes economic. People always attempt to habitualize their activities to achieve efficiency, and step by step the habits become embedded as routines in the general stock of knowledge. Habitualization provides the direction and the specialization of an activity, which makes it unnecessary for each situation to be repeatedly defined.

After a while the habits are *externalized,* and they spread through language and discourse to other people who were involved in the original habit. In other words, habits are knowledge that earlier generations have produced and that new generations learn through communication. From a psychological point of view, habits make it easier for humans to manage the uncertainty they experience in their lives. Cognitive dissonance, the uncertainty that people encounter in new situations, is reduced when people rely on habits or externalized knowledge. By ordering the social world people experience a sense of being part of a meaningful whole.

Habits also play an important role when people interact, and after a while typifications will evolve—certain typical motives for the actions that are ascribed to the other. In everyday life people use typificatory schemes in terms of which others are apprehended, in other words, "a business man," "an Arab," and "a cheerful boy." These typifications will strongly affect people's interactions with others and make people play different roles. The roles also make it possible to distribute work—the social actions—and different social institutions will progress. Institutionalization occurs as soon as there is a reciprocal typification of habitualized actions. In other words, any such typification is an institution.

In situations where people are about to learn the patterns of unfamiliar institutions, legitimations are fundamental. The legitimation explains the social and institutional order so it all makes sense. One method to legitimate social institutions is reification. It is the apprehension that products of human activity, for example organizations, are nonhuman and even something "suprahuman," such as the results of cosmic laws, natural developments, or expressions of the will of some God. Reification will make people forget that social institutions are products of human actions. Social institutions are, as a consequence of legitimations and reifications, *objectivated,* and will then appear as objective things "out there." People socially construct their reality when they repeatedly act in patterned ways and take these patterns for granted as their reality. Eventually, they forget that the social world is created.

When a child is born there are existing institutions that gradually appropriate it. Through primary and secondary socialization processes children learn, or in Berger and Luckmann's words *internalize,* how the social world is built and functions. The most important item of socialization is that language appears to the child as inherent in the nature of things, in other words, a thing is what it is called and could not be called anything else. As they internalize the norms and the institutions of the social world, they also become real social beings. Hence, through the process of socialization the objectified world acts back on human beings.

In Search of Guidelines

In the book *Modernity, Pluralism and the Crisis of Meaning* (1995) Peter Berger and Thomas Luckmann state that modernity and the following pluralism often will lead people to experience a crisis of meaning. In a modern society people constantly have to make different choices, at material, social, and intellectual levels: "Which career is the most appropriate?" "How should I raise my children?" and "What kind of house should we live in?" In developed industrial countries there are neither common values, which function as guidelines through the different stages of life, nor a single reality. And in the late modern society people's reality is complex and ever changing, or to use another term *raplex*—a fusion of rapidity and complexity. People constantly get new influences by traveling, media consumption, and organizations' colonization of different parts of life (Deetz, 1992). These factors will certainly affect people's identity and destabilize it. Berger and Luckmann underscore that the individual can no longer choose not to choose. In most cases crises of meaning take place at significant points in the life cycle, such as the onset of puberty, the end of schooling, entry into a new job, and death, but crises of meaning are also related to the never-ending flow of new consumer goods. Historically, organized religion has had a fundamental role in guiding people in their search for an understanding of the complexities of life and has helped save the individual from crises of meaning. The "secularization thesis," which is a product of modernity, implies that religious institutions have lost their credibility as institutions that can offer clear interpretations. Also, localized systems of meaning in the immediate society no longer act as guidelines because they are relativized through modern pluralism. The modern society's solution to helping people handle such crises is the invention of new institutions for the production and communication of meaning—such as psychotherapy or sexual counseling. Institutions offer different interpretations of reality and values, and the media select and package these solutions, transform them, and decide how they will be disseminated. Modern pluralism and the following choices and multiple interpretations make it difficult for people to create and develop a personal identity. During crises of meaning many people turn to organizations such as virtual communities for assistance in interpreting what has happened.

Critique of Berger and Social Constructionism

It is not easy to find explicit criticism of Berger's thinking and texts. The critiques one can find are directed to social constructionism in general. This criticism comes particularly from scholars that take a realist stance and praise objectivism as the overall goal for science. In a discussion of critiques of social constructionism, Burningham and Cooper (1999) maintain that realists are convinced that the objective of sociology is to reach an understanding of the real, objective, and "out-there" problems faced by society. Realists assume that material, natural, or nonsocial phenomena have causal efficacy and that it is possible to make objective statements of reality. Consequently, realists complain that social constructionists do not pay sufficient attention to "reality." The critique is focused on strong social constructionism or to use another word, *extreme* relativism; in other words, social constructionism as ontology where a physical reality is denied. However, most social constructionist scholars understand social constructionism as an epistemology or a mild constructionism, where attention is directed to social processes involved in the production and reproduction of institutions, epistemologies, and knowledge. The goal for mild constructionism is to understand how social reality is socially constructed (cf. Sismondo, 1993). Berger's thinking can be placed within the soft or mild version of social constructionism, with his interest in the social construction of reality and people's knowledge of their social reality. And as Hacking (1999) underscores, Berger does not claim that nothing can exist if it is not socially constructed.

To Sum Up on Berger

Berger wants to explain how modern society works by focusing on multiple levels of meaning. According to Berger, people participate in the production of their own perceived reality. Humankind is made up of acting beings, which means that people always try to change the figure of the given in order to produce a meaningful totality (Berger & Pullberg, 1965). We always try to understand what we have experienced and what is happening around us, and this process never ends and is never complete. As Berger and Pullberg (1965) maintain: "Totality…is never a *fait accompli*, but is always in the process of being constructed" (p. 201). The production of social reality is seen as an ongoing and dynamic process.

The world is never a given, and must be produced and reproduced over and over again. People understand the world as real only if others continually confirm it. Berger claims that people act on their interpretations and knowledge of a perceived reality, and thereby a social reality is reproduced and reinforced. The knowledge of the reality is taken for granted and perceived by people as a natural and an objective fact. Further, the process of producing a meaningful world is not an individual project; it is a social process.

Reflections on Essential Concepts

The main goal of scholars in social science, according to Berger, is to reveal the different layers of meaning. Following Berger's debunking motif, it is important to be suspicious of the standard way to understand and employ common conceptions in a field. Thus, it is important to "see through," "look behind," and question the taken-for-granted concepts that are used in a particular field. Therefore, I will reflect on the "practice" of some essential concepts in the field of crisis communication and uncover new levels of meaning. Three concepts are particularly important to this field, namely crisis, communication, and organization.

First, which I also mentioned above, in the traditional research on crisis communication, a *crisis* is often perceived as being a result of some external threat in the surrounding environment. Hence, a crisis is understood as an objective and "real" thing "out there," which hits an organization and affects its functioning. It is taken for granted that a crisis develops through fixed stages; for example, as described by Fink's (1986) four-stage model or Mitroff's (1994) five-stage model. There is also a tendency in research on crisis communication to exclusively focus on postcrises; in other words, scholars pay a lot of attention to the problems of handling a crisis that has already arisen. For that reason, the field can be characterized as action driven: materials are designed in preparation for a crisis, an existing crisis is coped with, and the goal is to restore order after a crisis has been settled (Kersten, 2005).

From a Bergerian perspective, a crisis does not just hit an organization like a thunderbolt from out of a blue sky, and an organization does not react and respond automatically to a crisis as an objective phenomenon. Rather, a crisis slowly evolves and takes a certain form. In newer research, a crisis is perceived as a process with no clear borders or stages (Murphy, 1996; Weick, 1988). If we apply Berger's reasoning to an organizational context, it would mean that organization members, like people in general—or to use Berger's expression "man [sic]"—do not react to an objective environment. Rather, they constantly try to make sense of events. From a social constructionist perspective it is assumed that members react to information in the surrounding environment, interpret the information, and enact a social reality which the members later act on. This implies that organization members will not react to changes in the environment in a causal way. The members are active in the construction of the social reality, and hence the reality of organizations can be seen as communication products. The result of the members' sense making processes depends on where they look, how they look, what they want to represent, and their tools of representation (Allard-Poesi, 2005). In general, a crisis is initiated by a trigger or when an organizational member notices and interprets certain information. A crisis does not just come up by itself; the member's sense making processes of changes in- or outside the organization slowly enacts a crisis. Thus, a crisis can then be seen as a result of the organization member's perception and sense making processes.

Second, there is a strong tendency in the literature on crisis communication, and among many practitioners, to have a rather simple view of *organization* as a phenomenon. In general, organizations tend to be reified in the crisis communication literature, in other words, seen as natural observable fact "out there" in the reality. According to Shotter (1993), this way of perceiving organizations had its origins in the Enlightenment and the dream of discovering "the real," already existing, orderly principles underlying people's behavior. The underpinning of those texts is a traditional view of system theory, with a rather static view of the relations between organizations and their publics. It seems that scholars, within the modernist (Alvesson & Deetz, 1996) or functionalist approach (Putnam, 1983), see organizations as "containers" in which organization members function, work, and interact with each other and with actors outside the organization. Consequently, the organization is either taken for granted or the internal processes are black boxed (Cheney & Christensen, 2001).

From a Bergerian perspective, an organization is not a stable phenomenon for more than a short while. Instead, it is continually transforming, progressing, and adjusting to changes in the environment (composed of information as was mentioned above). Berger (1963) understands society as a complex of human relations, and consequently organizations are also complexes of human relations. The social structure that constitutes an organization is produced and reproduced by the organizational members through communication (cf. Shotter, 1993). The language, Berger tells us, is both a vehicle to produce and reproduce the social reality, and a vehicle to understand the world around us. Language is a human product, but yet it is in most cases experienced as an external facticity, or as Berger and Pullberg (1965) express it: "things *are* that as which they are named" (p. 203). New members are socialized into the organization and internalize institutions within the organization. If organizations are regarded as social constructions, communication among the organizational members is the essence of the production and reproduction of the social structure. An important part of this sense making process is the production of social structures, which are parts of the objectified and produced world. A social structure has no reality apart from a human one; it is nothing but the product of human activity. Berger reasons that social structure is produced by people and in turn produces them (e.g., Berger & Pullberg, 1965). Karl E. Weick is an organizational scholar that clearly is inspired by Berger's reasoning on society as social construction. He is one of the most cited organization theorists and has introduced a social constructionist perspective to organizational theory. As early as 1969 Weick launched his organization theory that focuses on the continuous organizing processes, in the book *The Social Psychology of Organizing* (1969), which can be understood as a riff on Katz and Kahn's (1966) *The Social Psychology of Organization*. Like Berger, Weick focused on social life as a process—human activity constructing a reality that is taken for granted. Organization members are constantly engaged in structuring the world as a meaningful entity.

Third, in the bulk of literature on crisis communication it is presumed that *communication* and language can mirror the objective reality as a truth bearer. As a consequence, it is assumed that language stands in a clear and an unambiguous relation to reality; words have a certain known and agreed upon meaning. This perspective of communication, which James Carey (1988) calls the transmission view, is the most common in Western culture and inherent in most people's thinking. Communication is then described in terms such as *transmit, give, deliver,* and *send,* and it is assumed that words contain inherent meanings. The core element in the transmission view is the transportation of information through time and space, and effective communication is understood as a situation when receivers as quickly as possible get information via some medium from a sender.

In the eyes of Berger, communication and language do not mirror reality; rather, they create the social reality. Language is a social product and receivers of a communication construct the meaning. Through constant communication and interaction among the organization members, common meanings and a social reality are produced. It is here important to underline that Berger's social constructionist perspective does not question the existence of a reality "out there," but emphasizes people's relation to it—what it means to them. Carey (1988) calls this perspective on communication the ritual view. Thus, language does not describe the reality but is itself a form of action. Communication is a constitutive process where social realities, as organizations, are made. The social structures are externalized during communication and repeated communicative acts can lead people to internalize the social structure, the reality of an organization, so it is perceived as natural and objective. What people understand as a social reality, reflects the views and visions of those who are engaged in a communication process (cf. Gergen, 2003). Hence, there is a strong mutual relation between organization and communication.

Consequences for Crisis Communication

So, what are the consequences if we take a Bergerian, or social constructionist, perspective on crisis communication? During Peter Berger's career the concept of the institution has been at the center of his attention. However, social institutions and how they constrain public relations practices have not been focused on by public relations scholars (Leichty & Warner, 2001). Publics, for example, are often assumed to be reactive units that have developed in response to the actions of organizations. In reality, many publics exist before an organization enters the arena, and they are often independent and with own goals. Public relations is in itself an institution that affects several different dimensions of modern life, from such different aspects as the decisions of politicians to the identity of people in everyday life.

In contemporary research on crisis communication, crisis is seen as a part of an organization's life cycle (e.g., Kersten, 2005; Sellnow, 1993). A crisis is here seen as an important opportunity for development and learning. This means that an organizational crisis is not an anomalous situation, but a particular stage in the never-ending development of an organization. A social constructionist perspective on crisis gives a more holistic understanding, and emphasizes that both crisis and "business as usual" are normal parts of an organization's life cycle. Many scholars in the field, such as Coombs (1999) and Zoch and Duhe (1997), claim that crises in most cases are a result of poor communication between an organization and its publics. As was pointed out above, a crisis is not something that happens in extraordinary circumstances, but rather is "part of the game" for organizations. This means that both researchers and practitioners ought to be more interested in the precrisis phase, and not solely focus on the postcrisis phase. Further, this comprehension of crisis also means that the border between risk and crisis communication is not clear. According to Heath (1995), risk communication encompasses information exchange of the relative level of risk to different publics. Hence, risk communication is closely related to the precrisis stage. It is therefore an open question where a risk ceases and transforms into a crisis.

One can even wonder if it is defensible for two separate research fields to focus on the same phenomenon. If undeveloped and poor communication between an organization and its publics is a source of organizational crises, scholars in crisis communication should place more emphasis on and interest in communication and dialogue with publics, and consequently on relationship building. An interest in dialogues and relationships has already made an entrance in the contemporary research on public relations. Nowadays, there is a common understanding that public relations is a relationship-building professional activity (e.g., Heath, 2001), which stands in opposition to the traditional view of trying to change the opinions and behavior of different publics. Thus, from a Bergerian perspective there is a requirement for organizations to initiate mutual and long-lasting relationships with important publics in order to handle crisis situations in a flexible and smooth way. Communication and ongoing dialogues with publics is the only way to nurture and restore constructive relationships. The rationale behind this discussion is that dialogue is especially important in situations of crisis and that open community relationships with publics can prevent risk events or mitigate the force if they become a reality (Heath & Palenchar, 2000). Further, it is believed that stronger networks with publics are important resources for the gathering of relevant information in a crisis situation, and give better possibilities for a more accurate perception of the situation. In a crisis situation publics' trust tends to be fairly low, and messages are perceived as ambiguous and interpretations differ from those of the organization (Williams & Olaniran, 1998). Here it is also important to emphasize that communication from a Bergerian perspective enhances the function of communication from only being a tool for diffusion of information. In terms of research, there is a common assumption that crises can best be resolved through cooperation, not through manipulation or force (cf. Lee, 2005). Further, it is presupposed that organizations with developed, good relations with important publics should pay attention to their points of view, expectations, and demands for action. This means that public relations practitioners must acknowledge that people always create meanings in different situations, and their interpretation will inevitably be dissimilar to the sender's original meaning. Accordingly, communication is seen as a reciprocal process in which the participants—the members of an organization and representatives of a public—produce a mutual understanding of the reality. The communication is, in other words, a sense making process when a social reality is enacted.

A dialogic communication is an interaction in which a relationship exists (Kent & Taylor, 1998). Consequently, dialogue is closely related to community and this aspect gradually evolved in the contemporary public relations literature of the late 1990s. The interest in community has its origin in organizations' programs of corporate social responsibility, normally seen as a practice that benefits both organizations and society. According to L'Etang (1996), corporate social responsibility can be seen as a good investment in times of crisis. The resolution of a crisis and the result of the resolution has a close connection if the organization has developed good and stable relations with its main publics. Another reason for the increasing interest in communities is connected to the observation that people tend to be engaged in several informal communities in their private as well as in their professional lives. Communities are informal social configurations in which the members have some common and mutual interest, opinion, or practice (e.g., Lave & Wenger, 1991; Wenger, 1998). It has also been observed that publics emerge in communities rather than in disconnected anonymities; they strive for a social identity to share with the like-minded. Especially in a crisis situation, an individual's interpretation and construction of meanings is closely related to their community. Further, it is assumed that a mutual community relationship can lessen the threat of a risk and make a safer place for both the organization and the publics. With a Bergerian perspective on crisis communication, we ought to regard publics as a more complex entity than all too often seems to be the case. In American crisis communication literature it is common to discuss publics as activist groups, although in many countries and cultures activism is not an issue. Sriramesh (2002), for example, reports that in countries that are not characterized by pluralism or that do not foster open disagreement with authorities, activism by publics is nonexistent or restrained.

This discussion takes us further on to multiculturalism, which is a very pressing issue. For example, in 2004 22% of the Swedish population consisted of people with a foreign background (which of course is a rather low figure compared to the United States). According to Statistics Sweden, the term *foreign background* means that people were either born in another country, or that at least one parent was born abroad. From a crisis communication perspective, this social change will bring about new challenges to both theory and practice. It becomes clear to us that this new globalized and multicultural world consists of several often-competing systems of interpretation. Different cultures have their own habits and institutions that differ from the main culture or what Berger calls the respectable sector. If we apply Berger's thinking on this subject, it would mean that if we want to understand the world, we should follow his guide—the unrespectability and relativization motif. In other words, the goal for Berger is to be open minded about other cultures and to try to understand reality from several different perspectives. Hence, there is a need for greater diversity in our views of publics. There is a tendency among organizations not to appreciate and understand the value of minority groups' opinion, and really listen to them (cf. Deetz & Brown, 2004). If organizations want to follow Grunig's ideal of symmetrical communication, in other words, to see an organization and its publics as mutual participants in a communication process, they have to take a more long-term approach.

Conclusion

In this chapter, I have tried to promote a Bergerian, or social constructionist, perspective on crisis communication. From a Bergerian point
of view, public relations is an institution that constructs certain worldviews and realities through communication activities. Public relations
can be seen as a process of strategic disseminations of texts to maintain,
develop certain sociocultural practices and the preferred values and
attitudes of an organization.

A phenomenon that restricts an organization is an institutionalized
way to handle crisis and perform crisis management. Those ways, that
are taken for granted as the only right, have been developed throughout
the history of human society, and through externalization and socialization they have also been spread by different management discourses.
For example, once a crisis "hits" an organization it is most often handled
as a fire emergency response. To get a better understanding of public
relations as an institution, Berger asks us to look behind the façade and
inquire as to how public relations functions as producer of certain dominating realities in a society.

References

Allard-Poesi, F. (2005). The paradox of sense making in organizational analy-
sis. *Organization, 12*(2), 169–197.
Alvesson, M., & Deetz, S. A. (1996). Critical theory and postmodernism
approaches to organizational studies. In S. R. Clegg, C. Hardy, & W. R. Nord
(Eds.), *Handbook of organization studies* (pp. 191–217). London: Sage.
Beck, U. (1992). *Risk society: Towards a new modernity.* London: Sage.
Berger, B., & Berger, P. L. (1984). *The war over the family: Capturing the middle
ground.* Harmondsworth, UK: Penguin.
Berger, P. L. (1963). *Invitation to sociology: A humanistic perspective.* Garden City,
NY: Anchor Books.
Berger, P. L. (1987). *The capitalist revolution: Fifty propositions about prosperity,
equality, and liberty.* Aldershot, UK: Gower.
Berger, P. L. (1997). *Redeeming laughter: The comic dimension of human experience.*
Berlin: Walter de Gruyter.
Berger, P. L., & Luckmann, T. (1966). *The social construction of reality: A treatise in
the sociology of knowledge.* Garden City, NY: Doubleday.
Berger, P. L., & Luckmann, T. (1995). *Modernity, pluralism and the crisis of
meaning: The orientation of modern man.* Gütersloh, Germany: Bertelsmann
Foundation.
Berger, P. L., & Pullberg, S. (1965). Reification and the sociological critique of
consciousness. *History and Theory, 4*(2), 196–211.
Burningham, K., & Cooper, G. (1999). Being constructive: Social constructionism and the environment. *Sociology: The Journal of the British Sociological Association, 33*(2), 297–316.

Carey, J. W. (1988). *Communication as culture: Essays on media and society.* New York: Routledge.

Cheney, G., & Christensen, L. T. (2001). Public relations as contested terrain: A critical response. In R. L. Heath (Ed.), *Handbook of public relations* (pp. 167–182). Thousand Oaks, CA: Sage.

Cheney, G., & Christensen, L. T. (2006). What should public relations theory do, practically speaking? *Journal of Communication Management, 10*(1), 100–102.

Coombs, W. T. (1999). *Ongoing crisis communication: Planning, managing, and responding.* Thousand Oaks, CA: Sage.

Deetz, S. A. (1992). *Democracy in an age of corporate colonization: Development in communication and the politics of everyday life.* Albany: State University of New York Press.

Deetz, S. A., & Brown, D. (2004). Conceptualizing involvement, participation and workplace decision processes: A communication theory perspective. In D. Tourish & O. Hargie (Eds.), *Key issues in organizational communication* (pp. 172–187). London: Routledge.

Ewen, S. (1996). *PR! The social history of spin.* New York: Basic Books.

Fearn-Banks, K. (2002). *Crisis communications: A casebook approach* (2nd ed.). Mahwah, NJ: Erlbaum.

Fink, S. (1986). *Crisis management: Planning for the inevitable.* New York: American Management Association.

Gergen, K. J. (2003). Beyond knowing in organizational inquiry. *Organization, 10*(3), 453–455.

Giddens, A. (1991). *Modernity and self-identity: Self and society in the late modern age.* Cambridge, UK: Polity Press.

Gilpin, D., & Murphy, P. (2006). Reframing crisis management through complexity. In C. H. Botan & V. Hazleton (Eds.), *Public relations theory II* (pp. 375–392). Mahwah, NJ: Erlbaum.

Grunig, L. A., Grunig, J. E., & Dozier, D. M. (2002). *Excellent public relations and effective organizations: A study of communication management in three countries.* Mahwah, NJ: Erlbaum.

Hacking, I. (1999). *The social construction of what?* Cambridge, MA: Harvard University Press.

Heath, R. L. (1993). A rhetorical approach to zones of meaning and organizational prerogatives. *Public Relations Review, 19*(2), 141–156.

Heath, R. L. (1995). Corporate environmental risk communication: Cases and practices along the Texas gulf coast. In B. R. Burleson (Ed.), *Communication yearbook* (Vol. 18, pp. 255–277). Thousand Oaks, CA: Sage.

Heath, R. L. (2001). Defining the discipline. In R. L. Heath (Ed.), *Handbook of public relations* (pp. 1–9). Thousand Oaks, CA: Sage.

Heath, R. L., & Millar, D. P. (2004). A rhetorical approach to crisis communication: Management, communication processes, and strategic responses. In D. P. Millar & L. Heath Robert (Eds.), *Responding to crisis: A rhetorical approach to crisis communication* (pp. 1–17). Mahwah, NJ: Erlbaum.

Heath, R. L., & Palenchar, M. (2000). Community relations and risk communication: A longitudinal study of the impact of emergency response messages. *Journal of Public Relations Research, 12*(2), 131–161.

Katz, D., & Kahn, R. L. (1966). *The social psychology of organizations.* New York: Wiley.

Kent, M. L., & Taylor, M. (1998). Building dialogic relationships through the world wide web. *Public Relations Review, 24*(3), 321–334.

Kersten, A. (2005). Crisis as usual: Organizational dysfunction and public relations. *Public Relations Review, 31*(4), 544–549.

L'Etang, J. (1996). Corporate responsibility and public relations ethics. In J. L'Etang & M. Pieczka (Eds.), *Critical perspectives in public relations* (pp. 82–105). London: International Thomson Business Press.

Lave, J., & Wenger, E. (1991). *Situated learning: Legitimate peripheral participation.* Cambridge, MA: Cambridge University Press.

Lee, B. K. (2005). Crisis, culture, community. In P. J. Kalbfleisch (Ed.), *Communication yearbook* (Vol. 29, pp. 275–309). Mahwah, NJ: Erlbaum.

Leichty, G., & Warner, E. (2001). Cultural topoi: Implications for public relations. In R. L. Heath (Ed.), *Handbook of public relations* (pp. 61–74). Thousand Oaks, CA: Sage.

Mitroff, I. I. (1994). Crisis management and environmentalism: A natural fit. *California Management Review, 36*(2), 101–114.

Murphy, P. (1996). Chaos theory as a model for managing issues and crises. *Public Relations Review, 22*(2), 95–113.

Putnam, L. L. (1983). The interpretive perspective: An alternative to functionalism. In L. L. Putnam & M. E. Pacanowsky (Eds.), *Communication and organizations* (pp. 31–54). Beverly Hills, CA: Sage.

Seeger, M. W., Sellnow, T. L., & Ulmer, R. R. (2001). Public relations and crisis communication: Organizing and chaos. In R. L. Heath (Ed.), *Handbook of public relations* (pp. 155–165). Thousand Oaks, CA: Sage.

Sellnow, T. L. (1993). Scientific argument in organizational crisis communication: The case of Exxon. *Argumentation & Advocacy, 30*(1), 28–43.

Shotter, J. (1993). *Conversational realities: Constructing life through language.* London: Sage.

Shotter, J., & Gergen, K. J. (1994). Social construction: Knowledge, self, others, and continuing the conversation. In S. A. Deetz (Ed.), *Communication yearbook* (Vol. 17, pp. 3–33). London: Sage.

Sismondo, S. (1993). Some social constructions. *Social Studies of Science, 23*(3), 515–553.

Sriramesh, K. (2002). The dire need for multiculturalism in public relations education: An Asian perspective. *Journal of Communication Management, 7*(1), 54–71.

Weick, K. E. (1969). *The social psychology of organizing.* Reading, MA: Addison-Wesley.

Weick, K. E. (1988). Enacted sensemaking in crisis situations. *Journal of Management Studies, 25,* 305–317.

Wenger, E. (1998). *Communities of practice: Learning, meaning, and identity.* Cambridge, MA: Cambridge University Press.

Williams, D. E., & Olaniran, B. A. (1998). Expanding the crisis planning function: Introducing elements of risk communication to crisis communication practice. *Public Relations Review, 24*(3), 387–400.

Zoch, L. M., & Duhe, S. F. (1997). "Feeding the media" during a crisis: A nationwide look. *Public Relations Quarterly, 42*(3), 15–20.

Life and Work of Peter L. Berger

Peter Ludwig Berger was born in 1929 in Trieste, Italy, and raised in Vienna. In his late teens he immigrated to the United States. Berger graduated from Wagner College in 1949 with a bachelor of arts degree, and then studied at the New School for Social Research in New York where he obtained a doctorate in 1952. He was assistant professor at the University of North Carolina from 1956 to 1958, associate professor at Hartford Theological Seminary from 1958 to 1963. Berger has also held professorships at the New School for Social Research, Rutgers University, and Boston University. Since 1985 he has been director of the Institute on Culture, Religion and World Affairs at Boston University. He has written several books on sociological theory, modern society, and third world development, but he is probably best known for his texts on the sociology of religion.

Among his publications two stand out—*Invitation to Sociology* (1963), which for decades has been one of the most popular, and frequently referenced introductory texts in sociology, and *The Social Construction of Reality* (1966), coauthored with Thomas Luckmann, which is recognized as one of the most important contributions to the development of the social constructionism movement in the social sciences.

Peter Berger has written numerous books, including: *Redeeming Laughter: The Comic Dimension of Human Experience* (1997); *Modernity, Pluralism and the Crisis of Meaning* (with Thomas Luckmann 1995); *The Capitalist Revolution: Fifty Propositions About Prosperity, Equality and Liberty* (1987); and *The War Over the Family: Capturing the Middle Ground* (with Brigitte Berger 1984).

Chapter 4

On Bourdieu

Public Relations in Field Struggles[1]

Øyvind Ihlen

Abstract

According to Bourdieu, actors struggle and compete to position themselves in what he calls "fields" with the help of different forms of symbolic and material resources (capital). In this chapter, it is argued that public relations assists organizations in the struggle for such positions, and a typology of different resource types is developed. By extending the sociology of Bourdieu to an analysis of public relations, a more realistic perspective of the practice can be achieved and one that is based on a conflict perspective rather than on a consensus perspective of the world.

The sociology of Pierre Bourdieu implies that social actors struggle and compete to position themselves in *fields* with the help of different forms of symbolic and material resources (*capital*) (Bourdieu & Wacquant, 1992). The field is a social space of relations of dominance, subordinance, or equivalence, rooted in the types and amounts of resources that actors possess. Here, it is argued that public relations assists organizations in the struggle for such positions, and a typology of different resource types is developed using examples from the political field of energy and the environment. Extending the sociology of Bourdieu in this way means that a more realistic perspective of public relations than that provided by prevailing theories of the discipline can be obtained.

Liberal pluralism prevails in much public relations research, and the possibilities for harmony and consensus are emphasized (e.g., Grunig, Grunig, & Dozier, 2002; Heath, 1997). For scholars, a conflict perspective on society, such as that offered by Bourdieu, may produce a better understanding of the practice of public relations in society. For practitioners, the sociology of Bourdieu may help achieve a certain *cultural literacy* (Schirato & Yell, as cited in Webb, Schirato, & Danaher, 2001), which is necessary for their strategies to succeed.

This chapter presents an overview of selected parts of Bourdieu's work. This French scholar dealt with neither organizations nor public relations, so it is necessary to extend and reformulate some of his theoretical points. This endeavor is particularly helped by work in media sociology, which, in turn, is used to construct the typology of organizational resources that is suggested.

On the Sociology of Bourdieu

Pierre Bourdieu is considered to be among the most prominent contemporary social thinkers, and a number of books introduce and discuss his contributions to knowledge (e.g., Calhoun, LiPuma, & Postone, 1993; Elliott & Turner, 2001; Fowler, 2001; Jenkins, 2002; Robbins, 2000; Swartz, 1997, 1998; Webb et al., 2001). Here, a selection of some of his key concepts is made, based on what is deemed to be relevant to an analysis of public relations.

The focus of Bourdieu's sociology is uncovering the way in which the social world is structured, constituted, and reproduced through individual and collective struggle to conserve or transform the social world. Of particular interest are those struggles that "seek to impose the legitimate definition of reality" (Bourdieu, 1990b, p. 141). Bourdieu was originally trained as an anthropologist, but his research interest later veered toward sociology, and he became a truly multidisciplinary researcher, recognized not only in anthropology and sociology, but also in education, cultural theory, and philosophy, to mention just a few areas. Apart from this move from anthropology to sociology, however, it has been argued that it is difficult to recognize a specific theoretical "progression" or "stages" in the works of Bourdieu, due to their truly eclectic nature (Webb et al., 2001). This eclectic approach was also reflected in how he employed a whole range of different methods, from ethnography to statistical models, alongside metatheoretical and philosophical approaches. Throughout most of his work, however, a consistent interest in language and power is evident.

Language and Power

Bourdieu saw language as both a battlefield and a weapon. His perspective was that language structures our understanding of the world and that it is the medium by which these understandings are communicated. Language is both a *structuring structure* and a *structured structure*. In language and language use, traces of the social structure are expressed and reproduced (Bourdieu, 1991). The crucial point here is that language is a form of symbolic power that is often not recognized as power. As previously mentioned, the task of sociology is, according to Bourdieu, to uncover social structures and the mechanisms that help to reproduce or transform them (Bourdieu & Wacquant, 1992). It has also been claimed that by calling attention to such aspects, he continued the project of the Enlightenment. Bourdieu believed that scholarly work should be an intervention in the social world, rather than disinterested reflections. He was particularly critical of traditional authority and sought to demonstrate how certain mechanisms in society make positions of dominance appear to be "natural" or the result of personal choices. In his later years, Bourdieu began to engage directly in political action, challenging the ideology of neoliberalism generated by economists and administrators. Neoliberalism is sold to the public, he said, not in the form of policy documents, but in everyday language. An analysis of everyday language can help us to grasp what is taken for granted within a society, the *doxa*, or what is unquestioned universal opinion. Having a "doxic attitude," for instance, means "bodily and unconscious submission to conditions that are in fact arbitrary and contingent" (Webb et al., 2001, p. xi). An analysis of doxa and the stories that, for instance, the bureaucracy tells is thus a crucial activity for researchers to examine truth claims and the use of symbolic power (Webb et al., 2001). In other words, Bourdieu's work bears one of the most important hallmarks of critical social science—that of "identifying and challenging assumptions behind ordinary ways of perceiving, conceiving, and acting" (Brookfield, as cited in Alvesson & Deetz, 2000, p. 8).

At the same time, however, Bourdieu was also a fierce critic of another important modern scholar who has been linked to the Enlightenment project—Jürgen Habermas (see chapter 8, this volume). Bourdieu argued that false universalizations were present in the works of Habermas. He believed that Habermas failed to see that forms of symbolic violence have colonized the mind and that there are material conditions for reason. Such symbolic violence may include being denied resources or being treated as an inferior human being (Fowler, 2001; Webb et al., 2001). For Bourdieu, "linguistic relations [are] always relations of symbolic power" (Bourdieu & Wacquant, 1992, p. 142). Unlike many rhetoricians, linguists, and discourse analysts, however, he did not focus only on language itself, but also on objective structures, to explain and understand these power relations. To grasp his position, a foray into a key part of his sociology—"the theory of practice"—is necessary.

The Theory of Practice

Bourdieu's main contribution to social science has been his "theory of practice." He grappled with the classic antagonism concerning idealism and materialism, giving primacy to the structure or agency between subjectivism and objectivism. Subjectivism is here understood as the perspective "asserting that social reality is produced through the thoughts, decisions and actions of individual agents.... [Objectivism is] the idea that people's actions and attitudes are determined by objective social structures such as those relating to class, ethnicity, gender and language" (Webb et al., 2001, pp. xiv–xv).

Bourdieu ended up instead advocating that *relations* should be seen as the dominant factor (e.g., Bourdieu, 1972/1977, 1980/1990). It has been stated that his thinking began with Karl Marx, but that he drew more substantively from other classic sociologists, such as Emile Durkheim and Max Weber (see chapter 15 in this volume) (Swartz, 1997). Using the three concepts of *habitus*, *field*, and *capital*, he constructed a sociology that he argued made the opposition between subjectivism and objectivism obsolete.

Habitus

A habitus is a structuring mechanism that generates strategies for actors in the social world and through which actors relate to the social world. Habitus can be understood as a system of durable dispositions; that is, as an internalized mental or cognitive structure that functions both consciously and unconsciously and constrains what people should and should not do. A habitus is based on all of the situations through which dispositions are created and that an individual experiences throughout his or her lifetime (Bourdieu & Wacquant, 1992).

Bourdieu did not argue that the habitus *determines* actions or that the habitus pushes actors around and makes them passive. Reflection can help an actor to resist the habitus. As a system of durable dispositions, it is an open system; it produces society, but is at the same time produced by it. It is open for modification and "constantly subjected to experiences, and therefore constantly affected by them in a way that either reinforces or modifies its structures. It is durable but not eternal" (Bourdieu & Wacquant, 1992, p. 133).

The implications of this are discussed below, but an important point to note here is that people are not only consciously striving for clearly perceived goals. The strategies that are suggested by habitus must not be conflated with intentionality. Practices may be "reasonable without being the product of a reasoned purpose, and, even less of conscious computation" (Bourdieu & Wacquant, 1992, p. 120). Habitus here breaks with the notion of humans as rational agents through and through—as homo economicus. The calculation of interest is tacit.

Field

Field is the next important concept, and it has a dialectical relationship with habitus. A field is understood as a social space or network of relationships between the positions occupied by actors. These different positions are structured and anchored in forms of unequally shared power or capital. Conflict and competition characterize the relationships between the actors as they try to accumulate, conserve, or convert different types of capital. Actors take up positions of dominance, subordinance, or equivalence (homology), according to the types and amounts of capital they possess.

Capital

Capital as a concept is highly elastic, a trait that makes it quite compelling but also open to criticism. Bourdieu has written about several different types of capital, including political, personal, functional, professional, linguistic, intellectual, and scholastic capital (Bourdieu, 1991). Thus, the definition of capital is very wide and takes in both material and immaterial resources. However, in his article on the different forms of capital, Bourdieu narrowed them down to three fundamental types: economic capital (money, property), cultural capital (knowledge, skills, educational qualifications), and social capital (connections, membership of a group). At the same time, however, he argued that all of these forms of capital may also be apprehended as symbolic capital (prestige, honor) (Bourdieu, 1986).

Capital is considered to be accumulated labor: it is not a natural given, and it demands investment. In a sense, capital is the "energy of social physics" (Bourdieu, 1990b, p. 122). This implies that capital only functions relationally within a field. Capital is scarce, it is in demand, and it creates differences. Actors are distributed within the field in the first dimension according to the overall volume of the capital they posses. In the second dimension, they are distributed according to the composition of their capital—in other words, according to the relative weight of the different kinds of capital in their total set of assets (Bourdieu, 1991).

The social world is seen as being made up of several such fields that are more or less autonomous, but subsumed under the overarching field of power. This world is often referred to as comprising literary, business, scientific, and bureaucratic fields, among others. At the organizational level, a research center can be said to belong to the scientific field, a parent–teacher association to the educational field, a bank to the economic field, a theater to the cultural field, a ministry to the bureaucratic field, and so on. A typical trait of such fields is that they place a higher value on one type of capital than on another, although that type of capital may be worth less in another field. In the field of business, for example, economic capital is prioritized, but it has virtually no importance in the academic field. In the latter field, it is academic significance and one's rating by one's peers that counts. Such capital may only be appreciated properly within the academic field, although some kind of recognition can also be won outside of it (Bourdieu & Wacquant, 1992).

The limits of a field are "always at stake in the field itself, and therefore admits of no a priori answer" (Bourdieu & Wacquant, 1992, p. 100). One general pointer is that the limits of a field lie where its effects cease. To add further complexities to the theory, every field may be part of one or several other larger fields or may itself contain subfields. The aforementioned research center, for instance, may be part of the political field through its connections with a political agenda and political institutions. An environmental group could be said to belong to the political field at the same time that it has its own subfields with field-specific capital centered on certain environmental values. One could also talk about a field that encompasses all actors involved with issues concerning energy and the environment. The relationship between different fields, however, is not governed by any transhistoric laws. Therefore, each historical case must be investigated separately (Bourdieu & Wacquant, 1992).

Bourdieu also announced a certain "program" for proper field analysis and stressed that the field must be the focus of a research operation, as the "true object of social science is not the individual" (Bourdieu & Wacquant, 1992, p. 107). The researcher should focus on the competing interests, the conflicts they generate, and the whole logic of a field, which can only be done by plunging "into the particularity of an empirical reality, historically located and dated, but with the objective of constructing it as a 'special case of what is possible'" (Bourdieu, 1994/1998, p. 2). In other words, the study of particular historical conflicts on energy and the environment should contribute something other than "just" intrinsic insights into those conflicts.

Criticism

Bourdieu's often-impenetrable prose has invited a fair amount of criticism (Jenkins, 2002). It has also been remarked that his rhetorical strategy is particularly ironic, given his penchant for sociology as an instrument of struggle for circles beyond academia. That Bourdieu later started to use interviews as a mode of communication has been seen as his recognition of the problem (Swartz, 1997).

However, the most common theoretical criticism of his theory of practice is that it has not delivered on its promise to abolish the opposition between the micro and the macro, between the individual and the structure. The accusation is that the perspective is firmly rooted in objectivism, as Bourdieu presented his analyses as based in the "real" material world, "where behavior has its causes, but actors are not allowed to have their reasons" (Jenkins, 2002, p. 97). The role of deliberate decision-making is underemphasized, as habitus is given a prominent role. Most action is seen as reproducing a structure that gives privilege to the already dominant. Actors are given less "freedom" than they are granted by other sociologists (e.g., Giddens, 1984/1995). This position is also one of the reasons that it is difficult to apply the theories that Bourdieu espoused for linking rhetoric and capital (i.e., Bourdieu, 1991). I agree with this criticism and do not use the concept in public relations analysis.

The problem of intentionality surfaces, however, by rejection of the use of the concept of habitus. Bourdieu was not interested in decisions, actors, or strategies per se, but in *positions*. One of his arguments for the theory of practice is that it expands "the sphere of interest while reducing that of utility and consciousness" (Bourdieu & Wacquant, 1992, p. 25). In the context of public relations analysis, however, it is precisely the actors and their intentional and conscious strategies to influence thoughts and decisions that are of interest. What appears to one analyst to be well laid-out strategies, or what is presented as such by an interviewee, may in fact be the result of chance, as well as unconscious deliberation.

An additional problem with using the theory of practice is its claim that the notions of habitus, positions, field, and capital may only be understood as systemic concepts, that is, they can only be defined "within the theoretical system that they constitute, not in isolation" (Bourdieu & Wacquant, 1992, p. 96). However, there have also been arguments against attempts to achieve unambiguous meaning, as theories are believed to have a generative function. Here, this is interpreted as an invitation to borrow and expand, much like the kind of pragmatic relationship that Bourdieu himself had with other authors (Bourdieu, 1990a).

Relevance for Public Relations

Given the centrality that Bourdieu accords to communication, his work has become increasingly popular in media studies (e.g., Benson & Neveu, 2005; Webb et al., 2001). With a precious few exceptions (i.e., Edwards, 2006, 2007; Harris, 2005; Ihlen, 2002, 2004a, 2004b, 2005, 2007), however, his work seems to have been largely ignored within public relations. Here, it is argued that a reworked version of his sociology has a lot to contribute, although substantial breaks with, if not violations of, Bourdieu's work, beginning with a suggestion for a typology of organizational resources, are made. The concept of the field can be used loosely as a way of framing an organization's wielding of resources. That actors possess different types of resources is not an original notion. Several theorists have analyzed aspects of political processes, the strategies adopted by actors, and the resources they have drawn upon (e.g., Berry, 1977; Cobb & Ross, 1997; Rochefort & Cobb, 1994; Uhrwing,

2001). Thus, it may legitimately be asked what use can be made of the theory of practice if so much of its proposed framework is rejected. The advantage of drawing on Bourdieu, however, is his emphasis on relational and dynamic aspects. The positions of actors are seen in relation to each other and are explained as functions of their type and amount of capital, the field-specific appreciation of these forms of capital, and constant attempts to acquire, hold onto, or convert capital. The distribution of capital is also an expression of power relationships, which, in turn, are expressed in rhetorical strategies. A focus on these aspects is helpful in grasping the struggle and social space that actors are situated within. Public relations practice fits into this picture if it is regarded as a practice that assists organizational actors in various fields in pursuing their interests. In this sense, and as argued by Edwards (2007), public relations should drop its "façade of disinterestedness" (p. 3).

An Excursion in Media Sociology

One charge made against Bourdieu is that he treats individuals and institutions as entities with similar status and that he does not contribute a theorized model of institutions. Thus, institutions remain a "'black box' model," and habitus only partly fills the gap between the micro- and macrolevel, between actors and structure (Jenkins, 2002). In addition, several of the forms of capital with which Bourdieu operates are rather ill-defined or underdeveloped (Schuller, Baron, & Field, 2000). I read these traits as an invitation to borrow and elaborate. In this endeavor, media sociology that deals with source strategies is seen as useful in addressing the aforementioned problems. It must be emphasized that I do not see public relations only as media relations. However, the main advantage of the literature in this area is that it helps to analyze the symbolic struggles that take place with the assistance of public relations; that is, the way that sources compete for access to the media and for symbolic dominance in the media arena. The work of sources can be regarded as a continual struggle to mobilize unequally distributed resources to gain access (Cottle, 2003; Davis, 2002; Schlesinger, 1990; Schlesinger & Tumber, 1994). It is argued here, however, that the resources used in media relations also have relevance for other public relations activities, such as lobbying and community relations, to name two examples.

The struggle to gain media access is obviously related to the central position that the media have been accorded in modern society, both as material- and symbol-producing institutions. Media research has traditionally focused on the so-called agenda-setting function of the media and their influence on public attitudes. The media direct attention to certain issues at the cost of others, and they influence the ranking of these issues in hierarchies (Dalton, Beck, Huckfeldt, & Koetzle, 1998;

McCombs, 2004). In general, most of the research on the influence of
the media that goes beyond the agenda-setting function concludes that
the media are important for public attitudes, policy makers, and the
public policy process, but that their effects are complex and not necessarily direct (Ihlen, 2001a; McLeod, Kosicki, & McLeod, 2002; Waldahl,
1999). However, one crucial aspect here is that the media do orchestrate
debates about, for instance, the environment: some actors and perspectives are given space or time on the air, whereas others are not. Actors
also gain or lose legitimacy in this process.

The following sections draw together some of Bourdieu's writing on
resources with insights from media sociology. The importance of institutionalization, economic capital, knowledge capital, social capital, and
symbolic capital is also discussed.

Institutionalization

An organization's resources may be regarded as coming into play initially in the way it is institutionalized. One may question the degree
to which there exists "cognitive, normative, and regulative structures
and activities that provide stability and meaning" in an organization
(Scott, 1995, p. 33). Here, an organization is understood as encompassing attempts by a number of individuals to coordinate certain tasks,
including communication, to reach a goal (Bruzelius & Skärvad, 2000).
This implies a certain permanency and that certain types of roles are
assigned to participants in the simplest sense. Organizations may, however, differ in their degree of institutionalization. The simplest opera-
tionalization is to look at an organization's human resources; that is,
to ask whether an organization has employees and, if so, how many. In
the case of membership-based organizations, its number of members is
obviously relevant. One aspect of institutionalization in this sense could
also be called "human capital."

Stability is also an important aspect of institutionalization. An organization benefits from a high degree of stability when coping with
long-lived issues. Typically, the resources of a citizen group are drained
when a planning process is dragged out, as can be seen in a number of
environmental conflicts (Ihlen, 2004b). However, this may also give the
group the chance to build up its competence.

Other aspects of institutionalization include specialization and routinization. Permanent activity most often leads to routinization and to
different tasks being accorded to different members of the organization. An important indicator is whether an organization has routinized
its public relations activity or whether it has its resources bound up in
other day-to-day activities. This may also be seen as a question of prior-
ity, of course, and thus as an indicator of the level of sophistication with

regard to communication and its importance for an organization. In short, it becomes important to focus on how an organization handles its public relations and if it has a designated public relations manager or a public relations department. The relationship between the public relations function and management is also pivotal here. To what degree does management engage in public relations and see it as a major part of its role?

Economic Capital

Closely tied to the ability to institutionalize an organization is economic capital, which, in contrast to other forms of capital, may be disengaged from the same organization. Bourdieu saw this rather self-explanatory concept as being at the root of all of the other types of capital, but refrained from reducing everything to just this type, just as he rejected the notion that all social exchange could be reduced to communication (Bourdieu, 1986).

The importance of economic capital can be seen in the fact that, even in a free market system, free speech is only effective if actors can establish a substantial presence, and this most often requires resources, often of the financial kind (Condit & Condit, 1992; Coombs, 1993; Rakow, 1989). An important question is how much a source is willing or able to invest in, for instance, media relations. Is the organization able to supply information subsidies; that is, press packages, press releases, and other tools to facilitate journalists' write-up of stories (Gandy, 1980)? The blooming business of public relations agencies also gives rise to the question of whether organizations have the ability to hire such expertise.

However, public relations does not necessarily have to be expensive to be effective. The position and amount of media coverage that relatively resource-poor environmental organizations have secured over the years is a case in point. Public relations has, in general, given rise to two conflicting trends. On the one hand, already powerful sources have used it to consolidate their privileged access. On the other hand, alternative sources have also been able to utilize it to gain access (Davis, 2000). Public relations, or at least media relations, is relatively cheap and bound up in the cost of labor—something that even poor volunteer organizations can theoretically accommodate (Davis, 2002). The aforementioned degree of institutionalization, in this case active members, together with the form of capital discussed below, may act as a counterweight to the influence of economic capital. In a Norwegian study of a conflict over energy and the environment, simply due to its clever use of public relations (Ihlen, 2004b), a very poor environmental ad hoc organization was able to claim victory against its adversary, which was backed by the three largest Norwegian companies.

Knowledge Capital

A consistent focus in Bourdieu's work is on the field of education, as it is here that the values and relations of social space are passed on from one generation to the next (Bourdieu, 1984). In the field of education, cultural capital (or informational capital) is what matters. Cultural capital may be embodied, objectified, or institutionalized. That is, it may be related to individuals, by, for instance, professional knowledge, verbal facility, or general cultural awareness. It may be related to objects, such as books or computers. Moreover, institutions such as libraries and elite schools carry cultural capital (Bourdieu & Wacquant, 1992). In media sociology, however, cultural capital has been understood to take the form of "legitimacy, authoritativeness, respectability, and the contacts which these bring" (Schlesinger, 1990, p. 81).

It does seem, however, that cultural capital in Bourdieu's conception of it often has as much to do with refinement and, an extension of this, taste, as it does with a body of knowledge. In studying public relations strategies, the latter aspect is more interesting, and thus I write here of knowledge capital, rather than cultural capital. This is not to imply that culture is an unimportant resource for power, but, in this context, it is more a question of knowing the culture of politics and the media.

The importance of knowledge in a wider sense can be seen, for instance, when citizen groups meet with accusations that they do not know what they are talking about or that they must be "constructive" in their criticisms. Having "enough" education to pose the "right type" of (constructive) criticism seems to be an essential strategy for being taken seriously by actors who are struggling to present their definitions and perspectives (Kolbenstvedt, Strand, & Østensen, 1978). However, the greater responsibility for comprehensive research efforts clearly lies with the resourced, well-institutionalized party.

A particular type of knowledge capital concerns an acquaintance with the way in which the political process works and knowing how to lobby. Valuable knowledge includes insight into when politicians are most open to argument and most in need of counterexpertise to balance the information from the administration. An organization will be strengthened by its general ability to read the political power game, with its alliance building and competition for office and the need to appeal to certain constituencies that might be valuable for traditional or strategic reasons.

Another important type of knowledge is knowledge of how the media work. It has, for instance, been widely recognized that certain attributes are seen to make a story newsworthy. Events should, for instance, resonate with widely held cultural values, be recent, dramatic, conflict-oriented, tangible, illustratable, or tied to an action-oriented political agenda (Ihlen, 1999; Shoemaker & Reese, 1996). Appeals to news values are often pointed out as the most common source strategy, and they take the form of either creating events that conform to news values or of presenting events to journalists in ways that meet news values (Palmer, 2000). Many sources, for instance, acknowledge that the media appreciate hard-hitting rhetoric that intensifies conflicts (Ihlen, 2001b). By establishing a positive media profile, an organization may be able to overcome traditional institutional disadvantages. As noted above, public relations thus offers far greater potential for nonofficial sources than has previously been acknowledged. In fact, it could be argued that the dissemination of professional public relations has the potential to broaden, rather than restrict, media access for nonofficial source groups. A caveat is that there are also many interest groups and individuals who do not have access to even the minimum resources required (Davis, 2002).

It is, however, important to bear in mind that the importance of media coverage should not be overemphasized. First of all, as mentioned earlier in this section, media research has shown that there is no one-to-one relationship between media content and public attitudes. Furthermore, having "won" in the media arena does not guarantee the outcome of a political debate (Cracknell, 1993). This was illustrated in a study of how environmental organizations succeeded in getting their opposition to the development of a hydropower plant to dominate in the media. The politicians, nonetheless, ended up voting for the development, albeit for a smaller one than was initially planned (Ihlen, 2001b).

Social Capital

Social capital has been a social science buzzword for some time (e.g., Baron, Field, & Schuller, 2000; Field, 2002; Lin, 2002) (see also chapter 12 on Putnam in this volume). The concept is most often used to describe the resources and the degree of shared values and trust within the community. Social capital thus shifts attention away from an analysis of individual behavior to a focus on patterns of relationships between, for instance, individuals and organizations (Baron et al., 2000). This relational aspect is, of course, also important for Bourdieu, but he uses the concept differently:

> Social capital is the aggregate of the actual or potential resources which are linked to possession of a durable network of more or less institutionalized relationships of mutual acquaintance and recognition—or in other words, to membership in a group—which provides each of its members with the backing of the collectivity-owned capital, a "credential" which entitles them to credit, in the various senses of the word. (Bourdieu, 1986, pp. 248–249)

This definition has several important implications. Social capital must be understood as having two components: first, the size of the network that a person possesses, and second, the volume of the capital that the other components of the network have and to which a person obtains access through the network. Social capital is seen as the result of a conscious or unconscious investment strategy that involves exchanges of, for instance, gifts, services, words, time, attention, care, or concern. It also implies "obligations" or "credit." The members of a network can subjectively feel gratitude, respect, or friendship; the relationship can also be formalized in the form of legal rights and obligations. The credit can be called on, but without a guarantee that it will be recognized. Investment in social capital definitely involves risk. From a narrow economic perspective, investment in social capital seems to be pointless because it may yield interest only in the long run. However, there are several "goods" and "services" that cannot be obtained without social capital, and this capital must be well-established before the need for it appears, "as if for [its] own sake, and therefore outside [its] period of use" (Bourdieu, 1986, p. 252).

Social capital is also seen as important in that it can contribute to the bottom line of an organization. It may lead to increased and/or more complex forms of social capital, reduced transaction costs, and organizational advantage in the form of, for instance, increased productivity and efficiency (Hazelton & Kennan, 2000). To research an organization's social capital, it may be possible to pose several questions drawing on Bourdieu and other writings on social capital (e.g., Lin, 2002). It is, for instance, possible to ask what kind of investment an organization makes in social capital. How does it attempt to strengthen its connections with politicians, journalists, activist groups, bureaucrats, researchers, and other organizations? The number of meetings and the time and money spent organizing them could be used as an indicator.

Another question would be: What is the size of an organization's network? How many connections does the organization have to the publics mentioned above, and how does it compare with similar organizations? At the same time, one obviously needs to be sensitive to the fact that one "good" contact may be all that is needed to, for instance, shift a political decision. A study of a particularly successful public relations campaign showed how an environmental organization benefited from and worked actively to involve persons beyond the circle of what the activists themselves called "the usual suspects" (Ihlen, 2004b, p. 291).

Further general questions include the kinds of capital that an organization potentially has access to through its membership in a network. For instance, what professional standing (symbolic) or expertise (cultural) do the other organizations in this network have? How does the organization under study gain access to this through the network? Some organizations may, for instance, have good knowledge about lobbying and possess good political contacts. By sharing this knowledge and these contacts with other members in the network, a capital transfer takes place, which illustrates the value of social capital. In a huge conflict over a hydropower development in Norway, it was shown that a local ad hoc organization benefited from associating with an established environmental organization in terms of political contacts and lobbying know-how (Ihlen, 2004b).

Symbolic Capital

Among the pillars of Bourdieu's work is his judgment of taste. Here, symbolic capital is defined as "a reputation for competence and an image of respectability and honourability" (Bourdieu, 1984, p. 291). Elsewhere, it is stated that all other types of capital take the form of symbolic capital when they are "grasped through categories of perception that *recognize* its specific logic or, if you prefer, misrecognise the arbitrariness of its possession and accumulation" (Bourdieu & Wacquant, 1992, p. 119, original emphasis). Although symbolic capital has its roots in other types of capital, it is a form of "denied" capital, as it conceals the underlying interested relations. Symbolic capital is subjective, in contrast to other forms, and it is perceived as making legitimate demands for recognition. Symbolic capital legitimates power relations (Bourdieu, 1990b).

The roots of the symbolic capital within the other forms of capital can be elaborated upon. For instance, social capital always functions as symbolic capital, because it is "governed by the logic of knowledge and acknowledgement" (Bourdieu, 1986, p. 257). Indeed, the various forms of capital may often be difficult to separate, but the reputation that an individual or organization acquires for being "well-connected" is obviously symbolic capital. The same goes for the reputation for being knowledgeable. Furthermore, symbolic capital may be acquired with the help of knowledge capital (cultural capital) by way of a prestigious education.

As for institutionalization, it may be said that this is made into symbolic capital in the sense of the legitimacy and credibility that is accorded to institutionalized, official sources, which are taken more seriously by journalists. A concrete example concerning the aforementioned Norwegian environmental organization is the way in which an ad hoc group fighting against the building of a specific hydroelectric power plant received comparatively less coverage than did older and more established environmental organizations (Ihlen, 2001b). Thus, the older and more institutionalized an organization is, the better its chances of being established as part of the "naturalized" source network of journalists. With institutionalization comes symbolic capital.

Traditionally, it has been easier to acquire symbolic capital through cultural capital than through economic capital. The achievements and legitimacy of the latter may be weakened by inheritance.

The Reworked Typology of Capital

Drawing together the preceding section on different forms of capital, the following questions can be asked in an analysis of organizational public relations.

1. To what degree is an organization institutionalized? Questions can be asked about the nature of the organization's human resources, the size of its administration, the number of members or employees it has, the number of people engaged in public relations, and also how it compares to similar organizations or to its competitors.

2. What kind of *economic capital* does an organization have? This can be defined as the organization's budget. In addition, it is interesting to look at how much of this budget is channeled toward public relations. A large budget may make it possible to supply information subsidies or hire external public relations expertise. Figures can be presented and comparisons made between different organizations.

3. What kind of *knowledge capital* does an organization have? Knowledge capital is here defined as formal professional education or informal skills acquired through practice. This, then, is a broader category than the cultural capital or cultural refinement discussed by Bourdieu (Bourdieu, 1984). It is instead focused on the formal and informal education, skills, and experience that are represented in the organization. In particular, it is interesting to assess what kind of public relations expertise the organization has and how this compares with that of other organizations in the same field. Knowledge of how to lobby and how to gain media coverage is seen as pivotal; in the case of the latter, because the media are so central to modern society as both material- and symbol-producing institutions.

4. What kind of *social capital* does an organization have? For Bourdieu, social capital comprised, in essence, group membership and the credentials and credit that followed from it (Bourdieu, 1986). Important aspects are the size of the network an actor possesses and the volume of capital that can be accessed through the other parties in the network. The size of the investment that an organization has made in social capital is also of interest. This type of capital can also be assessed qualitatively, in terms of the type of connections that an organization has with competitors, politicians, journalists, bureaucrats, researchers, and other relevant groups. The nature of the capital that can be accessed through the network is also of interest, and, again, comparisons can be made among organizations.

5. What kind of *symbolic capital* does an organization have? Symbolic capital is defined as "a reputation for competence and an image of respectability and honourability" (Bourdieu, 1984, p. 291). This means that all of the other forms of capital may also function as and feed into the volume of symbolic capital that an organization has. Symbolic capital can be analyzed qualitatively as an organization's social standing, prestige, and legitimacy, most typically as expressed by other central actors or the media.

Summing up, the relevance of the above for public relations lies first and foremost in the possibility of analyzing the different forms of power positions that are constructed with the help of capital and public relations. An organization's resources can obviously be conceptualized in other ways than is done here. The most important point remains that current public relations theory often offers no good ontology; material existence has no role, as has been pointed out (Cheney & Christensen, 2001). This concern can be addressed with the concept of fields and a typology of resources or capital. Coupled with the concept of fields, the suggested typology is an important contribution to public relations theory.

It is also suggested that this theory can help to inform practice. Here, three brief points related to strategic thinking are made (Webb et al., 2001).

Self-reflexivity: first, to succeed, an actor needs a certain self-reflexive understanding (not understood in Luhmann's sense of the term, which is explored in chapter 10, this volume) of his or her position and resources within a field.

Understanding of social rules and regulations: second, an actor benefits from being aware of the rules, regulations, and official and unofficial forms of capital that characterize a field.

Ability to negotiate: third, an actor has to be able to maneuver and negotiate conditions within a field given its own forms of capital and those of its competitors.

These three elements together amount to what can be called *cultural literacy* (Schirato & Yell, as cited in Webb et al., 2001). They can also be seen as elements of a strategic and sophisticated public relations practice.

Conclusion

To frame an organization's public relations activities, the concept of field was borrowed from sociology and from the work of Pierre Bourdieu. In keeping with this perspective, an organization may be seen as located within one or several fields, in which they compete to position themselves in the social order. The actors seek to get their issues discussed, defined, and settled.

In this struggle within fields, an organization draws on different types of capital. It has been argued in this chapter that there is a need for a reworked typology that also incorporates insights from media sociology, as this discipline has focused more on the capital that organizations hold. A prime advantage of drawing on Bourdieu, rather than on other analyses of resources, is his emphasis on relational and dynamic aspects. The positions of actors are seen in relation to one another and explained as functions of the types and amounts of capital they hold, the field-specific appreciation of these forms of capital, and their constant attempts to acquire, hold onto, or convert their capital.

Further research should seek to develop richer and more stringent categories for an analysis of different forms of capital and their relations to the specific fields within which organizations operate. Because they are decisive to public relations practice, these forms of capital need to be better understood, better integrated, and further researched. Such studies would assist scholars and practitioners alike and help to bring about a more realistic perspective on the field of public relations.

Note

1. This chapter was published previously as: Building on Bourdieu: A sociological grasp of public relations, in *Public Relations Review, 33*(3), 2007. The article earned the author the 2008 Pride Article Award from the Public Relations-division of the National Communication Association.

References

Alvesson, M., & Deetz, S. A. (2000). *Doing critical management research.* London: Sage.

Baron, S., Field, J., & Schuller, T. (Eds.). (2000). *Social capital: Critical perspectives.* New York: Oxford University Press.

Benson, R., & Neveu, E. (Eds.). (2005). *Bourdieu and the journalistic field.* Malden, MA: Polity Press.

Berry, J. M. (1977). *Lobbying for the people: The political behavior of public interest groups.* Princeton, NJ: Princeton University Press.

Bourdieu, P. (1972/1977). *Outline of a theory of practice* (R. Nice, Trans.). Cambridge, UK: Cambridge University Press.

Bourdieu, P. (1990). *The logic of practice* (R. Nice, Trans.). Cambridge, UK: Polity Press. (Original work published 1980)

Bourdieu, P. (1984). *Distinction: A social critique of the judgement of taste* (R. Nice, Trans.). London: Routledge.

Bourdieu, P. (1986). The forms of capital. In J. G. Richardson (Ed.), *Handbook of theory and research for the sociology of education* (pp. 241–258). New York: Greenwood.

Bourdieu, P. (1990a). *In other words: Essays toward a reflexive sociology.* Cambridge, UK: Polity Press.

Bourdieu, P. (1990b). *The logic of practice* (R. Nice, Trans.). Cambridge, UK: Polity.

Bourdieu, P. (1991). *Language & symbolic power* (G. Raymond & M. Adamson, Trans.). Cambridge, UK: Polity Press.

Bourdieu, P. (1998). *Practical reason.* Cambridge, UK: Polity. (Original work published 1994)

Bourdieu, P., & Wacquant, L. J. D. (1992). *An invitation to reflexive sociology.* Cambridge, UK: Polity Press.

Bruzelius, L. H., & Skärvad, P. H. (2000). *Integrerad organisationslära* [Integrated organization theory] (8th ed.). Lund, Sweden: Studentlitteratur.

Calhoun, C., LiPuma, E., & Postone, M. (Eds.). (1993). *Bourdieu: Critical perspectives.* Cambridge, UK: Polity Press.

Cheney, G., & Christensen, L. T. (2001). Public relations as contested terrain: A critical response. In R. L. Heath (Ed.), *Handbook of public relations* (pp. 167–182). Thousand Oaks, CA: Sage.

Cobb, R. W., & Ross, M. H. (Eds.). (1997). *Cultural strategies of agenda denial: Avoidance, attack, and redefinition.* Lawrence, KS: University Press of Kansas.

Condit, C. M., & Condit, D. M. (1992). Smoking or health: Incremental erosion as a public interest group strategy. In E. L. Toth & R. L. Heath (Eds.), *Rhetorical and critical approaches to public relations* (pp. 241–256). Hillsdale, NJ: Erlbaum.

Coombs, W. T. (1993). Philosophical underpinnings: Ramifications of a pluralist paradigm. *Public Relations Review, 19*(2), 111–119.

Cottle, S. (Ed.). (2003). *News, public relations and power.* London: Sage.

Cracknell, J. (1993). Issue arenas, pressure groups and environmental agendas. In A. Hansen (Ed.), *The mass media and environmental issues* (pp. 3–21). Leicester, UK: Leicester University Press.

Dalton, R. J., Beck, P. A., Huckfeldt, R., & Koetzle, W. (1998). A test of media-centered agenda setting: Newspaper content and public interests in a presidential election. *Political Communication, 15,* 463–481.

Davis, A. (2000). Public relations, news production and changing patterns of source access in the British national media. *Media, Culture & Society, 22*(1), 39–59.

Davis, A. (2002). *Public relations democracy: Public relations, politics and the mass media in Britain.* Manchester, UK: Manchester University Press.

Edwards, L. (2006). Rethinking power in public relations. *Public Relations Review, 32*(3), 229–231.

Edwards, L. (2007). *Exploring power in public relations: A Bourdieusian perspective.* Unpublished doctoral dissertation, Leeds Metropolitan University, Leeds, UK.

Elliott, A., & Turner, B. S. (Eds.). (2001). *Profiles in contemporary social theory.* London: Sage.

Field, J. (2002). *Social capital.* London: Routledge.

Fowler, B. (2001). Pierre Bourdieu. In A. Elliott & B. S. Turner (Eds.), *Profiles in contemporary social theory* (pp. 315–326). London: Sage.

Gandy, O. H. (1980). Information in health: Subsidised news. *Media, Culture & Society, 2,* 103–115.

Giddens, A. (1995). *The constitution of society: Outline of the theory of structuration.* Cambridge, UK: Polity Press. (Original work published 1984)

Grunig, L. A., Grunig, J. E., & Dozier, D. M. (2002). *Excellent public relations and effective organizations: A study of communication management in three countries.* Hillsdale, NJ: Erlbaum.

Harris, R. (2005). When giving means taking: Public relations, sponsorship, and morally marginal donors. *Public Relations Review, 31*(4), 486–491.

Hazelton Jr., V., & Kennan, W. (2000). Social capital: Reconceptualizing the bottom line. *Corporate Communications: An International Journal, 5*(2), 81–86.

Heath, R. L. (1997). Legitimate "perspectives" in public relations practice: A rhetorical solution. *Australian Journal of Communication, 24*(2), 55–63.

Ihlen, Ø. (1999). *Medier og miljø: En skisse av norske avisers miljødekning 1977–1997* [Media and environment: A sketch of the environmental coverage in Norwegian newspapers 1977–1997] (Report No. 38). Oslo, Norway: Department of Media and Communication, University of Oslo.

Ihlen, Ø. (2001a). Medier, miljø og påvirkning [Media, environmental issues, and effects]. *Tidsskrift for samfunnsforskning, 42*(1), 65–88.

Ihlen, Ø. (2001b). Miljømakt og journalistikk: Retorikk og regi [Environmental power and journalism: Rhetoric and direction]. In M. Eide (Ed.), *Til dagsorden! Journalistikk, makt og demokrati* [To the agenda! Journalism, power and democracy] (pp. 304–328). Oslo, Norway: Gyldendal Akademisk.

Ihlen, Ø. (2002). Rhetoric and resources: Notes for a new approach to public relations and issues management. *Journal of Public Affairs, 2*(4), 259–269.

Ihlen, Ø. (2004a). Norwegian hydroelectric power: Testing a heuristic for analyzing symbolic strategies and resources. *Public Relations Review, 30*(2), 217–223.

Ihlen, Ø. (2004b). *Rhetoric and resources in public relations strategies: A rhetorical and sociological analysis of two conflicts over energy and the environment.* Doctoral dissertation. Oslo, Norway: Unipub forlag.

Ihlen, Ø. (2005). The power of social capital: Adapting Bourdieu to the study of public relations. *Public Relations Review, 31*(4), 492–496.

Ihlen, Ø. (2007). Building on Bourdieu: A sociological grasp of public relations. *Public Relations Review, 33*(3), 269–274.

Jenkins, R. (2002). *Pierre Bourdieu.* London: Routledge.

Kolbenstvedt, M., Strand, A., & Østensen, E. (1978). *Lokale aksjonsgrupper: Sammenfattende rapport* [Local citizen action groups: Summarizing report] (No. 44). Oslo, Norway: Norwegian Institute for Urban and Regional Research.

Lin, N. (2002). *Social capital: A theory of social structure and action.* Cambridge, MA: Cambridge University Press.

McCombs, M. E. (2004). *Setting the agenda: The mass media and public opinion.* Cambridge, UK: Polity Press.

McLeod, D. M., Kosicki, G. M., & McLeod, J. M. (2002). Resurveying the boundaries of political communication effects. In J. Bryant & D. Zillmann (Eds.), *Media effects: Advances in theory and research* (pp. 215–267). Mahwah, NJ: Erlbaum.

Palmer, J. (2000). *Spinning into control: News values and source strategies.* London: Leicester University Press.

Rakow, L. F. (1989). Information and power. In C. T. Salmon (Ed.), *Information campaigns: Balancing social values and social change* (pp. 164–184). Thousand Oaks, CA: Sage.

Robbins, D. (Ed.). (2000). *Pierre Bourdieu*. SAGE Masters in Modern Social Thought series. London: Sage.

Rochefort, D. A., & Cobb, R. W. (Eds.). (1994). *The politics of problem definition: Shaping the policy agenda*. Lawrence, KS: University Press of Kansas.

Schlesinger, P. (1990). Rethinking the sociology of journalism: Source strategies and the limits of media-centrism. In M. Ferguson (Ed.), *Public communication: The new imperatives: Future directions for media research* (pp. 61–83). London: Sage.

Schlesinger, P., & Tumber, H. (1994). *Reporting crime: The media politics of criminal justice*. Oxford, UK: Clarendon Press.

Schuller, T., Baron, S., & Field, J. (2000). Social capital: A review and critique. In S. Baron, J. Field, & T. Schuller (Eds.), *Social capital: Critical perspectives* (pp. 1–38). New York: Oxford University Press.

Scott, W. R. (1995). *Institutions and organizations*. London: Sage.

Shoemaker, P. J., & Reese, S. D. (1996). *Mediating the message: Theories of influences on mass media content* (2nd ed.). White Plains, NY: Longman.

Swartz, D. (1997). *Culture and power: The sociology of Pierre Bourdieu*. Chicago: University of Chicago Press.

Swartz, D. (1998). *Culture and power: The sociology of Pierre Bourdieu*. Chicago: University of Chicago Press.

Uhrwing, M. (2001). *Tillträde till maktens rum: Om interesseorganisationer och miljöpolitiskt beslutsfattande* [Access to the rooms of power: Interest organizations and decision-making in environmental politics]. Hedemora, Sweden: Gidlunds Förlag.

Waldahl, R. (1999). *Mediepåvirkning* [The media's influence] (2nd ed.). Oslo, Norway: Ad Notam Gyldendal.

Webb, J., Schirato, T., & Danaher, G. (2001). *Understanding Bourdieu*. London: Sage.

Life and Work of Pierre Bourdieu

Pierre Bourdieu (1930–2002) was born in Denguin, in the Béarn district of Southern France. He studied anthropology at the École Normale Supérieure from 1951 to 1954. Bourdieu conducted anthropological fieldwork among the Kabyle people in Algeria, and taught at the University of Algiers. His research interest veered toward sociology and his first book, published in 1958, was entitled *Sociologie de l'Algérie*. He returned to France in 1960 and thought for four years before becoming director of studies at l'École Pratique des Hautes Études. Bourdieu founded the Centre de Sociologie Européenne in 1968. His first major text was published in 1972, *Esquisse d'une Theorie de la Pratique* (*Outline of a Theory of Practice*, 1977). In 1979 Bourdieu published *La Distinction, Critique Sociale du Jugement* (*Distinction: A Social Critique of the Judgement of Taste*, 1984), which established his reputation outside of France. He was appointed professor of sociology at the Collége de France in 1981.

Other important works published in English include *The Logic of Practice* (1990), *Language and Symbolic Power* (1991), *The Field of Cultural Production* (1993), *Practical Reason* (1994), *The Rules of Art* (1995), and *On Television* (1998). Much of Bourdieu's writing is dense, and thus it may be useful to consult some of the introductory texts, such as Richard Jenkins's critical *Pierre Bourdieu* (2002), David Swartz's *Culture and Power* (1997), or the part-interview book *An Invitation to Reflexive Sociology* (1992). In 2000, Derek Robbins edited a four-volume work on Bourdieu in the series *Sage Masters in Modern Social Thought*.

Chapter 5

On Foucault

A Toolbox for Public Relations[1]

Judy Motion and Shirley Leitch

Abstract

Foucault's work provides both critical theory and methods for understanding public relations as a discourse practice with power effects. Within
this chapter we introduce the key theoretical concepts of Foucault's work,
focusing in particular on discourse, power/knowledge, and subjectivity. A
number of tensions that emerge from a Foucauldian consideration of public relations are highlighted and discussed. We then reflect on potential
applications of Foucault's theories for our understanding of the role public
relations in mapping discourse transformations and change, power effects
within relationship management, and identity work. This chapter contends
that Foucault's work can offer new critical insights into how public relations
works and why it works.

I would like my books to be a kind of tool-box which others can rummage
through to find a tool which they can use however they wish in their own
area…. I write for users, not readers. (Foucault, 1974, pp. 523–524)

Michel Foucault's work provides an intellectual toolbox for theorizing
the role of public relations in constructing and transforming societal
discourses and practices. It poses considerable challenges for those who
would seek simply to valorize or condemn the practice of public relations. Instead, the use of Foucault's work highlights some of the deeply
problematic, contradictory, and even questionable aspects of this complex profession by placing meaning production, power effects, truth
claims, and knowledge systems at the center of our thinking and investigations. A Foucauldian discourse perspective accentuates the production of meanings, the strategies of power, and the propagation of
knowledge (Foucault, 1978) at play within public relations and provides
a promising foundation for a critical theory of public relations.

Within this chapter we discuss the central concepts and tenets of
Foucault's work, reflect on the relevance and potential applications for
public relations scholarship, and highlight a number of tensions that
emerge from a Foucauldian consideration of public relations. Our focus

is on the major themes of Foucault's work: discourse, power/knowledge and subjectivity, and in particular, the ways in which Foucault's work may be applied to issues of change. We demonstrate the rich contribution that Foucauldian theory may make to public relations practice and scholarship by moving beyond a focus on excellence toward an understanding of public relations as a discourse practice with power effects.

The Work of Michel Foucault

Michel Foucault (1926–1984), a French philosopher whose work was influenced by political activism and commentary, emphasized the importance of challenge and critique. As chair of The History of Systems of Thought at the Collège de France, Michel Foucault was interested in the systems of thought or sets of knowledges that produce how we think about and understand the world (Rabinow, 1997). Although classification of his work has been contested and contradictory—for example, he is referred to as both a structuralist and poststructuralist scholar— Foucault described his work as belonging to the "critical tradition" of Kant (Foucault, 1994, p. 459). The problems he engaged with focused on the meaning-giving and organizing practices that objectify and subjectify individuals through his examination of the historical discursive practices and social effects (Dreyfus & Rabinow, 1982) of the relationships between institutions, power, and individuals.

Foucault is recognized, in particular, for his contribution to our understanding of discourse formations at a societal level, his conceptualization of power as a productive force, and his concern with subjectivity and the development of an ethic of the self. In the next section, we introduce the key terms and concepts that Foucault engaged with, starting first with his research approaches; we then provide an overview of the key philosophical concepts in his work and discuss the specific contributions of each of these approaches and concepts.

Research Approaches

Although Foucault is more often recognized for his contribution to theory, he also offered a number of radical methodological innovations to explore the history of ideas and the emergence of truth claims. Foucault used two research methods, "archaeology" and "genealogy," to interrogate or "problematize" institutional and social problems.

Archaeology

It is within *The Archaeology of Knowledge* that Foucault's primary methodology of exploring the history of the systems of thought is explained.

Foucault did not use the traditional historical approach of focusing on continuity. Instead, he problematized long term sociocultural and political trends, focusing on particular concepts, searching not for continuity but for shifts and rupture points in order to identify "displacements and transformations of concepts" (Foucault, 1972, p. 4), moments of discontinuity and change in political, economic, institutional, and societal practices. An archaeology focuses upon differences identified over time and avoids causal theories of change.

Genealogy

In contrast, the research approach of genealogy, or "writing a history of the present," was a mode of identifying, diagnosing, and tracing current situations and practices back to their historical roots (Dreyfus & Rabinow, 1982, p. 119). For Foucault, the objectivity of traditional history was part of the problem of identifying and understanding current situations so he sought, as an alternative, to undertake historically oriented interpretation, acknowledging the political interests in writing such a history. Whereas archaeology was language practices oriented, genealogy was focused on subjectivity or the constitution of the individual as a subject of and subject to institutional discourses and practices.

Problematization

A critique, according to Foucault, is not simply a matter of saying things are not right but "a matter of pointing out [on] what kinds of assumptions, what kinds of familiar, unchallenged, unconsidered modes of thought the practices we accept rest" (Foucault, 1988, p. 154). Like other critical social theorists, Foucault (1984) challenged scholars to think differently about problems and referred to the method that he used to interrogate shifts in the systems of thought as problematization. Problematization is a technique of posing questions in order to reflect upon and account for how certain systems of thought and practices come to be conceived in a particular way, to highlight paradoxes, difficulties, and "the conditions in which human beings 'problematize' what they are, what they do, and the world in which they live" (Foucault, 1984, p. 10).

Examples of how Foucault used problematization to underpin and integrate his study of discourse, power, and the subject are now briefly outlined. In his essay entitled "Politics and the Study of Discourse" (Foucault, 1991a), for example, Foucault provided an explanation of how he studied ensembles of discourse and the series of questions he asked to investigate systems of discourse formation and transformation. For example, Foucault problematized and investigated the criteria for discourse formation, transformation, and the relationship between discourses. As a consequence, a pluralist analysis of systems of discourse was developed and the linguistic systems that underpin them were also examined. In order to understand the second theme of Foucault's work, power, the collection of his essays and interviews in *Power/Knowledge* (Foucault, 1980), *Discipline and Punish* (Foucault, 1977), and his essay on "Governmentality" (Foucault, 1991b) should be consulted. Foucault posed a number of questions to problematize the notion of power and focused on issues of strategy, relations and power effects: "What took place here?" "Can one speak of interests here?" (Foucault, 1980, p. 204). "What does struggle mean here?" (1980, p. 209). Within *The History of Sexuality* series Foucault moved to his third major theme and provided an insight into his research methods and details of his investigation into subjectivity. Problematization thus formed the pivotal intellectual foundation for Foucault's inquiries into social and political systems of thought.

Discourse Production and Transformation

Within this section we turn from Foucault's research method to Foucault's work on discourse production and transformation. For Foucault (1972), discourse was embodied in sets of statements that formed the objects, concepts, subjects, and strategies of which they spoke. Foucault explained that discourses are "governed by analysable rules and transformations" (1972, p. 211) and can be identified according to the rules of formation for all of the objects, concepts, subjects, and strategies within the discourses. These rules constituted "systems of thought" that determined what could be said, who could speak, the positions from which they could speak, the viewpoints that could be presented, and the interests, stakes, and institutional domains that were represented. Accordingly, the primary task of discourse analysis was to focus on the formation and transformation of discourse or how ideas are "put into discourse" (Foucault, 1978, p. 11).

Discourse transformations occur within a set of historical conditions, form statements and concepts, and determine a complex group of power relations by "separating out from among all the statements which are possible those that will be acceptable" (Foucault, 1980, p. 197). Foucault (1984, p.12) explained that his analytical approach was to search for "instances of discursive production," "the production of power," and "the propagation of knowledge." A search for instances of discursive production focused on the formation, modification, and transformation of meaning, as well as focusing on the rules that define what may be said. The objective was to account for the fact that a discourse is talked about and what is said. A search for the production of power concentrated on power relations, in particular, an examination of what is at stake, the vested interests, acts of resistance, and contested truth claims. A search for the propagation of knowledge identified the process of establishing, normalizing, and legitimating certain concepts and theories and defining "the positions and functions that the subject could occupy in the diversity of discourse" (Foucault, 1972, p. 200). The inherent challenge for scholars is to integrate these three analytical approaches into a coherent critique of the discourse practices at work during a discourse transformation or period of "discontinuity."

Power/Knowledge and Truth

Power, as a central idea of political discourse, often carries negative connotations of domination. However, for Foucault (1980) power was both positive and productive:

> What makes power hold good, what makes it accepted, is simply the fact that it doesn't only weigh on us as a force that says no, but that it traverses and produces things, it induces pleasure, forms knowledge, produces discourse. (p. 119)

The exercise of power, Foucault argued, not only offered positive benefits to individuals and society but underlay all aspects of human existence. Foucault, then, was interested in the sites of modern power, the forms it took, and the ways in which it was exercised. He was also interested in the interrelationship between power and knowledge.

Foucault (1980) challenged the accepted view that knowledge was power, a view which saw knowledge as a scarce resource that conferred power on those who possessed it. In contrast, Foucault argued for the inseparability of power and knowledge: "The exercise of power perpetually creates knowledge and, conversely, knowledge constantly induces effects of power" (Foucault, 1980, p. 52).

Knowledge was, then, both a creator of power and a creation of power. Similarly, power was both a creator of knowledge and a creation of knowledge. The two concepts were inseparable and for this reason, Foucault coined the conjoint concept of "power/knowledge." In the above quote, Foucault also drew attention to the diffusion of power/knowledge throughout society and his work on the history of hospitals, prisons, and asylums for the mentally ill were all centrally concerned with the operation of power/knowledge (Foucault, 1972, 1974).

Foucault conceptualized power/knowledge as both organized and hierarchical within the context of clusters of relationships:

> The idea that there is either located at—or emanating from a given point—something which is a "power" seems to me to be based on

a misguided analysis...in reality power means relations, a more or less organized, hierarchical, co-ordinated cluster of relations. (Foucault, 1980, p. 198)

The notion of power/knowledge as relational was clarified by adding the element of strategy. That is, Foucault (1980) saw individuals and organizations as deploying various discourse strategies to conform with, circumvent, or contest existing power/knowledge relations. From this perspective, discourse may be seen as providing the vehicle through which power/knowledge circulates and discourse strategies as the means by which the relations of power/knowledge are created, maintained, resisted, and transformed (see also, Clegg, Courpasson, & Phillips, 2006; Davenport & Leitch, 2005).

The operation of power was also described by Foucault (1997) as "games of strategy" (p. 298). Successful games of strategy may achieve hegemonic status (Gramsci, 1971); in that the discourse within which they are played out becomes so pervasive that it is perceived as common sense. Hegemony is a macrolevel concept that is applied to systems of thought that arise from particular societal configurations of power/knowledge relationships. At a more microlevel, the power/knowledge relationship may be seen to operate through the production and acceptance of particular truths. Foucault (1980) explained that truth was

to be understood as a system of ordered procedures for the production, regulation, distribution, circulation and operation of statements. Truth is linked in a circular relation with systems of power which produce and sustain it, and to effects of power which it induces and which extend it. A "regime" of truth. (p. 133)

Foucault argued that there was a battle about the status of truth and the economic and political role it plays. Each society, according to Foucault (1980), had its regime of truth made up of the discourses which it accepted as "common sense" and which therefore functioned as truth. Foucault was interested in the rules that distinguished truth and falsehood and the power effects that were related to truth. This truth became indelibly linked with notions of discourse and power. In his later work, Foucault shifted his focus from the macrolevel concept of regimes of truth to the more microlevel "games of truth" through which individuals came to think of their own nature in particular ways and form themselves as subjects within particular discourses.

Governmentality

As part of his interest in power, Foucault also fixed his attention on what he termed *governmentality*. The term was used by Foucault to refer to a series of lectures on "Security, Territory and Population" (1991b, p. 102) which explored the increased centralized role that governments played in governing and regulating lives. He described governmentality as referring to the complex institutionalization of government power over populations and the formation of specific government apparatuses and knowledges. The problematic, as Foucault saw it, was to explore the integration of the management of the state and the instruments used by governments to control populations. One particular governmentality aspect that Foucault drew attention to was *Biopower* or the increasing levels of state intervention with the biological well-being of populations through the creation of public health systems. In the next section we extend the discussion of power into a consideration of Foucault's theory of subjectivity and the role that subjects play within discourse.

Subjectivity

There has been considerable debate about the tension between agency versus subjectivity in Foucault's work. Agency theories place an emphasis on the ability of individual and collective discourse actors to effect change. In contrast, theories of subjectivity are predicated upon the notion that individuals are subjects of and subject to discourse, thus emphasizing the structural elements of discourse that restrict or limit agency and thereby serve to reinforce existing relations of power/knowledge (Ainsworth & Hardy, 2004). Initially, Foucault saw individuals or subjects as being created or constituted through institutional discourse but in his later work, Foucault (1988) began to examine the technologies through which individuals constituted and transformed themselves as subjects. This interest in the constitution of the subject can be traced from his series on *The History of Sexuality* to his work on *Technologies of the Self*. Scholars drawing upon Foucault's work often overemphasize this dialectic of agency versus subjectivity, primarily focusing on the way that discourse constrains agency and limits how discourse subjects constitute and transform themselves. Yet, even within his earlier work on power it was possible to see that Foucault (1980) shifted to an acceptance of agency, in particular to the notion that power resides within relationships and that where there is power, there is always potential for resistance. Thus, from a Foucauldian perspective, individuals have the potential to choose beyond the range of subject positions offered within a discourse: "Everybody both acts and thinks" (Foucault, 1988, p. 14).

An Ethic of the Self

In his exploration of subjectivity, two interconnected threads of study were apparent: an ethic or care of the self and creating the self as a work of art. Foucault investigated the cultivation or ethos of self, that is, the way in which individuals constituted themselves as ethical sub-jects according to the practice of a moral code. He focused on "the dis-tinction between the code elements of a morality and the elements of ascesis" (Foucault, 1984, p. 31). The aim was to "look for the forms and modalities of the relation of the self by which the individual constitutes and recognizes himself qua subject" (Foucault, 1984, p. 6). In an inter-view entitled "The Ethics of the Concern for the Self as a Practice of Freedom" (Foucault, 1997), Foucault explained that his aim had been to clarify the relations between the subject and truth, focusing on the way in which knowledge and power systems act upon the self and create knowledge of the self. The forms of elaborating the self (Foucault, 1984, p. 32) included taking care of the self and self-formation as an ethical subject.

Foucault also considered that the aim of constituting and knowing the self was not to remain the same; it was to undertake a stylization of the self. Accordingly, Foucault (1988) stated that "The main interest in life and work is to become someone else that you were not in the begin-ning" (p. 9). He suggested that everyone's life could become a work of art or, quite literally, the self could be created as a work of art. "From the idea that the self is not given to us, I think there is only one practi-cal consequence: we have to create ourselves as a work of art" (Foucault, 1997, p. 262). Thus, it is possible to see that Foucault had moved to an appreciation of agency and the notion that the subject does indeed have the freedom to make choices.

Technologies of the Self

Foucault's work on the technologies of the self (those practices whereby individuals are transformed and transform themselves) fused notions of subjectivity and agency. He identified four discourse "technologies" that allowed people to understand and transform themselves: technol-ogies of production, sign systems, power, and the self. Each of these technologies comprised sets of discourse practices of domination and governmentality. Technologies of production "permit us to produce, transform, or manipulate things" (Foucault, 1988, p. 18) and contrib-ute to the constitution of a public identity for the self or subject. Fou-cault referred to the discourse strategies and practices that construct meanings as technologies of sign systems that "permit us to use signs, meanings, symbols or significations" (Foucault, 1988, p. 18). Foucault's technologies of power "determine the conduct of individuals and sub-mit them to certain ends or domination" (Foucault, 1988, p. 18). In terms of identity, for example, such technologies create sets of rules and norms for controlling and regulating identities. Technologies of the self "permit individuals to effect by their own means or with the help of others a certain number of operations on their own bodies and souls, thoughts, and way of being, so as to transform themselves in order to attain a certain state of happiness, purity, wisdom, perfection, or immobility" (Foucault, 1988, p. 18). Technologies of power are imposed whereas technologies of the self are chosen by subjects to construct, modify, or transform identity.

Foucault's unique contribution was to question how discourses and associated practices come to be accepted as true or legitimate and become objects for thought; to reconceptualize power as a productive force and to interrogate the normalizing institutional and societal practices associated with subjectivity and the development of an ethic of the self. These intellectual tools we have outlined offer methodological and epistemological options for researchers interested in problematizing aspects of public relations practice or scholarship.

Criticisms

Foucault's analytical approach of focusing on discontinuity has been subject to considerable criticism. In particular, his work has been criticised as factually inaccurate and lacking systematic research methods. However, it is important to remember that because Foucault's aim was to search for instances of change, he used examples of discontinuity from existing historical resources, along with philosophical concepts, to develop new understandings of the systems of thought. Such an approach necessitates an eclectic or "broad brush" orientation. In defense of his emphasis on discontinuity Foucault (1972) explained: "I reject a uniform model of temporalization, in order to describe, for each discursive practice, its rules of accumulation, exclusion, reactivation, its own forms of derivation, and its specific modes of connexion over various successions" (p. 200). This innovative approach has in fact provided an exemplar for discourse analysis that looks, not at microaspects of language, but instead at societal trends. Foucault (1988) argued that political and social processes were part of distinct historical changes and not readily apparent, and therefore the function of his emphasis on discontinuity was to reveal such processes.

Alongside the criticisms of method were critiques of a philosophical nature. Rather than provide a definitive theory, Foucault interrogated complex problems, shifting his focus of study in order to provide an ontological history of the present (McHoul & Grace, 1993). Furthermore, Foucault reconceptualized what his research focus was as his interests shifted. It was therefore somewhat difficult to pin down the exact nature of his contributions. However, one of the last explanations that Foucault (1988) offered of what he tried to achieve within his work was included in *Technologies of the Self,*

> What I have studied are three traditional problems: (1) What are the relations we have to truth through scientific knowledge, to those "truth games" which are so important in civilization and in which we are both subject and object? (2) What are the relationships we have to others through those strange strategies and power relationships? And (3) what are the relationships between truth, power and self? (p. 15)

The themes of discourse, power, and the subject were still evident but researched as integrated, rather than discrete, separate projects and his work evolved to incorporate notions of truth. Foucault's work does in fact offer a toolbox that may be brought to bear on complex societal and political problems in multiple ways and, like Foucault, scholars are able to modify and adapt his approaches to provide insights into the functioning of society.

Relevance for Public Relations

Foucault's work provides numerous tools for understanding public relations. The pluralist research approaches that he advocated guarded against a totalizing view of the "right way" to undertake research or of the "right way" to view any particular public relations practice. Rather, dipping into the Foucauldian toolbox enables multifarious insights to advance within the developing field of public relations. Indeed, within a Foucauldian tradition, attempts to impose a dominant model or advocate a specific approach would, themselves, become problematized and subject to critique. Specifically, Foucauldian concepts offer a number of tools for exploring the complex purposes of public relations and would lead us to conceptualize public relations variously as a knowledge system, a discourse technology, a power effect, and a subjectifying practice. The exploration of these intellectual avenues could potentially lead to new ways of thinking about public relations, expanding perceptions of public relations from the notion of it being primarily an institutional practice to include usage as a societal instrument for change. We now discuss in more depth how Foucault's work can help to problematize the purposes of public relations and outline some applications of Foucault's work in public relations.

Foucauldian Perspectives of Public Relations

For public relations scholars, problematization offers a technique for questioning and interrogating the role of public relations in society. A key question for understanding the origin and development of public relations, from a Foucauldian perspective, would be "How is it that we have come to think of public relations in this way?" Work of this nature has already been undertaken (e.g., Ewen, 1996; L'Etang, 2004, 2006; Motion & Leitch, 2001; Toledano, 2005). These historical perspectives advance our knowledge of the political, economic, and sociocultural development of public relations. However, a Foucauldian problematization of the evolution of public relations would bring the discursive role of knowledge production to the fore, critique the power relations and power effects of public relations strategies, and place notions of truth at the center of historical contextualizations of public relations. Historical trends and ruptures in public relations practice and scholarship could be identified. For instance, a critical history of the evolution of public relations could focus on the discourse practices of particular nations, organizations, or individuals; the techniques of power that underpin public relations strategies or maneuvers could be identified by mapping the stakes, interests, and values at play; and the relations between truth, power, organizations, and the self explored. In addition, networks of power and power effects could be delineated, and notions of regimes of truth and games of truth inherent within public relations investigated. An advantage of problematization is that it does not attempt to regulate what may be studied or how it may be studied, but instead, opens up the field of investigation. For example, a paradoxical problem that could also be investigated is: how is it that positive public relations efforts are excluded from common conceptualizations of public relations, yet negative conceptualizations prevail? How have we come to think about public relations in such a polemical manner? This problematization has the potential to turn our attention to the many positive attributes of public relations and reposition "public relations as the nexus between societal ideals and practice" (McKie, Motion, & Munshi, 2004, pp. 7–8).

Potential Applications of Foucault's Theories

Foucault's theories have particular salience for three key aspects of public relations practice and inquiry: meaning production and social change, relationship management, and identity work. From a Foucauldian perspective, public relations can be understood as a discursive process concerned with influencing the concepts and systems of thought that shape how we think about and understand the world. Application of Foucault's work to a relational approach to public relations highlights the power/knowledge relations between discourse actors or "stakeholders." The identity work undertaken by public relations professionals can be analyzed using a number of Foucauldian theories related to the creation and transformation of subject positions available to actors within discourse. Thus, a Foucauldian theoretical lens enhances both scholarly and practical understandings of the discursive, relational, and identity aspects of public relations. Our initial starting point for suggesting potential applications of Foucault's theories is to explore the conceptualization of public relations as a discursive meaning creation process.

Transforming Discourse and Mapping Social Change

Discourses may be contested, resisted, or transformed by any discourse actor (Hardy, Palmer, & Phillips, 2000; Hardy & Phillips, 1999) but this work often falls to public relations practitioners. The aim is to change the way people understand sociocultural and political phenomena by creating new meanings and rules "separating out from among all the statements which are possible those that will be acceptable" (Foucault 1972, p. 197). Although fragments of former discourses may remain, the underlying meanings, systems of thought, and discourse rules are changed. Changes in discourse, according to Foucault, can be determined by mapping the displacement of discourse boundaries, the new positions and roles made available for speaking subjects in the discourse, new modes of language, and new forms for circulating the discourse. For example, a public relations practitioner may attempt to change environmental discourse boundaries by introducing an economic discourse of growth and job security, position opponents as "greenie" radicals or ecoterrorists, focus on the language of business, finance, and job security, and attempt to influence unions. Or, conversely, public relations practitioners may attempt to overturn such efforts by reasserting the economic value of sustainability, position opponents as irresponsible corporations, and focus on climate change. Deploying this approach to map change, then, offers both a potential research agenda and methodical steps for inquiry into public relations practices concerned with meaning production.

Another potential application of Foucauldian theory to public relations emerges from Fairclough's (1992) analysis of discourse transformation, which drew upon Foucault's work, to analyze deliberate attempts to transform discourse in order to engineer sociocultural change. Fairclough (1992) referred to such attempts as the "technologization of discourse" by "professional technologists who research, redesign, and provide training in discourse practices" (p. 8). This insight has proved invaluable for our research into public relations. Within our scholarship we have been guided by the Foucauldian notion of problematization. Initially, we sought to understand the limits of the symmetrical model with its organizational orientation and find other ways of interpreting what appeared to be a more complex and differentiated practice (Motion & Leitch, 1996). A Foucauldian approach led us to place discourse and power at the center of our scholarship and investigations. Within later work we have focused on issues of truth, public interest, and public engagement. Our agenda has been to open up practice and scholarship to new ways of thinking about the role of public relations in society. For example, Motion and Leitch (1996) integrated Foucault and Fairclough's work on discourse technologization to theorize the role and practices of public relations practitioners in struggles to transform discourse and thus change sociocultural practices. The study concluded that public relations professionals facilitate the achievement of socio-cultural objectives through the transformation of discourse and thus change sociocultural practices. Motion (2005) deployed a Foucauldian lens to critique government attempts to transform a national economic discourse and the public relations practices that engage stakeholders in participative processes with predetermined outcomes. The work of Holtzhausen (2002) and Holtzhausen and Voto (2002) also fits within a Foucauldian tradition of interrogating hegemonic practices. Holt-zhausen and Voto (2002), for example, problematized the modernist corporate orientation of public relations and concluded that a postmod-ern activist perspective allows for critical empowerment and provides a postmodern agenda for public relations work.

Foucault's work on discourse has been extensively applied by orga-nizational scholars to analyze organizational issues and problems. The *Sage Handbook of Organizational Discourse* (Grant, Hardy, Oswick, & Putnam, 2004) provides a comprehensive overview of recent work in this area. Similarly, the work of critical organizational scholar, Livesey (2002a, 2002b), provides a Foucauldian-oriented critique of organiza-tional discourse practices, focusing on public relations efforts to main-tain organizational legitimacy and influence societal change, and thus serves as a useful resource for both scholars and practitioners wishing to understand or change public relations practices. We contend that Fou-cault's work on discourse has the potential to make a similar impact on critical public relations scholarship through problematization of mean-ing production and social change processes. For example, a potential objective could be to move beyond propaganda models to critique the deliberate technologization of discourse to achieve political and social change. We now discuss potential applications of Foucault's conceptual-ization of the relationship between power/knowledge and truth.

Managing the Power/Knowledge and Truth Aspects of Relationships

Public relations scholarship has neglected the concept of power to its detriment (Leitch & Neilson, 2001) and only more recently is the impor-tance of power being acknowledged and investigated (e.g., Berger, 2005; Edwards, 2006; Weaver, 2001; Weaver, Motion, & Roper, 2006). A significant development was the integrated circuit of culture model, by Curtain and Gaither (2005), which positioned power as a central concern for public relations because of its role in shaping discursive practices. Clearly, public relations practitioners are central actors in power/knowledge processes through their role as discourse technologists (Fairclough, 1992; Motion & Leitch, 1996). For example, public relations played a major role in the shift from a Keynesian to a neoliberal economic hegemony and in the accompanying ideological shift in Western societies during the last decades of the 20th century (Hall & Jacques, 1989). The networks of power that facilitate discourse production and transformation and the resultant power effects of ideological changes are an essential research area for further study.

Foucault's (1988) problematization of truth has intriguing implications for public relations work:

> Indeed, truth is no doubt a form of power. And in saying that I am only taking up one of the fundamental problems of western philosophy when it poses these questions: "Why in fact, are we attached to truth? Why the truth rather than lies? Why the truth rather than myth? Why the truth rather than illusion?" And I think that, instead of trying to find out what truth, as opposed to error, is, it might be more interesting to take up the problem posed by Nietzsche: how is it that, in our societies, "the truth" has been given this value, thus placing us in its thrall? (p. 107)

Public relations practitioners have frequently been accused of not being attached to the truth (Stauber & Rampton, 1995; Toth & Heath, 1992). In the above quote, Foucault raises a much deeper question as to why we should be attached to the truth. From a Foucauldian perspective, one would argue that the attachment to truth is central to the power/knowledge relationship. Particular knowledges gain the status of truths by virtue of their relationship to power. Indeed, truth itself is a concept/practice that needs to be problematized as a contingent and contextualized artifact or resource for particular discursive regimes. The notion of truth as a contingent, contextualized resource for the maintenance of or the struggle against particular power regimes and dominant coalitions emphasizes the mutuality and inextricable linkage between power, knowledge, and truth. For example, by the authority of the power vested in them the media may comment on societal events and thereby establish knowledge of and truth about events. In accepting the particular media perspective as truth, society then reinforces the power of the media system. In the background are the vested interests of various discourse actors whose perspectives are advocated by public relations professionals. Thus, we would contend that rather than being detached from truth, public relations has a central attachment to establishing and reinforcing particular truths. The public relations practices of establishing particular regimes of truth, the vested stakes and interests in such changes, and the power/knowledge struggles at play are all important potential opportunities for applying a Foucauldian critique.

Through their deployment of discursive strategies, public relations practitioners play a central role in shaping power/knowledge relations, which raises the fundamental question—what are the roles and responsibilities of public relations in society? By employing a critical Foucauldian discourse lens in public relations research, we are able to explore this question by problematizing the role of public relations practitioners as they attempt to establish particular truths and alter power/knowledge relations. The notion of public relations as a relatively innocuous system of business relationship management changes, when a Foucauldian approach is applied, to one that places power and influence at the center of both critique and practical considerations of the roles and responsibilities of public relations in society. Thus Foucault's work can be applied to rethink the nature, role, and influence of power in public relations practice.

Identity Work

Identity, for Foucault connoted neither a modernist fixed essential self nor a postmodern perpetual progression. Instead, Foucault's work on the subject emphasized that who one is emerges from practice, it is not a position or vantage point; rather, it is a "trajectory" (Rabinow, 1997, p. xix). Foucault's work on recreating the self can be deployed to theorize and critique the role of public relations practitioners in identity work or branding for individuals or organizations. Foucault (1982) espoused self-constitution and transformation, in contrast to the notion of an essential or unified self. Public relations professionals attempt to create and promote particular aspects of identity. However, the notion of commodifying and promoting identity, particularly in relation to individuals, raises questions about the ethics of self-promotion and whether there is an essential or authentic self. These questions have led to criticisms of public relations involvement in identity work or what is sometimes referred to as image or impression management. Here Foucault's (1984) work on an ideal of conduct and an ethic of the self would prove useful with personal ethics and values forming the core of the discursive positioning strategies adopted. In this way Foucault's work offers both a potential agenda and justification for ethical personal identity work.

Foucault's notion of constituting the self as a work of art, for example, fits neatly with the public relations concept of personal or celebrity branding. Public relations practitioners may assist individuals to undertake identity work such as personal public relations (Motion, 1999, 2000) or branding of the self by playing both formative and advisory roles. Drawing upon a Foucauldian approach, Motion (1999) identified two modes of personal public relations or identity work. Practitioners working in a formative mode were identified as actively forming the public identity, whereas within the advisory mode practitioners offered advice on how to discursively position the self, but the identity work was undertaken by the individual and potential ethical implications were explored. Further applications of Foucault's theories on constituting the self as a work of art could examine issues of how identity trajectories can be technologized, positioned within, and promoted through discourse; what it may mean to constitute the self as a work of art and the limitations of such an approach.

Foucault's (1988) discourse technology framework with its focus on technologies of production, sign systems, power and self also has implications for corporate identity work. For example, it has been applied to critique traditional approaches to corporate identity and develop a new semiotic model (Motion & Leitch, 2002) for understanding corporate identity as a discursive construct for the expression of all aspects of an organization and for assessing the congruence of those expressions. The framework could, in addition, be more broadly applied within public relations scholarship to understand how strategy and change practices are developed and implemented.

Conclusion and Implications for Research and Practice

Foucault (1974) described his work as a toolbox for use by other scholars. In this article we have given only a glimpse of the riches to be found within this toolbox and would argue that, in this sense, Foucault's oeuvre is more treasure chest than toolbox. Public relations scholars and practitioners can benefit equally from an understanding of the insights of a theorist who challenged us to "know how and to what extent it might be possible to think differently, instead of legitimating what is already known" (Foucault, 1984, p. 9). Unlike many other critical theorists, Foucault's work was not limited to simply taking apart the ideas offered by others. Rather, he offered new insights, new ways of understanding and making sense of the world.

By integrating Foucault's insights into our work as scholars and practitioners, we move beyond a focus on excellence and onto thinking about how public relations works and why it works. Foucault's work challenges us to problematize the role that public relations practitioners play within democratic societies, particularly in their role as discourse technologists. In doing so, we place the power/knowledge nexus at the centre of our thinking. Conceptualized from a power/knowledge perspective, public relations shifts from the discourse domain of business, where it is understood as a commercial practice, to the discourse domain of politics, where it is understood as a power effect that produces and circulates certain kinds of truths.

Note

1. A version of this chapter was published previously as: A toolbox for public relations: The oeuvre of Michel Foucault, in *Public Relations Review, 33*(3), 2007.

References

Ainsworth, S., & Hardy, C. (2004). Discourse and identities. In D. Grant, C. Hardy, C. Oswick, & L. Putnam (Eds.), *The Sage handbook of organizational discourse* (pp. 153–173). London: Sage.

Berger, B. K. (2005). Power over, power with, and power to relations: Critical reflections on public relations, the dominant coalition, and activism. *Journal of Public Relations Research, 17*(1), 5–28.

Bernauer, J., & Rasmussen, D. (Eds.). (1994). *The final Foucault.* Cambridge, MA: MIT Press.

Clegg, S., Courpasson, D., & Phillips. N. (2006). *Power and organizations.* London: Sage.

Curtin, P. A., & Gaither, T. K. (2005). Privileging identity, difference, and power: The circuit of culture as a basis for public relations theory. *Journal of Public Relations, 17*(2), 91–115.

Davenport, S., & Leitch, S. (2005). Circuits of power in practice: Strategic ambiguity as delegation of authority. *Organization Studies, 26*(11), 1603–1623.

Dean, M. (1994). *Critical and effective histories: Foucault's methods and historical sociology.* London: Routledge.

Dreyfus, H. L., & Rabinow, P. (1982). *Michel Foucault: Beyond structuralism and hermeneutics.* Chicago: University of Chicago.

Edwards, L. (2006). Rethinking power in public relations. *Public Relations Review, 32*(3), 229–231.

Ewen, S. (1996). *PR! A history of spin.* New York: Basic Books.

Fairclough, N. (1992). *Discourse and social change.* Cambridge, UK: Polity Press.

Foucault, M. (1972). *The archaeology of knowledge* (A. M. Sheridan Smith, Trans.). London: Routledge.

Foucault, M. (1974). Prisons et asiles dans le mécanisme du pouvoir [Prisons and refuges in the mechanism of power]. In *Dits et Ecrits* (Vol. 2, pp. 523–524). Paris: Gallimard.

Foucault, M. (1977). *Discipline and punish: The birth of the prison* (A. Sheridan, Trans.). London: Penguin.

Foucault, M. (1978). *The history of sexuality: An introduction* (R. Hurley, Trans.). London: Penguin.

Foucault, M. (1980). *Power/knowledge: Selected interviews and other writings 1972–1977* (C. Gordon, L. Marshall,, J. Mepham, & K. Soper Trans.). New York: Pantheon.

Foucault, M. (1982). On the genealogy of ethics: An overview of work in progress.

In H. L. Dreyfus & P. Rabinow (Eds.), *Michel Foucault: Beyond structuralism and hermeneutics* (pp. 229–252). Chicago: University of Chicago.

Foucault, M (1984). *The use of pleasure: The history of sexuality* (R. Hurley, Trans.). London: Penguin.

Foucault, M. (1988). Technologies of the self. In L. Martin, H. Gutman, & P. Hutton (Eds.), *Technologies of the self: A seminar with Michel Foucault* (pp. 16–48). Amherst: University of Massachusetts Press.

Foucault, M. (1991a). Politics and the study of discourse. In G. Burchell, C. Gordon, & P. Miller (Eds.), *The Foucault effect: Studies in governmentality with two lectures and an interview with Michel Foucault* (pp. 53–72). Chicago: University of Chicago.

Foucault, M. (1991b). Governmentality. In G. Burchell, C. Gordon, & P. Miller (Eds.), *The Foucault effect: Studies in governmentality with two lectures and an interview with Michel Foucault* (pp. 87–104). Chicago: University of Chicago.

Foucault, M. (1994). *Aesthetics: Essential works of Foucault 1954–1984* (J. D Faubion, Ed.; R. Hurley et al., Trans.). London: Penguin

Foucault, M. (1997). The ethics of the concern for the self as a practice of freedom. In P. Rabinow (Ed.), *Michel Foucault: Ethics, subjectivity and truth* (pp. 281–301). New York: New York University Press .

Gramsci, A. (1971). *Selections from the prison notebooks* (Q. Hoare & G. Nowell Smith, Eds. & Trans.). London: Lawrence & Wishart.

Grant, D., Hardy, C., Oswick, C., & Putnam, L. (Eds.). (2004). *The Sage handbook of organizational discourse.* London: Sage.

Gutting, G. (Ed.). (1994). *The Cambridge companion to Foucault.* Cambridge, UK: Cambridge University Press.

Hall, S., & Jacques, M. (Eds.). (1989). *New times: The changing face of politics in the 1990s.* London: Lawrence & Wishart.

Hardy, C., Palmer, I., & Phillips, N. (2000). Discourse as a strategic resource. *Human Relations, 53*(9), 1227–1248.

Hardy, C., & Phillips, N. (1999). No joking matter: Discursive struggle in the Canadian refugee system. *Organization Studies, 20*(1), 1–24.

Holtzhausen, D. (2002). Towards a postmodern research agenda for public relations. *Public Relations Review, 28*(3), 251–264.

Holtzhausen, D., & Voto, R. (2002). Resistance from the margins: The postmodern public relations practitioner as organizational activist. *Public Relations Review, 14*(1), 57–84.

L'Etang, J. (2004). *Public relations: A history of professional practice in the twentieth century.* Mahwah, NJ: Erlbaum.

L'Etang, J. (2006). Public relations as theatre: Key players in the evolution of British public relations. In J. L'Etang & M. Pieczka (Eds.), *Public relations: Critical debates and contemporary practice* (pp. 143–166). Mahwah, NJ: Erlbaum.

Leitch, S., & Neilson, D. (2001). Bringing publics into public relations: New theoretical frameworks for practice. In R. Heath (Ed.), *Handbook of public relations* (pp. 127–139). Thousand Oaks, CA: Sage.

Livesey, S. M. (2002a). Global warming wars: Rhetorical and discourse analytic approaches to ExxonMobil's corporate public discourse. *The Journal of Business Communication, 39*(1), 117–148.

Livesey, S. M. (2002b). The discourse of the middle ground: Citizen Shell commits to sustainable development. *Management Communication Quarterly, 15*(3), 319–349.

McHoul, A., & Grace, W. (1993). *A Foucault primer: Discourse, power and the subject.* Melbourne, Australia: Melbourne University Press.

McKie, D., Motion, J., & Munshi, D. (2004). Envisioning communication from the edge. *Australian Journal of Communication, 31*(3), 1–11.

Motion, J. (1999). Personal public relations: Identity as a public relations commodity. *Public Relations Review, 25*(4), 465–479.

Motion, J. (2000). Personal public relations: The interdisciplinary pitfalls and innovative possibilities of identity work. *Journal of Management Communication, 5*(1), 31–40.

Motion, J. (2005). Participative public relations: Power to the people or legitimacy for government discourse? *Public Relations Review, 31*(4), 505–512.

Motion, J., & Leitch, S. (1996). A discursive perspective from New Zealand: Another world view. *Public Relations Review, 22*(3), 297–309.

Motion, J., & Leitch, S. (2001). New Zealand perspectives on public relations. In R. L. Heath (Ed.), *Handbook of public relations* (pp. 659–663). Thousand Oaks, CA: Sage.

Motion, J., & Leitch, S. (2002). The technologies of corporate identity. *International Studies of Management & Organization, 32*(3), 45–64.

Rabinow, P. (Ed.). (1984). *The Foucault reader.* London: Penguin.

Rabinow, P. (Ed.). (1997). Introduction. In *Michel Foucault: Ethics, subjectivity and truth. The essential works of Michel Foucault 1954–1984* (R. Hurley et al., Trans.) (pp. xi–xlii). New York: New Press.

Stauber, J., & Rampton, S. (1995). *Toxic sludge is good for you: Lies, damn lies and the public relations industry.* Monroe, ME: Common Courage Press.

Toledano, M. (2005). Challenging accounts: Public relations and a tale of two revolutions. *Public Relations Review, 31*(4), 463–470.

Toth, E., & Heath, R. L. (Eds.). (1992). *Rhetorical and critical approaches to public relations.* Hillsdale, NJ: Erlbaum.

Weaver, C. K. (2001). Dressing for battle in the new economy: Putting power, identity, and discourse into public relations theory. *Management Communication Quarterly, 15*(2), 279–288.

Weaver, C. K., Motion, J., & Roper, J. (2006). From propaganda to discourse (and back again): Truth, power, the public interest and public relations. In J. L'Etang & M. Pieczka (Eds.), *Public relations: Critical debates and contemporary practice* (pp. 7–21). Mahwah, NJ: Erlbaum.

Life and Work of Michel Foucault

Michel Foucault (1926–1984) was born in Poitiers, France. He gained entry to the École Normale Supérieure, earning degrees in philosophy and psychology in 1950. Foucault lectured briefly at the École Normale and University of Lille, then left France in 1954 and held positions at the University of Uppsala, Warsaw University, and the University of Hamburg. In 1960 he returned to France taking up a position in philosophy at the University of Clermont-Ferrand and completed a doctorate on the history of madness in 1961 (*Folie et déraison: Histoire de la folie á l'âge classique*). In 1963 he published *Naissance de la clinique* (*Birth of the Clinic*) and *Raymond Roussel*. Foucault then moved to a position at the University of Tunis in 1965, published *Les mots et les choses* (*The Order of Things*) in 1966 which received popular acclaim. Foucault returned to France after the May 1968 student revolt where he published *L'archéologie du savoir* (*The Archaeology of Knowledge*) in 1969. In 1970 he was elected to the prestigious Collége de France as chair of the History of Systems of Thought. His work as a political activist was evident in the politicization of *Surveiller et punir* (*Discipline and Punish*), an examination of disciplinary power, control, and knowledge published in 1975. The *History of Sexuality* series focused on the discourse of the subject and care of the self. In addition, his lectures and seminars at the Collége de France that critiqued the will to knowledge and truth, technologies of power, and subjectivation of the self have been translated and published.

Useful references to consult about Foucault's work include Bernauer and Rasmussen (1994), Dean (1994), Gutting (1994), McHoul and Grace (1993), and Rabinow (1984).

Chapter 6

On Giddens

Interpreting Public Relations through Anthony Giddens's Structuration and Late Modernity Theory[1]

Jesper Falkheimer

Abstract

Using Giddens on public relations leads to a questioning of the dichotomy between the dominating agency-oriented public relations theories that neglect power structures, as well as critical theories that view public relations as a hidden strategic action used by elites to dominate the public sphere. The conclusion is that there are two major arguments for applying Giddens to public relations: (1) the theory of late modernity may enhance our understanding of public relations as an evolving practice in sociohistorical terms (linked to concepts such as trust, risk, expert systems, or legitimacy); (2) the structuration theory challenges the mass-oriented paradigm in public relations theory and enhances the holistic understanding of how public relations may be used in local contexts both as a reproductive and a transforming social instrument. Giddens's theory may in other words be used as a "third way public relations perspective": between managerial, functionalistic, and prescriptive traditions and critical and interpretative approaches.

Public relations has been an isolated theory and an undeveloped organizational subsystem for many years. From the perspective of strategy research, theory as well as practice has been dominated by classical, rational, and functionalistic approaches (Whittington, 2000). In concrete terms this has led to an overuse of rational plans and universal communication models instead of a more reflexive, process-oriented, situational, and flexible approach. The theories of Anthony Giddens may be useful in developing theory as well as practice in this direction, which I hope to show in this chapter.

Giddens is renowned for two theoretical systems of ideas: the structuration theory (1984) and the theory of late modernity and reflexivity (1990, 1991). In later years he has written about third way politics (1998) and globalization (2002). The concepts, analysis, and social frame constructed by Giddens have been used in several research areas. The broad approach makes his theories relevant to all sorts of social and cultural theories as well as social practices. Despite this fact, there have been few attempts to use Giddens's ideas in public relations theory and practice. In the closely related field of organizational communication the situation is similar (e.g., Yates & Orlokowski, 1992). This is strange, which I aim to show in this chapter, because there are good reasons for viewing structuration and late modernity theory as relevant tools for understanding why public relations has developed in a sociohistorical context, and how it may be interpreted as an instrumental organizational practice. On the other hand, social theory has been rather neglected in public relations research, so Giddens is not alone.

Considering the common critique in contemporary research that public relations has been dominated by mainstream and ethnocentric U.S.-biased perspectives (Sriramesh & Verčič, 2004; Verčič, van Ruler, & Flodin, 2001), it is interesting to see that the main contributors to a Giddensian public relations theory are Cozier and Witmer (e.g., 2001) from the United States. In various public relations case studies they have tried to apply structuration theory and focus on the interplay between human action and the nature of society.

From an applied perspective Giddens's theory may, based on a theoretical understanding, develop the professional identity of public relations practitioners from an ethical point of view. The popular and academic debate about the role of public relations in society has so far been limited to rather simple arguments. On the one hand critics such as Ewen (1996) and Stauber and Rampton (1995) have concluded that public relations is a corporate practice used to deceive the general public and to hide what is really going on. On the other hand, public relations researchers have showed little interest in analyzing public relations as a social institution, using social and cultural theory.

The structuration theory rejects the dichotomy between structure and agency in social theory. The theory of late modern reflexivity describes the social shift we are living in—with increasing uncertainty, individualism, identity work, globalization, and risk—from macro- as well as microperspectives. His "third way" politics, highly debated as a manifesto of "New Labour" and former prime minister Tony Blair in Britain, may be seen as an application of the structuration theory—an effort to adjust national politics to a late modern context.

Basically, his work may be viewed as a critique of sociological theory that is rooted in the classical dichotomies (Giddens, 1979). Giddens's theory is an attempt to go beyond the fundamental sociological traditions and the dichotomies of objectivism/subjectivism and structure/agency. The focus on the relations between micro- and macrolevels could be an argument for calling Giddens a social psychologist, since he interprets individual behavior and reflexivity as dialectic in relation to macrosocietal changes. There is certainly also a hermeneutic dimension in his works and he is critical toward structuralism, functionalism, and Marxism. But he is also critical toward theories that too strongly focus upon the human subject and action, since they neglect social structures. To handle these theoretical questions, Giddens draws on a time–space dimension that supports a dynamic and optimistic view of macro- and microsocial changes. The spatial perspective in Giddens's theory is of special interest to communication research as a whole, based on the notion that all forms of communication occur in space and that all spaces are produced through representations, which occur by means of communication (Falkheimer & Jansson, 2006). Giddens has not written explicitly about the role of public relations in these processes but it is not hard to find interesting crossroads.

Giddens—An Introduction

Giddens has become one of the most famous sociologists of our time together with Pierre Bourdieu, Jürgen Habermas, and Niklas Luhmann (see chapters 4, 8, & 10, this volume). There are several reasons for this. One reason is the massive scope of his academic writings. Since 1960 he has written approximately 35 books and hundreds of articles. His writings include metatheoretical books as well as textbooks and debate books; a critique of classical sociology as well as the formulation of a new social theory and analysis of social changes on macro- as well as on microlevels. The only subject that appears to have been neglected is research methodology. It is also a fact that despite his microsociological writings, there is a lack of empirical studies.

Another reason for his fame is his involvement in political life as an advisor to New Labour and former prime minister Tony Blair in Britain, as well as former American president Bill Clinton. Without a doubt, political leaders have been influenced by social scientists before, but probably not in the same and direct way. A third reason is the holistic and interdisciplinary approach that characterizes Giddens's work. The theoretical links to other fields—such as psychology, political science, economics, or human geography—are fundamental to his work.

Giddens's work may be split into three stages that also follow a logical chronology: (1) the critique of social theory; (2) structuration theory; and (3) late modernity theory. I will introduce Giddens from an epistemological perspective and thereafter discuss the content of these three theoretical stages. The presentations of the structuration and late modernity theories are linked to analysis of their relevance and consequence for public relations.

Giddens's Epistemology

Even though Giddens (1984) explicitly writes that his theory mainly draws on ontological concerns of social theory, he also develops an epistemological perspective. Obviously, he does not accept natural science as role model for social theory. Instead he promotes a hermeneutic approach that means that the individual and reflexive human being is placed at the center of theory. Human beings are capable of reflecting over their norms, intentions, and actions and may as a consequence also alter their lives. The active sense-making and interpretative communication process is also a hermeneutic process. One may also relate Giddens's theory to social constructionism that states that social reality is socially constructed (also see the chapter 3 on Berger, this volume). Linking the hermeneutic approach to a constructionist perspective means that the focus is shifted from individuals to the local social context that individuals interpret and act within. From a public relations perspective this perspective has been poorly developed in traditional research, which has mainly focused on practitioners' functions from a managerial approach. The constructionst perspective may be explained through four statements (Ahrensböll & Brinkmann-Petersen, 2002), that are easily related to the theory of Giddens:

1. Society is a human product. In other words, habits are acts that are made routines for one or more persons. Initially, these acts are constructed rationally but soon they are made nonreflective practices (externalization). As time passes and the habits are spread in institutions, action systems that influence social systems are constructed. In combination with other institutions, society is created.
2. Society is an objective reality. This means that institutions are legitimized through a process which leads to an objectification of their presence and relations to the environment. Moral standards are created as well as standardized action patterns.
3. Human beings are social products. This statement shifts focus to the individual and his or her socialization of norms and actions. Primary socialization agents are, obviously, the family, while secondary agents are other social institutions (that are influenced by public relations processes).
4. Face-to-face interaction is primary. In these local and everyday encounters between human beings meaning is constructed and acted upon. The interaction is based on language and the aim is to achieve mutual understanding. Social relations are the core of human existence.

The Critique of Social Theory

The first stage in Giddens's work (e.g., 1979) is based upon a reading and critique of three established traditions of sociology as well as the three "founding fathers," Durkheim, Weber, and Marx. Giddens is a true eclectic in the sense that he uses parts from several theories and traditions and builds a middle way theory of his own. Summarizing his critique is hard but necessary. Structuralism, functionalism, and systems theory lack theories of the subject and agency, even though they have some sound analysis of structural relations and systems. Interpretative and agency-based ideas of thought lack theories that show the relations between the subject and social structures. The strength of these interpretative theories is that they focus upon human reflexivity and relative freedom to act. Marxism has the best solution of the dichotomy between structure and agency but is based upon an idea of determinism and evolution and has low value in contemporary society. All together the critique of functionalism and structuralism has had certain effects on later writings by Giddens. There is, according to my interpretation, an increasing emphasis on the possibilities of conscious human agents to transcend structures.

There are several critical readings of this critique. As an example, Brante (1989) concludes that Giddens's argumentation vulgarizes the basic questions since it is superficial, too wide, and simple. One of the mistakes that Giddens makes, according to Brante (1989), is that he reads the sociologists too narrowly: "He is scared that structuralists don't understand that it is living human beings that produce as well as reproduce structures; that functionalists and evolutionists use concepts such as 'need' and 'social adaptation' not metaphorically but [because they] actually believe that societies are biological organisms with these qualities" (author's translation; p. 61). Another mistake, according to Brante, is the all-embracing approach. Giddens cannot accept that some aspects or social dimensions are not included, which leaves him juggling with too many balls at the same time.

Another critique was formulated in the early 1980s from a general systems theory platform (Archer, 1982). She supports the aim to combine old dichotomies but does not find the theory adequate in fulfilling this aim. Instead of structuration (introduced in the next section) she proposes a "Morphogenesis" theory, based on systems theory, that is more focused on interaction and a holistic approach: "I will seek to show not only that a better 'parts-whole' account results but also one which fulfils Giddens' desiderata of treating society as consisting of parts in tension and of understanding the totality as implicated in its parts" (Archer, 1982, p. 475). Giddens's theories obviously have limitations. But the grand scope of his ideas, his innovative analytical concepts, integration of spatial and temporal dimensions, as well as his progressive approach to traditional sociological theory, is inspiring for most readers.

The Structuration Theory

In the second stage, Giddens's critique and synthesis of the old classics is developed into a new theory—the structuration theory. This is done in a very complex way by using a spatial and temporal dimension in social analysis. The structuration theory does not focus on the individual actor or societal totality "but social practices ordered across space and time" (Giddens, 1984, p. 2). In fact, one of Giddens's main arguments against traditional social theory is that it does not position social institutions, structures, and agents in space and time. Space and time are basic conditions for social systems and social acts. The dualism between structure and agency is replaced with a relational approach. Social structures are reproduced or transformed through repetition (on a macrolevel) of individual acts. The conclusion is pragmatic: yes, there are social structures (traditions, institutions, rituals) but they are made by humans and may be replaced and changed through time and space. Social structures are medium of human agency as well as the result of this agency. It is an optimistic social theory that views social practice as processes rather than products or static states. Later I intend to focus upon this praxis as a mode of communication.

Social systems range from dyads to global formations (Giddens, 1979). Structuration processes are based on the condition that the development of these systems is open-ended. There are, as in Marxist thought or functionalist thought, no historical or functional structures that define the future. The structuration processes may lead to reproduction of existing structures as well as radical change. From an organizational

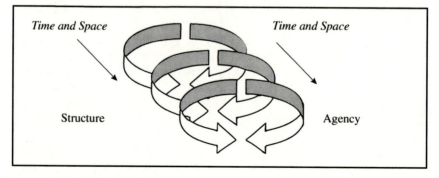

FIGURE 6.1 The Reproduction or Transformations of Institutions, Structures, and Agents in Space and Time.

perspective the theory is a sharp critique of the modernist notion of organizations as containers in which the organizational agents function and interact with each other and with agents outside the organization. There are here possible links between structuration theory and the epistemology of social constructionism that offers a shift from a focus on stable organization structures to ever-changing open-ended processes, crucial during crises (Falkheimer & Heide, 2006).

The Late Modernity Theory

In the third stage, Giddens's focus is on an analysis of modernity and the current social development. Bob Dylan was already singing "For the times they are a-changin'" in 1964. This quote might as well be used by Giddens, whose theory is framed by the notion that that we are living in a rapidly changing world. In one of his later texts, Giddens (2002) concludes that: "There are good, objective reasons to believe that we are living through a major period of historical transition. Moreover, the changes affecting us aren't confined to any one area of the globe, but stretch almost everywhere" (p. 1). Giddens's theory on historical transition differs from the radical postmodernists (e.g., Lyotard, 1986), since it does not view the social change as a total shift in time. From a radical postmodern perspective the modernity is overturned by a new social and cultural order in conflict with modern institutions and rational reason. The ideas of a coherent History, linear Progress, and systematic and objective Knowledge are viewed as social constructs with limited value. Instead of organizing lives around old authorities, postmodern humans organize themselves in new subcultures (like tribes), for instance, based on local myths, mass-mediated narratives, or transnational commercial brands. The postmodern relations between humans and these shifting signs or narratives are flexible and may change fast (nothing lasts in postmodernity). The focus on transnationality, globalization, multiculturalism, and decentralization may also be interpreted as postmodern consequences. The most radical postmodernists are leaning toward a solipsistic view on ontology but the concept of postmodernity (postmodernism is an aesthetic theory which was formulated in architecture and design during the 1970s) is seldom interpreted in such an extreme form nowadays. Anyway, from a Giddensian perspective, modernity is not at all overruled. Instead, we are living in a time where modernity has been radicalized. In other words: the social characteristics of late or high modernity have been there for centuries but have now become more radical and more global than ever.

Giddens (1990) points toward three interdependent sources of the modernity dynamic: (1) the separation of time and space; (2) the development of disembedding mechanisms; and (3) the reflexive appropriation of knowledge. The escalating separation of time and space has led to a higher speed of change (compared to premodern societies), expanding scope, and the growth of new modern institutions. All together, this has led to an increase in risk apprehension and uncertainty. Risk is distinguished into two types: First, external risks that are experienced as coming from the outside and are related to nature (e.g., floods or plagues); second, manufactured risks that refer "to risk situations which we have very little historical experience of confronting" (Giddens, 2002, p. 26), such as those connected to globalization (global warming) but also those connected to human beings' everyday life (e.g., traveling on the subway). In the same way as Ulrich Beck, the author of *Risk Society* (1992), Giddens bases his risk analysis from the perspective of a reflexive self, a late modern human that has to make more and more choices. The amount of objective risks is not the issue here, but the feeling among people that every step in life is related to different risk scenarios. "Living in a secular risk culture is inherently unsettling, and feelings of anxiety may become particularly pronounced during episodes which have a fateful quality" (Giddens, 1991, p. 182).

The increasing emancipation from old traditions and hierarchies has created a new lifestyle—"life politics" (Giddens, 1991, p. 214). The authorities in late modern societies are challenged, according to Giddens as well as Beck. As an example, scientists are losing their status. The scientific rationality has caused the risk society. The difference between Beck and Giddens appears when one asks how societies should handle and manage the risks. Giddens believes that it is important to reshape the trust in science, while Beck wants the expert systems to be democratized. Giddens (1998) points toward mass media spin, threats to the societal economy, and industrial scandals as reasons behind the decreasing trust. He proposes a strategy for creating new trust, for instance by teaching scientists to communicate with the public. The analysis of risk, uncertainty, and reflexivity, which I will discuss later, is of high importance to public relations. In late modernity the development leads to new relations between organizations, society, and the public concerning trust and legitimacy.

Giddens's concept of *disembedding* is used to describe how local social relations are restructured in unlimited spaces (in contrast to traditional and firm relations in premodern societies). The reason behind this process is the separation between space and place. Giddens uses two types of disembedding: symbolic tokens and expert systems. The symbolic tokens are "media of interchange which can be 'passed around' without regard to the specific characteristics of individuals or groups that handle them at any particular juncture" (Giddens, 1991, p. 22). His example is money and money transactions. Expert systems are "systems of technical accomplishment or professional expertise that organize large areas of the material and social environments that we live in today" (Giddens, 1991, p. 27). A technical example could be computer support. But the social expert systems are probably the most prevalent, especially with regard to mass media trends where instructive and therapeutic shows dominate contemporary television. Public relations is also a typical late modern expert system, a point which I will later discuss.

Public Relations and Structuration Theory

Structuration theory challenges the modernist notion of organizations and society as two different systems as well as the division into internal and external communication. The systems perspective analyzes organizations as organisms and "assumes that the survival of an organization is enhanced or constrained by consequences of the actions of its conflicting or relevant publics" (Cozier & Witmer, 2003, p. 4). Public relations then become a response system, an organizational subsystem (Grunig, 1992; Grunig & Hunt, 1984), especially used toward conflicting publics. The managerial choice between a symmetric and asymmetric approach has become the focus of interest in systems-related public relations theory.

Structuration theory is not in total opposition with the systems perspective, but has closer links to constructionist and critical perspectives. One first difference is that structuration describes rather than prescribes the role of public relations. A second difference is that the theory does not view organizations as stable, but rather as dynamic and transforming. The organizational as well as societal structures are produced and reproduced by the members of the organization through communication (cf. Shotter, 1993). The dualism between structure and agency is replaced with a relational approach that gives public relations a vivid role. "From a stucturationist perspective, public relations is a communicative force in society that serves to reproduce and/or transform an organization's dominant ideology, rather than solely adapting to a stakeholder group or public" (Cozier & Witmer, 2003, p. 16). A third difference is the focus on spatial and temporal contexts. The spatial (place) and temporal (time) dimensions in public relations theory are rather neglected. In the last decade there has been an increasing focus on international public relations but this has mostly meant national comparisons (e.g., van Ruler & Verčič, 2004). Giddens's stress on spatial dimensions is of a complex nature, focusing on local as well as regional spaces (in everyday life). The temporal dimension is in the same way directed toward micro- rather than macrotime. In other words, the historical models of public relations are not temporal in this sense (Grunig & Hunt, 1984).

Cozier and Witmer (2003) have made eight presuppositions for a structurationist public relations perspective, in which they mean to place public relations in the organizational center. Below I present a summary of these presuppositions:

1. The public relations core is communication processes that are dynamic, ideological, temporal, and spatial. There is a link to the ritual model of communication, focusing communication as sense-making rituals in contrast with the modernist transmission model (Carey, 1988). The focus is on shared meanings and sense making: organizational members mutually construct a social reality. In a methodological sense this presupposition is an argument for more ethnographic and qualitative research. In an applied sense it may be a support for a community-based approach through storytelling and rituals and an increasing support of informal communication systems.

2. Public relations is not a subsystem performed by public relations professionals, but by all members of the organization. "This means that the analysis needs to move away from roles and address the involvement of all organizational members in the enactment of ongoing public relations communication" (Cozier & Witmer, 2003, p. 23). In applied terms, this would mean that public relations is viewed more as a support process in the field, integrating all levels of the organization (such as the service encounters) than an isolated top management function.

3. Public relations needs to be analyzed as an ideological communication force that may have quite different outcomes. In the age of life politics, structuration theory supports the perspective on public relations as an important practice and profession that may lead to reproduction of social structures as well as emancipation and transformation.

The agent in the structuration process is reflective and active and may usually explain his or her actions. In other words: the agent may also, under different circumstances and in different aspects, change his or her actions and transform the structure. One may say that structures contain both constraints and resources. The agents are constrained by social norms and institutions and may reproduce as well as transform systems. From a communicative perspective changes of the rules in social systems may gain transformation. Public relations may be a contributing as well as a constraining practice.

Taken together, my interpretation is that structuration theory has advantages as well as disadvantages when it comes to public relations. A skeptic, and I would not totally disagree, would say that the structuration theory describes something simple in a very complicated way. That public relations is a communicative structuration force, transgressing the constructed borders in and between organizations and society, that either may reproduce or transform social structures is not really a surprise for most public relations researchers or professionals. On the other hand, structuration theory could be valuable as one part of a constructionist and communicative turn in public relations theoretical development. Drawing on interpretative, critical, as well as systems theory it advances the foundation and challenges modernist assumptions (e.g., between organizations and society, internal and external communication, public relations professionals and organizational members). The burning issue is, of course, in which way public relations must be organized and practiced to achieve the transforming function. There are no prescriptive answers to this grand question in Giddens's work. In fact, one may wonder if the main argument behind the increase of public relations practice in society is that organizational leaders want to hinder transformation and instead use public relations as a reproductive force. This question remains to be answered.

Public Relations in Late Modernity

The theory on late modernity is obviously connected to the structuration theory but also stands for itself. From a public relations perspective it gives an opportunity to leave the organizational framework of analysis and try to interpret public relations as a force in a rapidly changing society. In fact, it is possible to interpret public relations as one of the main strategies that different institutions and organizations implement when they try to handle and manage this development. The core issues of late modernity, discussed earlier, are also the core issues of public relations—risk, uncertainty, trust, and holistic reflexivity. From a professional standpoint, Giddens's late modernity theory may gain a societal understanding of the practice and its consequences. This may lead to a higher state of reflexivity (about the social context, ethics, and social responsibility). Reflexivity as a concept may also be used to argue for the role of public relations as an "interpretative" or "reflexive" profession, not only a work of transmission messages to publics. Below I will try to show the relations between late modernity and public relations regarding three main trends: the division between space and place, disembedding processes, and reflexivity.

When it comes to the spatial and temporal dimensions (e.g., globalization), the development of media and communication technologies have gradually challenged the time and space borders. This has gained the development of new symbolic spaces between humans, groups, and societies. Public relations may be viewed as a technique used for controlling, listening, and influencing these symbolic spaces. Historically, the main interest has been in formal symbolic spaces (e.g., news media) but the late modern development has created new, often informal, symbolic spaces that public relations now struggle with (e.g., blogs, e-mail, Listservs). Also, in modernity organizations have mainly related to national political and cultural contexts. But in late modernity these borders are transgressed and transnational publics, groups, or issues demand a multicultural and global approach.

When Giddens (1990) points toward the space and time compression as one of the central features of late modernity, he also concludes that this becomes a separation between what is seen and not seen. In a public relations context this separation is certainly important. Relations between what is formally communicated at the organizational front-stage (speaking with Goffman) and what is happening backstage are complicated. In fact, the bad reputation of public relations has evolved from the public notion that the practice only concerns the frontstage, trying to hide what happens behind. Despite exceptions and theoretical developments, one may presume that the majority of real-life public relations only work with frontstage and visual management in different symbolic spaces. All together, the increasing separation between place and space and importance of informal symbolic spaces are some of the reasons behind the expansion of public relations practice.

The second main trend of late modernity, processes of disembedding, are according to Giddens (1990) defined as "the 'lifting out' of social relations from local contexts of interaction and their restructuring across indefinite spans of time-space" (p. 21). From a public relations perspective, the disembedding processes of late modernity are also the main reasons for the evolvement of the practice. This is so because disembedding leads—beside symbolic spaces, which are mentioned earlier—to an increase of uncertainty and a need of systems that create trust and legitimacy. The knowledge specialization in all parts of society and the development of "manufactured risks," are putting people in tough situations where they have to make new choices all the time. Technical expert systems as well as service expert systems are there to help us. But from a holistic perspective, focusing relations between organizations and society, public relations could be interpreted as the main expert system for creating trust and legitimacy.

The third trend has been mentioned earlier—reflexivity. In the analysis on reflexivity Giddens leaves the macrolevel and tries to understand everyday human life from a social psychological point of view. The concept focuses on the continuous human process of reflecting upon how we act and what we think, a process that has evolved gradually in modernity. It is rooted in individualism, detraditionalization, and the informationalization of society: we know more about social life, have less "old" traditions and institutions to lean toward, and are forced to make individual choices all the time. This reflexivity may lead to different outcomes. In a debate book Giddens (2002) writes about how the detraditionalization and radical changes have led to an increase in religious, nationalist, or ethnic fundamentalism. Fundamentalists react toward threats to traditions and "to the fundamentalists, there is only one right and proper way of life, and everyone else had better get out of the way" (p. xiii). From a public relations perspective, the discussion on reflexivity is important because it concerns the sense-making processes of the public. In functionalist and mass-oriented theory the public, publics, or organizational members are usually not given active roles: they are receivers of messages, which they may or may not like. Viewing organizational members and the public as reflexive agents gains us an understanding of the relational aspects of public relations.

Conclusions

There are both advantages and disadvantages with using the theories of Giddens in analyzing public relations. The main advantage is that such an analysis may contribute to the understanding of public relations as a late modern societal phenomenon in relation to different political, economic, and cultural institutions. This is obviously a valid argument for using all kinds of social theory to understand public relations. The argument for using Giddens's theories specifically is that there are certain elements in these theories that are easy to link to public relations. First, such a theoretical perspective has a high degree of openness and does not necessarily lead to fixed and static conclusions. Compared to critical theory the theories of structuration and late modernity do not fix the analysis in a prewritten scheme of understanding. Compared to sense making and constructionist theories Giddens's theories do not limit the analysis to local practices. The dependence on interactions between structure and agency parallel with the spatial and temporal macrocontextualization makes a Giddensian public relations analysis dynamic and relevant.

The structuration theory may be used as a tool for developing new theory that transgresses traditional divisions and borders. Together with interpretative and critical theory it may give new insights. I especially find the late modernity theory relevant for a macroanalysis of public relations as a reflexive and social expert system, in a dialectical relationship to societies' norms and values. In an applied sense, Giddensian theory could be used to develop more dynamic and public-oriented strategies, focusing the public from a multicultural and reflexive view and challenging borders between constructed systems and subsystems.

The globalization has had massive implications for public relations practice but has so far seldom been integrated into analysis.

I find two main disadvantages of using Giddens in public relations theory. First, that—even though theoretically discussed—it lacks empirical grounding. Researching public relations practice from a structuration perspective soon becomes complicated. Applying late modernity theory may not be very much easier. Second, the dynamic, relational, and eclectic character of Giddens's theory makes it so wide that it may be used in all fields of social and cultural science in several ways. On the other hand, this may also be a sign of its true interdisciplinary and grand scope.

To sum up, according to my interpretation there are two main arguments for using Giddens's theories in public relations: (1) the theory of late modernity may enhance our understanding of public relations as an evolving practice in socio-historical terms; (2) the structuration theory challenges the mass- and systems oriented paradigm in public relations theory and enhances the holistic understanding of how public relations communication may be used both as a reproductive and a transforming social instrument. Giddens's theory may in other words be used as a "third way public relations perspective": between managerial, functionalistic, and prescriptive traditions and critical and interpretative approaches. A further development of a third way theory would lead to an increased focus on public relations everyday practice as situational, spatial and temporal. It would also lead to an increased interest in the qualitative dynamics of reflexivity processes in different publics, based on a social constructionist approach to practice and reality. In empirical terms this would motivate ethnographic research. From an applied perspective the third way theory may be used to develop dynamic and process-oriented communication strategies from a society-centric and public-oriented perspective.

Note

1. A previous version of this chapter was published as: Anthony Giddens and public relations: A third way perspective, in *Public Relations Review, 33*(3), 2007.

References

Ahrensböll, H., & Brinkmann-Petersen, C. (2002). *Prolog til et nyt paradigme? Glidninger mellem offentligheden og markedet fortolket udfra Anthony Giddens' teoretiske univers* [Prologue for a new paradigm? Shifts between the public sphere and the market in Anthony Gibbens' theoretical universe]. Unpublished Public Relations Speciale, Roskilde Universitetscenter, Denmark.

Archer, M. S. (1982). Morphogenesis versus structuration: On combining structure and action. *The British Journal of Sociology, 33*(4), 455–483.

Beck, U. (1992). *Risk society: Towards a new modernity.* London: Sage.

Brante, T. (1989). *Anthony Giddens och samhällsvetenskapen* [Anthony Giddens and social science]. Stehag, Sweden: Symposion.

Carey, J. W. (1988). *Communication as culture: Essays on media and society.* New York: Routledge.

Cozier, Z., & Witmer, D. (2001). Structuration analysis of new publics. In R. L. Heath (Ed.), *Handbook of public relations* (pp. 615–623). Thousand Oak, CA: Sage.

Cozier, Z., & Witmer, D. (2003, November 19–23). *A structurationist perspective of public relations: A metatheoretical discussion of boundary spanning.* Paper presented to the National Communication Association Convention, Public Relations Division, Miami Beach, FL.

Ewen, S. (1996). *PR! A social history of spin.* New York: Basic Books.

Falkheimer, J., & Heide, M. (2006). Multicultural crisis communication: Towards a social constructionist perspective. *Journal of Contingencies and Crisis Management, 4*(14), 180–189.

Falkheimer, J., & Jansson, A. (Eds.). (2006). *Geographies of communication: The spatial Turn in media studies.* Gothenburg, Sweden: Nordicom.

Giddens, A. (1979). *Central problems in social theory: Action, structure and contradiction in social analysis.* Berkeley: University of California Press.

Giddens, A. (1984) *The constitution of society: Outline of the theory of structuration.* Cambridge: Polity Press.

Giddens, A. (1990). *The consequences of modernity.* Cambridge, MA: Polity Press.

Giddens, A. (1991). *Modernity and self-identity: Self and society in the late modern age.* Cambridge, UK: Polity Press.

Giddens, A. (1998). *The third way: The renewal of social democracy.* Cambridge, UK: Polity Press.

Giddens, A. (2002). *Runaway world: How globalisation is reshaping our lives.* London: Profile.

Grunig, J. (Ed.). (1992). *Excellence in public relations and communication management.* Hillsdale, NJ: Erlbaum.

Grunig, J. E., & Hunt, T. (1984). *Managing public relations.* Orlando, FL: Harcourt Brace.

Lyotard, J.-F. (1986). *The post-modern condition: A report on knowledge.* Manchester, UK: Manchester University Press.

Shotter, J. (1993). *Conversational realities: Constructing life through language.* London: Sage.

Sriramesh, K., & Verčič, D. (2004). International public relations: A framework for future research. *Journal of Communication Management, 7*(1), 54–71.

Stauber, J., & Rampton, S. (1995). *Toxic sludge is good for you! Lies, damn lies and the public relations industry.* Monroe, ME: Common Courage Press.

van Ruler, B., & Verčič, D. (Eds.). (2004). *Public relations and communication management in Europe: A nation-by-nation introduction to public relations theory and practice.* Berlin: Mouton de Gruyter.

Verčič, D., van Ruler, B., & Flodin, B. (2001). On the definition of public relations: A European View. *Public Relations Review, 27*(4), 373–383.

Whittington, R. (2000). *What is strategy and does it matter?* London: Thomson International Business Press.

Yates, J., & Orlokowski, W. (1992). Genres of organizational communication: A structurational approach to studying communication and media. *The Academy of Management Review, 17*(2), 299–326.

Life and Work of Anthony Giddens

Anthony Giddens was born January 18, 1938 in Edmonton, London. His father was a clerk and he grew up in a middle-class family. He received his bachelor's degree at Hull University in 1959, his master's degree at the London School of Economics, and his doctorate from the University of Cambridge in 1974. Initially he taught social psychology at the University of Leicester, where he met and was inspired by Norbert Elias, a German sociologist who founded process or figurational sociology. This theory has a somewhat similar focus as Giddens's ideas of structuration: a temporal approach examining the connection between changes in human psychology (micro) and changes in social structures (macro).

In 1969 Anthony Giddens moved to the University of Cambridge where he was appointed full professor in 1987. He cofounded Polity Press, a major social science publishing house, and from 1997 to 2003 was Director of the London School of Economics. He has also been an advisor to former British prime minister Tony Blair and guided both him and former American president Bill Clinton in directing politics a "third way." He has been an active opinion leader supporting New Labour. He was given a life peerage in 2004 and became a Labour member of the House of Lords.

Chapter 7

On Goffman

Researching Relations with Erving Goffman as Pathfinder[1]

Catrin Johansson

Abstract

This chapter brings forth key concepts of Erving Goffman's sociology, which are advocated to be important to our understanding of social interaction and the study of interpersonal relationships with internal and external publics. The concepts of *impression management, framing, footing,* and *face* have bearing upon essential notions in public relations: relationships, identification, and image. Thus, it is predicted that development of these concepts in public relations research will deepen our understanding of communication processes that have important implications for the relation of publics in public relations.

When researching interpersonal relationships with internal and external publics, our understanding of social interaction is vital. In this chapter, key concepts of Erving Goffman's sociology; *impression management, framing, footing,* and *face* are developed. These concepts shed light upon processes of relationship building, identification, and image construction. The aim is to bring the previously neglected interpersonal communication with internal and external publics to the forefront.

The chapter is structured as follows. First, the use of Goffman's theories is situated in a public relations context. Second, an introduction to Goffman's contribution is made and concepts argued important to public relations are presented. Third, the development in public relations research and the call for more studies on interpersonal communication are commented upon. Fourth, the relevance and implications of the key concepts *impression management, framing, footing,* and *face* are discussed through a review of existing applications. Fifth, an empirical example is given, where the application of framing, footing and face is illustrated.

The building and maintenance of strategic ethical relationships are the essence of public relations research and practice today, state Vasquez and Taylor (2001). However, with few exceptions, interpersonal relationships and communication have not yet attracted much attention. Toth (2000) advocates interpersonal communication theory as one type of communication practice in managing relationships. Coombs (2001) suggests that we should analyze interaction patterns in order to understand how organization and stakeholder words and actions affect the development of their relationship. The empirical study of interpersonal relations in a PR context is indeed wanting.

Erving Goffman's sociological work is centered around theories of social interaction derived from his empirical work in different settings. He analyzes the relationship between interpersonal meanings and social structure, paying attention to both the symbolic value of what is said and done and the more abstract forms of social life. A comprehension of Goffman's ideas will deepen our understanding of how the social world is experienced and reproduced. This understanding is vital to our efforts to improve our institutions and social environment, according to Manning (1992). In other words, to improve the functioning of organizations and their stakeholder relations we will benefit from what Goffman offers.

Identity and relationships, personal, as well as organizational, are coconstructed in face-to-face interaction. The concepts of impression management, framing, footing, and face could serve as a theoretical foundation to the empirical study of social interaction in organizational settings. Approaching a "discursive turn" (cf. Alvesson & Kärreman, 2000; Fairhurst & Putnam, 2004) in public relations research will add new perspectives in the field.

Erving Goffman's Contribution

Erving Goffman was both influential and controversial within the discipline of sociology. His sociology develops the ideas of several classic sociological theorists, and applies them to a domain of social life whose structural complexities had (before Goffman's work) gone largely unnoticed: face-to-face social interaction. With his focus on social interaction, he provides a description of how language is situated in particular circumstances of social life, and how it reflects and adds meaning and structure in those circumstances.

His ideas later became incorporated into the work of general theorists such as Giddens and Habermas. His thinking also impacted on the work of scholars outside sociology; for example, in political science, philosophy, anthropology, linguistics, and psychology. His ideas about "impression management" became adopted by journalists and writers of popular studies of interpersonal conduct.

Goffman's methods are determined by his central object, face-to-face interaction in which Goffman sees predominantly a world of implicit knowledge that actors can barely articulate or "say" because of its habitual nature (Willems, 2004). In his early works, Goffman uses "naturalistic observation." He observes, on the one hand, normal everyday life. On the other hand, he invokes particular, remarkable, and separate worlds beyond the layperson's everyday world. In his later work Goffman sees an important option for naturalistic observation in the use of audiovisual recording equipment. Goffman's observational, analytical, and descriptive strategy also consists of using metaphors, concepts, and models as well as contrast and imagery (Willems, 2004).

However, his work has also received criticism for being lightweight and inconsequential (Smith, 1999). Goffman's methods, to generate new concepts from rather unsystematic observations, have been questioned. Smith concludes that overall, the corpus of Goffman's writings has a fragmentary character. Goffman gave the impression of always wanting to race on to the next issue or topic, rather than consolidate what he had achieved. From the outset he himself emphasized the exploratory character of his work (Smith, 1999). Thus, his theories have been tested and his concepts have been more thoroughly developed subsequently by his interpreters (cf. Schiffrin, 1994).

Key Concepts: Impression Management, Framing, Footing, and Face

In his early book *The Presentation of Self in Everyday Life*, Goffman develops a drama metaphor concerning an individual's presentation of her or his public self (Goffman, 1959). He meant the book to serve as a handbook, detailing one sociological perspective from which social life can be studied—especially the kind of social life that is organized "within the physical confines of a building or plant"—or any "concrete social establishment, be it domestic, industrial, or commercial." We could translate these directions into the study of organizations.

By producing the drama metaphor, Goffman compares face-to-face interaction to parts played by actors in front of audiences. When an individual enters the presence of others, they seek to acquire information about this person. Information about the individual helps to define the situation, enabling others to know what is expected from them, and what they may expect (1959). Moreover, many crucial facts lie beyond the time and place of interaction or lie concealed within it. Consequently, the "true" or "real" attitudes, beliefs, and emotions of the individual can be ascertained only indirectly. The expressiveness of the individual (and therefore his or her capacity to give impressions) appears to involve two radically different kinds of sign activity, according to Goffman: the expression that the individual *gives,* and the expression that is *given off.* The first involves verbal symbols which are used admittedly and solely to convey the information that are known to attach to these symbols. This is communication in the traditional and narrow sense. The second involves a wide range of action that others can treat as symptomatic of the actor, the expectation being that the action was performed for reasons other than the information conveyed in this way (1959). The individual does intentionally convey misinformation by means of both of these types of communication, the first involving deceit, the second feigning.

Goffman also employs notions like *front* versus *backstage, setting,* and *appearance.* He argues that the self is a social construction or, more specifically, an interactive construction—an idea that has been developed at great length in different research traditions like discourse theory and organizational communication.

Impression management signifies that people use communication deliberately and strategically to create desired impressions of themselves. In interaction with others, a person uses communication to manage other people's impressions of him- or herself (Goffman, 1959). This communication may be divided into two parts: a part that is relatively easy for the individual to manipulate at will, verbal communication, and a part that is more unconscious and difficult to control, nonverbal communication. The audience check upon the validity of what is said in words and what is expressed by other means. Thus, a fundamental asymmetry is demonstrated in the communication process, the individual being aware of only one stream of communication, the others of both (Goffman, 1959).

Accordingly, different positions toward the impression that is communicated may be taken: an individual may be sincere, believe in the impression, or be cynical about it. We also can expect to find natural movement back and forth between cynicism and sincerity.

In interpersonal communication, interactants are coconstructing the definition of the situation. However passive the role of an audience or a listener may seem to be, every person will define the situation by virtue of the response to the individual, and the communicated impression. First impressions and initial information are important, since they form the basis which is later developed and modified by the participants. Normally, a working consensus, a level of agreement, is established in an interaction setting (Goffman, 1959). However, the working consensus established in one setting will be quite different in content from the working consensus established in a different type of setting. In many interaction settings some of the participants cooperate together as a team. The interaction can be analyzed in terms of the cooperative effort of all participants to maintain a working consensus (Goffman, 1959).

The notion of *front* or *frontstage* signifies that part of the individual's performance regularly functions in a general and fixed fashion to define the situation for those who observe the performance. A formal presentation of the company's activities and economic status, could work this way. This is contrasted with the notion of *backstage*, which is a place where the impression fostered by the performance is knowingly contradicted. Here, illusions and impressions are openly constructed. Here, the communication strategy is planned. Here, persons behave "out of character," the team can run through its performance, checking for offending expressions when no audience is present to be affronted by them. Here, poor members of the team, who are expressively inept, can be schooled or dropped from the performance. Here, eventually, the performer can relax and drop the official front (1959).

The vital secrets of a show are visible backstage, and because performers behave out of character while there, it is natural to expect that the passage from the front region to the back region will be kept closed to members of the audience or that the entire back region will be kept hidden from them. This is a widely practiced technique of impression management, according to Goffman (1959).

Framing is another important concept that has been developed and gained ground in public relations and media research. Bateson (1972) originally pointed out that frames are essential to understanding communicative moves. Bateson discussed why some activities are interpreted as serious, while other activities are not. The framing of the action is important for us in order to know whether it is "play" or "the real thing" that is occurring. Goffman (1974) expands on Bateson's definitions and describes the significance of frames in interaction. Framing is, according to Goffman, a way to explain the background parties' need to interpret the ongoing conversation. In other words to form an answer to the question: "What is it that's going on here?" (Goffman, 1974, p. 8).

The "frame" in frame analysis refers to this inevitably relational dimension of meaning. A frame, in this sense, is only a particularly tangible metaphor for what other sociologists have tried to invoke by words like *background, setting, context,* or a phrase like *in terms of* (1974, p. xiii).

We tend to perceive events in terms of primary frameworks, and the type of framework we employ provides a way of describing the event to which it is applied. The idea of a primary framework is, then, the first concept that is needed. However, the concept is quite complex—Goffman recognizes "the embarrassing fact" that during any one moment of activity, an individual is likely to apply a multitude of frameworks, or none at all (1974, p. 26).

An activity that is meaningful in its own right through a primary framework, may be transformed or "keyed" into having a socially constructed meaning: for fun, deception, experiment, rehearsal, dream, fantasy, ritual, demonstration, analysis, and charity. Expectations facilitate our comprehension and interpretation of objects and events. At the same time they influence our perception. Frames are expressed in discourse and subject to collective construction. "Taken all together, the primary frameworks of a particular social group constitute a central element of its culture" (1974, p. 27).

In many situations the meaning of an event can be ambiguous—the ambiguity will be translated into felt uncertainty and hesitancy. According to Goffman, the various kinds of ambiguity, including vagueness and uncertainty, have their counterpart in error. That is in beliefs, uninduced and erroneous, as to how events at hand are to be framed. Instead of merely stopping short to try to figure out what is happening, the individual may act on the basis of wrong premises. This is one plausible explanation of how rumors may be created in an organization.

It is obvious that a given appearance on different occasions have different meanings. But usually the context rules out wrong interpretations. Activities which must be predicated on a small amount of information are especially vulnerable to misguided framing. This insight complies with public relations practitioners' experiences that restricted access to information may cause problems with fabricated stories that spread quickly through the grapevine.

Goffman (1974) provides numerous examples of framing in everyday life, revealing how people transform activities in systematic ways and cue such transformations. He argues that the framing of activity establishes its meaningfulness for the individual.

Frames, furthermore, organize more than meaning; they also organize involvement (1974). During an activity, participants will ordinarily not only obtain a sense of what is going on, but will also (to some degree) become spontaneously engrossed, caught up, involved, or committed. Facial expressions often reveal the level of involvement of participants (1974).

Footing is a concept which concerns participants' stance or posture in interaction, in Goffman's own words: "Participant's alignment, or set, or stance, or posture, or projected self is somehow at issue" (Goffman, 1981, p. 128). This implies that footing includes both verbal and nonverbal signals representing participants' attitudes toward the issue of communication. Furthermore, Goffman states that footing may "be held across a strip of behavior that is less long than a grammatical sentence" and that it may vary: "A continuum must be considered, from gross changes in stance to the most subtle shifts in tone that can be perceived" (Goffman, 1981, p. 128). Changes in footing are marked by sound markers like "pitch, volume, rhythm, stress, tonal quality" (Goffman, 1981, p. 128). If we think of a manager speaking in a meeting, he or she might present different reactions toward different subjects discussed in the meeting.

Moreover, Goffman divides the footing of a speaker into three parts: *animator, author,* and *principal. Animator* is the person speaking, *author* is the person who chose the content and form of what is said, and *principal* is the person who is behind the utterance and whose attitudes are brought forward (Goffman, 1981). When using the term *speaker*, one often implies that the individual who animates is formulating his or her own text and that animator, author, and principal are one and the same person. But, according to Goffman, exceptions from this scenario are extensive.

This distinction sheds light upon the creation of an image of trustworthiness and authenticity in interaction. Plainly reciting a fully memorized text or reading aloud from a prepared script allows us to animate words we had no hand in formulating, and to express opinions, beliefs, and sentiments we do not hold. Accordingly, small cues in written and spoken interaction, for example hedges and qualifiers introduced in the form of performative modal verbs (*I wish, think, could, hope*), are creating intimacy or distance between speakers and utterance. Trustworthiness can be severely damaged by these small cues, something that analyses of interaction may reveal. Thus, the footing, in other words, the relation between the spokesperson and the message, is important to consider, for instance when appointing organizational spokespersons, both in external and internal contexts.

Levinson (1988) developed and extended Goffman's theory on footing and participation roles. He points out that participation roles cover both production and reception roles, and discusses Goffman's proposed reception roles (addressed recipient, unaddressed recipient, over-hearers and eavesdroppers).

Face is "the public self-image" that individuals want to claim for themselves, and a tool to describe social relations (Brown & Levinson, 1987; Goffman, 1959). Initially introduced by Goffman (1959, 1967), this concept was later more thoroughly developed by Brown and Levinson (1987): "face is something that is emotionally invested, and that can be lost, maintained, or enhanced, and must be constantly attended to in interaction" (p. 61).

Face is constantly negotiated when communicating. In general, it is in every participant's best interest to maintain each others' faces. Furthermore, while the content of face will differ in different cultures, Brown and Levinson (1987) still assume that the mutual knowledge of members' public self-images or faces, and the social necessity to orient oneself to them in interaction, are universal. The concept of face is intertwined with power and personal prestige and the study of face in interaction can be used to trace hidden or overt conflicts. Brown and Levinson (1987) treat the aspects of face as basic wants, and see two components of the concept; *negative face*—the want of every "competent adult member" that his or her actions be unimpeded by others, and *positive face*—the want of every member that his or her wants be desirable to at least some others.

Relationships are rarely symmetrical, but mostly asymmetrical, and these power differences are uncovered and possibly also managed by face threatening and face saving acts. Among acts that threaten the addressee's face are orders and requests, advice, threats, and warnings that put pressure on the addressee to do something (Brown & Levinson, 1987). Acts that indicate that the speaker does not care about the addressee's feelings or wants do include: expressions of disapproval, criticism, complaints, accusations, and insults.

In the context of the mutual vulnerability of face, any rational participant will seek to avoid these face-threatening acts, or will employ certain strategies to minimize the threat. The actor might go "on record" in doing an act A if it is clear to participants what communicative intention led the actor to do it. In contrast, if an actor goes "off record" in doing an act A, then the actor cannot be held to have committed himself to one particular intent. Doing an act baldly, without redress, involves doing it in the most direct, clear, unambiguous, and concise way possible (for example, for a request, saying, "Do X!"). By redressive action, Brown and Levinson (1987) mean action that "gives face" to the addressee; that is, that attempts to counteract the potential face damage of the face threatening act by doing it in such a way, or with such modifications or additions, that indicate clearly that no such face threat is intended or desired.

It is in action and interaction that the most profound interrelations between language and society are to be found, according to Brown and Levinson (1987). For them, communicative intentions have built-in social implications, often of a threatening sort. Language usages are tied to strategies rather than directly to relationships, although relationships will be characterized by the continued use of certain strategies. Accordingly, a key to understanding the nature of relationships is communication and language use.

Relevance for Public Relations

Public relations practitioners today experience a multifaceted profession, which comprises communication and relationship building with internal as well as external publics, and face new challenges driven by development in communication technology and continuously changing organizations. Interpersonal relations is a promising research field, given that the building and maintenance of strategic ethical relationships are fundamental in public relations research and practice today (cf. Vasquez & Taylor, 2001). The relationship paradigm provides a framework in which to explore the linkage between public relations objectives and organizational goals, for constructing platforms for strategic planning and tactical implementation, and approaching programmatic evaluation in ways understood and appreciated by the ruling management group (Ledingham & Bruning, 2000). The relational perspective builds upon and transfers ideas based on interpersonal relationship initiation, development, maintenance, and dissolution from the individual level to organizations and publics.

A significant development in public relations research is the transition from a functional perspective to a cocreational one (cf. Botan & Taylor, 2004). The bulk of studies in public relations researching relations depart from a functional perspective. A *functional perspective*, prevalent in the early years of the field, sees publics and communication as tools or means to achieve organizational ends. The focus is generally on techniques and production of strategic organizational messages. An issue of principal concern to many writers is how to *manage* relationships in order to maximize outcomes. Research plays a role only insofar as it advances organizational goals. The major relationship of interest is between the public relations practitioner and the media with a corresponding emphasis on journalistic techniques and production skills.

The *cocreational perspective* sees publics as cocreators of meaning, and communication as what makes it possible to agree to shared meanings, interpretations, and goals. This perspective is long term in its orientation and focuses on relationships among publics and organizations. Research is used to advance understanding. The major relationship of interest is between groups and organizations, and communication functions to negotiate changes in these relationships. In the cocreational perspective, publics are not just a means to an end. Publics are not instrumentalized but instead are partners in the meaning-making process (Botan & Taylor, 2004).

One way of approaching the study of relations closely related to the cocreational perspective is interpersonal communication (c.f. Toth, 2000). Coombs (2001) reviewed past uses of interpersonal communication and discussed trends that favor the increased use of interpersonal communication theory in public relations. Interpersonal communication has previously been seen merely as a channel or medium that helps to produce behavior change in a campaign. However, it is suggested for the future that relationship dimensions of each major category of stakeholder be identified, and interaction patterns analyzed in order to understand how organization and stakeholder words and actions affect the development of their relationship. Departing from a stakeholder model, Coombs points out that organizations have to manage multiple relationships simultaneously.

In a critical response to Coombs, Cheney and Christensen question if organizations can approach stakeholders as individual persons and understand them in meaningful terms (Cheney & Christensen, 2001). Likewise, it is questionable to treat stakeholders, publics, and organizations as entities and homogeneous groups. Organizations, publics, and stakeholders are groups made up by individuals. These individuals may have certain knowledge, attitudes, and values in common, but the common traits may vary due to time, composition of groups, and issue under discussion. Jahansoozi (2006) comments that, "Public relations practitioners do not have relationships with publics; they build and nurture relationships with individuals within publics" (p. 62).

The view that publics are homogeneous groups is also rejected by Leitch and Neilson (2001). They see publics as groups of individuals who develop their own identities, and perhaps representations of their collective interests, in relation to the system. Individuals are not members of single publics but instead participate in the multiple sites of the public sphere as members of diverse publics. Individuals may simultaneously hold a number of different subject positions within these sites and publics. These multiple subject positions may overlap, intersect, or conflict and will always be in a state of flux. Taken together, they provide the context within which individuals must negotiate their own public identities.

As is commented by Jahansoozi (2006), many models and theories of public relations involve the concept of communicating with groups, group dynamics, and behavior, and building relationships with specific groups or publics, a bias resulting from an emphasis on the media relations function. The conceptual move from a mass communication foundation to a relationship-building orientation leads to a new emphasis on understanding the communication dynamics of relationship building (Vasquez & Taylor, 2001). Following from this stance is the need for greater emphasis on interpersonal communication. For this purpose, Goffman's theories and concepts concerning social interaction could be applied and further developed. Only on rare occasions have they been used and developed in public relations research before.

A theoretical work permeated by the Goffmanian influence, although only occasionally stated explicitly, is Mickey's (1995) book *Sociodrama: An Interpretive Theory for the Practice of Public Relations*. The goal of sociodrama is to understand public relations as interaction rather than as simply sending out messages to a target audience. Mickey's (1995) axiom number two clearly communicates the influence from Goffman: "Sociodrama is not concerned with only content or agency in communication but how people use the words to define themselves" (p. 28). As a consequence, the sociodrama model calls for research methods in which the subjects are allowed to express themselves in their own words.

Impression Management in Public Relations

There are problems ensuing a comparison of organizations and individuals, as discussed above. Nevertheless, in a way, organizations, like individuals, can be seen as "actors" engaging in "performances" in various "settings" before "audiences" (Allen & Caillouet, 1994). Although much research into corporate image has assumed that image is managed and created by the organization, findings conclude that image is also determined by environmental and personal factors of the audience member (Williams & Moffitt, 1997).

In public relations, Goffman's notion of *impression management* has previously been referred to as image or reputation management (cf. Coombs, 2001). Impression management studies considering interpersonal communication has so far been studied in relation to organizational crises (Allen & Caillouet, 1994) and impression management strategies used by employees when discussing their organization's public image (Caillouet & Allen, 1996). Through analysis of statements consisting of written and spoken discourse expressing the organization's public image, Allen and Caillouet (1994) developed a typology of impression management strategies of an organization in crisis. The study builds upon both the interpersonal and organizational impression management research. It was concluded that strategies similar to those used by individuals emerged in the organization's external discourse as employees drew upon their own repertoire of communication strategies. The authors argue that it is important to study the actual complex milieu of messages occurring in the public arena because these messages potentially build and shape public perceptions of legitimacy. In this way, their research strategy follows Goffman's methodology of making observations in the actual setting, taking into consideration the notion of context that is important for the construction of meaning.

The study by Allen and Caillouet (1994) addresses both some constraints upon and the complexity of corporate discourse by identifying how corporate actors use different impression management strategies with different stakeholders to acknowledge institutional norms. The rich collection of images that emerged did not always coincide with the public images desired by organizational leaders or seem logical given the goal of legitimacy. The authors therefore suggest that the impression management literature may be extended by a focus on corporate impression management that emphasizes how the setting shapes strategic communication offered by employees speaking as agents.

In a later study, Caillouet and Allen (1996) interviewed employees in order to generate accounts where impression management strategies (IMS) were supposed to be embedded. IMS identified were factual distortion, denouncements, ingratiation, excuses, and justifications. Results reported an evident difference in strategy use between interviewed employees and organizational spokespeople. Justifications were the most frequent strategies to appear in interview data, which was a dramatic difference from what emerged in other media. Furthermore, interviewed managers and non managers differed in the IMS embedded within their interview statements. Although not significantly different, managers offered twice as many excuses as nonmanagement personnel. In turn, nonmanagers offered almost twice as many distortion strategies (Caillouet & Allen, 1996). The authors recognize that although messages are shaped or constrained by the medium, it appeared as if the interview context itself carried a potential for the generation of more justifications than any other strategy. Consequently, strategy use within its natural environment ought to be studied in the future (Caillouet & Allen, 1996).

Impression management is furthermore an interesting phenomenon in internal communication between managers and organizational members. In order to understand how organizational identity is created and why change efforts are met with resistance, it is important to study organizational communication processes and interpersonal relationships between significant actors.

A leader communicating an image of the corporation to employees might be viewed in a positive sense as an actor trying to reduce ambiguity and help get a clear picture of the context of the work situation, of the organization, its character, and its product. In a critical sense, the increased difficulty that people in organizations have of obtaining a clear picture, might be viewed as the basis for leaders' campaigns designed to anchor favorable views of the organizational reality in the minds of the employees (Alvesson, 1990).

Irrespective of whether a functional, cocreational, or critical perspective is chosen, public relations research would benefit from more research in this area. Questions for future research may be: What impressions do public relations practitioners and individual managers consciously and unconsciously create and communicate in different organizational settings? How are these impressions managed front stage and back stage? What impressions are apprehended and perceived by different audiences or publics?

Implications of Framing for Public Relations

Hallahan (1999) finds that framing is a potentially useful paradigm to examine public relations, although it suffers from a lack of coherent definition. The concept of framing has also been employed and developed in analyses of media discourse, and thus influenced theories on agenda setting, framing, and priming in media and communication science (Entman, 1993; Hallahan, 2005; Rice & Bartlett, 2006; Scheufele, 1999; Wicks, 2005).

Hallahan (1999) identifies seven distinct types of framing applicable to public relations. These involve the framing of situations, attributes, choices, actions, issues, responsibility, and news. According to Halla-han, framing also implicitly plays an integral role in public relations. If public relations is defined as the process of establishing and maintaining mutually beneficial relations between an organization and publics on whom it depends, the establishment of common frames of reference about topics or issues of mutual concern is a necessary condition for effective relations to be established (Hallahan, 1999).

Lundy (2006) studied the effect of message framing on cognitive processing by employees of an internal organizational message. Subjects were asked to list the thoughts they had while reading messages presented. Interpretations were shown to vary according to frame. Expanding this research to face-to-face interaction, for instance a physical meeting, where frames are constructed in communication, will shed more light on the process of framing and interpretation of messages according to perceived frame. Since framing is context dependent, it is very important also to research messages in their actual context.

In *The Art of Framing*, Fairhurst and Sarr (1996) stress that an important aspect of leadership is to manage meaning, in other words, influence people's interpretations of messages:

> To hold the frame of a subject is to choose one particular meaning (or set of meanings) over another. When we share our frames with others (the process of framing), we manage meaning because we assert that our interpretations should be taken as real over other possible interpretations. (p. 3)

An important, but still neglected, area for public relations practitioners working with internal communication is the coaching of leaders on their communicative behavior. Here framing, but also footing and face are important concepts to consider.

Other examples of important areas of research on framing are how alternative frames and rumors come into being and spread through the grapevine; and how frames of corporate identity, values, and brand are coordinated in internal and external communication. Informal or backstage communication has rarely been studied, although research in leadership has confirmed that informal leaders play an important part when situations are defined, and when decisions are taken on which organizational rules groups will follow or ignore.

Applying Footing and Face in Public Relations

The concepts of footing and face seem so far not to have been applied in public relations research. Footing also has important implications for the communication between organizational leaders and employees.

Seen from a public relations perspective, the understanding of differing speaker and listener roles and their implications in communication processes is an important aspect of interpersonal relationships. As discussed above, coaching managers on internal communication issues requires knowledge of the impact of footing and different roles enacted by managers.

Internal communication campaigns, concerning mission statement and goals, corporate values, or organizational change are implemented by leaders appointed for this purpose. These campaigns could be the focus of research, thus extending knowledge on relationship building between internal publics. The actual quality of the relationship, focusing on relational elements of trust, satisfaction commitment, control mutuality, dialogue, and transparency could be assessed as commented by Jahansoozi (2006; cf. Hon & Grunig, 1999).

In public relations literature, publics are often considered to be equal participants in the dialogue or relationship. When power is omitted from the relationship, it is possible to assume that an organization and its publics are able to meet on equal terms and are able to develop mutually beneficial outcomes for recognized problems (Jahansoozi, 2006). However, it is not defensible to ignore the concept of power, which in fundamental ways affects relations and communication in organizations (cf. Leitch & Neilson, 2001; Mumby, 1988, 2001).

In communication between public relation practitioners and journalists, between managers and employees, and between groups of employees, *face* is an important dimension and can also serve as an analytical tool for studies of power differences in interaction. The often discussed status of communication managers and their claims for legitimacy could be analyzed in empirical studies of group management meetings (cf. Johansson, 2003). An alternative to model and idealize communication as for instance two-way symmetrical, is to engage in empirical studies of interaction and include concepts that reveal power differences. In order to develop our understanding of the process of relationship building, whether the purpose is to create strategic ethical relationships or to take on the role of organizational activists, face is a concept that could be further developed and applied in public relations.

Goffman in Practice: Analyzing Communication on Corporate Strategy

An empirically based illustration of how to implement Goffman's theories can be provided by the case study of communication on corporate strategy that I have conducted and reported at length elsewhere (Johansson, 2003). Here I analyze internal communications between managers and coworkers in a longitudinal qualitative study. Communication about strategy (encompassing vision, strategic objectives, and common values) in a company followed a top-down process from CEO down the hierarchy of managers to employees. Different methods: interviews, observations, and discourse analysis were combined to find important factors influencing the strategy communication process. The analysis demonstrates how visions formulated by top managers met different realities constructed by subordinate managers. Discourse dimensions of framing, footing, and face reveal the importance of individual experience, attitudes, and power for sense making in the strategy communication process. Accordingly, this method is considered to enhance analyses of sense making and communication problems in organizations.

Framing is particularly important in the opening of meetings. Here the chair of the meeting often highlights the purpose of the meeting, and in this way also directs the wanted outcome of the discussion. The following discourse example is from a group management meeting, where the CEO frames how the process of communicating strategy is supposed to be interpreted:[2]

> CEO: The reason why we are running this is eh to find a way to have a better understanding of the strategies we have produced. Group Strategy, divisional strategies. And to have it implemented in the organization. Understand, first of all, understand, and then have it implemented. (Johansson, 2003, p. 162)

The framing of the strategy process made by the CEO in this meeting: "to have a better understanding," could be compared to the framing made by the business area manager in a meeting on the next hierarchical level in the organization. This meeting represents a new context with new participants, which according to Goffman affects the establishment of the working consensus or level of agreement. Here, the business area manager A (BA-A), who participated in the group management meeting above, has the role of chair. He frames the process somewhat differently compared to the CEO:

> BA-A: [Welcome to] our Business Area...global management meeting. As you see from the agenda, today is related to the strategy. ...

> BA-A: And so, what will be our day today, so that's eh will be Balanced Scorecard. It's eh what, what, how we see it, that's a, that's a tool to implement our our strategy for the whole organization. And why we have come to this is that of course when we have thought about our strategy, so generally it's not so easy to communicate to the organization, and we have after studying different possibilities found out that this is hopefully a good way to do that. Get the

message to our organization that what really is the strategy, and how we can work according that, and set also certain targets. (Johansson, 2003, p. 178)

Business area manager A is using the name of the management tool they are using (Balanced Scorecard), and frames the process as more problematic than the CEO does: "not so easy to communicate." He uses the word *hopefully*, which may give the impression that he is not convinced himself that this method is the right way. The repetitions in these lines imply that he is seeking the right words. In addition, they strengthen the impression that the manager is hesitant and obviously finds it hard to explain what Balanced Scorecard is.[3] The Balanced Scorecard method employed to communicate the strategy is something new and unknown to him. This interpretation gets support in the next excerpt:

BA-A: I'm not going to tell anything more about it [laughs + laughter among participants in the meeting] but we have professionals here and the floor is yours. (Johansson, 2003, p. 179)

Finishing his introduction in this way, curtly, his tone and words implying that he is no expert, which causes laughter, while stepping aside, the manager leaves the floor to two consultants, hired to implement the process. During the rest of the meeting he is not taking the role as chair. This role is taken by the consultants.

His framing of Balanced Scorecard as "hopefully a good way" to communicate the strategy is quite weak compared to business area manager B (BA-B), who chaired a comparable meeting with participating division managers and consultants in his business area:

BA-B: you must see this as—I have to stand up [he stands up and turns to face the participants] It's easier to speak. You must see the scorecard, the corporate scorecard is a way for Group Management to communicate, to, to, define the way, the direction which the company is going. (Johansson, 2003, p. 196)

Business Area manager B stands out as convinced of the usefulness of Balanced Scorecard. He frames it strongly employing words like *must*, as a way to define the direction of the company. In this episode he is standing up, gesticulating in front of his managers, eager to bring them along. His appearance is quite different from that of business area manager A, who sits down and quickly calls on the consultants to speak.

The *footing* of the managers in the meetings could also be discussed out of the examples shown. Perhaps the excerpts reveal too little context here, but since I was present as an observer throughout the whole process, I could conclude that the CEO and Business Area manager B clearly acted as *principals*, and gave the impression of being whole-heartedly committed to the goal of communicating the strategy to the employees. Business Area manager A, on the other hand, merely takes the role of *animator*, as illustrated above. By acting this way, he gives the impression that Balanced Scorecard is something outside his authority and expertise. The consequences are that his trustworthiness in front of his managers could deteriorate (Johansson, 2003).

A department manager in Business Area A (Dep-a1), comments in an interview the process of creating involvement and enthusiasm:

> Dep-a1: Management must be present and it has to be run by man-agers who are enthusiastic. How could you get employees enthusias-tic if they do not see management enthusiastic? (Johansson, 2003, p. 150)

The concept of *face* is useful in that it reveals power in relations between interactants. Position and power could be formal and informal. Through discourse analysis it is possible to disclose who has informal power in a meeting. One example of this is an open conflict between department manager a1, who leads a technology development depart-ment, and a sales manager, during a meeting at division A. They are discussing product strategy:

> Department manager a1: we have divided our products into seven areas, actually now it will be eight areas. And for each of those areas there is a clear vision and goal.... So it's quite defined for each area, where we stand and what—where we want to go and what we are doing....
>
> Sales manager: you think, OK you have divided into your seven boxes, that's OK. But if I look at from the sales department, I look in another eyes than you.[1]
>
> Department manager a1: You don't look very much in another eyes than I do first of all, [gets angry and raises his voice] and second of all if I would listen to you [Sales manager], I'm sorry I have to say, then I would change product strategy every time we lose an order. We have a clear product strategy, and you have agreed to it, it has been presented on the product committee. [lowers his voice again] We have all agreed to it. (Johansson, 2003, p. 216)

Open conflicts were rare in the observed meetings, probably to some extent depending on the observer effect. Although these managers are equals in terms of formal power, both of them are department managers, department manager a1 here demonstrates his superiority to cut the sales manager short. He publicly offends him by shouting that the sales manager is wrong and can't be listened to. This is what Brown and Levinson (1987) call a face threatening act on record with redressive action employing negative politeness. In other terms the most threatening act of all. Episodes like this during the communication process, may severely damage trust and confidence between these managers, which also may have negative consequences for the communication and cooperation between departments.

In general, interaction patterns illustrated that subordinates tried to avoid face-threatening acts and that superiors lead discussions by taking initiatives; for example, to open and close episodes and to change frames. Consequently, it is concluded that power structures and respect for participants' faces (Brown & Levinson, 1987) might prevent an honest and pertinent communication that could solve many problems. Very rarely does someone openly criticize a superior manager, since that could jeopardize the individual's personal position. This is a well-known explanation as to why opinions from lower levels do not reach top management. In public relations this is known as ingratiation theory (Jones, 1990).

Given that staff–management relationships and relationships between managers from different hierarchical levels in the organization are a core concern for communication management (cf. Tourish, 2003), the concepts of framing, footing, and face are useful when studying these relations.

Conclusion

Only on rare occasions have Goffman's theories been used and developed in public relations research. Undoubtedly, his theories and concepts can be applied to analyze relationships, where the establishment of mutual trust and confidence are important components. I see Goffman's sociology, treating social interaction and relationships, as an inspiring resource for developing public relations theory. His concepts are linked to essential notions in public relations: relationships, identification, and image. As argued by Hallahan (1999), framing plays an integral role in public relations. Furthermore, framing puts information in a situational or cultural context that delineates how people evaluate information, comprehend meanings, and take action (Hallahan, 2005). The concept of impression management has been used and developed in studies of crisis communication and employees statements (Allen & Caillouet, 1994; Caillouet & Allen, 1996). The two other concepts discussed in this article, footing and face, have been used by Johansson (200, 2007) to study internal communication on corporate strategy, vision, goals, and values. However, all four concepts could be further developed and contribute to research of face-to-face interaction in the relational perspective focusing on interpersonal communication with internal and external publics. As long as predominant methods employed in public relations research are quantitative, we are not provided with a rich description or understanding of the organization–public relationship including interpersonal communication, as would be the case if qualitative methods were used instead (cf. Jahansoozi, 2006).

In conclusion, Goffman's concepts are developed out of observations in empirical settings, and I would like to emphasize that by analyzing at a microlevel, the social interaction that continuously shapes relations inside and outside organizations, we will deepen our understanding of communication processes that have important implications for the relation of publics in public relations.

Notes

1. A previous version of this chapter was published as: Goffman's sociology: An inspiring resource for developing public relations theory, in *Public Relations Review, 33*(3), 2007.
2. No translation of the transcripts has been made because these meetings were originally held in English. However, none of the managers is a native English speaker.
3. The analysis made here departs from recordings and transcripts but also from observations of nonverbal language during the meetings. The author participated in all meetings as an impartial observer.
4. The "Swenglish" expression "in another eyes" is a direct translation from Swedish, meaning "in another way." The managers are not native speakers of English.

References

Allen, M. W., & Caillouet, R. H. (1994). Legitimation endeavors: Impression management strategies used by an organization in crisis. *Communication Monographs, 61,* 44–62.

Alvesson, M. (1990). Organization: From substance to image? *Organization Studies, 11,* 373–394.

Alvesson, M., & Kärreman, D. (2000). Taking the linguistic turn in organizational research. *The Journal of Applied Behavioral Science, 36,* 136–158.

Bateson, G. (1972). *Steps to an ecology of mind.* New York: Ballantine.

Botan, C., & Taylor, M. (2004). Public relations: State of the field. *Journal of Communication, 54,* 645–661.

Brown, P., & Levinson, S. C. (1987). *Studies in interactional sociolinguistics: Vol. 4. Politeness: Some universals in language use.* Cambridge, UK: Cambridge University Press.

Caillouet, R. H., & Allen, M. W. (1996). Impression management strategies employees use when discussing their organization's public image. *Journal of Public Relations Research, 8*, 211–227.

Cheney, G., & Christensen, L. T. (2001). Public relations as contested terrain. A critical response. In R. L. Heath (Ed.), *The handbook of public relations* (pp. 167–182). Thousand Oaks, CA: Sage.

Coombs, T. W. (2001). Interpersonal communication and public relations. In R. L. Heath (Ed.), *The handbook of public relations* (pp. 105–114). Thousand Oaks, CA: Sage.

Entman, R. (1993). Framing: Toward clarification of a fractured paradigm. *Journal of Communication, 43*, 51–58.

Fairhurst, G., & Sarr, R. (1996). *The art of framing: Managing the language of leadership.* San Francisco, CA: Jossey-Bass.

Fairhurst, G., & Putnam, L. (2004). Organizations as discursive constructions. *Communication Theory, 14*, 5–26.

Goffman, E. (1959). *The presentation of self in everyday life.* Garden City, NY: Doubleday.

Goffman, E. (1967). *Interaction ritual: Essays on face-to-face behavior.* Garden City, NY: Doubleday.

Goffman, E. (1974). *Frame analysis.* Boston: Northeastern University Press.

Goffman, E. (1981). *Forms of talk.* Oxford, UK: Blackwell.

Hallahan, K. (1999). Seven models of framing: Implications for public relations. *Journal of Public Relations Research, 11*, 205–242.

Hallahan, K. (2005). Framing theory. In R. L. Heath (Ed.), *Encyclopedia of public relations.* (Vol. 1, pp. 340–343). Thousand Oaks, CA: Sage.

Hon, L. C., & Grunig, J. E. (1999). Guidelines for measuring relationships in public relations. Retrieved January 27, 2007 from http://www.instituteforpr. org/index.php/IPR/research_single/guidelines_measuring_relationships/

Jahansoozi, J. (2006). Relationships, transparency, and evaluation: The implications for public relations. In J. L'Etang & M. Pieczka (Ed.), *Public relations: Critical debates and contemporary practice* (pp. 61–91). Mahwah, NJ: Erlbaum.

Johansson, C. (2003). *Visioner och verkligheter: Kommunikationen om företagets strategi.* [Visions and realities: A case study of communication on corporate strategy]. Uppsala, Sweden: Uppsala University.

Johansson, C. (2007). Research on organizational communication: The case of Sweden. *Nordicom Review, 28*, 93–110.

Jones, E. (1990). *Interpersonal perception.* New York: Freeman.

Kim, K. (2003). *Order and agency in modernity. Talcott Parsons, Erving Goffman, and Harold Garfinkel.* Albany, NY: State University of New York Press.

Ledingham, J. A., & Bruning, S. D. (Eds.). (2000). *Public relations as relationship management. A relational approach to the study and practice of public relations.* Mahwah, NJ: Erlbaum.

Leitch, S., & Neilson, D. (2001). Bringing publics into public relations. New theoretical frameworks for practice. In R. L. Heath (Ed.), *Handbook of public relations* (pp. 127–138). Thousand Oaks, CA: Sage.

Lemert, C., & Branaman, A. (Eds.). (1997). *The Goffman reader.* Oxford, UK: Blackwell.

Levinson, S. (1988). Putting linguistics on a proper footing: Explorations in Goffman's concepts of participation. In P. Drew & A. Wooton (Eds.), *Erving Goffman: Exploring the interaction order* (pp. 161–227). Cambridge, UK: Polity Press.

Lundy, L. K. (2006). Effect of framing on cognitive processing in public relations. *Public Relations Review, 32,* 295–301.

Manning, P. (1992). *Erving Goffman and modern sociology.* Stanford, CA: Stanford University Press.

Mickey, T. J. (1995). *Sociodrama: An interpretive theory for the practice of public relations.* Lanham, MD: University Press of America.

Mumby, D. (1988). *Communication and power in organizations: Discourse, ideology and domination.* Norwood, NJ: Ablex.

Mumby, D. (2001). Power and politics. In F. M. Jablin & L. L. Putnam (Eds.), *The new handbook of organizational communication* (pp. 585–623). Thousand Oaks, CA: Sage.

Rice, S., & Bartlett, J. (2006). Legitimating organisational decisions: A study of media framing of the Australian Government's legitimacy strategy and public opinion on the war in Iraq. *Journal of Communication Management, 10,* 274–286.

Scheufele, D. (1999). Framing as a theory of media effects. *Journal of Communication, 49,* 103–122.

Schiffrin, D. (1994). *Approaches to discourse.* Oxford: Blackwell.

Smith, G. (Ed.). (1999). *Goffman and social organization: Studies in a sociological legacy.* London: Routledge.

Toth, E. L. (2000). From personal influence to interpersonal influence: A model for relationship management. In J. A. Ledingham & S. D. Bruning (Eds.), *Public relations as relationship management. A relational approach to the study and practice of public relations* (pp. 205–219). Mahwah, NJ: Erlbaum.

Tourish, D. (2003). Critical upward feedback in organisations: Processes, problems and implications for communication management. *Journal of Communication Management, 8,* 150–167.

Vasquez, G. M., & Taylor, M. (2001). Public relations: An emerging social science enters the new millennium. *Communication Yearbook, 24,* 319–342.

Wicks, R. H. (2005). Message framing and constructing meaning: An emerging paradigm in mass communication research. *Communication Yearbook, 29,* 333–361.

Willems, H. (2004). Erving Goffman. In U. Flick, E. von Kardorff, & I. Steinke (Eds.), *A companion to qualitative research* (pp. 24–28). Thousand Oaks, CA: Sage.

Williams, S., & Moffitt, A. (1997). Corporate image as an impression formation process: Prioritizing personal, organizational, and environmental audience factors. *Journal of Public Relations Research, 9,* 237–258.

Life and Work of Erving Goffman

Erving Goffman (1922–1982). Born in Canada, Goffman obtained a bachelor's degree in sociology and anthropology from the University of Toronto in 1945. He moved to Chicago for graduate work, which led to a doctoral dissertation about social interaction on a small island community off the coast of Scotland: *Communication Conduct in an Island Community*, Department of Sociology, University of Chicago (1953). He was appointed an assistant professor in the Department of Sociology at the University of California, Berkeley, in 1958 and became a full professor in 1962. In 1968 he obtained the Benjamin Franklin chair in anthropology and sociology at the University of Pennsylvania. In 1969 he became a Fellow of the American Academy of Arts and Sciences.

He wrote 13 books and 29 articles and book chapters. For a full bibliography of Goffman's own writings and a comprehensive list of secondary literature see Lemert and Branaman (1997). His major, and most influential works include:

- *The Presentation of Self in Everyday Life* (1956/1959)
- *Frame Analysis* (1974)
- *Forms of Talk* (1981)

Goffman's work is illustrated, explained, and commented on in Smith (1999), Manning (1992), Lemert and Branaman (1997), and Kim (2003).

Chapter 8

On Habermas

Understanding and Public Relations[1]

Roland Burkart

Abstract

In his seminal work *The Theory of Communicative Action* Habermas reconstructs universal conditions of understanding within the human communication process. The chapter applies Habermas's concept of understanding
for the purposes of planning and evaluation. A model for *Consensus-Oriented Public Relations* (COPR) is suggested. This model assumes that the process of understanding between public relations practitioners and affected
publics plays a central role in public relations management. Especially in
conflict situations, practitioners have to take into account that a critical
public might question their messages and disbelieve their validity claims.
The message recipients might doubt the *truth* of propositions, the *truthfulness* and *legitimacy* of communicators. This necessitates discourse and the
COPR-model shows how practitioners can facilitate this.

Jürgen Habermas is a prominent German critical philosopher and
sociologist who, as a research assistant to the philosopher Theodor W.
Adorno in the 1950s, joined the so-called Frankfurt School of German
critical theory. The Frankfurt School refers to a group of German social
theorists (e.g., Max Horkheimer, Theodor W. Adorno, Herbert Marcuse) who founded the Institut für Sozialforschung (Institute for Social
Research) in 1925 at the University of Frankfurt/Main in Germany for
analyzing the changes in Western capitalist societies with reference to
the classical theory of Karl Marx (Wiggershaus, 2001). They developed
a critical social theory for a very practical purpose: "to liberate human
beings from the circumstances that enslave them" (Horkheimer, 1982,
p. 244). The members of the Frankfurt School analyzed the system of
cultural production dominated by film, radio broadcasting, newspapers, and magazines (e.g., Horkheimer & Adorno, 1972). Their point
was that mass media, controlled by advertising and commercial imperatives, serve the needs of dominant corporate interests and play a major
role in ideological reproduction in creating subservience to the system
of consumer capitalism. The output of the Frankfurt school included

several critical cultural studies dealing with processes of cultural production (Kellner, 1989, 1995).

Habermas tried to historicize this analysis of the culture industry undertaken by Adorno and Horkheimer. In the early 1960s he published his postdoctoral dissertation *Strukturwandel der Öffentlichkeit* (published in English as *The Structural Transformation of the Public Sphere* in 1989), which made him a well-known scholar in the German speaking and reading world, and later within the Anglo-American social scientific community too. In this work "he seeks to draw from political and intellectual history certain core normative ideas about the nature of democracy" (Edgar, 2005, p. 31). For this purpose he developed a historically grounded theory of the "public sphere." According to Habermas a "public sphere comes into existence when citizens communicate, either face to face or through letters, journals, and newspapers and other mass media in order to express their opinions about matters of general interest, and to subject these opinions to rational discussion" (Edgar, 2005, p. 31). In order to get an impression about the origin status of the "political public sphere" he goes back to the emergence of the "bourgeois democracy" from the late 17th to the 18th century. In his opinion, during this period the bourgeois public sphere was most developed in Britain, "as a sphere which mediates between society and state, in which the public organizes itself as the bearer of public opinion, accords with the principle of the public sphere—that principle of public information which one had to be fought for against the arcane policies of monarchies and which since that time has made possible the democratic control of state activities" (Habermas, 1974, p. 50). A central point connected with the concept of the public sphere was the idea of a rational debate on political matters—first in literary salons (therefore he also identifies a *literary* public sphere) and later on in the print media that promoted the Enlightenment ideals of equality, justice, and human rights. In short, the bourgeois public sphere was seen as an era where a critical and rational discussion took place—in a certain way a forerunner of the parliamentary democracy.

However there has been a peculiar weakening of the critical functions of the political public sphere of the social welfare state:

> At one time the process of making proceedings public was intended to subject persons or affairs to public reason, and to make political decisions subject to appeal before the court of public opinion. But often enough today the process of making public simply serves the arcane policies of special interests; in the form of "publicity" it wins prestige for people or affairs, thus making them worthy of acclamation in a climate of non-public opinion. The very words "public rela-

tions" (*Oeffentlichkeitsarbeit*) betray the fact that a public sphere must first be arduously constructed case by case, a public sphere, which earlier grew out of the social structure. Even the central relationship of the public, the parties and the parliament is affected by this change in function. (Habermas, 1974, p. 55)

The idea of Habermas's "public sphere" was not only widely acknowledged but also criticized—often it is argued that the quality of the created idea of the public sphere "was only ever an approximation" (Crossley & Roberts, 2004, p. 4).

Nevertheless the ideas of a political public sphere are conceived by Habermas "as a category that is typical of an epoch" (1989, p. xvii). Although those ideas were not realized as they had been conceptualized one can "argue that the concepts and their preconditions are still relevant and should be further developed to reflect on public relations as a profession in its societal context" (Jensen, 2001, p. 134).[2] The present article takes this seriously—especially in view of Habermas's magnum opus, published in English as the *Theory of Communicative Action* (*TCA*; 1984, 1987).

A central effort of TCA is to reconstruct universal conditions of understanding within the human communication process. A major issue in this context is semiotics and its well-known dimensions syntactics, semantics, and pragmatics (Morris, 1938). While syntactics deals with the grammatical rules for concatenating signs, semantics refers to the aspects of meaning that are expressed in a language. The pragmatic perspective—the third component—focuses on the relation of signs to interpreters. This is a very central perspective in Habermas's thinking: his assertion is that social life fundamentally can be explained in terms of the ability of actors to communicate and to use what he, referring to the philosophers Austin (1962) and Searle (1969), calls "speech acts." In Austin's famous phrase, speakers "do things with words," which is to say "that speech is approached as a form of social practice, realizing social relationships between actors" (Edgar, 2005, p. 139). When we use language we make assertions, give orders, ask questions, make promises. Speech acts are seen as the smallest units of verbal communication.

This exactly is the point where Habermas sets in with his TCA. In this seminal work he analyzes the conditions of the human communication process by means of an examination of speech-acts because he views language as the specifically human means of understanding. "Reaching understanding"—according to Habermas—is the "inherent telos of human speech" (Habermas, 1987, p. 287).

As a philosopher, Habermas intends to make "understanding" (and thus communication) discernable as a fundamental democratic process.

He wants to demonstrate that, as a measure for the solution of social conflicts, violence can be replaced by the rational consensus of responsible citizens.

My intention is to utilize this aspect of Habermas's theory for public relations research. This is not really a new idea. There have been several attempts to employ the Habermasian communication theory for public relations. In most of those cases, however, the issue has mainly been to transfer the ideal type conditions of the dialogue to the public relations process, and to formulate, based upon this context, "an ethical imperative for public relations" (Pearson, 1989a, p. 127) or, respectively, the necessary conditions for ethical public relations (Pearson, 1989b).[3] Similar ideas can be found in more recent publications, too. For example, Leeper (1996) points out the importance of the study of public relations ethics; Meisenbach develops "five steps of enacting discourse ethics" (2002, p. 46) using Habermas's theory as a moral framework for organizational communication, and Holmström (1997) discusses normative ideals for public relations practice.

This chapter, however, focuses neither on ethical principles nor on morally based directives. Nor will I (naively) try to apply the Habermasian principles of understanding directly to the reality of public relations. The aim of my approach is rather to gain suggestions for the analysis of public relations from the perspective of Habermas's concept of understanding. In particular, one can use this perspective to illuminate the relation between public relations experts offering information and members of target groups who receive this information. As a result of this attempt, a so-called *consensus-oriented public relations* (COPR) approach for planning and evaluating public relations-communication has been established (Burkart, 1993, 1994, 2004, 2005). This approach will be presented in this chapter.

The practical background is that economic acting in developed industrial societies is no longer solely determined by or reliant on money. Businesses willing to remain profitable have to ask themselves if and how they want to reach their targets in relation to their responsibility to society and often have to rely on explaining their methods to the public (Münch, 1991). Economic acting is becoming more and more *also* a form of communicative acting.

The reason for this lies partially in the complex problematic nature of the development of scientific and technical progress in the second half of the 20th century. Since the well-known publication by Ulrich Beck (1986) and the concurrent nuclear reactor accident at Chernobyl, the label of a "risk society" has been established in this context. In modern industrialized societies the production of wealth is systematically linked to the production of dangers (Beck, 1986), and these risks from modernization go hand in hand with the almost fatal tendencies of globalization. Using the motto "Need is hierarchical, smog is democratic" —author's translation of this and the following German quotes—(Beck, 1986, p. 48), Beck shows that the results of worldwide industrialization such as air pollution, deforestation by acid rain, the hothouse effect, nuclear catastrophes, or floods are neither related to a social stratum nor a specific geographical location.

The anxiety about a life-threatening disruption of our environment together with the distrust in politics and science (Rödel, Frankenberg, & Dubiel, 1989) has brought about a multitude of public initiatives, occupations, blockages, and other forms of "civil disobedience" (Kleger, 1993). Many people feel betrayed in a certain way because decisions of managers seem to be made behind their backs (Röglin, 1994). At the same time, these organizations have come under pressure to identify their positions—that means: they have to be able to justify their actions.

Today, the consequences that result from this for public relations are well known as *corporate social responsibility*, a term originally coined by Bowen (1953). It suggests that organizations have an obligation to consider the interests of customers, employees, and other stakeholders in all aspects of their operations (Carroll & Buchholtz, 2003). Generally speaking, organizational managements have to keep "an eye on the effects of their decisions on society as well as on the organizations" (Grunig, 1992, p. 17). In Germany Volker Nickel, the then spokesperson of the umbrella organization of the German advertising industry (ZAW), voiced a similar point in 1990. Businesses, according to Nickel (1990), move in a reactionary manner when they only use their public relations work as a strategy to increase sales. He therefore pleads for a "social responsibility" of the modern entrepreneur that should comprise interacting with the public to resolve conflicts reasonably. He talks of a "responsibility to hear or listen" after which the company can address the demands and criticisms of various groups and take these points seriously. He recommends a "responsibility to correct" that includes taking up the concerns and implementing them into the internal decision-making process of the company.

My central thesis is this: Public relations is well advised to take its basic principal of communication seriously. More than this, I dare to say: Public relations must not neglect its communicative nature.

Especially in situations with a high chance of conflict, companies and organizations are forced to present good arguments to communicate their interests and ideas—in other words: they must make the public *understand* their actions. Therefore, in the view of COPR, understanding plays an important role within the public relations management process. This point of view is similar to the position of James E. Grunig and his two-way symmetrical model of public relations, which emphasizes "mutual understanding" as a purpose of public relations (Grunig & Hunt, 1984, p. 22).

It needs to be emphasized that in this context communication must not be seen as a general means for conflict solution. It would be erroneous to believe that perfectly planned communications are able to eliminate conflicts. The latter normally arise when opposite interests collide—especially in democratically organized societies where such situations are quite common. Modern conflict sociology refers to *rational* or *coordinated dissent* (Miller, 1994, 2006), which mainly comprises the joint identification of controversial issues.

The Perspective of Understanding in Habermas's Theory of Communicative Action

According to the *Theory of Communicative Action* (Habermas, 1984, 1987), communication always happens as a multidimensional process and each participant in this process needs to accept the validity of certain quasi-universal demands or claims in order to achieve understanding.

This implies that the partners in the communication process must mutually trust that they fulfill the following validity claims:

* *Intelligibility* (being able to use the proper grammatical rules);
* *Truth* (talk about something which the partner also accepts exists);
* *Truthfulness* (being honest and not misleading the partner);
* *Legitimacy* (acting in accordance with mutually accepted values and norms).

These four validity claims are mapped by Habermas onto three domains of reality the three "worlds": The "objective world" of external nature (about which true statements can be made); the "subjective world" of internal nature (which consists of individual experiences and is only accessible to the respective speaker); and the "social world" of society (i.e., the world of social relations controlled by values and norms).

As long as neither of the partners has doubts about the fulfillment of these claims, the communication process will function without interruption.

However, these ideal circumstances are an ideal type of imagination—they hardly ever occur in reality, Habermas argues. Often, basic rules of communication are violated and therefore discourse is needed as a "repair-mechanism." The term *discourse*, as used by Habermas, implies that all persons involved must have the opportunity to doubt the truth of assertions, the truthfulness of expressions, and the legitimacy of interests. Only when plausible answers are given, the flow of communication will continue.

Basically, Habermas distinguishes between three types of discourse (see Table 8.1):

- In an "explicative" discourse we question the intelligibility of a statement,
- in a "theoretical" discourse we question the claim of truth, and
- in a "practical" discourse we question the normative rightness (legitimacy) of a speech-act by doubting its normative context (Habermas, 1984).

A fourth aspect, that is, the claim of truthfulness, is an exception as it cannot be subject to discourse because the communicator can prove his truthfulness only by subsequent actions and not by arguments (Habermas, 1984).

Discourses, however, are subject to special standards: they must be free of internal and external constraints because they are there to build a consensus about a claim of validity that has become problematic, but that is based on nothing more than the "unforced force of the better because more plausible argument" (Habermas, 1995, p. 116). Such a consensus requires another prerequisite that Habermas labels "the ideal speech situation." The main particular characteristic of an ideal speech

Table 8.1 Claims and Types of Discourses According to Jürgen Habermas's Theory of Communicative Action

Claim	Consent	Type of discourse	Question leading the discourse	Answer
Intelligibility	Mutual intelligibility of a statement	Explicative	How do you mean this? How shall I understand this?	Interpretation
Truth	Shared knowledge about the content	Theoretical	Is it really as you said? Why is that so?	Assertion / Explanation
Truthfulness	Trust toward each other	—	Will this person deceive me? Is he/she mistaken about himself/herself?	—
Legitimacy	Mutual acceptance of norms	Practical	Why have you done this? For what reason didn't you act differently?	Justification

situation is that all persons participating in the discourse have an equal opportunity to choose and use "speech-acts" (Habermas, 1984, p. 177). But this is "contra-factual" because the ideal speech situation does not arise in real discourse practice: it is not an empirical phenomenon and is also "not only a construct, but also, a reciprocal prerequisite assumption that is unavoidable in discourse…a workable fiction necessary in an operative communicative process" (Habermas, 1984, p. 180). Habermas talks of anticipation or premature action before the ideal speech situation: it is part of the argumentation prerequisites that we use "contra-factually," whilst carrying out the speech-act, acting as though the ideal speech situation is not fictive but a reality. That normative fundament of verbal communication is therefore both anticipated, but, as an anticipated basis, also effective (Habermas, 1984).

Understanding is not only an end in itself of communication, but also, in the rule, a means of realization of interests (Burkart, 2002): Verbal communication is only the mechanism that merges the action plans and the action purposes of those involved.

However, the point of the prerequisites for communicative action described by Habermas is not the unconditional imposition of interests, but that those involved in the process of communication:

> [F]ollow their individual goals, subject to the condition that their plans of action are based on a common definition of the situation to be coordinated amongst the participants. From that point of view the negotiating of definitions of the situation is a major part of the interpretation-effort necessary for communicative action. (Habermas, 1984, p. 385)

Habermas distinguishes between "strategic" and "communicative action." Strategic action is success-oriented. "Acting strategically," means to orient one's behavior exclusively towards intended consequences. The acting person attempts to achieve his or her goals without regard to the others involved (e.g., by using gratifications, tricks or force).

Communicative acting, on the other hand, is consensus-oriented. The acting person meets his or her counterpart without using tricks or having a hidden agenda. He or she allows the actions to match the intentions and interests of the opponent. In this case communication is only used for understanding, not for influencing. In my opinion, however, this is a somewhat misleading differentiation because it implies that consensus oriented acting cannot be considered as success-oriented. This critical point has been mentioned by others too (e.g., Greve, 1999, 2003; Skjei, 1985; Tugendhat, 1992; Zimmermann, 1985).

The public relations theory presented here draws its inspiration from the Habermasian concept of understanding. However, its intention is not to transfer this concept onto public relations straightaway. It cannot be denied that all public relations pursue certain goals—but this needs not to exclude, in principle, a striving for understanding.

As mentioned above, Jürgen Habermas in his book *The Public Sphere* (1964/1974) held a very negative view of public relations. His judgment, however, referred to the 1960s; in the preface to the new edition of his work (1964/1990) Habermas made some of his positions less absolute. Without making specific reference to public relations, Habermas nevertheless admits that some of his views would be less pessimistic if his study were made again.

With regard to the public relations theory presented in this chapter it should be mentioned that when particular interests are involved, at least in democratic societies, conflicts are likely to get resolved through negotiation that results in compromise. Compromise is, in reality, not only widespread but also, according to Habermas, "has a not inconsiderable value" and that the "procedure of building a compromise can be evaluated from a normative standpoint. One cannot expect a fair compromise, if the participants do not have the same position of power or do not have the same threat potential" (1985, p. 243).

Anyway, it remains to note that only after a communication process that has gone on without a hitch, a common definition of the situation becomes possible. On this basis it is possible to decide what should be done.

Public Relations as a Process of Understanding

The model of COPR focuses on the above prerequisites. Public relations managers who reflect on the basic principles of communication will always orientate their activities in accordance with possible criticism maintained by the public.

However, the COPR-model is not a naive attempt to transfer Habermas's conditions of understanding directly onto the reality of public relations—although some German critics (wrongly) insinuated this in the past (i.e., Jarren & Röttger, 2005; Merten, 2000; see also my reply, Burkart, 2000a). In view of the theory's contrafactual implications this would be inadequate. It was, rather, a goal to gain new ideas for the analysis of public relations from Habermas's concept of understanding. The main impact of creating the COPR-model is the possibility to differentiate communicative claims, so that this process of questioning can be analyzed more systematically.

Especially in situations when conflicts are to be expected public relations practitioners have to take into account that critical recipients might question their messages. Looking at the communicative claims of validity this questioning can be analyzed and systematically differentiated:

public relations professionals can count on being publicly doubted by the involved members of the public and that the truth of propositions, the truthfulness of communicators, and the legitimacy of each of the interests to be realized of the participants be scrutinized.[4]

When, for example, the establishment of a hazardous waste facility is proposed, it can be expected that the prospective neighbors, at least, are not going to be happy. Usually, a citizen's action group will be formed with the target of stopping the proposal. Conflict is inevitable. The public relations practitioners working for the operators of the potential depot can expect that: (1) Any proposition that they put forward will be scrutinized for the *truth* of it's content. (2) They can also expect that the people (companies and organizations, etc.) involved will be actively *mistrusted*. (3) They can calculate that the intention of building a hazardous waste facility or landfill will be doubted in principle.

Based on these distinctions, public relations practitioners are able to analyze the situation and the ante of incipient conflicts and can focus on how to present the *truth* of their assertions, the *truthfulness* of the communicators involved and the *legitimacy* of the interests under discussion, and, if applicable, substantiate these claims.

On the one hand, it seems to be obvious that such considerations should be applied to such conflict situations where doubt is clearly articulated and made public, not least through media coverage of the conflict. Practitioners must have considered their replies and have to answer with arguments. It is hard to argue against early inclusion of consensus-oriented deliberation in the public relations management process, regardless of how the potential conflict situation is interpreted. Only if such deliberation is included early on can it help in setting public relations targets and be checked for efficacy in reaching those goals.[5]

Aims of Consensus-Oriented Public Relations

The overriding aim of consensus-oriented public relations is to facilitate what one hopes will be a smooth communication process between the public relations client and the relevant members of the public. This is the case if the three different levels of communication between the communicating parties are in agreement. It should be pointed out that in the present context there could be a misunderstanding of the definitions taken from Habermas's theory, namely "agreement" and "consensus." A usual misunderstanding is to equate agreement with approval or consent of something in dispute. Here, however, "agreement" only means agreement about validity claims.

Agreement about validity claims means that: (1) the subject of the issue matter must be clearly understood, that is, *what* can be represented under the subject, and it should be a consensus about the *truth* of the propositions and explanations provided by the client; (2) the communicators have to be clear about *who* is responsible for the plans and aims of the enterprise and the *truthfulness* of the organization and its spokesperson must be indisputable; (3) the positions held or represented must be comprehensible—*why* the (client's) interests should be pursued—and it should be a consensus about the *legitimacy* of the interest. This is illustrated in Figure 8.1.

A breakdown in the communication process can happen when the relevant members of the public doubt one or more of the claims of validity (made by the public relations client). This necessitates discourse, according to the theory of communicative action. Consensus-oriented public relations then has to take the need for discourse seriously and make attempts to facilitate this discourse.

How this can be achieved is shown in the following passages. Though this phase of discourse is only one of the steps in the COPR-process, in total, four main phases are suggested as crucial and help to measure the results. In the following section, the relevant parts of my Viennese evaluation study of the planning of two hazardous waste facilities in Lower Austria (Burkart, 1993) is used as an example of the questions that should be posed in relation to the four phases.

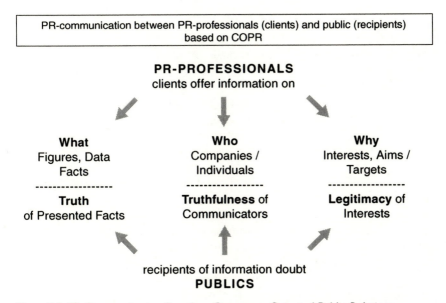

Figure 8.1 PR Communication Based on Consensus-Oriented Public Relations

Public Relations Aim: Information

Prerequisite to being able to make a rational judgment on a subject is the need to have a fairly good issue-specific knowledge. A public relations practitioner therefore has to have the relevant facts of the respective projects and make them available to members of the publics affected.

Success, in this information phase, comprises then, from the communicators' perspective, that precise level of *quality of the information* on offer must be met. The COPR model implies that the quality of information has to be relatively clearly determined on three levels:

At the first level, the planners of a waste depository should collect and present the facts of the case in a clear manner. In addition to purely technical information (which type of material will be deposited, the depository volume, the security of the stored waste, etc.) that is relevant for waste disposal, the planners should also detail the next planning steps (if neighbors will be included in the planning, when there are to be expert witnesses or evaluations made, etc.).

At the second level, the involvement of institutions (i.e., the state government) or organizations (the waste disposal firm) should be presented in order to given an idea of who has the responsibility for making decisions, who is responsible for which decisions, and with whom one has to deal (for instance who does one have to see for which decision and how does one contact them, etc.).

And finally, at the third level, the legitimacy of the entire project should be highlighted. This would include arguments that justify the project by discussing the chosen variation of waste disposal (i.e., deposition instead of burning), the choice of location, and the order of the planning of events.

In this information phase, successful public relations means that there will be positive media coverage, and, from the perspective of recipients of the information, that relevant members of the public can take up sufficient information (in the sense of communicative claims of validity). Only then can the central question be asked, namely, if and, for which issue, the recipients still need explanations and justifications if the enterprise is considered to be trustworthy.

The evaluation of the public relations success indicates various different subjects to be examined and various methodical ways to access this information. First of all an evaluation of all the public relations messages, including information press releases, circulars, handouts, posters, and information packages, as well as public announcements and paid advertising. Content analysis can be applied here.

Furthermore, a media resonance analysis has to be carried out, a particular type of content analysis, asking how the media used the public relations material. And, finally, the state of knowledge (about the subject) as well as the degree of consensus of relevant members of the public has to be examined. A (representative) survey of the members of the relevant public should be made. With these interviews, the degree of consensus can be assessed in relation to the claims of communicative validity. Only after this assessment has been carried out can one decide whether to go on to the next phase of the COPR-process.

Public Relations Aim: Discussion

When an issue is controversial, and that means when claims of validity are seriously doubted, it is time to start a "discussion-phase." It is not primarily thought that a direct discussion between members of the public and representatives of the client should take place. Rather, the focus should be on the classic methods of media information directed at selected journalists who are provided with specific information. If, in the case of planning a hazardous waste landfill, the results of a survey show that there are strong doubts about the legitimacy of the choice of a site for the facility, the journalists should primarily be supplied with information on the pros and cons for the selection of the site. Other aspects of concern, such as the types of waste that will be deposited or the organization of the waste disposal enterprise, plays only a marginal, if any, role at this stage.

Furthermore, it is surely sensible to plan for other forms of discussion: expert hearings, discussion evenings, civic assemblies, or consulting time with the project planners or the decision makers of the waste disposal firm. In addition, the Internet offers new possibilities for online dialogue (Burkart, 2000b) that could not have been imagined a few years ago.

Success in the discussion phase means that the public relations clients, when there is criticism or a need for explanation, should not appear to be "closed," but really involve themselves with these discussions and organize so that contact between members of the affected publics and the organization can take place. This requirement can be realized in many ways. At the time when the case of the hazardous waste facility project was analyzed, the potential waste disposal enterprise set up a citizens' advice office on the site, giving the publics a specific contact person to discuss the project with. In addition, information events were organized where experts who had carried out surveys and viability studies could be directly questioned. These days an Internet homepage would be created to provide interaction and information.

All these initiatives by the communicators are done with the intention of creating resonance or a "virtual discussion" in the media. An example for the latter would be a discussion between journalists and project planners (or other experts) where different viewpoints would be made visible to the public.

Yet again, the success of the discussion phase has to be evaluated. With regard to the method, a media resonance analysis has to be conducted in order to find out if and how far a virtual discussion of the issue has taken place in the media, and what image of the enterprise has been communicated. In addition, the public relations practitioners can consider use of participating observation (in civic meetings or in public hearings), qualitative reception analysis (or also a quantitative log file analysis) of an Internet page (if launched), as well as conducting a representative survey. The crucial question to be asked is: Are the claims of communicative validity being questioned and if yes, to what extent?

Public Relations Aim: Discourse

In principal, it is imaginable that the discussion phase could lead to a communicative consensus between the public relations client and members of the affected publics affected. In relation to highly controversial issues, however, this is not normally the case. This implies that the public relations practitioner has to assess which validity claims are in dispute and necessitate discourse. Using the example of the controversial hazardous waste landfill this would mean that the public relations practitioner has to focus on:

1. Doubts about the validity claim of the truth of statements, for instance: "The report by evaluator X is false";
2. Doubts about the *truthfulness* of the communicators, for instance, "The dump planners are hiding relevant facts";
3. Doubts about the *legitimacy* of the project, like, "Burning waste is a better solution than burying waste."

In the sense of TCA, the claims of communicative validity are here "truth" and "legitimacy," and accessible by means of a discursive debate. The practitioner using the COPR model should therefore consider which public relations needs arise from a "theoretical" and a "practical" discourse.

In theoretical discourse, the object is the evidence of truth of objective judgments, in other words, it focus on disputed details (numbers/data/facts), evidence of objectivity or truth must be presented with the aim of eliminating doubts. Objective judgments are based, in the rule, on technical or scientifically provable facts that appear in reports that are (mainly) more or less objectively determinable (numbers and measures).

In *practical discourse* the object is the *justification* of interests, objectives, or decisions, whereby value-judgments are up for discussion. That means that grounds for the decisions must be given: why or more explicitly, on the basis of what norm and value context can the individual objective be pursued? Value judgments are not provable in the classical scientific sense. They are anchored in the appropriate context of social norms or result from moral rules or ethical principles.

Here it should be pointed out, as mentioned above, that it is not the primary aim (of discourse) to mediate between the public relations client and affected members of the publics in actual face-to-face disputes. Again, public relations practitioners have to pay attention to media coverage: This is particularly true in conflict situations in which discussion or discourse is necessary and that also provoke higher media interest. Journalists are not only interested in newsworthy issues, but also in competent interviewees who can give explanations and develop arguments for the justification of positions. When public relations management can provide such interviewees a "virtual discourse" can happen—a reflection on objectives and values or value judgments between relevant experts in different journalistic genres (reports, interviews, commentaries, etc.).

Success in this discourse phase means that consensus can be achieved on both the level of objective judgment (regarding the validity claim *truth*) and the level of value judgment (regarding the appropriateness of the reasons referring to the validity claim *legitimacy*). More realistically, one can expect that doubt in the objective and value judgments will be minimized.

Methodically, as before, media resonance analysis is useful, and it can be tested if and how far this (meaningful) discourse argumentation has been used in the media coverage. The same can be done by surveying the relevant members of the public, to inquire about their level of understanding of the subject matter and the degree of their communicative consent.

Public Relations Aim: Situation Definition

In this last COPR-phase, what remains is to establish the status quo of the communication achieved and to inform the relevant members of the public, which again indicates the importance of media coverage as well as the attitudes/positions of the publics affected. It has to be asked if the claims still are doubted (and if so, to what extent) in relation to the following:

1. The *truth* of the declared facts (as well as omnipresent debatable objective judgments);

2. The *truthfulness* of the organization or the persons involved;
3. The *legitimacy* of the interests represented (as well as any debatable value judgments) by the members of the relevant public that could be dismissed or minimized and how far consensus could be established.

Full agreement or unrestrained approval on all three levels of claims of communicative validity is never going to happen and it is not implied by TCA. It may be worth pointing to a position from the sociology of conflict, that of "rational dissent" (Miller, 1992), that sees this as a major stage toward coping with social conflict: one knows the points about which one has not (yet) agreed, and then when the points of dissent can be identified precisely. This is exactly what can be achieved by using the COPR-model and focus on the distinctions of communicative validity claims.

When the analysis of the hazardous waste project was carried out, most of the people had believed the claims made by the planners of the depot (they had not doubted the truth of these claims) and had also considered the project planners to be trustworthy. Still, the legitimacy of the choice of the site was not seen as valid; on the contrary, most people disagreed with the choice of their region for a hazardous waste site.

The term *situation definition* (loaned from TCA) goes over and above the sense used in the COPR-model. At this stage, the organization has to decide what it wants to do. The decision will, without doubt, be easier when the degree of agreement is high and broad acceptance of the project targets can be expected. This was the result in the case of the study of the hazardous waste depot (i.e., Burkart, 1993).

COPR criteria were used to analyze the procedural method of the project planners and the following deficiencies in the information offered were identified: Both public relations publications and the media coverage contained relatively few facts about the planned facility and no argument about the legitimacy of the selection of the sites. The results of the survey fit with the results that the landfill project did not find approval with the majority of the public.

With the help of a representative survey, in which the participants were questioned about how much they understood about the criteria that were relevant to the matter, it became clear that the potential acceptance of the facility was combined with a better understanding of the criteria for successful communication. "Potential" here means that the question of acceptance of the facility was considered to be subject to a positive environmental impact assessment. Those who supported the site, were, often not only better informed but also seldom doubted the truthfulness of the project planners and the legitimacy of the choice of site. In summing up: the COPR-model has proven its worth as an instrument of diagnosis to evaluate public relations communication.

Conclusion: The COPR-Model as a Public Relations Evaluation Program

Evaluation, the measurement and judgment of the quality and success of public relations, has been widely discussed at least since the mid-1990s (i.e., Baerns, 1995; GPRA, 1997). In evaluation research (i.e., Fuhrberg, 1995; Lindenmann, 2003; Pavlik, 1987) two different methods of measurement can be found: Summative research, that uses measurement at the end of a public relations program or campaign, and formative research that requires continuous measurement in which "the individual work procedure (process) is continually assessed and evaluated" (Fuhrberg, 1995, p. 55) to arrive at an improvement of the situation analysis of planning, the implementation and the final summative evaluation.

In the COPR model, the final summative evaluation is located within the situation definition phase. Table 8.2 illustrates that in the first three of the COPR phases, the formative method of evaluation, meaning the continuing control of the success of the taken measures, should be adopted as the basis for work. The decisions to be taken during the next steps of the model rely to a high degree, on the knowledge gained from accomplishment of targets.

Table 8.2 illustrates the described levels and phases of COPR and the central questions to be asked to evaluate using the criteria of the model in relation to the three communicative levels (objective, subjective, and social world). Additionally, the objects of analysis for each phase are specified.

Despite the evidence from the case study mentioned above, the COPR-model should not be thought of as a model to obtain acceptance as such. Agreement with one project cannot be generated by public relations "pressing the right public relations button" but has to be generated by the persons concerned. "Who ever wants acceptance must not wish for it," is a handy phrase of Röglin (1996, p. 235). In addition, Röglin argues that *transparency* has to become the new central keyword for public relations.

Although, it can be added, that approval develops when the communicative acceptance is high between the organization and the involved members of the public. Development of such approval is strengthened when the organization and the public relations practitioners take the need for discourse seriously, particularly in those instances when the affected public feels threatened or limited by the action or interests of the organization. Here, the COPR model can assist practitioners.

Table 8.2 COPR-Planning and Evaluation (from Burkart, 2005): Questions for Planning and Evaluation

Levels of understanding COPR-phases		Objective world What Facts, Figures, Data	Subjective world Who Enterprises/Persons	Social world Why Grounds
Information	C	Have the relevant facts been presented?	Has the central information about the company been presented?	Have the aims of the project been justified?
	M	Which of the facts or issues were mentioned in the media (and how)?	Which of the company data were mentioned in the media (and how)?	Which of the project goals and grounds were reported (and how)?
	R	How far does the IMP know the facts?	To what extent are the IMP informed about the company?	How far does the IMP know the project related grounds?
	V	Is there a need for explanation for either the IMP or the media and if yes for which issues?	Is there a need for further information about the company for either the IMP or the media and if yes for which issues?	Is there a need for justification for either the IMP or the media and if yes for which grounds?
Discussion	C	To what extent have the project instigators made a issue-related discussion possible or lead one?	—	To what extent have the project instigators made a project targets related discussion possible or lead one?
	M	How have the fact related discussion been reported in the media?	Which image of the company has been created by the media coverage?	How have the discussions about project goals been reported in the media?
	R	How has the IMP participated in or received these factual discussions?	What type of image has the relevant IMP formed about the company?	How far has the IMP followed the discussion on legitimacy or taken part and received it?
	V	Is there doubt on the part of the IMP or the media of the truth of data and facts?	Is there doubt on the part of the IMP or the media about the truthfulness of the company?	Is there doubt on the part of the IMP or the media of the legitimacy of the project goals?

Levels of understanding COPR-phases		Objective world What Facts, Figures, Data	Subjective world Who Enterprises/Persons	Social world Why Grounds
Discourse	C	Have factual judgments been presented as proof for doubted facts?	—	Have value-based judgments been presented as proof for doubts about legitimacy?
	M	Have factual judgments or proof of truth found mention in the media coverage, and if so, how?	Has the (quality of) company communication been made issue in the media coverage, and if so, how?	Have value based judgments or doubts about legitimacy been presented in the media coverage, and if so, how?
	R	How far has the IMP received these factual judgments and/or proof of truth?	Did the IMP take notice of (the quality of) the company communication?	How far has the IMP received the value based judgments or legitimacy proof?
	V	Do doubts exist on the part of the IMP or the media coverage about the truth of the factual judgments?	Do doubts exist on the part of the IMP or the media coverage about the discourse-quality of company communication?	Do doubts exist on the part of the IMP or the media coverage about the value judgments or legitimacy proof?
Definition of the situation	M R V	To what extent is there consent about the facts and fact based judgments?	To what extent is there consent about the truthfulness of the company and (client)-communicators?	To what extent is there consent about the project goals and value based judgments?
	C	Has the result been adequately communicated?		

C: Communicator or Client
M: Media coverage
R: Recipient or "involved members of the publics" (IMP)
V: Claim of validity

Further research should focus on how the respective validity claims are connected to each other. In particular the importance of truthfulness needs to be studied. As mentioned above, truthfulness is the very validity claim that cannot be the subject of a discourse. It should be examined how far the emergence of trust in public relations clients depends on believing in their statements or considering their intentions as acceptable. In other words: Does the trust in public relations clients lead to a reduction of doubts about the truth of their assertions and the legitimacy of their intentions? In the context of the COPR model the connections (interrelations) between the respective validity claims are rather unclear. For this reason, results of trust research should be taken into account in future studies.

Notes

1. The author would like to thank the anonymous reviewers for a number of helpful suggestions, and his colleague O. C. Oberhauser for some help with the English version. A previous version of this chapter was published as: On Jürgen Habermas and public relations, in *Public Relations Review, 33*(3), 2007.
2. Jensen (2001) for instance refers to these preconditions of a democratically organized public sphere and develops an analytical framework for reflecting specific functions of the contemporary public sphere.
3. The mentioned conditions could "involve the communicator's understanding and satisfaction with rules concerning 1) 'opportunity for beginning and ending communicative interaction;' 2) 'length of time separating messages;' 3) 'opportunity for suggesting topics and initiating topic changes;' 4) 'a partner in communication has provided a response that counts as a response;' 5) and 'channel selection'" (Pearson, 1989b, pp. 82–84, quoted in Leeper, 1996, p. 142).
4. This is also valid for the claim of "understandability." But it is not comparable to other far-reaching consequences and is, as a result, ignored in this context.
5. The typical ideal work routine in public relations comprises the four steps of situation analysis, planning, implementation and evaluation (e.g., Cutlip, Center, & Broom, 2000; Fuhrberg, 1995).

References

Austin, J. L. (1962). *How to do things with words.* Oxford, UK: Clarendon Press.

Baerns, B. (Eds.). (1995). *PR-Erfolgskontrolle. Messen und Bewerten in der Öffentlichkeitsarbeit: Verfahren, Strategien und Beispiele* [PR-evaluation: Measuring and evaluating: Modes, strategies and examples]. Frankfurt, Germany: IMK.

Beck, U. (1986). *Risikogesellschaft. Auf dem Weg in eine andere Moderne* [Risk society: Towards a new modernity]. Frankfurt am Main: Suhrkamp.

Bowen, H. R. (1953). *Social responsibilities of the businessman.* New York: Harper & Row.

Burkart, R. (1993). *Public Relations als Konfliktmanagement: Ein Konzept für verständigungsorientierte Öffentlichkeitsarbeit. Untersucht am Beispiel der Planung von Sonderabfalldeponien in Niederösterreich.* Vienna [Public relations as conflict management: A model for consensus-oriented public relations. Based upon research about planning a hazardous waste facility in Lower Austria]. Wien: Braumüller.

Burkart, R. (1994). Consensus oriented public relations as a solution to the landfill conflict. *Waste Management & Research, 12,* 223–232.

Burkart, R. (2000a), Die Wahrheit über die Verständigung: Eine Replik auf Klaus Merten [The truth about understanding: A reply to Klaus Merten]. *Public Relations Forum für Wissenschaft und Praxis, 2,* 96–99.

Burkart, R. (2000b). Online-Dialoge: eine neue Qualität für Konflikt-PR? [Online dialogs: A new quality for conflict-PR?] In B. Baerns & J. Raupp (Eds.), *Information und Kommunikation in Europa. Forschung und Praxis* [Information and Communication in Europe: Research and Practice] (pp. 222–230). Berlin: Vistas.

Burkart, R. (2002). *Kommunikationswissenschaft: Grundlagen und Problemfelder. Umrisse einerinterdisziplinären Sozialwissenschaft* [Communications: Basics and fields of problems. A profile of an interdisciplinary science]. Vienna: Böhlau.

Burkart, R. (2004), Consensus-oriented public relations (COPR)—A conception for planning and evaluation of public relations. In B. van Ruler & D. Verčič (Eds.), *Public relations in Europe: A nation-by-nation introduction to public relations theory and practice* (pp. 446–452). Berlin/New York: Mouton De Gruyter.

Burkart, R. (2005). Verständigungsorientierte Öffentlichkeitsarbeit: Ein Konzept für Public Relations unter den Bedingungen moderner Konflikt gesellschaften [Consensus-oriented public relations: A PR-model for modern conflict-societies]. In G. Bentele, R. Fröhlich, & P. Szyszka, (Eds.), *Handbuch Public Relations: Wissenschaftliche Grundlagen und berufliches Handeln* [Handbook for public relations: Academic basics for professional actors] (pp. 223–240). Wiesbaden, Germany: VS.

Calhoun, C. (Ed.). (1992). *Habermas and the public sphere.* Cambridge, MA: MIT Press.

Carroll, A. B., & Buchholtz, A. K. (2003). *Business and society: Ethics and stakeholder management.* Mason, Ohio: Thomson.

Crossley, N., & Roberts, J. (Eds.). (2004). *After Habermas: New perspectives on the public sphere.* Oxford, UK: Blackwell.

Cutlip, S. M., Center, A. H., & Broom, G. N. (2000). *Effective public relations* (8th ed.). Englewood Cliffs, NJ: Prentice Hall.

Edgar, A. (2005). *The philosophy of Habermas.* Chesham, UK: Acumen.

Finlayson, J. G. (2004). *Habermas: A very short introduction.* New York: Oxford University Press.

Fuhrberg, R. (1995). Teuer oder billig, Kopf oder Bauch—Versuch einer systematischen Darstellung von Evaluationsverfahren [Expensive or cheap—

head or stomach—An attempt of a systematical description of evaluation models]. In B. Baerns (Ed.), *PR-Erfolgskontrolle: Messen und Bewerten in der Öffentlichkeitsarbeit* [Control pf PR success. Measuring and evaluating public relations] (pp. 47–69). Frankfurt am Main, Germany: IMK.

GPRA/Gesellschaft Public Relations Agenturen. (Eds.). (1997). Evaluation von Public Relations: Dokumentation einer Fachtagung [Evaluation of public relations: Documentation of a symposium]. Frankfurt, Germany: IMK.

Greve, J. (1999). Sprache, Kommunikation und Strategie in der Theorie von Jürgen Habermas [Language, communication and strategy within the Theory of Communicative Action by Jürgen Habermas]. *Kölner Zeitschrift für Soziologie und Sozialpsychologie, 51*(2), 232–259.

Greve, J. (2003). *Kommunkation und Bedeutung. Grice-Programm, Sprechakttheorie und radikale Interpretation* [Communication and meaning: Grice program, speech act theory and radical interpretation]. Würzburg, Germany: Königshausen & Neumann.

Grunig, L. (1992). Activism: How it limits the effectiveness of organizations and how excellent public relations departments respond. In J. Grunig (Ed.), *Excellence in public relations and communication management* (pp. 503–530). Hillsdale, NJ: Erlbaum.

Grunig, J., & Hunt, T. (1984). *Managing public relations.* New York: Holt, Rinehart & Winston.

Habermas, J. (1962). *Strukturwandel der Öffentlichkeit. Untersuchungen zu einer kategorie der bürgerlicjen gesellschaft* [The structural transformation of the public sphere: An inquiry into a category of bourgeois society]. Darmstadt und Neuwied: Luchterhand

Habermas, J. (1974). The public sphere: An encyclopedia article (S. & F. Lennox, Trans.). *New German Critique, 3,* 49–55. (Original work published 1964)

Habermas, J. (1984). *The theory of communicative action: Vol. 1. Reason and the rationalization of society* [Die Theorie des kommunikativen Handelns. Handlungsrationalität und gesellschaftliche Rationalisierung]. Boston: Beacon Press.

Habermas, J. (1985). *Die neue Unübersichtlichkeit. Kleine politische Schriften V* [The new conservatism: Cultural criticism and the historians' debate]. Cambridge, MA: MIT Press.

Habermas, J. (1987). *The theory of communicative action: Vol. 2. Lifeworld and system: A critique of functionalist reason* [*Die Theorie des kommunikativen Handelns. Zur kritik der funktionalistischen Vernunft*]. Boston: Beacon Press. (Original work published 1981)

Habermas, J. (1989). *The structural transformation of the public sphere: An inquiry into a category of bourgeois society.* Cambridge, MA: MIT Press.

Habermas, J. (1990). *Moral consciousness and communicative action.* Cambridge, MA: MIT Press.

Habermas, J. (1990). Vorwort zur neuauflage (Preface to new edition). In J. Habermas (Ed.), *Strukturwandel der Öffentlichkeit. Untersuchungen zu einer kategorie der bürgerlicjen gesellschaft* [The structural transformation of the public sphere: An inquiry into a category of bourgeois society] (pp. 11–50). Frankfurt am Main: Suhkamp.

Habermas, J. (1992). Further reflections on the public sphere., In C. Calhoun

(Ed.), *Habermas and the public sphere* (T. Burger, Trans., pp. 421–461). Cambridge, MA: MIT Press.

Habermas, J. (1995). *Vorstudien und Ergänzungen zur Theorie des kommunikativen Handelns.* Frankfurt, Germany: Suhrkamp.

Holmström, S. (1997). The inter-subjective and the social systemic public relations paradigms—Two basically differing roles for public relations in the corporate practice of social responsibility. *Journal of Communication Management, 2*(1), 24–39.

Horkheimer, M. (1982). *Critical theory.* New York: Seabury Press.

Horkheimer, M., & Adorno, T. W. (1972). *Dialectic of enlightenment.* New York: Herder & Herder.

Jarren, O., & Röttger, U. (2005). Public Relations aus kommunikationswissenschaftlicher Sicht. In G. Bentele, R. Fröhlich, & P. Szyszka (Eds.), *Handbuch Public Relations: Wissenschaftliche Grundlagen und berufliches Handeln* [Handbook for public relations: Academic basics for professional actors] (pp. 19–36). Wiesbaden, Germany: VS.

Jensen, I. (2001). Public relations and emerging functions of the public sphere: An analytical framework. *Journal of Communication Management, 6*(2), 133–147.

Kellner, D. (1989). *Critical theory, Marxism, and modernity.* Cambridge, UK & Baltimore: Polity & John Hopkins University Press.

Kellner, D. (1995). *Media culture: Cultural studies, identity, and politics between the modern and the postmodern.* London & New York: Routledge.

Kleger, H. (1993). *Der neue Ungehorsam. Widerstände und politische Verpflichtung in einer lernfähigen Demokratie* [The new disobedience: Resistances and political obligations in an adaptive democracy]. Frankfurt/New York: Campus.

Leeper, R. V. (1996). Moral objectivity, Jürgen Habermas' discourse ethics, and public relations. *Public Relations Review, 22*(2), 133–150.

Lindenmann, W. K. (2003). Guidelines for measuring the effectiveness of PR programs and activities. In *The Institute for Public Relations.* Retrieved June 18, 2006, from http://www.instituteforpr.com

Meisenbach, R. J. (2006). Habermas' discourse ethics and principle of universalization as a moral framework for organizational communication. *Management Communication Quarterly, 20*(1), 39–62.

Merten, K. (2000). Die Lüge vom Dialog: Ein verständigungsorientierter Versuch über semantische Hazards [The lie about the dialogue: A consensus-oriented essay on semantic hazards]. *Public Relations Forum für Wissenschaft und Praxis, 6*(2), 6–9.

Miller, M. (1992). Rationaler Dissens: Zur gesellschaftlichen Funktion sozialer Konflikte [Rational dissent: Social functions of conflicts]. In H.-J. Giegel (Ed.), *Kommunikation und Konsens in modernen Gesellschaften* [Communication and consensus in modern societies] (pp. 31–58). Frankfurt am Main, Germany: Suhrkamp.

Miller, M. (1994). Intersystemic discourse and coordinated dissent—A critique of Luhmann's concept of ecological communication. *Theory, Culture & Society, 11*(2), 101–122.

Miller, M. (2006). *Discourse learning and social evolution*. London/New York: Routledge.

Morris, C. W. (1938). *Foundations of the theory of signs*. Chicago: University of Chicago Press.

Münch, R. (1991), *Dialektik der Kommunikationsgesellschaft* [Dialectics of the modern communication society]. Frankfurt am Main: Suhrkamp.

Nickel, V. (1990, April-May). Umweltorientierte Öffentlichkeitsarbeit [Environmentally oriented public relations]. In *Werben und Verkaufen* (w&v), 15–17.

Outhwaite, W. (1994). *Habermas: A critical introduction*. Cambridge, UK: Polity.

Pavlik, J. (1987). *Public relations: What research tells us*. Newbury Park, CA: Sage.

Pearson, R. (1989a). Business ethics as communication ethics: Public relations practice and the idea of dialogue. In C. H. Botan & V. Hazelton (Eds.), *Public relations theory* (pp. 111–131). Hillsdale, NJ: Erlbaum.

Pearson, R. (1989b). Beyond ethical relativism in public relations: Coordination, roles and the idea of communication symmetry. *Public Relations Research Annual, 1*, 67–86.

Rödel, U., Frankenberg, G., & Dubiel, H. (1989). *Die demokratische Frage: Ein Essay* [Questioning democracy: An essay]. Frankfurt am Main, Germany: Suhrkamp.

Röglin, C. (1994). *Technikängste und wie man damit umgeht* [Technology anxiety and how to address it]. Düsseldorf, Germany: VDI.

Röglin, C. (1996). Die Öffentlichkeitsarbeit und das Konzept der kühnen Konzepte [Public relations and the concept of the venturous models]. In G. Bentele H., Steinmann, & A. Zerfass, *Dialogorientierte Unternehmenskommunikation* [Dialogue-oriented corporate communication] (pp. 229–244). Leipzig, Germany: Vistas.

Searle, J. R. (1969). *Speech acts*. Cambridge, UK: Cambridge University Press.

Skjei, E. (1985). A comment on performative, subject, and proposition in Habermas' theory of communication. *Inquiry, 28*(2), 87–105.

Tugendhat, E. (1992). Habermas on communicative action. In G. Seebass & R. Tuomela (Eds.), *Social action* (pp. 179–186). Dodrecht, Germany: Reidel.

Wiggershaus, R. (2001). *Die Frankfurter Schule: Geschichte, Theoretische Entwicklung, Politische Bedeutung* [The Frankfurt School: History, theoretical development, political importance]. Munich: Hanser. (Original work published 1986)

Zimmermann, R. (1985). *Utopie—Rationalität—Politik* [*Utopia—rationality—politics*]. Freiburg /Munich, Germany: Alber.

Life and Work of Jürgen Habermas

Jürgen Habermas was born in Düsseldorf, Germany in 1929. He studied philosophy, history, psychology, and German literature at Göttingen, Zürich, and Bonn and earned his doctorate in 1954 with a dissertation about Schelling. Until 1956 he worked as a freelance journalist, then from 1956 to 1959 he was an assistant to Theodor W. Adorno at the Institute for Social Research in Frankfurt. In 1961 he wrote his postdoctoral dissertation *The Structural Transformation of the Public Sphere* and was offered a professorship in philosophy at the University of Heidelberg, which he accepted in 1962.

From 1971 to 1983 he served as director of the Max Planck Institute at Starnberg (near Munich). During this period he published his magnum opus *The Theory of Communicative Action*. Habermas then returned to Frankfurt and became professor of social and historical philosophy. He became professor emeritus in 1994.

Habermas is the recipient of several awards. In 1986 he received the Gottfried Wilhelm Leibnitz Award of the German Research Foundation (Deutsche Forschungsgemeinschaft); in 2001 he received the Peace Prize of the German Book Trade (Friedenspreis des deutschen Buchhandels); in 2004 he was the 2004 Kyoto Laureate in the arts and philosophy section; and in 2005 he received the Holberg International Memorial Price. Habermas is also a permanent visiting professor at Northwestern University, Evanston, Illinois. He lives in Starnberg, Bavaria and is a world-renowned public intellectual.

The secondary literature on Habermas is quite huge and includes among others Calhoun (1992), *Habermas and the Public Sphere*; Outhwaite (1994), *Habermas: A Critical Introduction*; and Finlayson (2004), *Habermas: A Very Short Introduction*.

Chapter 9

On Latour

Actor-Network-Theory (ANT) and Public Relations

Piet Verhoeven

Abstract

In this chapter the actor-network theory (ANT) or the sociology of associations, as developed by the French sociologist/philosopher Bruno Latour, is described and summarized. Central concepts like actor-network, the construction of (scientific) facts, the association of humans and nonhumans, the Nonmodern Constitution, and the central position of controversies in the theoretical perspective are discussed. The relevance of these concepts for public relations is explored in general and in combination with empirical examples taken from the societal debate on external risk around Amsterdam Schiphol Airport in the Netherlands. ANT as an analytical perspective promises a more complex and a more detailed insight in the practice of public relations and its role in the collective. It gives room for a more realistic picture of the role public relations practitioners play in the construction of reality and how they participate in and influence the decision making processes in a democracy.

The French sociologist/anthropologist/philosopher Bruno Latour is a leading and at the same time controversial social thinker. His social theory, under the heading actor-network theory (ANT), originated in the small subfield of sociology, science, and technology studies (STS) as a theoretical perspective from which to study scientists and engineers in society (Callon 1986; Callon & Latour, 1981; Latour, 1987; Latour & Woolgar, 1979; Law 1986). Over the years it has developed into a sociology of associations, an alternative social theory, a theoretical perspective from which to study not only scientists and engineers in action but to follow all kinds of other actors as well while they are associating themselves to other actors or to things, often in a controversy, trying to form a collective with a shared definition of a common world. The tracing of these associations is the main task of the social scientist, according to Latour, wherein the social is defined as a type of connection between all kinds of heterogeneous elements (Latour, 2005b).

Although concepts like network, actor, and controversy are used in public relations research, Latour's ANT does not share the same philosophical foundation with the concepts normally used in public relations research. ANT is a form of constructivism that should not be carelessly thrown together with social constructivism (see below) (Latour, 2005b). Constructivism here relates to the construction of facts, particularly scientific and technological facts. In the field of social studies of science and technology, constructivism means that scientific knowledge is considered as constructive instead of descriptive and that social structure is "at best the consequence but never the cause of what people do" (Hagendijk, 1990, p. 44).

Constructivism is not frequently used in the study of public relations practices; functionalistic and normative perspectives prevail (Berger, 1999), with the exception of Holmström who uses Luhmann's constructivist system theory (see chapter 10 of this volume) for analyzing public relations. ANT seems very well suited for developing constructivism-based research into activities undertaken by public relations actors as an elaboration of the perspective of *reflective communication* as proposed by van Ruler and Verčič (2005).

This chapter will introduce a selection of the key terms and concepts of ANT and their possible relevance for public relations research. First a more or less chronological overview of the development of Latour's theory will be given; starting with his laboratory studies in the 1970s and 1980s to his nonmodern constitution in the 1990s and his current political ecology and sociology of associations. In the second part of this chapter the relevance of Latour's theory for public relations will be discussed by looking at public relations from an ANT perspective and by comparing some of the ANT notions with the notions usually used in public relations theory

On the Sociology of Latour

Coming as he did from a subfield of sociology, science and technology studies (STS), it will come as no surprise that the development of science and technology is at the heart of Latour's work. Latour started off in this field as an anthropologist doing participant observation of scientists at work in Roger Guillemin's laboratory at the Salk Institute in California in the 1970s. The results of this research were published with coauthor Steve Woolgar in *Laboratory Life: The Construction of Scientific Facts* (1979). From then on Latour completed many other studies of scientists and engineers at work; for example, on Louis Pasteur (Latour, 1983, 1988). In the 1980s, all these studies led to a proposition regarding a set of principles and rules of method for use in "follow[ing] scientists and engineers through society" (Latour, 1987), ideas which were developed in *Science in Action* (1987). Gradually his work builds up to a more general analysis of modern society, or the modern Constitution as it is called, in

We Have Never Been Modern: A Plea for a Symmetrical Anthropology (Latour, 1993). This symmetrical anthropology refers to symmetry of humans and nonhumans, in other words a plea for the recognition of the many hybrids that inhabit our world. In *Pandora's Hope* (1999) Latour worked out his position on science studies further and broadened his analysis of the modern world into a political philosophy of nature or a political epistemology in *Politics of Nature: How to Bring the Sciences Into Democracy* (Latour, 2004b). In that text a connection between the sciences and democracy is made.

Building on the sociology of science, Latour (2005b) proposes in *Reassembling the Social: An Introduction to Actor-Network Theory,* a social science that "should be able to reclaim an empirical grasp, since it travels wherever new associations go rather than stopping short at the limit of the former social" (p. 251). In this book he lays out a "travel guide" (Latour, 2005b, p. 7) for ANT-scholars to go on a journey through the social landscape feeding off "controversies about *what* this universe is made of" (Latour, 2005b, p. 21). In the following section some aspects of this ANT or sociology of associations and its history will be introduced en explained.

"Give Me a Laboratory and I Will Raise the World" (Latour, 1983)

ANT starts from the premise that nature and society are constructed in one process of attributing meaning. Phenomena are to be explained by the *process* by which they are made and the strength and length of the *network* in which they are embedded and not by "Nature" or "Society." The representation of nature and the stability of society are the result (and not the cause) of the settlement of controversies around scientific facts and technological artifacts like machines. For example, the difference between a scientific fact and a nonscientific fact can, in this perspective, be explained by the scale of the construction: scientific facts are large scale constructions, nonscientific facts are small scale constructions (Latour, 1987). Scientific truth is to be found in strong networks of humans and *nonhumans*, networks strong enough to resist criticism and time. It is also important to take the nonhumans (for example viruses, microbes, and machines) in the network into account, although always in relation to their association with humans.[1] To include the performances of the nonhumans in the network sometimes the word *actant* is used, instead of actor, making actor-network theory *actant*-network theory (Latour, 1999).

The construction of scientific facts is by definition a collective process: it happens within a network. Fact construction is so much a collective process that isolated persons can only build dreams, claims, and feelings, not facts (Latour, 1987). Scientists try to transform their own position into a *black box*. In the beginning of this process controversies might arise, dissidents (other scientists or outsiders) might question the position of the scientist involved. In order to establish a firm scientific fact, scientists strengthen their position by many means, aiming at isolation of dissidents. The key factor in this process is *rhetoric*: texts in scientific media. The texts will gradually become more technical, containing different levels and extended visualizations, to prevent contradiction and to be sure of a large number of supporters, in the form of citations. Scientific texts are the result of a long process in the laboratory with instruments, registrations, and tests. Scientists thereby become the spokespeople of the registrations of the instruments by means of these texts (Latour, 1987).

Dissidents who don't agree with the assertion presented by scientists can either give up, go along with the assertion, or try to open the black box or build a new one. In order to do that they will have to go back to the starting point of the texts: the *laboratories*. Dissidents can build a counterlaboratory to start building counterclaims (Latour, 1987).

One of the most important questions therefore is: what is happening inside the laboratory, "the place where scientists *work*" (Latour, 1987, p. 64). Laboratory practices should be studied from an anthropological perspective following scientists and engineers *in action* (Latour, 1987), while they are in the process of constructing scientific facts, technological artifacts, and as a result of that the construction of reality. This process starts with capturing the interests of others outside the laboratory for the work that is taking place inside the laboratory (Latour, 1983). These interests are not a given, translation is necessary. Others will have to participate in the scientist's construction process, their interests have to be translated in order to form alliances and to establish facts. Scientists have to become a compulsory and "logical" step in the problem solving process of large groups of people; they have to be mobilized (Latour, 1987). Important elements of this mobilization process are scaling down and scaling up. Problems, like diseases, are reformulated and scaled down to the level of a laboratory. There, because of the small scale, the problem can be varied, studied, and solved (or partially solved). In order to understand and to solve problems laboratories become indispensable. But for the solutions to work, the solutions constructed in the laboratory have to be scaled up to the level of the world outside the laboratory. To solve the problems the conditions in the small scale laboratory have to be extended to other parts of the world as well: *"if this means transforming society into a vast laboratory, then do it"* (Latour, 1983, p. 166). As a consequence laboratories destabilize or undo the differences of scale between the micro- and the macrolevels in society and between the inside and the outside of the laboratory (Latour, 1983). In this perspective there is no micro- or macrolevel in society, no inside or outside of the laboratories. There are only transformations, displacements, and differences of scale produced by actors, not only by scientists and engineers but also by CEOs of big corporations, politicians, and journalists, to name a few other actors. They all will become part of the extending network (Latour, 1983, 1987). The work in the laboratories here refers to natural scientists and to technicians who have laboratory practices. Latour analyses their actions as an example of the construction process of facts and of reality. Although not all scientists use laboratories, the construction process is exemplary for the sciences in general. Latour, for example, says that in sociology the text can be seen as a "functional equivalent of a laboratory" (Latour, 2005b, p. 149).

In the process of scaling up, mathematical centers, as Latour calls all kinds of statistical institutions in society, play a decisive role in connecting all the allies in the network. Through what is called *metrology*, a process of registering, summarizing, and totaling, those centers create registrations (registrations to the nth-order), which are scaled up to the world. Thereby the outside world is transformed into an inside world where facts and machines can survive (Latour, 1983, 1987). The network then is further extended and firmly established.

The notion of *translation* plays an important role in ANT. It is contradictory to the notion of *diffusion* (Latour, 1987, 2005b). In the language of diffusion, facts and machines have a "*vis inertia* of their own" (Latour, 1987, p. 133) and are moving around by themselves, without people. Technical and scientific determinism are coupled here with the notion of discovery. Some actors are labeled as great inventors of facts or technical discoveries and receive all the credits for it. Their ideas or their inventions only need to be *diffused* to a society, defined as "a medium of different resistances *through which* ideas and machines travel" (Latour, 1987, p. 136). Groups that resist the ideas or discoveries are invented in order to persuade them to accept the ideas, inventions or discoveries. It is obvious that this diffusion model does not account for the actions of the many people involved in the construction of facts and machines. Nor does it account for the negotiations between all those people and the associations and alliances between humans and nonhumans that are made through that. As Latour (1987) concludes about the difference between translation and diffusion:

> Understanding what facts and machines are is the same task as understanding who the people are. If you describe the controlling elements that have been gathered together you will understand the groups which are controlled. The only question in common is to learn *which associations are stronger and which are weaker.* (p. 140)

The belief in the existence of a society and a nature separated from science and technology in the making,[2] the belief in "Nature" or "Society" as the cause of the settlement of controversies between actors, is the product of the diffusion model. The translation model gives a very different picture (Latour, 1987).

The Nonmodern Constitution

By means of translation the networks create all kinds of new mixtures of forms of being, the so-called hybrids of nature and culture. In debates about the world, three repertoires are used: one about facts (scientific knowledge of nature), one about power (politics in society), and one about language (the discourse that gained independence from nature and from society). Through concealing the connections between those facts, power and language, and by splitting processes of translation and purification, the modern Constitution is created, a constitution where nature and society are two distinct zones; where objects and subjects become dichotomized (Latour, 1993). The modern Constitution denies the production and the proliferation of hybrids, simultaneously allowing them to expand. Latour says that as soon as we study in detail the production of these hybrids as well as the way they are being eliminated, we will notice that we have never been modern (Latour, 1993).

That's why Latour proposes that we are *nonmodern;* and that there is a need to study the world from a symmetrical starting point in order to make official what the modernists have always denied. That means to give representation to the undividable *quasi-objects* and *quasi-subjects*, the hybrids of nature and society. It than becomes clear that nature and society are the result of a continuous collective process of mediation and translation. That also opens up the possibility "to replace the clandestine proliferation of hybrids by their regulated and commonly agreed upon production" (Latour, 1993, p. 142). Hybrids then can become matters of democratic debate and democratic decision making (Latour, 2004b).

In the nonmodern Constitution, which is also called the *new* or the *ecological* Constitution, the collective of humans and nonhumans (a new name for the network, the heir to the old nature and the old society which were divided) is given room to compose a common world (Latour, 2004b). In this new Constitution the indisputable matters of *fact* from the old Constitution will always first be disputable matters of *concern*, because it is acknowledged that all beings are manufactured and are part of a public life where humans and nonhumans become associated. In the new Constitution the sciences can be made compatible with democracy (Latour, 2004b, 2005a).

A Sociology of Associations

In order to follow what is being assembled in the collective and what kind of associations are made between heterogeneous elements, a sociology that will trace these associations is needed. Latour proposes a sociology of associations as a resumption of the sociology of the social in order to do that. The sociology of the social seeks to explain all kinds of activities by the "social" or by "society," where according to Latour the explanation is confused with what should be explained (Latour, 2005b). A sociology of associations as a synonym for ANT, and it follows the actors themselves while they are associating and moving.

As mentioned earlier such a sociology feeds off controversies about "*what* this universe is made of" (Latour, 2005b, p. 21).[3] The sociology of associations is constructivist theory, not to be confused as Latour (2005b) warns with social constructivism—and especially not confused with the meaning assigned to social constructivism in the critique that came after the notion the "social construction of scientific facts" had been used. This expression has been misunderstood as meaning that scientific facts were not real, could be made up, or were not true. No such meanings were ever implied by ANT when speaking about the construction of facts. "Unwittingly, constructivism had become a synonym of its opposite number: deconstruction" (Latour, 2005b, p. 92). Latour reclaims the term *constructivism*—in *Reassembling the Social* (2005) he does the same with relativism—strongly linking it to an "*increase* in realism" (Latour, 2005b, p. 92) and argues that these have been synonyms all along:

> When we say that a fact is constructed, we simply mean that we account for the solid objective reality by mobilizing various entities whose assemblage could fail; "social constructivism" means, on the other hand, that we replace what this reality is made of with some other stuff, the social in which it is "really" built.... To bring constructivism back on its feet it's enough to see that once social means again association, the whole idea of a building made of social stuff vanishes. (pp. 91–92)

Relevance for Public Relations

Latour never writes about public relations or the role of public relations people in the collective. He seems to refer to it once when he is explaining the different loops in the circulatory system of scientific facts; a more detailed description of the translation process done by scientists. He proposes to call the fourth loop in this process *public representation*, after the loops of mobilization of the world, autonomization, and the building of alliances, "if we can free this expression from the stigma associated with PR" (Latour, 1999, p. 105). This reference to public relations activities and public relations practitioners seems simultaneously to set public relations apart from public representation as part of the translation process. In the theory of Latour, public relations therefore means public representation. Although he also almost never pays explicit attention to processes of mass communication or the role of journalists in the translation process, this public representation is described as a very important loop for scientists because the other three loops largely depend on it. "Thus," Latour (1999) says, "far from being a marginal appendage of science, this loop too is part and parcel of the fabric of facts and cannot be left to educational theorists and students of media" (p. 106).

These remote remarks about public relations and public representation might be the reason why Latour's theories are almost completely ignored by public relations theorists and practitioners with the exception of Sommerville (1999). When actor-network theory meets public relations, Sommerville has suggested that, new perspectives may open up in public relations theory, especially by resisting and disputing some presuppositions in the current public relations theories and by including nonhuman actors or actants, which are being ignored in public relations (Sommerville, 1999).

Latour does write quite a lot about other actors in organizations though. Apart from scientists and engineers, CEOs and other people with managerial tasks frequently appear in his studies (e.g., Latour, 1987, 1996). That might be the reason that the theories of Latour have been used more frequently by scholars of organizational communication, especially by the so-called Montreal School and its most prominent representative, James R. Taylor. Latourian concepts such as translation, interobjectivity, and mediation are here used to theorize about "organizations-in-communication" (Cooren & Taylor, 1997; Taylor, Cooren, Giroux, & Robichaud, 1996).

In the rest of this section we will look at public relations through the lens of actor-network theory and explore the question what the relevance of Latour's theory might be for public relations. First we will look at ANT as an analytical perspective to study the practice of public relations, followed by some considerations about the presuppositions in the normal public relations practice and theory in relation to ANT. At the same time questions will be raised about the role of public relations in the collective.

Studying Public Relations in Action

First and foremost ANT can be considered as an analytical perspective to study public relations people in action on the analogy of following scientists and engineers through society. At the end of his book *Science in Action* (1987) Latour warns that "bureaucrats, managers, paper-shufflers or, in brief, this tertiary sector that completely dwarfs the size of technoscience" (Latour, 1987, p. 255) should not be despised and should be studied using the same methods that were applied to the study of scientists and engineers. By technoscience he means science and technology in the making (see note 3), which in his later work is referred to as "the sciences." The bureaucrats, managers, and paper-shufflers, as Latour ironically calls them, should be studied with the same method as well because "a stable state of society is produced by the multifarious administrative sciences exactly like a stable interpretation of black holes is provided by astronomy" (Latour, 1987, p. 256). The administrative networks should therefore not be overlooked in the role they play in the construction of facts and in the stabilizing or destabilizing of the sciences. Their position seems to have strengthened since the early 1980s, a time wherein science has invaded our daily lives; science and technology are everywhere. They have become banalized and are even better connected to all kinds of other elements in the networks than before, as Latour stated in an interview with the Science and Education section of the Dutch newspaper *NRC Handelsblad* (Gewoner, 2007).

Since the early 1980s, the administrative networks have increasingly been populated with public relations people, public information managers, communication managers, or whatever names they give themselves (Cottle, 2003; van Ruler & Elving, 2006). Of all these public relations and communication people we can ask the question as to what they contribute to the construction of reality in the collectives they participate in. What associations do they form? With what kind of humans and nonhumans do public relations people associate themselves and why? Answers to these kinds of questions about the relative position of public relations people in the collective could be found with a research program using participant observation as a methodology and ANT as an analytical perspective. Although Latour stresses that ANT is not suitable to be applied to all kinds of situations, it can be used as a perspective to study the traces, movements, and results produced by all kinds of human and nonhuman actors (Latour, 2005a).

Studying public relations from an ANT perspective first of all moves debates and controversies about social issues to the heart of public relations research. After all, public relations people often play an important role in these debates, on stage or behind the scenes, as research has shown. We can think of environmental issues (Meznar & Nigh, 1995), the famous battle between Shell and Greenpeace about the Brent Spar (Tsukas, 1999), medicine (Anderson, 2001; Berger, 1999), and biotechnology (Kleinman & Kloppenburg, 1991). An ANT perspective on these kinds of discussions can show that they are about science and technology in the making, that they are controversies about "*what* this universe is made off" (Latour, 2005a, p. 21). As we have seen earlier, ANT feeds off those kind of controversies (Latour, 2005a) and can also make a good starting point for analyzing the part public relations people play in these controversies.

Second, an ANT perspective can help to shed a light on the way tensions between the interests of different actors are created and handled by public relations people. The tensions between partisan and nonpartisan interests are difficult to overcome for many in the field of public relations. That is why "ethical relativism is a common moral stance among practitioners" (Pearson, 1989, p. 67). Since the objective moral standards are not to be known or do not exist, ethical relativism or pragmatism seems the only frame of reference for public relations actions. Pearson (1993) suggested a way to move beyond this relativism; focus on the ethical dimensions of the communication processes themselves with concepts like coorientation, communication rules, and the idea of communication symmetry (Pearson, 1989; Van Osch, 2003). An ANT perspective on public relations can also help to move beyond the ethical relativist position. This perspective will make visible the construction of partisan and nonpartisan interests and the way they are brought into the collective. It will show the role of public relations people in those construction processes of the inside and outside boundaries of the issue at stake.

Third, studies from an ANT perspective will show how public relations people create and handle public representation; how do public relations actors work with concepts like openness, public opinion, and democratic decision making? These classical concepts of public relations when connected with working in the public sphere (van der Meiden & Fauconnier, 1994) can take a central position in research on public relations (again). An ANT perspective therefore connects with the reflective communication management view as proposed by van Ruler and Verčič (2005). The view takes a constructionist position in looking at society and communication, defining communication management (here taken as a synonym of public relations) as being engaged in:

> [C]onstructing society by making sense of situations, creating appropriate meanings out of them and looking for acceptable frameworks and enactments...concerning itself with maximizing, optimizing, or satisfying the process of meaning creation, using informational, persuasive, relational and discursive interventions to solve managerial problems by co producing societal (public) legitimation. (p. 266)

Actor network theory can help to extend the theory of reflective communication by taking a microsociological perspective to study public relations people in action.

Five Types of Controversies

Tracing associations is the main task of a scholar working from an ANT perspective and that can be done by asking questions about five types of controversies that take place. Latour calls them the five major uncertainties (Latour, 2005a): the nature of groups, the nature of actions, the nature of objects, the nature of facts, and the nature of the study itself. In the following section the five uncertainties will be discussed in general in combination with empirical examples. These examples are taken from a societal debate in the 1990s in The Netherlands. The debate was about how the Dutch should handle the external risk problem of the major international airport, Schiphol in Amsterdam. External risk is the risk that people living in the vicinity of an airport run of becoming victims of an aircraft accident (Verhoeven, 1996). This case study shows very well that societal debates are very often controversies about what reality is made of and the formation of a collective around the issue at stake. Latour's sources of uncertainty will be exemplified with this case study.

The first source of uncertainty is the *nature of groups*; there are no fixed groups, there is only group formation. On the construction site of the nonmodern or new Constitution all kinds of members of the collective assemble and contribute to the process of composing the common world. There are contributions from the sciences, from the politicians, from economists, and from moralists, all performing the same tasks now[4] instead of performing the different tasks that were attributed to them in the modern or old Constitution. In the new Constitution reality becomes represented after, speaking in a political metaphor, two *representative powers* have been able to do their work: the so-called *upper house* by articulating "with how many are we in the collective" and the so-called *lower house* by articulating "who are we" in the collective (Latour, 2004b, p. 181). In the case of external risk around Schiphol the group formation started in 1989 when a small group of politicians, people from the aviation industry, and some engineers began working on this question. In the following years this small group gradually extended to include scientists, other experts, commercial researchers, more politicians, members of parliament, more industrialists, economists, journalists, medical doctors, representatives of nongovernmental organizations, surviving relatives, people from action committees, and pressure groups and individuals (Verhoeven, 1996). These people together made up the common world of the risk of living close to a big airport. With regard to public relations, the question will be what the role of public relations people is in such a formation of different groups and of a collective: how do they contribute, are they group makers, group talkers, or group holders? Who do they enroll in the groups that are formed, or are they themselves enrolled in certain group formation processes? Public relations people could be considered one of the mediators in the group formation process and the question can be asked as to what they are mediating in these processes; what do they transform and how are they themselves being transformed (Latour, 2005a)?

The second source of uncertainty is the *nature of actions*; who are the acting agents and when they act, who else is acting? In the sociology of association, action cannot be taken over by a social force, as in the sociology of the social; actors are made to act by many others, by the associations that are produced. In the case of external risk around Schiphol associations were produced by many means. For example, by creating steering committees and working groups that meet to discuss the issue, formulate research questions, political solutions, and write reports. Action is also taken through setting up and reporting on several laboratory studies regarding the risks and social-psychological studies into people's perception of risks. Other actions included the creation of leaflets and newspaper articles about the issue and so on. After a few years the actors not only are connected in their communication at meetings and debates but also through the texts that the emerging collective produces around external risk (Verhoeven, 1996). The central question about public relations here will be how public relations people are made to act and what kinds of other actors they force to act. How do they produce associations with other actors?

The third source of uncertainty is the *nature of objects*; the central questions in this controversy are what type of agencies are participating and can objects also have agency . It is about the role of nonhumans and about symmetry. As we have seen, not only humans act, nonhumans can be made to act as well, and we have to be symmetric in the analysis. Latour (2005a) stresses that ANT is not to be understood as "some absurd 'symmetry between humans and nonhumans'. To be symmetric...simply means *not* to impose a priori some spurious *asymmetry* among human intentional action and a material world of causal relations" (p. 76).

In a case of external risk, objects like runways and their position in the landscape, houses, and the layout of the districts around the Amsterdam airport, and obviously all kinds of aircraft can be taken into account as objects. Objects like these have played an important role in the debate about external risk, even having been central in making the debate a controversy. This is so, not only because in 1992 during the debate a Boeing 747 crashed in one of the Amsterdam suburbs, but also because the external risk debate was being connected to the future of the airport and the future layout of the runway system (Verhoeven, 1996). In that sense objects do have agency and can be seen as part of the network. The central question here will be if, and if so, how public relations people produce associations with objects. What is their role in making objects talk, for example?

The fourth source of uncertainty is the *nature of facts*: what scientific facts about nature (and also about society) are constructed and how did they become facts? In an ANT perspective the matters of fact of the old Constitution are replaced by matters of concern of the new Constitution (Latour, 2004a, 2005a). These matters of concern are "highly uncertain and loudly disputed, these real, objective atypical and above all, *interesting* agencies are taken not exactly as object but rather as *gatherings*" (Latour, 2005a, p. 114). The traces of these matters of concern are everywhere since scientific facts are no longer only made in laboratories, "it is hard to follow a course of action anywhere in industrial societies without bumping into one of their outcomes" (Latour, 2005a, p. 119). Not only their outcomes are to be found everywhere, also their production is often debated publicly in intense "controversies over 'natural things'" (Latour, 2005a, p. 119). Defining external risk started off as in the old Constitution: some engineers were asked to calculate the risk in the standardized measures of risk calculation: individual risk (the chance an individual on the ground dies due to an air crash) and group risk (the chance that a group of people on the ground die due to an air crash). After the plane crash external risk became a matter of concern, with the aircraft in the middle of the discussion. New and additional laboratory studies were done and after the societal and political discussion only the individual risks became facts; the calculations of group risks were considered too uncertain by most of the collective. Group risk was excluded from political policy making. Individual risk was considered to be the factual external risk, and on the basis of that safety zones were installed and 17 houses in the vicinity of the airport had to be demolished (Verhoeven, 1996).

The fifth source of uncertainty in an ANT account is the *uncertainty about the study itself*. The texts produced by social scientists, also by sociologists of associations, are "the social scientist's laboratory" (Latour, 2005a, p. 127) and they can fail like experiments in the natural sciences often do too. Since in the sociology of associations the word *social* is defined as "a trail of associations between heterogeneous elements" (Latour, 2005a, p. 5), the social is a trace. A good ANT text is, according to Latour, a text that "traces a network" (Latour, 2005a, p. 128). A network is, as we have seen, not a thing out there but a concept, a tool to help describe something. A good ANT account is therefore a story about actors that are doing something, that are treated as mediators and thereby making the social visible by showing the movements of the mediators. An ANT study of public relations actors should do the same.

These five uncertainties, the nature of groups, of actions, of objects, of facts, and of social science are debated by actors and as the contro-

versy ends the uncertainties are stabilized in a collective. Often this stabilization is temporary until a new controversy starts. After stabilizing
the facts of external risk around Schiphol airport, about three years
later a new controversy started but now the problem of external risk
became defined as a health problem (Vasterman, 2004). In order to be
able to show how this stabilization in the collective comes into being,
the ANT scholar, Latour says, has to make three corrective moves in
addition to examining the controversies about the five uncertainties.
The ANT scholar has to start with keeping the social landscape completely flat[5] in order to be able to see what is being located where;[6] "to
relocate the global so as the break down the automatism that leads from
interaction to 'Context'" (Latour, 2005a, p. 172). That is the first corrective move. In the second corrective move, the local will be redistributed
by transforming every local site that's built by the actors into a provi-
sional endpoint of some other local site. Third, "we will connect the sites
revealed by the two former moves, highlighting the various *vehicles* that
make up the definition of the social understood as association" (Latour,
2005a, p. 172). In that way there will be enough room for the collective
to collect itself and enough space for the ANT scholar to follow what the
actors are doing.

The Basic Principles of ANT and the Study of Public Relations

An ANT perspective on studying public relations practices not only
means to follow public relations people in action; it means especially to
accept the basic principles of ANT, most of them being incommensu-
rable with the functionalistic and normative perspectives that are dominant in the field. In the following section a few of those principles will
be discussed.

The most important principle is that ANT is a *constructivist* theory;
it starts, as we have seen, from the premise that phenomena have to be
explained by the process by which they are made. Concepts like nature,
society, the social, but also facts, truth, being right or being wrong are
the result and not the cause of the settlement of controversies. The stabilization of the uncertainties explains what a collective holds for a fact
and what not. Furthermore in the collective not only humans, but also
nonhumans can be made to act, this possible role for nonhumans is
an important part of ANT in contrast with functionalistic and normative accounts of public relations where nonhumans are not considered
problematic or are ignored. As is the central role of science and technology, an ANT account of public relations places the collective process of
constructing reality by the sciences, politicians, economists, and moralists together at the heart of studying public relations. Central questions
then are what role public relations people play as accomplices in the

construction of reality, why they are playing such a role, and how they did acquire their role in the network?

The *notion of diffusion* often used in public relations theory and practice (Rogers, 2003) loses much of its meaning in an ANT account of public relations. Interest, facts, machines, to name a few examples, are not a given to be diffused to different target groups; instead the interest, facts, and machines are the results of *translation processes*, as are the target groups that are said to resist or embrace the new ideas or inventions. We can ask by means of what kind of translations public relations people became enrolled in the networks and what kind of translations do they use themselves?

The same goes for the *notion of intermediaries*, also often used in public relations theory and practice, not only as the means of producing the social, but also as a conceptualization of all kinds of different communication media. One of the main differences between the sociology of associations and the sociology of the social lies in the conceptualization of the *means* to produce the social: are they to be seen as *mediators* or as *intermediaries*? In the sociology of the social those means are often taken as intermediaries while in ANT they are taken as mediators. An intermediary can be defined as a black box; it transports meaning without transforming it and the input equals the output. Mediators on the contrary, "transform, translate, distort, and modify the meaning they are supposed to carry" (Latour, 2005b, p. 39) and can therefore not be seen as a black box where the input predicts the output. The contrast between them is big, as Latour (2005b) says:

> To sum up the contrast in a rudimentary way, the sociologists of the social believe in one type of social aggregates, few mediators, and many intermediaries; for ANT, there is no preferable type of social aggregates, there exists endless number of mediators, and when those are transformed into faithful intermediaries it is not the rule, but a rare exception that has to be accounted for by some extra work—usually by the mobilization of even more mediators! (p. 40)

In an ANT perspective there are many more *mediators* than there are intermediaries; transforming, translating, distorting, and modifying meaning, as mediators do, seems to be the rule rather than the exception. The question could be raised when do public relations people have the position as mediators and when do they have the position as intermediaries in the networks. The same question, for that matter, can be raised about the position of journalists and other actors in the realm of the mass media in the collective. How and when do they mediate? Are they ever an intermediary?

Finally in an ANT perspective of public relations, the *nonmodern* Constitution has to be acknowledged as opposed to the modern Constitution where many of the standard public relations theorists work. The nonmodern Constitution has to be accepted as one of the basic principles to analyze the construction processes done by the collective, with an open eye for the hybrids, the quasi-objects, and the quasi subjects. What is the role of public relations people on the *construction site* of the nonmodern Constitution? Do they play a role, and if so what role, in, for example, the articulation of the propositions made by the sciences, the politicians, the economists, and the moralists? What is their role in public life where humans and nonhumans become associated in the debates about matters of concern? And last but not least what is their role in the democratic debate and the democratic decision making about the sciences? All these questions can be raised and answered in an ANT perspective on public relations.

Conclusions

The sociology of associations or actor-network theory from Bruno Latour has, as an analytical perspective, a lot to offer to public relations theory and practice compared to the functionalistic and normative theories that are more common in public relations. First of all it promises a more complex and a more detailed insight in the practice of public relations and its role in the collective. On top of that the basic principles of ANT give room for a more realistic picture of the construction site of the nonmodern Constitution where public relations practitioners play their part in the construction of reality, associating themselves with other humans and nonhumans. That will also be the main relevance of this social theoretical perspective for practitioners; a better or a more real understanding of their own acting. It moves science and technology and controversies about related issues to the heart of the analysis of public relations activities. This could give scholars and practitioners a better insight in how public relations activities contribute to the construction of reality, in controversies and after closing the controversies. In such a perspective public relations is not perceived as something that follows strategy or already determined policies of organizations; it will show that public relations and communication activities are constituent to these strategies and policies. It will also show the political dimension of public relations activities and could shed a light on how practitioners create circumstances to engineer consent (Bernays, 1955; Ewen, 1996) while they participate in a democratic process. After all, an ANT approach could make public relations more reflective and studies of public relations more real, and, might help to move the discipline beyond ethical relativism.

As already stated, ANT cannot be used directly or be applied to practical situations, but for the theoretical development of the field it can generate many questions for empirical research; for participant observation of the many "communication people" working in all kinds of administrative networks. Research like that can be one of the elaborations of the perspective of reflective communication as proposed by van Ruler and Verčič (2005) a constructivist perspective away from the functionalistic and managerial perspectives so common in the field, and into the direction of studying public relations practices in the public sphere. In Latourian terms that will mean following public relations people in action to trace the associations and the type of connections they are making with humans and nonhumans and the role they play in the formation of a collective with a shared definition of reality and of a common world.

Notes

1. The concept of nonhuman only has meaning, says Latour, in the "difference between the pair 'human-nonhuman' and the subject-object dichotomy" (Latour, 1999, p. 308). By using the pair human-nonhuman instead of subject-object and by focusing on the changing and developing associations of humans and nonhumans in a network Latour bypasses the political war to make a hard distinction between a world of subjects on one side and a world of objects on the other side.

2. Science and technology in the making is used here as a substitution for the term *technoscience*. In *Science in Action* (1987) Latour distinguishes between technoscience to "describe all the elements tied to the scientific contents no matter how dirty, unexpected or foreign they seem, and the expression 'science and technology', in quotation marks, to designate *what is kept of technoscience* once all the trials of responsibility have been settled" (p. 174).

3. A sociology of associations examines five major uncertainties: the nature of groups, the nature of actions, the nature of objects, the nature of facts, and the nature of the science of the social itself. To give the collective enough room to collect itself and not confusing the already formed society with the construction site of the new Constitution, the ANT scholar has to make three corrective moves in addition (see the paragraph "Studying Public Relations in Action").

4. Seven tasks or functions are identified: perplexity, consultation, hierarchy, institution, the separation of powers, the scenarization of the whole, and the power to follow through. See chapters 3 and 4 of *Politics of Nature* for a description and an explanation of these tasks (Latour, 2004a).

5. Where Latour explains this, in *Reassembling the Social* (2005b), he advises readers to "consult online Latour and Hermant, *Paris the Invisible City*" (p. 172).

6. This refers to the micro/macrodebate in the social sciences. Latour does

not present ANT as a compromise to solve the micro/macro debate or the actor/system debate in the social sciences. The debate addresses the question whether the actor is in a system or whether the system is in an actor. Latour suggests deciding that it is impossible to stay at one of those two sites for a long period, and therefore the social landscape should be made flat to enable observers to see what dichotomies between micro and macro or actor and system are being constructed.

References

Anderson, W. (2001). The media battle between Celebrex and Vioxx: Influencing media coverage but not content. *Public Relations Review, 27,* 449–460.

Berger, B. K. (1999). The Halcion affair: Public relations and the construction of ideological world view. *Journal of Public Relations Research, 11*(3), 185–203.

Bernays, E. L. (Ed.). (1955). *The engineering of consent.* Norman, OK: University of Oklahoma Press.

Callon, M. (1986). Some elements of a sociology of translation domestication of the scallops and the fishermen of St Brieux Bay. In J. Law (Ed.), *Power, action and belief: A new sociology of knowledge?* (pp. 196–229). London: Routledge & Kegan Paul.

Callon, M., & Latour, B. (1981). Unscrewing the big leviathans: How do actors macrostructure reality? In K. Knorr & A. Cicourel (Eds.), *Advances in social theory and methodology: Toward an integration of macro and micro sociologies* (pp. 277–303). London: Routledge.

Cooren, F., & Taylor, J. R. (1997). Organization as an effect of mediation: Redefining the link between organization and communication. *Communication Theory, 7*(3), 219–260.

Cottle, S. (2003). News, public relations and power: Mapping the field. In S. Cottle (Ed.), *News public relations and power* (pp. 3–24). London: Sage.

Ewen, S. (1996). *PR! A social history of spin.* New York: Basic Books.

Gewoner, maar niet begrijpelijker. Bruno Latour over het belang van wetenschap in de huidige cultuur [More common, but not more understandable: Bruno Latour about the significance of science in contemporary culture]. (2007, February 24). *NRC Handelsblad,* p. 6.

Hagendijk, R. P. (1990). Structuration theory, constructivism, and scientific change. In S. E. Gozzens & Th. F. Gieryn (Eds.), *Theories of science in society* (pp. 43–69). Bloomington: Indiana University Press.

Kleinman, D. L., & Kloppenburg, J. Jr.(1991). Aiming for the discursive ground: Monsanto and the biotechnology controversy. *Sociological Forum, 6*(3), 427–447.

Latour, B. (1983). Give me a laboratory and I will raise the world. In K. Knorr-Cetina & M. Mulkay (Eds.), *Science observed: Perspectives on the social study of science* (pp. 141–170). London: Sage.

Latour, B. (1987). *Science in action: How to follow scientists and engineers through society.* Cambridge, MA: Harvard University Press.

Latour, B. (1988). *The pasteurization of France* (A. Sheridan & J. Law, Trans.). Cambridge, MA: Harvard University Press. (Original work published in 1984)

Latour, B. (1993). *We have never been modern* (C. Porter, Trans.). Hertfordshire, UK: Harvester Wheatsheaf. (Original work published in 1991)

Latour, B. (1999). *Pandora's hope: Essays on the reality of science studies.* Cambridge, MA: Harvard University Press.

Latour, B. (2004a). *La fabrique du droit. Une ethnographie du Conseil D'État* [The fabrication of law]. Paris: La Découverte.

Latour, B. (2004b). Politics of nature. How to bring the sciences into democracy (C. Porter, Trans.). Cambridge, MA: Harvard University Press.

Latour, B. (2005a). From Realpolitik to Dingpolitik or how to make things public. In B. Latour & P. Weibel (Eds.), *Making things public: Atmospheres of democracy* (pp. 14–41). Cambridge, MA: The MIT Press.

Latour, B. (2005b). *Reassembling the social: An introduction to actor-network-theory.* Oxford, UK: Oxford University Press.

Latour, B. (2006). *Paris invisible city.* Retrieved March 1, 2007, from http://www.bruno-latour.fr/virtual/index.html#

Latour, B., & Woolgar, S. (1979). *Laboratory life: The social construction of scientific facts.* London: Sage.

Law, J. (1986). On the methods of long distance control: Vessels, navigations and the Portuguese route to India. In J. Law (Ed.), *Power, action and belief: A new sociology of knowledge?* (pp. 234–263). London: Routledge & Kegan Paul.

Lee, N., & Brown, S. (1994). Otherness and the actor-network theory: The undiscovered continent. *American Behavioural Scientist, 37*(6), 772–790.

Meznar, M. B., & Nigh, D. (1995). Buffer or bridge? Environmental and organizational determinants of public affairs activities in American firms. *Academy of Management Journal, 38*(4), 975–996.

Pearson, R. (1989). Beyond ethical relativism in public relations: Coorientation, rules, and the idea of communication symmetry. *Public Relations Research Annual, 1,* 67–87.

Pinch, T. J., & Bijker, W. E. (1987). The social construction of facts and artifacts: or how the sociology of science and the sociology of technology might benefit each other. In T. J. Pinch & W. E. Bijker (Eds.), *The social construction of technological systems* (pp. 17–50). Cambridge, MA: MIT Press.

Rogers, E. M. (2003). *Diffusion of innovations.* New York: Free Press.

Roosen, P. (1997). The social construction of mountain bikes: technology and postmodernity in the cycle industry. *Social Studies of Science, 23*(3), 479–513.

Sommerville, I. (1999). Agency versus identity: actor-network theory meets public relations. *Corporate Communications: An international journal, 4*(1), 6–13.

Taylor, J. R., Cooren, F., Giroux, N., & Robichaud, D. (1996). The communicational basis of organization: Between the conversation and the text. *Communication Theory, 6*(1), 1–39.

Tsukas, H. (1999). David and Goliath in the risk society: Making sense of the conflict between Shell and Greenpeace in the North Sea. *Organization, 6*(3), 499–528.

van der Meiden, A., & Fauconnier, G. (1994). *Public relations.* Groningen: Martinus Nijhoff Uitgevers.

van Osch, D. C. (2003). Co-oriëntatie: truc of troef? Symmetrische communicatie als managementinstrument.[Coorientation: trick or trump? Symmetrical communication as a management instrument]. Alphen aan de Rijn, The Netherlands: Kluwer.

van Ruler, B., & Verčič, D. (2005). Reflective communication management: Future ways for public relations research In *Communication Yearbook 29* (pp. 239–273). New Brunswick, NJ: Translation Books.

van Ruler, B., & Elving, W. (2006). *Trendonderzoek Communicatieberoepspraktijk 2005–2006* [Trend research communication professionals 2005–2006]. Netherlands: Amsterdam School of Communications Research (ASCoR).

Vasterman, P. (2004). *Mediahype.* Amsterdam: Aksant.

Verhoeven. P. (1996). *Strijd rond technowetenschap: Metanarratief als concept voor de analyse van technowetenschappelijke debatten op basis van de empirische case study "Risico rond Schiphol"* [Fighting technoscience: Metanarrative as a concept for the analysis of debates around technoscience on the basis of the empirical case study; "Risk around Schiphol"]. Unpublished master's thesis, University of Amsterdam, Amsterdam, The Netherlands.

Life and Work of Bruno Latour

Bruno Latour (1947–) was born in Beaune, Burgundy in France. He studied philosophy and anthropology and is now professor at Sciences Po Paris, after being professor at the Centre de Sociologie de l'Innovation at the École Nationale Supérieure des mines in Paris from 1986 to 2006. Central to his work is the study of scientists and engineers at work and controversies about scientific and technological questions in democratic societies.

His most important works, in which he proposes his theoretical perspectives and which are translated into English, are *Laboratory Life: The Construction of Scientific Facts* (1979) in cooperation with Steve Woolgar, *Science in Action* (1987), *We Have Never Been Modern* (1993), *Pandora's Hope: Essays on the Reality of Science Studies* (1999), *The Politics of Nature* (2004b), and *Reassembling the Social* (2005b). Other important works describing empirical research into specific cases or essays are *The Pasteurization of France* (1988), in which Louis Pasteur plays a central role, *Aramis or the Love of Technology* (1996), about the rise and fall of the guided-transportation system Aramis intended for Paris.

Some crucial studies using an actor-network approach have been done in the field of technology studies; for example, the study of the development of the penny-farthing bicycle by Pinch and Bijker (1987) and the study of the development of the mountain bike by Roosen (1993).

In 2002 and 2005 Latour was curator of two major expositions in the ZKM (Center for Art and Media Technology) in Karlsruhe, Germany: *Iconoclash* (Latour & Weibel, 2002) and *Making Things Public* (Latour & Weibel, 2005).

In addition, Latour has published many chapters in books about science studies and social theory, books and articles in French about the consequences of science studies for other social scientific topics; for example, *La Fabrique du Droit* (Latour, 2004a) and an electronic book, *Paris Invisible City* (Latour, 2006).

Chapter 10

On Luhmann

Contingency, Risk, Trust, and Reflection[1]

Susanne Holmström

Abstract

Niklas Luhmann's epistemological sociology is counterintuitive, relentless in its abstraction and scope, and empties society of human beings as well as any teleology or content apart from the highly improbable ability to reproduce itself. Paradoxically, exactly these qualities constitute the empirical sensitivity to the interrelation between organization and society in today's hypercomplex society. Luhmann never theorized on public relations; yet his theories enable identification of frames for understanding public relations in relation to society's overall coordination processes. Contemporary society apparently tries to solve problems activated by the blind reflexivity of modernization by activating reflective forms of coordination.

According to Niklas Luhmann, to fulfill its task of analyzing empirical problems, sociology requires a theoretically founded description of society with sufficient complexity to grasp contemporary society. From his first works in 1964 to his death in 1998, he reformulates sociology by developing a comprehensive, universal theory with flexible networks of interrelated concepts that can be used to describe the most diverse social phenomena. His theory recognizes all knowledge—including itself—as contingent and forces observations to constantly take into account that reality is reconstructed in the observation and that the way this observation is conditioned determines how reality appears.

The fundamental premise of Luhmann's theory is to dissociate itself from anthropocentric understandings of society which see the individual as the ultimate reference. Society is constituted by subjectless communications, vanishing events in time that, in producing the networks that produce them, constitute emergent orders of temporalized complexity in continuously changing self-referential social systems. Contemporary society is seen as a complex system of communication that has differentiated itself into a network of interconnected social subsystems through which the world is recognized. Society lacks any "supersystem" to ensure coordination, let alone direct it teleologically to a better future.

We are presented with a "recursive universe" characterized by disorder, nonlinear complexity, and unpredictability. Evolutionary dynamics are driven only by the compulsion of communicative processes to continue themselves. This approach turns traditional notions of systems upside down—in relation to machine metaphors as well as to teleological thinking, conservative, legitimizing, or functionalist ideologies.

Communication, Observation, and Distinction

To grasp contemporary society, Luhmann questions most intuitive notions and radically reconstructs concepts such as society, communication, observation, reflection, trust, and system. An introduction to his comprehensive theoretical groundwork will always be extremely reductive. Key concepts are *communication* and *observation* based on *distinction*. They are the social mechanisms within which highly complex systems are reproducing, and, as Baecker observes, "Though this is a very simple and 'mathematical' account of communication, it leads to an envisioning of its most subtle complexities since we now begin to look into the fabrication of the set of possibilities in social situations" (2001, p. 66).

Communication: The Circular Dynamics

Communication consists of the social processes constituting anything social—society, organization, interactions—and the concept is not confined to linguistic processes. For instance, payment processes are seen as communication. Luhmann defines communication as a synthesis of three selections: information (a selection from the specific referential horizon), utterance (a selection from various forms of expression), and understanding (the observation of the distinction between utterance and information): "Communication grasps *something* out of the actual referential horizon that it itself constitutes and leaves *other things* aside. Communication is the processing of selection" (Luhmann, 1984/1995b, p. 140). Understanding is not the purpose of communication. Like in any autopoietic (self-reproducing) system, the processes are primarily concerned with their own continuation. Understanding simply implies that the third selection activates further communications and thus continues the system's autopoiesis (self-reproduction).

Communication takes on its own life in closed, self-referential communication circuits—social systems—and is guided solely by its own horizon of meaning, not the intentions and hermeneutic capacities of a communicating subject. Accordingly, meaning is defined as communication's perpetually recursively self-constructed horizon of possibilities for connection, as "the continual actualization of potentialities" (Luhmann, 1984/1995b, p. 65) which is constantly changed by communication.

Meaning is "the universal medium of all psychic and social, all consciously and communicatively operating systems" (Luhmann, 1997a, p. 51). Both types of systems are self-referentially closed and operate simultaneously without interfering with each other at the level of their respective autopoiesis, yet they are structurally coupled. No social system could exist without the environment of psychic systems, and correspondingly, as Knodt observes, "a consciousness deprived of society would be incapable of developing beyond the more rudimentary level of perception" (1995, p. xxvii). The interrelation between thoughts and communications activates a complex coevolution; however, it is not linear. The communicative resonance provoked by a psychic system is always self-referentially conditioned by the social system, and vice versa.

For Luhmann, the intransparency of consciousness from the viewpoint of the social is not an obstacle to be removed but the very condition that activates communication. Systems rationality is about establishing and stabilizing structures of expectation in an otherwise infinite, immense world by reducing complexity and thus rendering probable communication: "Every social contact is understood as a system, up to and including society as the inclusion of all possible contacts" (Luhmann, 1984/1995b, p. 15). The limits of society are established by the limits of communication. Organizations exist only as long as decisions—the specific communicative processes constituting organizations—are being made.

Luhmann's concept of communication sharpens the focus on the self-referential circular dynamics of social processes which are means as well as ends. This apparently simple—but counterintuitive—dynamics is the basic frame for empirical analyses based on Luhmann.

Observation and Distinction: The Empirical Object of Analysis

With the concepts of *observation* and *distinction* Luhmann develops the epistemological position and clarifies the *distinction theoretical approach*. Since Luhmann held that communication could not be observed directly, only inferred, the object of systems theoretical analyses are *observations*. Observations are part of communicative processes by generating the information which is uttered. Consequently, with Luhmann we talk of *observers* where action theoretical approaches talk of *actors*.

The term observations refer neither to human beings nor to sight, but are social operations. Observation always distinguishes something as distinct from something else; otherwise the observer would be unable to indicate what it is that he or she wishes to observe (Luhmann, 1993b). The formula of observation is based on the logical calculus of Spencer-Brown (1969/1979): "We cannot make an indication without drawing a distinction" (p. 1)—for example, the distinction "system/environment" where system is indicated as distinct from the unmarked counterconcept of environment. When the same phenomenon can always be observed with different distinctions, and since the distinction determines what the observer observes—then the distinction becomes decisive to any observation. Analyzing public relations processes using the basic distinctions of "social/psychical" and "system/environment" will lead to observations of something else than analyses based on the distinctions between "system/life world" or "particular interest/common interest." Different distinctions give different meaning to the apparently same indication. For instance, the indication of "communication" will mean something different depending on whether the unmarked counterconcept is (1) discontinuation of society, (2) consciousness, or (3) "strategic action" (Habermas, 1981). In other words, empirical analyses have to look at both sides of the distinction: at the selection being selected and the set of possibilities from which the selection is made.

A system—whether a society or an organization—can observe and realize only according to the distinctions at its disposal; that is, its complexity. Consequently, *first*, as Luhmann observes:

> [A] system can see only what it can see, it cannot see what it cannot. Moreover, it cannot see that it cannot see this. For the system this is something concealed "behind" the horizon that, for it, has no "behind". What has been called the "cognized model" is the absolute reality to the system. (Luhmann 1986/1989, pp. 22–23)

Second, what it sees is reconstructed by the systems-specific operations. When information is brought into the system's communicative processes, it is recoded and changes its meaning as a systems-internal construction of a systems-external world. The sufferings of millions of Africans afflicted by AIDS cannot be observed directly by society, since they are not social, but organic and psychical processes. However, communication can thematize pain, disease, and poverty insofar as society has developed distinctions for observing such matters. Correspondingly, within society, social systems observe and reconstruct each other from each of their perspectives. For instance, the political system sees steering objects, news media reconstruct their environment as information, and business sees markets.

Like any other social system, organizations can observe only a segment of the world, depending on the complexity not of the world, but of the organization. The more complex, the better the organization is geared to recognize and relate to a turbulent environment. In order to continuously reduce world complexity, organizations have to develop their own complexity and open up to the environment in their observations. With Luhmann, organizations are closed in order to be open, open in order to be closed. If the open observation is not founded in a specific social filter, which is established exactly by means of the closed boundary, then there is nothing to guide the observation; the organization drowns in indeterminate complexity. It cannot separate itself from the environment. It cannot determine any premises for its decision processes—for instance whether being a business company or a humanitarian organization. They come to a halt. The organization dissolves.

So, the closed meaning boundaries have a vital function, and "When put under a pressure of selection, the system principally synchronizes itself with itself, however [it] can do this in forms that are more or less sensitive to the environment" (Luhmann, 2000c, p. 162). Consequently, in systems theory we can never talk of a linear causality and direct adjustment to the environment, only of a social system's adjustment to itself. Hence, the conditionality of an observation and the difference between the first order observation characterized as *reflexivity* and the second order observation of *reflection* become decisive to the analysis of contemporary ideals of organizational legitimization. *Reflexivity* implies a monocontextual, narcissistic perspective from within which applies distinctions blindly, and from where the organization takes its own worldview for given, takes what it sees to be the one reality, the only truth—and consequently conflicts blindly with different worldviews. In *reflection*, the organizational system sees itself as if from outside and reenters the distinction between system and environment within the system. "This higher layer of control is attained by social systems' orienting themselves to themselves—to themselves as different from their environments" (Luhmann, 1984/1995b, p. 455). The organization observes itself as an observer applying certain contingent distinctions, and further, it sees differently from other perspectives.

Consequently, reflection is the production of self-understanding in relation to the environment. So, where the reflexive organization is inattentive to the broader context and consequently to the unintended, often far reaching side-effects involved in its decisions, reflection enables the organization to understand itself in a larger, interdependent societal context and to develop self-restrictions out of consideration for its environment in order to secure its own independence and self-referential development (autopoiesis) in the long term.

The concepts of observation and distinction enable an extensive empirical sensitivity to the conflicts and constraints within which organizational legitimacy is embedded, and supply tools for analyzing and categorizing the ideal types of organizational legitimization.

Society's Differentiation

Based on his theory on social systems as unfolded in particular in his first main work *Social Systems* in 1984, Luhmann develops his theory on society in *Society's Society* (1997a). In Europe, since the 1600s a new form of primary societal differentiation gradually replaced stratification, which differentiates society into hierarchical layers. In the *functionally differentiated society*, the communicative processes of diverse functional systems are conditioned by specific *symbolic media* and *binary codes*.

The Luhmannian theory focuses on process more than on structure and does not claim a once-and-for-all differentiation of certain functional systems. Function does not—as for instance with Parsons (1951)—imply any legitimation but an analytical focus: a system's function is seen as an offer of meaning which is achieved by its specific reduction of the complexity of the world. Luhmann describes a principle which he demonstrates in several analyses of some of the more prominent functional systems; for example, politics (2000c), law (1969/1993a), science (1981/1990a), economics (1999), art (1995/2000a), mass media (1996/2000b), education (2002), and religion (2000c). The function of economy is identified as a reduction of scarcity, the medium as money, the binary code as "+/÷ pay, own," and the communicative processes as payments. In line with the theory's fundamental idea, profit is not an end but a means to the continuation of communicative processes. The function of politics is identified as enabling collectively binding decisions over the medium of power and the code of govern/governed. The function of mass media is identified as diffusion of information and a collective reality by means of the highly dynamic medium of information. Medium and code are invariant, whereas evolutionary variations in functional systems are located in their *programs*: "The economic system will never doubt that there is a distinction between payment and nonpayment. Programs, on the other hand, can be varied" (Luhmann, 1997b, pp. 52–53). For instance, formerly extra-economic considerations such as concerns for nature and human rights appear today to be included in economy's programs without the imperative of profit being afflicted.

Society and Organization

Functional systems each produce their specific realities which are incompatible and indifferent to each other, "but this indifference is used as a protective shield to build up the system's own complexity, which can be extremely sensitive to irritations from the environment as long as they can be internally perceived in the form of information" (Luhmann, 1998, pp. 35–36). By accelerating a pronounced growth of complexity, functional differentiation has facilitated industrialization and today's knowledge society. This complexity also implies that what in previous societies just happened over the course of time now "demands explicit couplings in the form of decisions in order to secure a connection between past and future" (Luhmann, 2003, p. 53). So, as functional differentiation evolved, it required a supplementing principle of system formation: organization. Organizations establish a social identity (i.e., stable expectations over time), which bridges the gap between past and future.

In a Luhmannian optic, organizations are constituted not by employees, factory buildings, products, or services, but "'consist' of nothing but communication of decisions" (Luhmann, 1997a, p. 833). This means that just as society would deteriorate if the communicative processes slowed down—then organizations depend on strong and dynamic decision processes: "Consequently, the maintenance and improvement of the competence of deciding (instead of rationality) become the actual criteria of effective organizations" (Luhmann, 2000c, p. 181). Again, the driving dynamics with Luhmann is the continuation of communication—not rationality, neither specific objectives (although this is what is thematized by organizations).

Even if all organizations refer to several functional systems (and almost all in some way to economy), they predominantly identify themselves by means of a primary reference to one of society's functional systems—a research institution to science, a court of justice to law, and so forth. Each functional reference constitutes specific expectations: it facilitates decision-making processes and strengthens expectations when you know whether you deal with a hospital (health system as functional primacy), a business company (economic system), a humanitarian organization (care system), a law court (law system), a newspaper (mass media system), or a political party (political system).

Conflicts of Globalization

From Europe, functional differentiation spread to Europe's former colonies, and today with globalization it is found worldwide. We find various stages of differentiation and various societal forms of regulating the differentiated functional spheres with implications to the interrelation between society and organization. The insensitivity of a functionally differentiated society to group belonging created alternative forms of diversity treatment, such as pluralism, modernism, and individualism. This led to ideals of free decision making, individual choice, and to the attribution of responsibility within the framework of political democracy, free economic markets, modernist education, and positive rights (cf. Baraldi, 2006). However, functional differentiation continues to face stratified societies where hierarchical relationships are basic and group belonging is the predominant way of giving meaning to individual identities (cf. Luhmann, 1997a, pp. 678–706), with significant implications to the legitimate space for organizational decision making.

Counterintuitivity, Complexity, and Criticism

A theory so denaturalized, counterintuitive, and immediately provocative by its dissociation to tradition, and so "ambitious in its scope and
relentless in its abstraction" (Knodt, 1995, p. xvi), is bound to activate
some objection. General criticism can be traced back mainly to three
positions: (1) normative positions based in moralizing, politicizing or
traditional critical orientations; (2) a lack of knowledge with the extensive and complex theory; (3) misconceptions of the theory, based on
readings from more traditional positions (cf. e.g., King & Thornhill,
2003).

The latter can be illustrated in the somehow peculiar attacks on
Luhmann for conservatism, functionalism, antihumanism, and legitimization of systems. Rather, as Knodt observes, "the theoretical rigor
with which Luhmann thinks through and embraces the consequences
of modernization—*not* because the society in which we live is the best
of all possible worlds, but because an acceptance without any nostalgia
of the structural limitations of modernity—is a precondition, and possibly the only way, of finding creative solutions to its problems" (1995,
p. xxxvi).

As to systems, "Niklas Luhmann did not believe in systems. He used
the notion of system as a methodological device" (Baecker, 2001, p. 71).
As to "antihumanism," Reese-Schäfer notes: "Luhmann is about methodological, but not normative antihumanism" (1999, p. 78). Baecker
(2006) comments that

> this does not mean that you, when you read Luhmann, refer noth-
> ing to the psychical, but only to the social: but it means that you
> can do both, and in any case have to make a decision. That alone
> enriches the analytical potential enormously and…makes you aware
> of ambivalence as the basic state of affairs of individual and social
> life.

The level of abstraction, complexity, and artificial language of Luhmann's theories has intimidated many scholars. It seems, however,
exactly these qualities which "contest the epistemological relevance of
an ontological presentation of reality" (Luhmann, 1990c, p. 37) dissolve
the compactness of language and force to a second glance. Traditional
semantics reflects a society inhabited by acting individuals, whereas
Luhmann's semantics endeavors to represent social self-organization,
and, as Qvortrup notes, we "are compelled to develop a social semantics
which matches society's structure—otherwise we are no longer capable
of reducing complexity" (1998, p. 12).

Part of Society's Learning Processes

Luhmann never theorized specifically on public relations; however, so far, particularly in German-speaking and Scandinavian countries, Luhmann's theories are increasingly applied in studies regarding public communication processes or the interrelation between society, state, and organization. Ronneberger and Rühl supplied the most comprehensive German attempt so far of a Luhmann-based public relations theory in 1992. They analyze public relations as a subsystem of "the public communications system" with the specific societal function of strengthening public trust—"at least to regulate the drifting-apart of particular interest and prevent distrust to arise" (Ronneberger & Rühl, 1992, p. 252). The most extensive analyses of and theoretical developments on organizational legitimization based on Luhmann's theories are undertaken by the author of this chapter. In interrelated parts of her research program, she focuses on:

1. The coevolution of societal coordination and organizational legitimization from 1700s early modernity up until today, and on corresponding changes in ideals of organizational legitimacy (Holmström, 2006, 2008);
2. The specific evolution of a reflective paradigm as the ideal in the late 1900s transition from modernity's stable order to late modernity's flux (Holmström, 1997, 1998, 2002, 2003, 2004, 2005a, 2005b);
3. The interrelation between different forms of societal regulation and organizational legitimization today, and conflicts activated by globalization (Holmström, 2008).

Analyses from this research program will be applied in the remaining part of this chapter to illustrate the potential of Luhmann's theories. The main empirical point of departure is changes since the 1960s in the legitimating notions and legitimizing practices which mediate the interrelations between organization and society, with a main focus on Northern Europe's old democracies characterized by full functional differentiation, pluralism, and the flux of late modernity.

Analyses show how society deals with the increasing strains of modernization, and how the increase of public relations structures is part of society's evolutionary learning processes. The notions of evolution and learning processes are not value-laden. Luhmann's "evolution theory is no theory of progress" (Luhmann, 1997a, p. 428). Society's self-continuing dynamics will endeavor to strengthen the functional differentiation constituting modern society since "a society can only imagine a change

of its principle of stability and that is to say its form of differentiation…
as disaster" (Luhmann, 1996, p. 104).

During the latter half of the 20th century the functionally differentiated society reached its full development with firmly stabilized functional systems. As modernity rigidifies in reflexivity and self-referential
social processes, the autonomized dynamics of the functional systems
strain each other as well as society's environment, from bribery and
restrictive law to pollution and stress. A growing turbulence seems to
threaten the established structures of society with vehement protests
and repeated legitimacy crises.

However, applying the Luhmannian optics, centuries of turbulence,
protests, and legitimacy crises seem to help society—including the business community—adjust and preserve itself rather than to threaten it,
and protect society "against rigidifying into repeated, but no longer
environmentally adequate patterns of behavior. The immune system
protects not structure but autopoiesis, the system's closed self-reproduction" (Luhmann, 1984/1995, p. 372). In this sense, the evolutionary
learning processes from reflexivity to reflection identified in the theory
of a reflective paradigm for organizational legitimization are part of
society's self-continuing endeavors. Reflection is manifested in ideals
of a legitimizing practice characterized by notions such as "dialogue,"
"stakeholder engagement," "triple bottom line," "symmetrical communication," "sustainability management," and so on—as "communication-
based processes of coordination…formed by the need for decentered
processes of mutual observation and coordination among social sub-
centers [in a polycentered society] in which the stabilizing factor is not
a central guiding body or social ideology," as Qvortrup (2003, p. 4)
observes based on Luhmann's theories.

Even if we may ultimately trace back problems to the functional differentiation of society, then society's conflicts surface in organizations.
Organizations "equip society with ultra-stability and with sufficient
local ability of absorbing irritation" (Luhmann, 2000c, p. 396). The
adjustments of society mainly take place in organizations and provoke
new coordinating structures such as public relations, and new legitimating notions. Where such notions no longer support the continuation of the communicative processes constituting society (including
organizations), they gradually change. Legitimacy is understood as "a
generalized preparedness to accept decisions within certain boundaries of tolerance; decisions which are still undecided as regards contents"
(Luhmann, 1969/1993a, p. 28). Holmström (2005b, 2006, 2008) identifies four interconnected societal features which activate new legitimating notions and learning processes within legitimizing practice.

Society vs. Environment: The Triple Bottom Line[2]

The first feature is the theoretical premise that society has to reconstruct its environment into social processes according to society's functional filters—for example, economy, politics, family, science, education—in order to observe, interpret, and communicate organic, chemical, biological, psychical, and physiological processes, as for instance "obesity," "life quality," "climate changes," or "animal welfare." This implies a highly selective resonance to the well-being of nature and human beings. The economic filter will automatically activate questions such as: Does it pay? Does it improve our competitiveness? The economic rationale cannot see its strains on nature and human beings until economic criteria are influenced. And what is seen is then automatically reconstructed from economic premises. A corresponding (in)sensitivity goes for all social dynamics. Politics: Will we gain votes, power? Science: Does it generate new knowledge? News media: Is it new information?

Empirically, during the latter half of the 20th century, a critical mass of unintended side-effects of the blind reflexivity of society's functional filters strains society's environment, such as deforestation and oppression of human rights. The perspective of protest organizes in social movements and catches on to mass media's selection criteria of sensation and conflict. Society's functional differentiation is questioned. Decades of numerous legitimacy conflicts seem to activate a general reprogramming of functional systems into reflection which increases society's sensitivity to its environment. Taking the economic system as the example, formerly extra-economic matters are gaining resonance within the meaning boundaries of business, expressed, for example, in the concept of the triple bottom line of people, planet, profit.

Necessity vs. Contingency: Responsibility and Trust[3]

The second feature is that with full functional differentiation, basic norms over the centuries have grown naturalized, anthropologized, and integrated as tacit assumptions and a priori constructs in the self-description of society. During the late 1900s, protests against the rigid authorities that dominate society were increasingly activated and gradually provoked communication on communication and a second order perspective which sees social filters as results of contingent choices. The general acknowledgment of contingency causes insecurity and uncertainty, and consequently increases worry and fear. However, as Luhmann (1991/1993b) suggests as a criticism of Beck's *Risk Society* (1986/1992), we cannot explain fear in the dangers we "really" face (the fact dimension)—but partly in the temporal dimension in regard to the principally unknown future, and partly in the social dimension in regard to who makes the decision which endangers others. Luhmann changes the distinction of risk/security applied in most observations on "the risk society" to risk/danger, and with this distinction the problem with which the topic of risk confronts society is seen differently: risk cannot be transformed into security, but is a question of attribution. From the dangerous position of potential victims the legitimacy of organizations' risky decisions are continuously questioned. Everything from global warming to AIDS and obesity is attributed to decisions.

The increasing acknowledgment of contingency has several implications for society's predominant decision makers: organizations. First, the premises of decisions are no longer given but have to be generated along with the decision processes. The identity and legitimacy of an organization are continuously regenerated, and formerly tacit values are explicated.

Second, when decisions are seen not as based in natural norms and common consensus but as products of contingent choice they are made socially responsible for their consequences. Companies today must explicitly assume responsibility for the consequences of their decisions in the broader perspective—mantra: social responsibility. They must be able to account for companies' decision processes—cue: transparency. The demand for sustainability makes companies responsible for the future.

Third, the whole social order is based on structures of expectations. In the normative society of yesterday, control and socialization guaranteed stability. Confidence prevailed and alternatives were unconsidered. With the recognition of contingency, norms and values grow unstable (cf. also Jalava, 2003). In unfamiliar, unpredictable, and uncertain situations we need trust, which makes it possible to interact on uncertain premises, without firm knowledge. So, relations between organization and environment are no longer mediated by passive confidence, but by active trust. Moreover, organizations have to be constantly prepared for random "trust checks" by the mass media.

Fourth, when universality is replaced by diversity and univocality by ambiguity—then it grows increasingly evident that what different observers consider to be the same thing generates different information for each of these positions.

Fifth, when the environment is no longer given, but is acknowledged as contingent—then it has to be continuously reconstructed by the organization. A new environmental sensitivity is brought into focus for instance in the form of stakeholder models which grow increasingly dynamic and fluid.

Independence vs. Interdependence: New Stakeholder Sensitivity[4]

The third feature is the increasing conflict between independence and interdependence as functional differentiation stabilizes. The higher the independence of functional systems, the higher is their interdependence. The level of knowledge, competency, and specialization in today's full differentiation requires cooperation across multiple and diverse positions. On the one hand, the development of new medicine involves science, which depends on the educational system for qualified scientists and the health system for clinical tests, which depends on economics, which depends on law for intellectual property rights, which depends on the political system, and so forth. On the other hand, tight shutters are needed between, for instance, the rationales of economics and of science for the individual dynamics to function adequately. Verdicts of illegitimacy lurk in the event of suspicion of economically biased scientific research results. Full differentiation on the one hand increases the mutual negligence of functional systems. However, on the other hand it increases the sensitivity and motivation to develop self-restrictions and coordinating mechanisms in recognition of the interdependence.

The reflective perspective exposes the paradoxical interrelation between independence and interdependence. To maintain its independence—its autopoiesis—a system has to take into consideration the interdependence with other systems. Consequently, reflection implies that organizations intensify their sensitivity to diverse perspectives, and the primary functional rationale of an organization is no longer an undisputed trump in the decision-making processes. In the case of business companies, the economic rationale conventionally determining business operations is increasingly being filtered through other rationales such as science, education, family, care, politics, health, and mass media.

Law vs. Legitimacy: Polycontextreferential Self-Restriction[5]

The third interrelated feature is that with full differentiation new political forms emerge which constitute new challenges to organizational legitimization. Analyses show how the intervening law of the welfare state gradually grows overburdened and inadequate for flexibly containing the accelerated speed and complexity of social process, and for simultaneously securing the interdependence and the independence of functional dynamics. Part of this picture is national legislation's impotence in the wake of globalization. Based on Luhmann's theories, these emerging forms of regulation are conceptualized as *supervision state* (Andersen, 2004; Willke, 1997), *polycontexturality* (Sand, 2004), and *polycontextualism* (Holmström, 2006, 2008). In polycontextualism, conventional law and authorities are substituted by increasing communicative complexity. For an organization to navigate legitimately it must be reflectively sensitive to several rationales and take an active part in society.

Key features of polycontextualism are first, that the political system relieves the pressure on its own risky decision making and increasingly passes the responsibility on to the economic system. This is primarily done by means of political initiatives which aim at internalizing the societal horizon within the business community. Corporations should take coresponsibility for society and should impose a sensitive self-control (European Commission, 2001). Still more organizations become involved in policy networks and partnerships with other private organizations, public institutions, and a multitude of NGOs to solve societal issues by producing tools for organizations' reflective self-restriction.

Second, political initiatives not only endeavor to intervene from *outside* by conventional law—but increasingly influence organizations' *internal* reflections on their own role and responsibility, acknowledging that "any system can steer itself only, with the modification that other systems can regulate it not against, but exactly through its self-regulation" (Luhmann, 1997b, p. 53). In this context we may understand, for example, corporate governance guidelines, political incentives to environmental and social considerations and reporting, and encouragement to voluntary compliance with ethical standards.

Third, political regulation relies on the regulating force of polycontextual interplays between the public perspective, news media, various NGOs, and an increasing number of stakeholders. Correspondingly, sanctions take new, polycontextual forms such as mass mediated legitimacy crises and failing support from stakeholders.

Fourth, when politics and responsibility are decentralized, the traditional legitimating reference of the political system, public opinion, increasingly grows relevant to organizations outside the political system. We see a pronounced increase of public relations structures.

The Evolution of a Reflective Paradigm

Empirical analyses of the social learning processes activating new ideals of organizational legitimization show how society tries to solve its problems activated by the blind reflexivity of modernization by gradually activating reflective forms of coordination. The process is characterized by three distinctive features: the elevation from reflexivity to reflection; polycontextual interplays between society's differentiated perspectives; and an evolutionary process in specific stages.

From Reflexivity to Reflection

Holmström (2004, 2005) locates the difference between reflexivity and reflection in three interrelated functions in organizations: sensitivity, self-observation, and self-presentation. The reflexive as well as the reflective organization are ideal types. Empirically, findings show grey zones and combinations.

Sensitivity deals with how an organization sees its environment; that is, how is the organization open? "As environment counts only what can be constructed within the organization" (Luhmann, 2000c, p. 162). In reflexivity, the perspective is self-centered from within, and the reflexive organization sees only its inherent environment—which to business is the markets of consumption, investment, and employment. In reflection, however, the organization sees itself in the sociodiversity, and sees a larger and more complex environment as relevant. Linear stakeholder models are replaced by increasingly dynamic models in which the company attempts to see itself as if from outside and no longer sees itself as the center, but as one of several polycentered interacting social perspectives. Where the reflexive organization tends to see an environment to be managed, the reflective organization sees an environment to be respected.

Self-observation deals with the organization's view on itself and with the premises of its decision processes and the self-referential processing of the environment; that is, how is the organization closed? In reflexivity, the organization takes its worldview as a given. Premises of decisions are seen as resting in natural social norms, and as automatically socially responsible. In reflection, in contrast, the contingency of decision premises is acknowledged: The responsibility of being a decision maker is explicitly assumed. The organization continually questions its role, identity, and responsibility in stakeholder-oriented processes. The "whys" are continuously debated—instead of the "whats" of reflexivity.

In reflexivity, decision processes tend to be blindly and monocontextually mediated by one functional primate. In reflection, we see how the polycontextual sensitivity is integrated in the decision-making processes. Business companies endeavor to balance financial growth with corporate responsibility, short-term gains with long-term profitability, and shareholder return with other stakeholder interests—basically to continue their autopoiesis.

By means of *self-presentation,* the organization facilitates the observation by the environment and influences patterns of expectations. The reflexive organization relies on passive confidence from the environment, whereas the reflective organization sees that it has to actively earn stakeholder trust. When legitimacy cannot be justified in naturalness or necessity, then consistent but sensitive and consequently constantly changing self-presentation is required to signal what is to be expected from the organization. It serves the purpose of generating trust since one will "be more likely to resort to distrust than to trust [when] one lacks opportunities for learning and testing one's trust" (Luhmann, 1984/1995b, p. 129).

The reflexive organization is characterized by blind self-presentation from within. It does not see conflicts, or tries to silence them, or believes that they can be dissolved by information. The reflective organization, on the contrary, is sensitive to social diversity, sees the potential of conflicts, exposes their background, and facilitates exchange of views. Conflicts are systematically looked for to increase the dynamics of partnerships and multistakeholder dialogues and the sustainability of problem solving.

Polycontextual Interplay

Feature two is that these evolutionary learning processes take place in a polycentric society where "descriptions can no longer converge, but you have to observe the observer when you want to determine what is reality to whom" (Luhmann, 2000c, p. 449). Unlike the monocentric ideas of state, public sphere, or civil society as in earlier societal forms, Luhmann describes a contemporary society with no top, center, privileged position, or commonly shared reasoning. Society's coordination processes take place in a highly complex interplay between multiple perspectives. We can basically distinguish between the dominating, functionally differentiated perspectives: economy, science, news media, law, health, education, and so forth, and other perspectives which provoke society to continuously readjust itself: in particular the public perspective, moral (Luhmann, 2008a), fear (Luhmann, 1991/1993b), and protest (Luhmann, 1996).

The public perspective[6] questions the contingency of otherwise taken-for-granted social filters by implying a specific observation which indicates social boundaries without crossing them. The public perspective questions without making decisions, without judging, without intervening. It is not rooted in a particular interest or a specific social filter with which it will automatically try to dominate what it observes. So, in a Luhmannian reconstruction the public perspective becomes a reflective principle for society's self-description, a perspective which questions the naturalness of social boundaries and thereby continuously makes society readjust itself. However, when social filters are questioned as contingent, social irritation and insecurity are aroused, and society activates defense and relief mechanisms. Among these we may understand public relations structures.

A system can respond to disturbances in the environment only in a way which is compatible to the continuation of its own autopoiesis. Empirical analyses show societal learning processes during the latter half of the 20th century where the perspectives of public, fear, moral, and protest are gradually absorbed and transformed into a new range of code-consistent legitimizing structures within the programs of functional systems, such as ethical codes, sustainability certification, and social reporting guidelines (cf. also Krohn, 1999).

Evolutionary Stages of Practice

Feature three is that these learning processes from reflexivity to reflection take place in evolutionary stages with each having its form of legitimizing practice, each its specific relationship between organization and environment, and each its perception of legitimacy. Systems are continuously changing in evolutionary processes; however, they are subject to a high degree of inertia. Luhmann bases evolution on three consecutive mechanisms: (1) suggested *variation* of stabilized structures from previous evolutions; (2) *selection* of variation and *retention*; upon which follows (3) *stabilization* provided that the selected variation can be integrated into the system's structural characteristics.

In a *conventional* stage, the reflexive boundaries of the functional systems dominating society and the premises of organizations' decision making are challenged by the suggestion of variations, in particular from the perspectives of fear and protest organizing in social movements. They match the mass media's selection criteria and gain resonance. For example, when focus on profit seems to risk the welfare of nature and human beings, variations as to the legitimacy of business are suggested. The economic system identifies socially responsible practice with making profits: "social responsibility/no profit," whereas the critical environment suggests the distinction of "social responsibility/profit." At first, the business community ignores these attacks on the conventional economic assumption of responsibility. Systems can react upon disturbances in the environment either by variations of their structures or by an increase of their indifference.

In the *counteractive* phase of conflict and prejudice in the 1970s and 1980s the turbulent environment gains resonance as it catches on to functional criteria of relevance—in the economy when markets are influenced. The counteractive phase witnesses a pronounced growth of public relations structures. Reflexive rationales, including the idea that the social responsibility of business is to increase its profits, are justified as necessary. A moralizing discourse is intensified from conflicting positions. The contingency-setting public perspective, instead of being pacified, is spurred when facing justifications based on unambiguous declarations of necessity. And as the positions of victim and decision maker systematically produce opposite views on the same matter, the business community's strategic counteraction of more information with the objective of "mutual understanding" is doomed to fail.

Gradually, a *reflective* response is provoked primarily in major, exposed organizations. From interrelations being characterized by prejudice and locked positions, reflection opens up attempts at mutual respect and consequently to practices such as stakeholder engagement and partnerships. Gradually, it grows accepted as a precondition of profit to be societally responsible in this broader sense. New distinctions are selected when they stimulate communicative processes; that is, the system's autopoiesis. In the economic system, with Luhmann (1999) this means processes of payment. So, when it pays to take into consideration formerly extra-economic matters, they are integrated into the programs of the economic system. Distinctions change from, for instance "considerations of people and planet/profit" to "considerations of people and planet/no profit." Former opposites are now increasingly seen as mutual preconditions. Profits are maximized through sustainable development and balanced growth. Economy is strengthened through extra-economic considerations. Shareholder values presuppose stakeholder trust. Competitiveness requires social responsibility.

Distinctive features of a reflective organization are: the organization takes on responsibility as decision taker in a societal context, respects the sociodiversity, acknowledges interdependence, and refers to several rationales in the decision processes without losing sight of the primary rationale—which to business is economy. The reflective organization involves itself in partnerships and policy networks with conflicting rationales to deal with common issues—ranging from child labor to global warming. This does not mean that relations between reflective systems are now free of conflicts. On the contrary, the basic condition of late modernity is conflict. Reflection implies a larger mutual toleration of the differences and the diversity, and consequently the possibility to transform conflicts into productive dynamics.

However, reflection is a risky and resource demanding form of communication. It is risky, because it may raise doubts within an organization about its own boundaries and *raison d'être*. It demands resources because reflection doubles the communicative processes and makes decision processes far more ambiguous than reflexivity. Gradually, as reflective processes diffuse, they are relieved into *best practice* routines which are adaptable to basic existing structures in the form of, for instance, certification, verification, sustainability accounts, and business guidelines for social responsibility.

In the final, *neoconventional* stage of the evolution, the variations as to organizational legitimacy have stabilized in a reflective paradigm. Society canalizes its polycontextual self-regulation from unstable, hyperirritable conditions into more secure patterns of expectation. It returns second order observations to the level of first order observations, and "it is by no means the old naïveté of direct common belief in the world but of finding a solution to inextricable entanglements in communication" (Luhmann 1991/1993b, p. 229). Although reflection has grown into reflex, the ideals established in the reflective phase are still active.

Hyperirritation and Indifference

In the immediate analysis, reflection may seem a panacea. However, a prominent quality of Luhmann's theories is the unrelenting and unsentimental sensitivity to new problems resulting from solutions to previous problems. The backcloth of a reflective society is the acknowledgment of contingency and a hyperirritated state of society which apparently cannot be suspended by more knowledge, or more information. Where organizations are forced, on the one hand, to make decisions, these decisions can, on the other hand, refer to no ultimate reason. These traits lead to public attention being continuously alerted; the position of fear being stimulated over and over, and prejudices and worries about the future prevailing. Consensus is not possible: partly because society is differentiated in irreconcilable perspectives; and partly because, since future consequences cannot be known in advance, there can be no unambiguously right solutions. Reflection copes with contingency; however, it also increases the perception of flux, and may lead to hyperirritation, feelings of powerlessness and indifference, paralyzing of decision processes or distorted resonance, such as, for instance, extensive resources spent on social reporting and media alertness. So, after this adjustment of modernity we may expect a gradual return to reflexivity; however, with new perceptions of legitimacy stabilized—upon which new evolutions can take their start.

Legitimacy Conflicts in Globalization

To varying degrees, the trends analyzed above are identifiable in most regions characterized by functional differentiation. Different societal, political, and cultural forms, however, foster different notions, ideas, and ideals as to the interrelation between society and organization. As globalization creates interdependence between societal, cultural, and political forms which were previously independent of each other, previously latent conflicts of legitimacy are activated. The ultimate conflict is localized between fully functionally differentiated societies and societies dominated by stratification, where functional differentiation plays only a secondary role, as experienced by Scandinavian dairy cooperative Arla Foods in 2006. Because of a Danish newspaper's cartoons of Muslim prophet Mohammed, publicized as "a test of freedom of expression" (Rose, 2005, p. 3), first, the company was boycotted in Arab countries dominated by stratified structures. Later, after having tried to legitimize itself in Arab countries by publicly expressing respect for local values, Arla Foods was threatened with a boycott back home in Scandinavia for betraying modernist values.

Based on Luhmann's analyses of the differences between a functionally differentiated society and a stratified society, decisive differences of organizational legitimacy and legitimizing practice can be identified. First, a functionally differentiated society values individual performances and expressions of personal diversity, whereas in a stratified society individual identity and social identity overlap, and consequently dissolve the boundary between a private and a public sphere. Second, in functional differentiation, modernist ideas prevail of a public sphere with equal access for a diversity of individual expressions. In stratification, the public sphere is regulated from above (or from a center) with the function of maintaining a common collectivist identity. Third, the coordination of a functionally differentiated society takes place in continuous legitimating and legitimizing processes in polycontextual, pluralist interplays without any center or top. In a stratified society, societal coordination is hierarchical, most often with religion as the fundamentally legitimating reference of society. Notions of legitimacy are dictated rather than debated. Fourth, in functional differentiation, intermixture of functional rationales is illegitimate, such as, for instance: (1) of politics and mass media: it is illegitimate if the political system dictates the boundaries of expression to mass media; (2) of religion and politics: it is illegitimate if any religion dictates to the government and law of a nation; and (3) of economy and politics or law: bribery of politicians or public servants is illegitimate. In contrast, the stratified society implies no distinct boundaries between the social systems of religion, politics, economy, mass media, family. Even economics, politics, law and market mechanisms are subject to religion and stratified group affiliation. Fifth, the modernist values of functional differentiation breed a culture of contingency as opposed to necessity, inevitability. Social norms and institutions tend to be acknowledged as contingent; that is, as choices which could have been taken differently, and consequently as potential subjects to intentional change through reflection and discussion. In contrast, in a primarily stratified society social relations are based on perceptions of necessity, orthodoxy, and belief in authorities; norms are assumed as inevitable and necessary to maintain society, as unquestionably accepted self-evidences. Freedom of expression without boundaries of necessity is illegitimate.

Conclusion

With Luhmann, we are forced to a counterintuitive perspective. Sources of social transformations are localized within the constantly changing self-referential social processes which constitute society and organizations. The frames of explanation developed from Luhmann's theories share the analysis that in late modernity, society no longer sees justification as based on natural norms or on institutionalized roles and conventions, but on contingent choice. Consequently, organizations must continuously legitimize their decisions. In this context, we can explain the emergence of public relations structures during the 20th century, and identify the core of the new ideals of legitimization as the ability of reflection as opposed to reflexivity as part of society's self-continuing endeavors. The analysis identifies different categories of practice based on the difference between reflexivity and reflection.

Some of the benefits to research in public relations—and, more generally, in organizational legitimization—implied by the scope and nature of Luhmann's theories are, first, that we can identify the specific function within society's learning processes. Second, we can undertake our analyses at all societal levels, and furthermore analyze interrelations between these levels; that is, the larger societal dynamics and organizations or even specific group interactions. Third, the focus is the social and temporal dimensions which continually change the fact dimension: how do perceptions of legitimacy, of what is seen as real, relevant, and right change in various interplays between different social perspectives? Luhmann's theories facilitate in-depth analyses of the polycontextual interplays within which an organization is involved. Fourth, with Luhmann's analyses of organizations as social systems, we are given a sensitive optic on the conditions and constraints of organizations' sensitivity and complexity. Fifth, Luhmann's theories can help us categorize and interrelate different forms of societal coordination and of organizational legitimization, and identify conflicts activated by globalization.

As demonstrated, based on Luhmann's theories, public relations practice may find a unity and a function in contemporary society and understand the premises on which its legitimacy rests—without the theory attaching any legitimizing, delegitimizing, or otherwise normative qualities to practice. Luhmann's theories are not intended to give guidelines to any practice. However, exactly the insight gained by Luhmann's counterintuitive abstractions and in-depth analyses of the social processes that surround us may help facilitate perceptive practice.

Notes

1. A previous version of this chapter was published as: Niklas Luhmann: Contingency, risk, trust and reflection, in *Public Relations Review 33*(3), 2007.
2. This analysis in particular applies to the theoretical optic provided in Luhmann (1986/1989, 1996).
3. This analysis in particular applies to the theoretical optic provided in Luhmann (1968–1975/1982, 1991/1993b, 1997a, 1998).
4. This analysis in particular applies to the theoretical optic provided in Luhmann (1997a).
5. This analysis in particular applies the theoretical optic provided in Luhmann (1981/1990a, 2000b).
6. Luhmann only deals with the concept of "public" to a limited extent, and this reconstruction of the public perspective is based mainly on Baecker (1996); moreover on Luhmann (1995a, 1996/2000b, 1997a, 2000c).

References

Andersen, N. Å. (2004). Supervisionsstaten og den politiske virksomhed [The supervision state and the political corporation]. In C. Frankel (Ed.), *Virksomhedens politisering* (pp. 231–260). Copenhagen: Samfundslitteratur.

Baecker, D. (1996). Oszillierende Öffentlichkeit. In R. Maresch (Ed.), *Medien und Öffentlichkeit* (pp. 89–107). Munich, Germany: Klaus Boer Verlag.

Baecker, D. (2001). Why systems? *Theory, Culture & Society, 18*(1), 59–74.

Baecker, D. (2006). Niklas Luhmann. *Systemagazin.* Retrieved May 1, 2006, from http://www.systemagazin.de/beitraege/luhmann/baecker_luhmann.php

Bakken, T., & Hernes, T. (Eds.). (2003). *Autopoietic organization theory.* Oslo, Norway, Copenhagen, Denmark: Abstrakt Liber, Copenhagen Business School Press.

Baraldi, C. (2006). New forms of intercultural communication in a globalized world. *The International Communication Gazette, 68*(1), 53–69.

Beck, U. (1992). *Risk society: Towards a new modernity.* London: Sage. (Original work published 1986)

Becker, K. H., & Seidl, D. (Eds.). (2005). *Niklas Luhmann and organization studies.* Copenhagen, Denmark, Malmö, Sweden: CBS Press/Liber.

European Commission. (2001). *Promoting a European framework for corporate social responsibility.* Luxembourg: Directorate-General for Employment and Social Affairs.

Habermas, J. (1981). *The theory of communicative action.* London: Heinemann.

Holmström, S. (1997). An intersubjective and a social systemic public relations paradigm. *Journal of Communications Management, 2*(1), 24–39.

Holmström, S. (1998). *An intersubjective and a social systemic public relations paradigm* Roskilde, Denmark: Roskilde University Press. Retrieved from http://www.susanne-holmstrom.dk/SH1996UK.pdf (Original work published 1996)

Holmström, S. (2002). Public relations reconstructed as part of society's evolutionary learning processes. In B. van Ruler, D. Verčič, I. Jensen, D. Moss, & J. White (Eds.), *The status of public relations knowledge in Europe and around the world* (pp. 76–91). Ljubljana, Slovenia: Pristop.

Holmström, S. (2003). Grænser for Ansvar [Limits of Responsibility]. Doctoral dissertation 41/2003 ISNN 0909-9174, Roskilde University, Roskilde, Denmark.

Holmström, S. (2004). The reflective paradigm. In B. van Ruler & D. Verčič (Eds.), *Public relations in Europe, a nation-by-nation introduction of public relations theory and practice* (pp. 121–134). Berlin/New York: de Gruyter.

Holmström, S. (2005a). Fear, risk, and reflection. *Contatti (Udine University: FORUM), 1*(1), 21–45.

Holmström, S. (2005b). Reframing public relations: The evolution of a reflective paradigm for organizational legitimization. *Public Relations Review, 31*(4), 497–504.

Holmström, S. (2006). The co-evolution of society and organization. In S. Holmström (Ed.), *Organizational legitimacy and the public sphere* (Vol. 1, pp. 54–72). Roskilde, Denmark: Roskilde University Press.

Holmström, S. (2008). Reflection: Legitimising late modernity. In A. Zerfass, B. van Ruler, & K. Shriramesh (Eds.), *Public relations research: European and international perspectives and innovations* (pp. 235–250). Wiesbaden, Germany: Westdeutscher Verlag.

Jalava, J. (2003). From norms to trust—The Luhmannian connections between trust and system. *European Journal of Social Theory, 6*(2), 173–190.

King, M., & Thornhill, C. (2003). Will the real Niklas Luhmann stand up, please. *The Sociological Review,* 276 –285.

Knodt, E. M. (1995). Foreword. In *Niklas Luhmann: Social systems* (pp. ix–xxxvi). Stanford, CA: Stanford University Press.

Krohn, W. (1999). Funktionen der moralkommunikation [(Functions of moral communication]. *Soziale systeme, 5*(2), 313–338.

Luhmann, N. (1982). *Trust and power.* Hoboken, NJ: Wiley. (Original work published 1968–1975)

Luhmann, N. (1989). *Ecological communication.* Cambridge, UK: Polity Press. (Original work published 1986)

Luhmann, N. (1990a). *Political theory in the welfare state.* Berlin, New York: de Gruyter. (Original work published 1981)

Luhmann, N. (1990b). *Die Wissenschaft der Gesellschaft* [Society's science]. Frankfurt, Germany: Suhrkamp.

Luhmann, N. (1990c). *Soziolohische Aufklärung 5. Konstrucktivistische Perspekiven* [Sociological clarification 5]. Opladen, Germany: Verlag.

Luhmann, N. (1993a). *Legitimation durch Verfahren* [Legitimation through procedure]. Frankfurt, Germany: Suhrkamp. (Original work published 1969)

Luhmann, N. (1993b). *Risk: A sociological theory.* Berlin, New York: de Gruyter. (Original work published 1991)

Luhmann, N. (1993c) *Das Recht der Gesellschaft* [Socerty's law]. Frankfurt, Germany: Suhrkamp.

Luhmann, N. (1995a). *Brent Spar oder Können Unternehmen von der Öffentlichkeit lernen?* [Brent Spar or could companies learn from the public perspective?]. Frankfurt, Germany: Zeitung.

Luhmann, N. (1995b). *Social systems.* Stanford, CA: Stanford University Press. (Original work published 1984)

Luhmann, N. (1996). *Protest.* Frankfurt, Germany: Suhrkamp.

Luhmann, N. (1997a). *Die Gesellschaft der Gesellschaft* [Society's society]. Frankfurt, Germany: Suhrkamp.

Luhmann, N. (1997b). Limits of steering. *Theory, Culture & Society, 14*(1), 41–57.

Luhmann, N. (1998). *Observations on modernity* (W. Whobrey, Trans.). Stanford, CA: Stanford University Press.

Luhmann, N. (1999). *Die Wirtschaft der Gesellschaft* [Society's business] (3rd ed.). Frankfurt, Germany: Suhrkamp.

Luhmann, N. (2000a). *Art as social system* (E. M. Knodt, Trans.). Stanford, CA: Stanford University Press. (Original work published 1995)

Luhmann, N. (2000b). *The reality of the mass media.* Cambridge, UK: Polity Press. (Original work published 1996)

Luhmann, N. (2000c). *Die Religion der Gesellschaft* [Society's religion]. Frankfurt, Germany: Suhrkamp.

Luhmann, N. (2000d). *Die Politik der Gesellschaft* [Society's politics]. Frankfurt, Germany: Suhrkamp.

Luhmann, N. (2002). *Das Eziehungssysstem der Gesellschaft* [Society's educational system]. Frankfurt, Germany: Suhrkamp.

Luhmann, N. (2003). Beslutningens paradoks [The paradox of decision]. In H. Højlund & M. Knudsen (Eds.), *Organiseret kommunikation—systemteoretiske analyser* [Organized communicatoin—systems theoretical analyses] (pp. 35–61). Copenhagen, Denmark: Samfundslitteratur.

Luhmann, N. (2008a). *Die Moral der Gesellschaf* [Society's moral]. Frankfurt, Germany: Suhrkamp.

Luhmann, N. (2008b). *Ideenevolution* [Evolution of ideas]. Frankfurt, Germany: Suhrkamp.

Parsons, T. (1951). *The social system.* New York: Free Press.

Qvortrup, L. (1998). *Det hyperkomplekse samfund.* Copenhagen, Denmark: Gyldendal.

Qvortrup, L. (2003). *The hypercomplex society.* New York: Peter Lang.

Reese-Schäfer, W. (1999). *Niklas Luhmann zur Einführung* [Introduction to Niklas Luhmann]. Hamburg, Germany: Junius Verlag.

Ronneberger, F., & Rühl, M. (1992). *Theorie der Public Relations* [The theory of public relations]. Opladen, Germany: Westdeutscher Verlag.

Rose, F. (2005, September 30). Freedom of expression: The face of Mohammed. *Jyllands-Posten,* p. 3.

Sand, I.-J. (2004). Polycontexturality as an alternative to constitutionalism. In C. Joerges, I.-J. Sand, & G. Teubner (Eds.), *Transnational governance and constitutionalism.* Oxford: Hart.

Spencer-Brown, G. (1979). *Laws of form.* New York: E.P. Dutton. (Original work published 1969)

Thyssen, O. (1995). Interview with Professor Niklas Luhmann. *Cybernetics & Human Knowing, 3*(2), 24–26.

Willke, H. (1997). *Supervision des Staates* [The state's supervision]. Frankfurt, Germany: Suhrkamp.

Life and Work of Niklas Luhmann

Niklas Luhmann (1928–1998) was born and lived in Germany. He became a doctor of law in 1949, and for some years worked as a civil servant, before he gradually surrendered completely to academia. Between 1968 and 1993 he was professor of sociology at Bielefeld University. Luhmann's theories literally changed the language and the ways of seeing the world for many (above all for German and Scandinavian) intellectuals.

Luhmann published more than 50 books and 400 articles. So far, only a minor but increasing part is translated into English. Below, the titles of translated works are in English, and the year of the English publication follows the original German publication.

His main works are *Social Systems* (1984/1995b) and *Die Gesellschaft der Gesellschaft* (1997a). Other monographs are *Die Wirtschaft der Gesellschaft* (1999), *Die Wissenschaft der Gesellschaft* (1990), *Das Recht der Gesellschaft* (1993), *Art as a Social System* (1995/2000a), *The Reality of Mass Media* (1996/2000b), *Die Politik der Gesellschaft* (2000d), *Das Erziehungssystem der Gesellschaft* (2002), and *Die Religion der Gesellschaft* (2000c).

His major work on organization theory is *Organization und Entscheidung* (2000); on society's structure and semantics *Gesellschaftsstruktur und Semantik* (4 volumes) 1980–1995, *Love as Passion* (1982/1998); on enlightenment/modernity: *Soziologische Aufklärung* (6 volumes) 1970–1995, *Observations on Modernity* (1998), *Ideenevolution* (2008a).

Other relevant works on public relations research: *Trust and Power* (1968–1975/1982), *Ecological communication* (1986/1989), *Risk* (1991/1993b), *Protest* (1996), *Die Moral der Gesellschaft* (2008a).

An extensive number of introductions to Luhmann have been published in German and in various Scandinavian languages; however, so far, only a few have appeared in English. Knodt provides a perceptive introduction in her foreword to *Social Systems* (Knodt, 1995). The anthologies *Autopoietic Organization Theory* edited by Bakken and Hernes (2003) and *Niklas Luhmann and Organization Studies* by Becker and Seidl (2005) develop Luhmann's organization theory. The journal *Soziale Systeme* in German and English focuses mainly on Luhmann-based research.

Chapter 11

On Mayhew

The Demonization of Soft Power and the Validation of the New Citizen

Richard C. Stanton

Abstract

Toward the end of the 20th century, American sociologist Leon Mayhew impugned public relations as applying persuasion and influence, inexorably altering the shape of public opinion and thus the public sphere. The influence of public relations created a "New Public," which, unlike Habermas's mythical public of the Enlightenment, was incapable of differentiating real and fabricated information. Consequently, this New Public was unable to form genuine opinions or interpret public policy. Two of Mayhew's theories have the capacity to influence poststructural public relations; the rhetoric of presentation and the redemption of tokens of influence. This chapter explains Mayhew's argument and provides an introduction to the relevance of his work as the field of public relations struggles with the triangular instruments of globalization, regionalization, and localization along with its own social relationships to communities, "tribes," and the news media of the early 21st century.

In the late 20th century, Leon Mayhew, a U.S. sociologist, set out to prove that public relations[1] exerts enormous persuasion and influence upon the mass public of Western culture, and that the consequent rationalization "erodes the social organization of public opinion" (Mayhew, 1997, p. ix). To support his argument, he drew deeply from the work of German philosopher Jürgen Habermas and, to a lesser extent, American systems theorist Talcott Parsons. Habermas, in terms of the Mayhewian position, questioned separately the validity of existence of modern differentiated society without the input of the opinions of an integrated mass public. Mayhew visualized his "New Public" as hybrid, emerging from Habermas's generalist public sphere. Mayhew forged his idea in Jürgen Habermas's overheated furnace. He applied heat to Habermas's mythical public sphere, strenuously beating and hammering, until he had reshaped it into his own public sphere. In doing so he argues from two competing, and at times unsupportive, viewpoints. His first is that public relations has the capacity to persuade and influence without revealing the truth or reality of what it is that is the subject of the influence (thus implying that a mass public receives inaccurate information with which to frame its opinions). Second, he implies the mass public of the late 20th century, while unable to provide inputs to social policy, were sufficiently informed to develop sound opinions and make rational decisions. This dichotomy rests on an assumption that journalism is not persuasive or influential, a consideration we shall return to shortly.[2]

Mayhew's New Public is caught up in a modernity surrounded by sociopolitical and economic products and services which it is unable to differentiate, thus placing it in harm's way; a position that is manipulated by public relations' intent on delivering maximized profits to sociopolitical and economic clients. The communicators most reviled by Mayhew are public relations counselors, advertisers, and marketers, all representing client-based communication as consumable product, and seeking immunity from any "redemption of tokens" most often associated with "solidarity" between client and consumer. By imagining historical mass publics in a particular way, Mayhew at once is able to imagine his own New Public in which mass opinion is cogniscent of the aims and goals of public relations working on behalf of clients, refusing thus to be persuaded and influenced. In this there lies a dichotomy which I will attempt to ameliorate. On one hand Mayhew demonizes public relations for acting as agents of persuasion and influence, shielding the truth and reality of their clients' social and political actions and strategies, while at once presenting an argument that citizens are sufficiently informed to see through these strategies. Mayhew's argument is built upon the idea that public relations dominates public opinion, displacing the "free" public of the Enlightenment (in which, Habermas argues, objective discussion forms public opinion) with a New Public subject to systematic persuasion and influence. Mayhew's New Public is therefore a "refeudalized" Habermasian public sphere in which the processes of rationalization of persuasion, developed in advertising and market research, dominate public communication and thus, dominate the sociopolitical processes through the rhetoric of presentation. His interest in public relations as social and political communication was sparked by the 1988 presidential election campaign. From this he attempted to develop taxonomies for various groups of communicators and to refer to them generally as "professional." The professionalization of public relations, however, is a global issue with various regional and local discourses. While L'Etang and Pieczka (2006) suggest professionalization requires the triangulation of a body of knowledge with a code of ethics and certification, there can be no doubt that public relations is a very different pursuit to those Western practices which are professionalized; law, medicine, engineering, and accountancy (Stanton, 2007a). It can also be argued that it is a separate field from advertising, marketing, and market research.

Grounding Mayhew's Thought

While he was not a prolific writer in sociological or public relations terms, Mayhew's thought can be viewed as nonsecular, seeking to establish two-way discourse in pursuit of truth and a stable social order. His quest for a new model of a mass public (in Western terms) that is fully apprised of the rhetorical techniques of the communication of modernity, is grounded in his lifelong faith in the Church of Jesus Christ of Latter Day Saints, or Mormonism, coupled with a desire for human beings to act in harmony and to live within communities of peace and good will. Evidence for this appears in *The New Public* in chapter 6, "The Differentiation of Rhetorical Solidarity." In this Mayhew is not altogether extraordinary. The practice of public relations has itself been transformed in recent years to become dominated by conservative, nonsecular actors (Stanton, 2007b) for whom earlier practices associated with propaganda and deception are alien concepts.[3]

In his preface to *The New Public*, Mayhew reveals information which assists us to understand his role as a protagonist in relation to public relations and indeed, toward most forms of mass communication. Watching the 1988 contest between U.S. Republican candidate vice president George Herbert Walker Bush and democratic challenger, governor Michael Dukakis, Mayhew began thinking about a number of aspects of mass society and mass communication that had been the subject of debate and thought since Aristotle. As a sociologist he considered reasonable the sociological proposition that mass publics are not vulnerable to elite persuasion and influence, or at least, not as vulnerable as suspected. Media coverage of the presidential campaign appears to have provided him with enough evidence to build his own argument that might prove the earlier theories required "substantial revision" (Mayhew, 1997, p. ix).

An earlier, less developed exploration of his argument appeared as *Political Rhetoric and the Contemporary Public* (1992). One of the ironies of Mayhew's work lies in his Habermasian acceptance of the media—particularly journalism—as a respectable "profession"; one that lies between the public and the manipulators and attempts to present news and information in a truthful and meaningful fashion. His unquestioning acceptance of the Habermasian ideal is evident from his treatment of all other communicators and his setting aside of a deeper investigation into the coverage of the election that led him down his New Public path. Indeed his analysis of the 1988 candidates is contained in one page.

Rhetorical Tokens and the Redemption of Influence

Rather than seeing rhetorical tokens as instrumental, Mayhew attempts to present them as a way for a variety of stakeholder publics to insinuate themselves into public policy debates and therefore, into the public sphere. In this, and its associated idea of the capacity for publics to redeem rhetorical tokens promised by others, lies the significance of the theories for public relations. The prospect of redemption (setting aside the religious overtones), however, has no basis in truth. Mayhew himself expresses a desire that "to redeem a rhetorical claim is to respond to demands for clarification, specification and evidence" (Mayhew, 1997, p. 13). He laments the capacity of a candidate (social or political) to make promises on the basis of truth; the promises will never be able to be truthfully redeemed at some point in the future given that they are contingent upon contestable criteria and unknown future circumstances. He attempts to balance his dismay with the assertion that the use of undifferentiated rhetoric within his New Public is now so diffuse that "symbolic" information and vague assertions have completely replaced discursive contests. It is this assertion that has the most profound weight for the theory and practice of public relations in both social and political contexts. The difficulty for Mayhew lies not in the evidence that the discursive contests have been replaced by symbolic representation. It lies in his capacity to offer solutions through his idealized forums for the redemption of these tokens. We will see in the conclusion that the proposed forums have been overrun by technology. But this does not mean that they cannot be reinvigorated to engage with these technologies.

Some of his ideas for the redemption of rhetorical tokens include deliberative forums such as direct debate, third party, diffuse citizen forums in which competing material is placed in the same medium (Mayhew, 1997). On balance we can accept that his valid contribution is an appeal for fluid mechanisms to ameliorate the redemption of rhetorical tokens, rather than in the provision of soluble forums.

Imagining Public Relations

The public relations of the Mayhewian imagination emerged in the 1980s as a discipline with little theoretical foundation, relying on empiricism to establish its position. Public relations straddles the two competing spheres of public and private. Australian political scientist Hugh Emy (1976) suggests there is a need for a clear distinction between the public sphere and the private sphere if there is to be a better understanding of the relationship between public policy and public opinion. As Mayhew points out, other media sociologists (Schudson, 1992) have commented on the need for the news media to play an active role by investigating and reporting decisions made in the private sphere that have implications and effects in the public sphere (Mayhew, 1997). For Mayhew, the community (or electorate) is the legitimate bearer of public opinion, which in turn is the creator of public policy, and thus the source of legitimate governing power. Modern public opinion is a product of democracy rather than of the persuasion and influence of professional communicators (see Fishkin, 1997; Fraser, 1992). A strategic difference can be detected in the origins of public opinion epistemology, which has its genesis in Lippmann's eponymous early 20th century work. Lippmann provided a rigid platform onto which could be bolted a body of work with clear definition, despite its elitist perspective (Fishkin, 1997; Lane & Sears, 1964; Qualter, 1989; Stretton & Orchard, 1994). In contrast, public policy literature appears to have no similar foundation. Its modern emergence can be traced to a reaction by the left in the United States against conservative foreign policy (see Chomsky, 1969; McChesney, 1997) and to a shift of focus from development of theories of public administration—examination of the structure of government—to observation of the effects of government (see Davis, Wanna, Warhurst, & Weller, 1993; Davis & Weller, 2001; Howlett & Ramesh, 1995; Sharp, 1999; Stewart, 1999; Stone, 1997). Ihlen and van Ruler (2007) argue that public relations has a social dimension that is inherently more important than others and that the quest for one great theory to encompass and embrace the field is an impossible dream. They suggest the field of public relations and its theoretical development has been framed historically by U.S. hegemony.

Habermasian Persuasion

While the work of Jürgen Habermas and its influence on public relations has been examined in detail in another chapter in this book and elsewhere, the relevance of his argument underpins Leon Mayhew's theory and demands brief discussion. Habermas, in his widely recognized work on 18th century London as a mythologized model of a public sphere, aligns the modernist politics of advertising—in which forms of democratic social order were displayed through contested elections—with 18th century European dramatic spectacle. Habermas considered these spectacles removed from authentic public dialogue. Mayhew took this in a different direction and argued that sociopolitical communication was a "direct outgrowth of public relations and the methods of influence developed in advertising and market research" (Mayhew, 1997, p. 209). Actors as participants in the public communication process are, for Mayhew, distinct and overwhelmingly commercially focused. They are public relations counselors, media specialists (though not journalists), public opinion pollsters, specialist lobbyists, focus group organizers, and demographic researchers (Mayhew, 1997). There is no flexibility in this list. Each is a product of the market. Similarly, he believes there is no system of checks and balances for these communicators as that identified and coupled to the role of the journalist as communicator and ideologue. There is nothing more than commercial gain for the individual and the firm. In this sense Mayhew has adopted elements of Habermas's argument for the benefit of his own position, stating that mass publics are not engaged with the establishment of social and public policy, and that policy is framed solely through the influence of communicators acting on behalf of the influential; in effect that public relations actors dominate discursive processes within the democratic public sphere (Habermas, 1989).

Habermas's mythical public sphere should, however, be imagined as a meeting place or public forum—a mediating environment—that occurs between citizens and the state and in which there is open and objective discussion of issues. Mayhew argues that persuasion and influence through public relations now dominate public communication, displacing Habermas's free public of the Enlightenment, and setting up a New Public which is subject to systematic mass persuasion. Fraser (1992) and others (see Garnham, 1992; Schudson, 1992) repudiate (as does Habermas himself) the notion that such an ideal public sphere ever existed. The importance of the possibility of there having been such a sphere is vital to Mayhew's argument that an enormous transfer of power has occurred from the public within such a sphere, to communicators whose primary focus is the manipulation of the opinions of the public within. Just as Leon Mayhew makes subjective claims that the public today is easily influenced, he too appears to have been easily influenced by the works of Jürgen Habermas.

Had Mayhew lived longer, he would have been confronted by Habermas's own admissions of doubt about his mythical 18th century public sphere. But for the moment we shall look to the Habermasian influence on Mayhew (and indeed upon his continuing influence over Western scholarship) to see what it was that Mayhew was able to draw out, thus providing the opportunity for us to investigate his claims and to tease out positive aspects from his ideas on rhetorical tokens and the redemption of influence.

Habermas's shaping of the mass public into a particular form also offers Mayhew the opportunity to imagine his own fictional New Public in which mass opinion is aware of the objectives of client-sponsored professional communicators, and that consequently the New Public refuses to be influenced or persuaded. As mentioned above, Mayhew's New Public can be viewed as a refeudalized Habermasian public sphere in which the processes of rationalization of persuasion, developed in advertising and market research, dominate public communication and the sociopolitical process through the rhetoric of presentation. But there are alternative views on this, notably those of Norris who suggests the unquestioned orthodoxy which frames advertising and marketing in terms of control of the sociopolitical process, is an inaccurate reflection of the public's perception (Norris, 2000). As previously stated, Habermas aligns the modernist politics of advertising with 18th century European dramatic spectacle. He defines and conceptualizes the public sphere within a sociological paradigm, thus creating the platform from which Mayhew launches his investigation. Mayhew attributes the origin of scholarly writing on sociopolitical communication to Habermas in the 1950s and 1960s, a not unreasonable attribution (see Garnham, 1992; McNair, 2000).

Mayhew's New Public Sphere

Much has been written and debated about the public sphere. In Western democracies, it is viewed from competing positions and presented as a variety of alternative spheres, depending upon the worldview of the protagonist. Some view it as being in crisis (see Baudrillard, 1998; Blumler & Gurevitch, 1995; McNair, 2000; Michie, 1997) while others argue it is maintaining stability and developing its own weapons against the onslaught of such things as "new media" (see Berelsen, Lazarsfeld, & McPhee, 1954; Stretton & Orchard, 1994). A third position argues there are competing spheres offering ideologically based positions such as feminism, materialism, and postmaterialism (see Fraser, 1992; Papadakis & Grant, 2001). For others, such as McNair (2000) it is the news media which contributes the information that is central to an analysis of a dynamic public sphere while Stretton and Orchard (1994) argue economic theories of government should be more central to its existence than social or political theories. Earlier, Lippmann (1922) defined the public sphere in terms of public opinion and stereotypes, while Packard (1957), continuing the sociological metaphor, focused on the relationship between the public and advertising. As Mayhew argues, there has always existed a rhetoric of presentation in which the display of symbols outweighs discursive argument. In attempting to define this argument more specifically, stating that public relations specialists have produced anti-discursive models which present high levels of information as being dangerous, he acknowledges the positive presence of the news media within his New Public sphere, with its capacity to "filter" specialist rhetoric of presentation. But instead of arguing that the news media are objective and thus provide the mechanisms by which the New Public can filter information to form objective opinion, he argues that the news media have the same potential as the average citizen to be persuaded and influenced by sources and the antidiscursive models invoked by public relations. He argues that it is standard practice in public relations to advocate a positive position for an issue or event without specifying exactly how promised benefits from that position will materialize. Such syllogistic techniques were evident in the advertising campaigns of most of the political candidates in Australia at the national election in late 2007. Candidates and parties adapted collective techniques directly from the then current Democratic presidential nomination campaign in the United States. At first blush, Mayhew appears to be suggesting that members of his New Public are unable to grasp the nature of the artifice in this type of persuasion, eager as they are to elect a candidate on the basis of implication and the perceived redemption of a candidate's promised tokens. These tokens are frequently based on narrow or ill-defined reputational capital rather than any substantive future action.

In general terms, Mayhew's argument has credence that the rhetoric of *pathos*, or the emotions of citizens, can be measured as the dominant form of persuasion in the United States. It must be viewed, however, in its narrower sociological perspective, as there is compelling evidence to suggest that outside a mass urban paradigm, especially in a rural sociopolitical environment, the first of Aristotle's principles of persuasion— *ethos*—still prevails. As Kavanagh notes, most people find sociopolitical actions and events difficult and complex compared to the simplicity of their household budget or the normal daily decision-making process (Kavanagh, 1995). Schumpeter and others (e.g., Blumenthal, 1992; Bowler & Farrell, 1992; Freidenberg, 1997; Kavanagh, 1995) have found that citizens as voters in the sociopolitical act appear to be more interested in the image of a candidate or political party than in policies (Schumpeter, 1976). This "horse race" scenario is a point that Mayhew draws from his viewing of the 1988 U. S. presidential campaign.

For Habermas the true notion of public discourse meant the communicative action of discursive contests on public policy, functioning specifically to allow citizens the opportunity to understand and formulate opinion without "perceived' rhetorical influence. Mayhew, however, argues that his New Public has little interest in such contests, imagining them in terms of the rhetoric of persuasion; less forums for the redemption of tokens than forums in which sociopolitical persuasion will overwhelm the underlying issues.

Public Relations through Candidature: Citizen as Communicator

While Mayhew formed his argument from the perspective of the citizen as observer in his New Public, the citizen as participant is an equally natural action and thus requires apprehension from the "client" perspective. Mayhew made no assumptions about citizens as candidates for office—how they transfer their actions from observers to participants other than that they use public relations methods and techniques. But political candidates—other than elite candidates for presidential office—come from within the New Public that Mayhew identifies and across the Western world their deliberative participation in the democratic policy process is increasing (see Habermas, 2006). Within this sociopolitical communication environment there are a number of factors that differentiate these candidates and their campaigns. Central to a successful campaign is an understanding of electoral systems, voting, and the issue of representation of minority interests. Farrell (1997) argues that the presumption of minority interest representation resting on stability is fallacious and that in fact an electoral system can cope with maximum representation of those interests without a threat being imposed on the stability of government. Farrell's argument allows us to contemplate the true nature of Mayhew's New Public as a sphere in which citizen communicators represent their own actions and in so doing, contribute to the level of poor-quality information inputs because they are equally unable to offer any true redemption of their promises or rhetorical tokens. Mayhew argues, however, that it was the birth of public relations and the emergence of the sociopolitical communication consultant, along with attendant tools of opinion polling, market-driven election campaigning, political advertising, and lobbying that created the necessary circumstances for the transformation of the discursive public sphere to his New Public; an amorphous mass of citizens subject to persuasion and influence through systematic processes, replacing the more acceptable modern public of the Enlightenment in which discursive processes in public places embodied the "good" in each society (Mayhew, 1997, p. 189).

Habermas (1989) argues that persuasion and influence, transferred from the "honorific" avocation of the politician to the paid professional, brought about the structural transformation of his public sphere. A society circumscribed by communication produces observable limitations, he says, the consequence of which is a communicative-theoretic model in which "actors orient their own actions by their own interpretations" (Habermas, 1989, p. 118). Such is the position of the politician as actor through either an interpretation of his or her own actions, or an interpretation by a second actor (public relations counselor) of the interpretation of the actions of the politicians.

Plasser (2000) argues that rejection of global models of communication is conscious and that candidates will adopt tactics if they feel they will work, similar to how they "shop" when buying goods and services, a point that lends weight to Mayhew's redemption of tokens theory. But this argument is more relevant to a global market than a local social issues or political market. I suggest that local candidates, with limited budgets and limited knowledge of the availability of a "basket" of campaign tactics, enter the public sphere as "communicators in ignorance," relying on unsophisticated ideas based loosely on the reinforcement of friends and relatives that they have a "chance" rather than "shopping" for the right combination of tools to do the job effectively. These citizens as candidates create the negative circumstances Mayhew argues are created by public relations professionals. The reliance of a communal interpretation of communicative action and the relativization of utterances within a valid framework presents the fledgling candidate with a logical direction in which to enact a social or political election communication campaign.

Schlesinger (1994) suggests an inescapable promotional dynamic lies at the heart of contemporary sociopolitical culture. Within this culture, marketers rely on the identification of aggregates of preferences in determining potential sales of goods and create frameworks in which these aggregates are measured against the supply of goods and services from industry. Social and political communication campaigns on the other hand, rely on values, opinions, and attitudes which are almost impossible to aggregate in an attempt to find a state of equilibrium which can be measured against the supply of redeemable tokens (Moloney, 2006).

Justifying Commodification of Public Relations

If, as Mayhew argues, a contemporary sociopolitical public relations campaign is crafted along the same lines as a marketing campaign, there is justification for consultants offering campaign solutions. It is not, however, a simple step from drawing assumptions about the use of marketing to concluding that public relations has subsumed sociopolitical campaigning within an economic framework. Indeed, in early 2008, when the European Parliament was considering the idea of registering the 15,000 political communicators, or lobbyists, working in Brussels, it was suggested by a number of Members of the European Parliament that their existence contributed positively to policy development (http://www.europarl.europa.eu/).

Marketing is by its nature, based on tactics designed to sell products and services. Some marketing tools have made a transition to the sociopolitical public sphere. They include direct mail, telephone surveys, database management, and list selling which Mayhew describes in negative terms (Mayhew, 1997).

Overall, however, effective marketing campaign measurement does not equate with similar success in sociopolitical communication campaigns. Marketing as a subset of economics, uses quantitative modeling as a predictive tool. As part of the process of commodifying politics, public relations practitioners have turned in recent years to the use of marketing and marketing communication tools to assist sociopolitical clients. Market research, targeting voters and measuring opinion polls, permeates national election campaigns in Western democracies but are not widely used in local social or political issue campaigns due to prohibitive costs. The application of marketing tools has a different effect on the electorate to the employment of advertising and public relations. Advertising provides direct image comparison. The candidate who uses the local newspaper to advertise a policy, accompanied by a picture, allows the electorate to read its own message into the image.

Public relations campaigns which include dissemination of published material, such as newsletters, create a more direct relationship with the electorate. The main functions of communicating politics, for the campaigning politician, are to affect the allocation of resources and to avert, divert, or convert social change (Nimmo, 1978). Quite frequently however, candidates begin their campaign unequipped. They present their credentials as they relate to places of employment, community affiliations or family. It is not unusual for a candidate to run on a platform of family, work, and religious affiliation. Mayhew, however, fails to differentiate elite communicators and local grassroots communicators, which is a flaw in his argument. Intuition and a "feeling" for the electorate may provide the initial impetus or motivation to nominate, but the development of a strategy and the application of tactics within the strategy will not always impel that initial motivation toward elected representation.

The Development of Persuasive Leadership

It is relevant at this point to discuss the notion of leadership, which Mayhew calls prolocution, and its emergence and nurturing in fledgling candidate communicators. I will investigate below his decision to set aside a detailed analysis of journalism as a contributing factor in the persuasion of his New Public, but he also chose to leave alone the main actors; the candidate in the sociopolitical event, those either seeking elected office or other positions which may attract influence. Candidates cannot be viewed collectively nor do they share a common set of communication skills. In fact, some candidates for local elections from Norway to Japan or New Zealand have an image of themselves as being capable of "making a difference" (the one common piece of rhetoric) and view themselves as activist or special interest communicators. But they employ few public relations techniques and rarely engage the prohibitively costly services of public relations consultants. Indeed, these candidates are members of his New Public rather than manipulators of it; they are not elites and they have no access to elite methods or financing of strategy.

It served Mayhew's purpose to observe the communication of elites because that is where most news media coverage lies, but in reality the majority of candidates communicating their proposals and policies come from within the New Public itself. These candidates practice elementary technological public relations and develop their skills at campaign level.

Candidates frequently communicate their narrow ideas and views without developing and framing them in epistemological or methodological terms so that their stakeholder publics can form opinions of both the policy and the candidate. These candidates rarely act beyond a single campaign (Stanton, 2005). Others, however, use events such as local committee elections to develop elementary public relations techniques that assist them in sociopolitical elections or activist events. Activists can be separated into group spokespersons and opinion leaders (Nimmo, 1978) but it is arguable whether both can be considered to be prolocutors (Mayhew, 1997).

Political leadership and political motivation can be described as two distinct styles, task motivation and relationship motivation (Nimmo, 1978) which provide two types of leadership roles involving one based on tasks and outcomes, the other on development of emotional responses in group members. Popularity among individual sociopolitical communicators provides a link to their capacity for leadership. Candidates, unless they have achieved some success in becoming known in the public sphere, must run information campaigns designed to register them within the broader public sphere as someone trustworthy, at the very least, and someone who has a legitimate right to stake a claim on the contest. Legitimacy embraces the capacity for policy formulation and issues management as well as an understanding and application of the elements of public relations communication which play a role in the candidate's election.

The Role of Prolocutor

Momentary relief from Mayhew's attack rests on the foundation of prolocution. But this too is ambiguous. He argues that spokespersons with evident capacity and nonaffiliation, may provide opinions which are capable of being truthfully assessed by citizens. Mayhew defines prolocutors as the bearers of influence in society. Some are appointed to speak on behalf of groups, while others become prolocutors through independent advocacy. A prolocutor is defined as one who speaks for another or others, but it is a term that is now rarely used in everyday language. Prolocution is defined in the *Oxford English Dictionary* as "the use of ambiguous language so as to mislead" (p. 2364). There is some ambiguity between Mayhew's use and that described by the OED. Prolocutors, Mayhew suggests, use persuasion to capture free-floating disposable loyalties with success dependent upon their rhetorical capacity to present, create, and adapt appeals to new social situations. He adds however, that until the appeals are accepted by stakeholders, leadership claims are not valid. In this Mayhew was focusing on the larger picture of U.S. presidential elections. A different picture emerges when we contemplate lesser contests. Nimmo (1978) asserts that each member of a social structure is effectively a communicator (and thus potentially a prolocutor?) by virtue of participation as an individual with an opinion. But evidence suggests that few citizens deploy their opinions in the available public spheres (Stanton, 2007a). For each taxonomy of communicator (these include public relations practitioners, advertisers, political advisers, and journalists) Nimmo identifies divisions between representation and persuasion (Nimmo, 1978). Representation of the viewpoint between sources and stakeholders is the role of party officials and journalists, while persuading stakeholders of the value in changing their opinion is left to ideologists, public relations counselors, and opinion makers. Lippmann (1922) argues that stereotyping allows us to maintain order, to represent a consistent picture within our worldview, and thus to remain comfortable in our habits and tastes. Persuasion, however, is dialectical and is therefore determined by an investigation of truth through discourse. In its purest form, persuasion as dialectic is a foundation argument. In real terms, persuasion is influenced by deadlines, alternative viewpoints which are powerful through their stereotype, and images of those attempting to pursue the dialectic.

Mayhew's investigation of public relations did not include a substantial examination of the role or actions of journalism. Curiously, following Habermas, his argument supports their veracity. He attempts to provide objectivity by developing a link between elites and the mass media, illuminating corresponding patterns of influence. Journalism itself, he argues, is influenced profoundly by its "professionalism" and its desire to produce objectivity (Mayhew, 1997). In grounding this professionalism in his New Public's reality, Mayhew acknowledges the reliance placed on news sources and the "problem" with sources based on the opinion of the source and the potential to influence. He does not, however, present a realistic image of a news source (as public relations) and of the capacity or otherwise of a journalist to determine the veracity of the source, the information and thus, the story's legitimacy.

We need look no further than the world's leading news medium, *The Economist*, to gauge the ranking of social issues and how, with the support of public relations soft power, they become news. Mayhew was unwilling or unable to investigate these tensions nor to apply "heat" to the journalist as persuader. Every day, global news media record social issues as news; Renaissance 2010, an education initiative in Chicago (*The Economist*, May 10, 2008, p. 44), betting and gambling in New York (*The Economist*, January 26, 2008, p. 41), Sumo wrestling in Japan (*The Economist*, February 16, 2008, p. 36). Each one receives news treatment similar to material on politics and economics; the two pillars of global news values. What is interesting is that these social stories are more often received from unsolicited public relations sources.

Mayhew's reflection on the lost "center" of society[1] supports his concern that citizens are incapable of understanding their position due to a constantly shifting focus provided by public relations. Public opinion is partly shaped by information obtained from the news media. For Mayhew this reality locks in to "reputation" and "prestige"; into the confidence in and the capacity of the individual citizen to accept as a token of faith the opinions of those who display reputation and prestige (Mayhew, 1997, p. 65). The legitimation of the need to validate information and opinion received from others relative to their standing in the sociopolitical order supports this notion.

Stone argues that information is never "fully and equally available to all participants in politics" (Stone, 1997, p. 29). It is from this position that social policy, while based on the notion of democracy and equality, is mostly about the retention of information for one's own purposes rather than sharing and dissemination for good. This position rejects the notion of the "rational" in the policy process and places it firmly in the framework of conflict and cleavage. Conflict and cleavage, however, are ideological. In Mayhewian terms, public relations, seeking to trade warrants of solidarity, must make judgments by acting out what has been promised. A record of consistency of statements and acts builds a reputation for sincerity (Mayhew, 1997).

Conclusion

The question we must attempt to answer is not whether Leon Mayhew has contributed positively or negatively to the development of the sociology of public relations. Rather it is to question whether his theories, seen previously as a minor sociological representation of public relations, are of greater epistemological, methodological, or technological value. His theory of the redemption of tokens of influence must be seen as crucial to the ethical practice of public relations, while his ideas on the rhetoric of presentation offer interesting practical ways forward.

For Mayhew, the problem lay not in life, but in death. Had he lived a decade beyond the publication of his major work he would have witnessed a partial transformation of his New Public through the instrument of wireless communication. Third places, as those public spaces defined by Habermas have become known, have been transformed from those in which humans interact with each other, to those in which humans engage in other first (home), second (office), or third spaces using wireless technology—PDA or laptop—to access e-mail, send text messages, or watch video news downloads. Such a transformation has altered the way sociopolitical activity is constructed, with some interesting consequences, as we have seen on a Mayhewian large scale in election campaigns in the Philippines, Spain, and Sierra Leone. The introduction of specific sociopolitical communication sites such as YouTube, MySpace, and FaceBook into campaign communication at national levels has been significant in shaping and altering public opinion (these forms of communication may have already been transformed by the time this book is published). At the Australian national election in 2007, for example, the use of social networking sites assisted a socialist opposition coalition (Labor and Greens) in the overthrow of a conservative government that had held office for 11 years. The strategies used by the candidates and their public relations strategists were adopted as "big box" strategies from those being employed at the time in the campaigns for the U.S. presidential nominations (an irony that would not have escaped Mayhew's glance). They were not adapted or reframed for local conditions. They were successful because they were applied to the technologies that have been absorbed unconditionally by a new generation of New Public. The relevance of instant widespread communication is important to the continuity of Mayhew's thesis. At one level, it appears to offer a substantial opening for individual citizens to access exhaustive amounts of information upon which to form an opinion. Given that this information is arriving at the citizen in forms they themselves have encouraged, it is reasonable to assume the veracity of the information will be more acceptable to them than it would have been had it been transmitted and distributed through orthodox, less acceptable media such as television or newspapers. At another level, for public relations defined by Mayhew, these new channels provide the perfect opportunity to continue to influence without the need for the presentation of tokens of redemption, and to act within a public sphere in which there is no open, accountable discourse governed by "good reason" (Mayhew, 1997, p. 118). Warrants of solidarity, in which the communicator and the citizen share equally, appear to be embedded in technology: if you use a Blackberry and I use a Blackberry, and we are both sitting in Starbucks cafés in different countries communicating with each other, then the information we are communicating must also be part of our solidarity. It is here, at this point, that the redemption of rhetorical tokens again comes into play in the Mayhewian sense, and in the sense that his thesis has the potential to make a significant contribution to the theory of public relations.

Notes

1. Throughout his work Mayhew uses the term *professional communicator*, but a close reading of the text indicates he is most interested in public relations as it is applied in social and political situations rather than other types or fields of communication.
2. In support of his argument, Mayhew acknowledges both the left-of-center theories of Jürgen Habermas, and the more conservative, right-of-center

systems theories of Talcott Parsons. As we shall see, Mayhew himself is more comfortable in the conservative arena, a position which assisted him in his endeavors. He employs conservative Parsonian systems theory, acknowledging briefly that its own existence was flawed. The Habermasian theory of the transformation of the public sphere, however, is the real foundation of his argument. For reasons of space constraints, I have not dwelt on the Parsonian influence on Mayhew. While this chapter examines the Habermasian influence on Mayhew, Parsons plays an interesting but briefer role. I would argue that Mayhew made a vain attempt to resurrect Parsons through his New Public, as an acknowledgment to his former mentor.

3. A close reading of *The New Public*, written during a time of personal physical distress (Mayhew suffered for the last 12 years of his life from viral pneumonia leading to pulmonary fibrosis) reveals a level of personal irritation embedded within his argument. A Mormon publication, reporting on his death in 2000, stated that

> [Mayhew] was deeply concerned about the reputation and fame of the institution of the university. Embedded in that sense of integrity, that concern for the institution, was a strong commitment to a set of fair rules, to mechanisms for ensuring that all relevant parties knew the rules, and the procedures that ensured the just application of the rules. He participated in a system-wide group that worked to bring clarity and even-handed implementation of the academic personnel system. In his performances both as vice chancellor and as dean of the College of Letters and Science he strove to ensure that the institution be, as much as human frailty would allow it to be, above reproach. (LDS, 2008)

This statement goes some way to providing an understanding of his concern for the overt use of persuasion and influence as manipulative instruments upon hapless citizens to which there are attached no accessible redemptive forums.

4. Mayhew invokes a literary metaphor originating with 20th century Irish poet W. B. Yeats. Yeats, however, appears to be less pessimistic in "The Second Coming," the poem from which Mayhew draws, than Mayhew wants us to believe. Yeats imagines the possibility of a new world in which

> Things fall apart; the centre cannot hold;/Mere anarchy is loosed upon the world,/The blood-dimmed tide is loosed, and everywhere/The ceremony of innocence is drowned;/The best lack all conviction, while the worst/Are full of passionate intensity. (Yeats, 1990)

He is, though, unwilling to offer an image of the future as bleak as that offered by Mayhew.

References

Aristotle (1991). *The art of rhetoric* (H. Lawson-Tancred, Ed.). London: Penguin.

Baudrillard, J. (1998). *The consumer society: Myths and structures.* London: Sage.

Berelson, B., Lazarsfeld, P., & McPhee, W. (1954). *Voting: A study of opinion forma-tion in a presidential campaign*. Chicago: University of Chicago Press.

Blumenthal, S. (1992). *The permanent campaign*. New York: Touchstone Books.

Blumler, J., & Gurevitch, M. (1995). *The crisis of public communication*. New York: Routledge.

Bowler, S., & Farrell, D. (1992). *Electoral strategies and political marketing*. London: Macmillan.

Chomsky, N. (1969). *American power and the new mandarins*. New York: Penguin.

Davis, G., Wanna, J., Warhurst, J., & Weller, P. (Eds.). (1993). *Public policy in Aus-tralia*. Sydney, Australia: Allen & Unwin.

Davis, G., & Weller, P. (Eds.). (2001). *Are you being served? State, citizens and govern-ment*. Sydney, Australia: Allen & Unwin.

Economist. (2008, January 26). All bets may be off, p. 41.

Economist. (2008, February 16). Heavy hitters, p. 36.

Economist (2008, May 10). Red ties and boys pride, p. 44.

Emy, H. (1976). *Public policy: Problems and paradoxes*. Melbourne, Australia: Macmillan.

Escott, T. (1911). *Masters of English journalism*. London: T. Fisher Unwin.

Farrell, D. (1997). *Comparing electoral systems*. Rugby, UK: Prentice-Hall.

Fishkin, J. (1997). *The voice of the people: Public opinion and democracy*. New Haven, CT: Yale University Press.

Fraser, N. (1992). Rethinking the public sphere: A contribution to the critique of actually existing democracy. In C. Calhoun (Ed.), *Habermas and the public sphere* (pp. 109–142). Boston, MA: MIT Press.

Freidenberg, R. (1997). *Communication consultants in political campaigns*. West-port, CT: Praeger.

Garnham, N. (1992). The media and the public sphere. In C. Calhoun (Ed.), *Habermas and the public sphere* (pp. 359–376). Cambridge, MA: MIT Press.

Habermas, J. (1989). *The structural transformation of the public sphere*. Cambridge, MA: MIT Press.

Habermas, J. (2006). *Arenas of political communication*. Paper presented at the 56th Annual Conference of the International Communication Association, Dresden, Germany.

Howlett, M., & Ramesh, M. (1995). *Studying public policy: Policy cycles and policy systems*. Oxford: Oxford University Press.

Ihlen, Ø., & van Ruler, B. (2007). How public relations works: Theoretical roots and public relations perspectives. *Public Relations Review, 33*(3), 247–248.

Kavanagh, D. (1995). *Election campaigning*. Oxford: Blackwell.

Lane, R., & Sears, D. (1964). *Public opinion*. Upper Saddle River, NJ: Prentice-Hall.

LDS (Church of Jesus Christ of Latter Day Saints). (2000, May 21). Retrieved March 2008, http://www.mormonstoday.com.

L'Etang, J., & Pieczka, M. (Eds.). (2006). *Public relations: Critical debates and con-temporary practice*. Mahwah, NJ: Erlbaum.

Lippmann, W. (1922). *Public opinion*. New York: Free Press.

Mayhew, L. (1992). Political rhetoric and the contemporary public. In P. Colomy (Ed.), *The dynamics of social systems*. London: Sage.

Mayhew, L. (1997). *The new public: Professional communicators and the means of social influence.* New York: Cambridge University Press.

McChesney, R. (1997). *Corporate media and the threat to democracy.* New York: Seven Stories Press.

McChesney, R. (1999). *Rich media poor democracy.* Champaign: University of Illinois Press.

McNair, B. (2000). *Journalism and democracy: An evaluation of the political public sphere.* London: Routledge.

Michie, D. (1997). *The invisible persuaders: How Britain's spin doctors manipulate the media.* London: Bantam.

Moloney, K. (2006). *Rethinking public relations: PR propaganda and democracy.* London: Routledge.

Murphy, D. (1976). *The silent watchdog: The press in local politics.* London: Constable.

Nimmo, D. (1970). *The political persuaders: The techniques of modern election campaigns.* Englewood Cliffs, NJ: Prentice-Hall.

Nimmo, D. (1978). *Political communication and public opinion in America.* Tucson, AZ: Good Year.

Norris, P. (2000). A virtuous circle: Political communicators in post industrial societies. *Harvard International Journal of Press Politics, 5*(1), 1–12.

Packard, V. (1957). *The hidden persuaders.* Harmondsworth, UK: Penguin.

Papadakis, E., & Grant, R. (2001). Media responsiveness to old and new politics issues in Australia. *Australian Journal of Political Science, 36*(2), 293–309.

Plasser, F. (2000). American campaign techniques worldwide. *Harvard International Journal of Press Politics, 5*(4), 33–54.

Qualter, T. (1985). *Opinion control in the democracies.* New York: St. Martin's Press.

Schlesinger, P. (2000). The nation and communicative space. In H. Tumber (Ed.), *Media power, professionals and policies* (pp. 99–115). London: Routledge.

Schudson, M. (1992). Was there ever a public sphere? If so, when? Reflections on the American case. In C. Calhoun (Ed), *Habermas and the public sphere* (pp. 143–163). Cambridge, MA: MIT Press.

Schudson, M. (1995). *The power of news.* Cambridge, MA: Harvard University Press.

Schumpeter, J. (1976). *Capitalism, socialism and democracy.* London: Allen & Unwin.

Sharp, E. (1999). *The sometimes connection: Public opinion and social policy.* Albany, NY: SUNY Press.

Stanton, R. (2005). *Leon Mayhew and the sociological impact of political public relations.* Paper presented at the 55th Annual Conference of the International Communication Association, New York.

Stanton, R. (2007a). *All news is local: The failure of the media to recognize world events in a globalized age.* Jefferson, NC: McFarland.

Stanton, R. (2007b). *Economic and social index of public relations practitioners in Australia.* Unpublished pilot survey, The University of Sydney, Australia.

Stewart, R. (1999). *Public policy: Strategy and accountability.* Melbourne, Australia: Macmillan.

Stone, D. (1997). *Policy paradox: The art of political decision-making.* New York: Norton.

Stretton, H., & Orchard, L. (1994). *Public goods, public enterprise, public choice: Theoretical foundations of the contemporary attack on government.* London: Macmillan.

Weaver, D. (1987). *Media agenda-setting and elections: Assumptions and implications.* In D. Paletz (Ed.), *Political communication research* (pp. 176–193). New York: Ablex.

Weaver, D. H. (Ed.). (1998). *The global journalist.* Creskill, NJ: Hampton Press.

Wilcox, D., Ault, P., Agee, W., & Cameron, G. (2000). *Public relations strategies and tactics.* New York: Longman.

Yeats, W. B. (1990). *Collected poems.* London: Pan.

Life and Work of Leon Mayhew

Leon Mayhew was born on May 15, 1935 in Ogden, Utah. Some years later his family moved to Berkeley, California where he attended Berkeley High School. He went on to earn a bachelor's degree in sociology from the University of California, Berkeley. Around the time he joined the Navy, serving two years in Hawaii, he married Janet Ellsworth, with whom he had three children. He entered the graduate program in social relations at Harvard, earning a master's degree in 1960 and a doctorate in 1965. At Harvard, Mayhew studied with Talcott Parsons, and most of his subsequent publications built on Parsonian themes. In 1962 he joined the sociology faculty of the University of Michigan as a lecturer. In 1968 he was invited to Berkeley as a visiting associate professor. He joined the University of California, Davis sociology department in 1969 as professor and chair. In addition to 16 scholarly articles on a wide range of topics, he wrote four books. His last book, *The New Public: Professional Communication and the Means of Social Influence* (Cambridge University Press, 1997), has been described as "a difficult and successful synthesis of the ideas of Parsons and Habermas" (LDS Web site newsletter).

Chapter 12

On Putnam

Bowling Together—Applying Putnam's Theories of Community and Social Capital to Public Relations

Vilma Luoma-aho

Abstract

Although the concept of *social capital* is by no means new, it has certainly spread more widely due to the writings of Robert D. Putnam. His writings have underlined the importance of civic engagement and social ties for the welfare of individuals and societies at large. Putnam's theory of social capital posits that the success of societies greatly depends on the horizontal bonds of collaboration: only long-term relations, such as associations and clubs, are able to generate the cohesion that brings societal benefits such as lower crime rates, increased health, happiness, and even economic prosperity. Putnam's writings are timely in a world of increased uncertainty and increasingly fractured publics. The creation and maintenance of organizational social capital can be seen as a foundation for public relations and as spanning the boundaries of public relations through topics such as stakeholder thinking, corporate social responsibility, and relationship management.

The field of public relations is tightly intertwined with society and its functions, yet this connection has often been overlooked by public relations scholars in theory development. Although Robert Putnam's writings on social capital and community building are well-known, his work has rarely been applied to the study of public relations (Putnam, 1993, 2000; Putnam, Feldstein, & Cohen, 2003; Putnam, Leonardi, & Nanetti, 1993). Accordingly, organizations with reciprocal, trusting stakeholder networks could be understood as having high amounts of social capital

The topic of community building is timely, as corporations struggle to survive in a globalized, unpredictable, and fractured "reputation society" (Luoma-aho, 2005; Pizzorno, 2004). This chapter argues that the aim of public relations should be to create and maintain organizational social capital. The chapter is structured as follows: First, the work and theories as well as the criticism of Robert Putnam are introduced. Second, Putnam's contributions for public relations theory and practice are discussed through exploring its previous applications and suitability. Third, a model deriving from Putnam's thinking on social capital

creation is presented and finally conclusions are drawn on the usefulness of his theories for theory and practice of public relations.

Robert Putnam and the Art of Bowling

Robert Putnam (1941–) is an American political scientist famous for coin-
ing the phrase *Bowling alone*, first in an article (1995a) and later in a book
(2000). Putnam's studies have concentrated on democracy and society at
large, and he argues that society today has seen a decrease in a sense of
community. Despite technological development and the new media, and
in fact partly because of them, people today have fewer interpersonal
relationships than ever before. There has been a generational shift, and
people have become isolated; they no longer belong to clubs and associations or do things together, but instead they even bowl alone. Putnam
argues that people today have lost a sense of community, which makes
collaboration and relationships difficult to establish and maintain.

According to Putnam (2000) the reasons behind this decline are several. Putnam identifies the biggest causes to include the changing family structure toward living alone, suburban sprawl that has fractured
people's spatial integrity and affected their free time. Moreover, the
introduction of electronic entertainment has "privatized" leisure time,
and the newer generations value communal activities less than did earlier ones. All these trends are responsible for diminishing interaction
and hence slowly eroding the social networks vital for the welfare of
societies and individuals.

Bowling Alone (2000) describes the disintegration of civic tradition
in America, but similar trends can also be found elsewhere. In fact, the
ideas were originally developed in Putnam's study on Italy—*Making
Democracy Work* (Putnam et al., 1993). Putnam conducted a comparative study of successful and unsuccessful regional governments in Italy
that had been established around the same time. Putnam was interested
in these differences and offered empirical evidence for the reasons
behind them. He argued that the blame resided in the civic traditions
and histories of the local populations. He emphasized the importance
of informal collaboration: a society with strong civic traditions and a
participating population made for successful government as well as a
successful economy, whereas a weak and un-civic-minded society would
only foster a corrupt government and lead to a cycle of poverty. Success
was due to the social networks that generated trust and trustworthiness
among people.

What Putnam has been able to describe is a link between institutional
performance and the character of civic life (Putnam et al., 1993), and he
has thereby also contributed to the ongoing structure–agent controversy.
While Putnam's theory is mostly about structure, he makes it clear that

agency is the creator of structure: a civic community is characterized by civic engagement, political equality, solidarity, trust, and tolerance as well as a strong associational life (Putnam et al., 1993; Putnam, 2000). For Putnam, civic engagement is not only about politics, but refers to the different connections people have with the life of their communities. Putnam sees clubs and associations as being the places where the functioning of democracy is learned and built on: he claims that the social networks formed in associations generalize trust across society at large. In short, learning to trust people on a small scale will enable trust even on the societal level. This learning to collaborate and formation of trust, however, are not quick processes, but take place gradually over time, and as in the case of regional governments in Italy, even centuries (Putnam et al., 1993).

For Putnam, working together requires a bottom-up approach: what is important is not only how governments or organizations are managed, but how people in general behave. The key ingredient, what makes or breaks societies and different forms of organizations, can hence be seen as what Coleman (1988) and Bourdieu (1980/1995) have earlier described as social capital. Putnam and colleagues (1993) define social capital as "features of social organization, such as trust, norms, and networks that can improve the efficiency of society by facilitating coordinated actions" (p. 167). Social capital not only benefits those involved, but also bystanders and society at large; the benefits vary in nature from decreased tribal conflict to voter turnout, lower transaction costs, and satisfied citizens (Putnam et al., 2003). In short, social capital builds and maintains a thriving community, and when there is a decrease in social capital, a sense of society is lost.

Defining Social Capital

Social capital can be understood as a metaphor derived from other types of capital.

> Whereas physical capital refers to physical objects and human capital refers to the properties of individuals, social capital refers to connections among individuals—social networks and the norms of reciprocity and trustworthiness that arise from them. In that sense social capital is closely related to what some have called "civic virtue." The difference is that "social capital" calls attention to the fact that civic virtue is most powerful when embedded in a dense network of reciprocal social relations. A society of many virtuous but isolated individuals is not necessarily rich in social capital. (Putnam, 2000, p. 19)

In other words, social capital enables people to collaborate, socialize, establish communities, and live together.

Social capital owes its origin to such concepts as social connectedness, referring to formal memberships as well as informal social networks, and generalized reciprocity, social trust, and tolerance. Putnam (1996) clearly links social capital with collaboration and community: "By 'social capital' I mean features of social life—networks, norms, and trust—that enable participants to act together more effectively to pursue shared objectives. (Whether or not their shared goals are praiseworthy is, of course, entirely another matter.)" (p. 34). On this basis, social capital is understood to consist of beneficial connections among individuals.

For Putnam, social trust, norms of reciprocity, and networks of civil engagement are mutually enforcing. "Effective collaborative institutions require interpersonal skills and trust, but those skills and that trust are also inculcated and reinforced by organized collaboration" (Putnam et al., 1993, p. 180). Moreover, norms and networks of trusting behavior contribute to economic prosperity and are in turn reinforced by that prosperity (Fukuyama, 1995). Collaboration makes no sense if you do not trust others to reciprocate. In societies where generalized trust in other people is low, collaboration is difficult and scholars speak of the social trap (Platt, 1973; Rothstein, 2003; Rothstein & Stolle, 2002). According to Putnam (Putnam et al., 2003), it is possible to build trust even in societies lacking in collaboration. The key is to get people involved with each other on a smaller scale; for example, through associations. These grass-root level experiences of working together are the building blocks of trust in society at large (Putnam et al., 1993).

The Role of Social Networks

For Putnam's understanding of social capital, networks play a special role. They not only foster reciprocity, but also facilitate coordination and communication and amplify information about the trustworthiness of individuals or organizations; that is, their reputation. Networks are for Putnam the embodiment of past success at collaboration. In fact, reputation can be described as the value of public awareness in the social networks important to the organization; "an intertemporal identity" (Pizzorno, 2004), a record of trustworthy or untrustworthy behavior (Luoma-aho, 2005). According to Putnam's logic, importance is placed on "particularly the historical trustworthiness of parties in previous interactions with others, and it is the social context that makes reputational effects possible" (Rousseau, Sitkin, Burt, & Camerer, 1998, p. 397). Previous experiences of working together create expectations for the future.

However, not all social networks are alike nor do they serve the same functions. Putnam (2000) applies the distinction made between two different types of social capital: bridging or inclusive, and bonding or exclusive, social networks. Bonding social capital is the type that furthers in-group cohesion, whereas bridging social capital is understood as relationships with those outside the group. In Putnam's view both are needed.

Bridging and bonding networks represent different types of relationships. If a relationship is a way to survive possible threats posed by the surroundings, people, and the environment, bonding social capital is for Putnam (2000) the superglue of groups and societies. It reinforces exclusive identities, and promotes in-group cohesion. It is easily formed, but runs the risks of becoming excessive. In fact, bonding social capital is often formed without any effort: like minds tend to gather together. Bonding social capital is necessary for organizational cohesion and collaboration, as it enables the organization to function. However, as it is exclusive by nature, its consequences are not always positive (Ojala, Hakoluoto, Hjorth, & Luoma-aho, 2006). Negative consequences of social capital include, for example, insider trading or exclusion from social groups, both of which are beneficial for their members, but not for those who are outside the particular group, nor for the society at large.

On the other hand, bridging social capital, the kind that is the most beneficial for a healthy but diverse society, is difficult to create (Putnam et al., 2003, p. 3). Bridging social capital is like oil for groups and societies; it smoothes relations between groups and individuals. Bridging social capital is close to what Granovetter (1973) calls weak ties, and related to what Burt (2002) calls structural holes. Bridging social capital identifies networks that bridge social divides and promote heterogeneity in groups and societies. It reinforces inclusive identities, and thus runs less risk of excess.

Putnam's theories operate on a macrolevel of societies and collaboration. He argues that recent societal changes have disintegrated social bonds, and diminished people's sense of community. As a result, trust in societies has diminished, which has contributed to problems in health, wealth, and wisdom. What is needed, is more trust and collaboration that allows people to resolve collective problems, share information, transact smoothly, stay healthy, be social, and build a we-feeling of belonging: to conclude, more social capital. Social capital is formed over long periods of time and as a result of repeated interactions, and increasing it is more complex that forming a bowling club: "Social capital is usually developed in pursuit of a particular goal or set of goals and not for its own sake" (Putnam et al., 2003, p. 10).

Critique of Putnam's Works

Putnam's theories have been widely supported, but also widely criticized. The central tenets of his theories have attracted perhaps most criticism; critics are quick to point out that there is little convincing empirical evidence that getting people to work together and trust each other on a smaller scale would result in social capital for the whole community (DeFilippis, 2001; Patulny, 2003). Moreover, he has been called naïve and illusionary to propose that reestablishing community would solve large societal problems.

Social capital is intangible, and thus difficult to measure and prove of value. Putnam's attempt to introduce narrative and quantitative history and compare it to his present-day empirical data has been greatly admired because by that means he has been able to tell a story of historical development and their influence on present-day social networks. However, the direction of causality has never been satisfactorily demonstrated: does social capital result from cohesive societies or does it cause societies to become cohesive? Moreover, Putnam is taken to task for divorcing power from his concept of social capital, and for oversimplifying history, especially by ignoring many significant developments for the formation of social capital. Although there may be a correlation between active communities and societies that flourish, it has been argued that Putnam's social capital does not tell the whole story (DeFilippis, 2001).

Putnam has since addressed many of his critics, and there is a clear evolution from his earliest theorizing on social capital and community to his most recent publications on the creation of social capital. For example, after *Making Democracy Work* was criticized for holding true only in Italy, Putnam published *Bowling Alone* in which he argued that the same concepts held true in the United States. Now, Putnam's thinking was criticized by those who felt that he was ignoring new organizations and forms of social capital. Others further argued that many of the organizations included were responsible for the suppression of civil rights movements and the reinforcement of antiegalitarian social norms. By way of atonement, Putnam published *Better Together* in 2003 with Feldstein and Cohen.

Critics also complain that the historical-based civic community and measures of social capital Putnam describes serve as a form of predestination. Putnam has also been accused of bringing a forlorn message: in areas with a low sense of community and little social capital, the process of reestablishing either a sense of community or social capital is almost impossible. If the social trap has been shut, creating trust becomes almost impossible (Putnam, 1993; Rothstein, 2003).

While Putnam's message has not changed due to this critique, he has recently directed his interest away from the description of social capital toward finding ways of creating and maintaining social capital. *Better Together* (Putnam et al., 2003) and Putnam's active role in the annual meetings of the Saguaro Seminar on Civic Engagement in America represent a search for new possibilities of social capital creation. In *Better Together* he describes 12 different social capital creators, from clubs, churches, and organizations to networks and neighborhood pressure groups, that all "involve making connections among people, establish bonds of trust and understanding, building community.... They all involve creating social capital: developing networks of relationships that weave individuals into groups and communities" (Putnam et al., 2003, p. 1).

Putnam's writings spell out that individualism has overtaken communitarism, social capital is diminishing, and a sense of community is fading. If society is to prosper in the long run, a sense of community must be rebuilt and social capital created (Putnam et al., 2003). The next chapter discusses the contributions of Putnam's work for the theory and practice of public relations, and gives insight into the processes of creating social capital.

Putnam *for* Public Relations

Public relations in a changing world requires a more holistic approach than most public relations theories have thus far provided. Putnam's theories are important because they are able to explain the deeper meanings of relationships for not only individuals and organizations, but also society at large. In Putnam's view, the vitality of a community can be estimated based on its social interaction, and this can be seen to hold true for organizations as well (Luoma-aho, 2006). Putnam's thinking broadens the view of public relations, as he shows the long-term effects of social relationships and that communities and publics form also without and despite organizational existence and action (Hallahan, 2004; Putnam et al., 2003): a common interest in itself is able to give birth to communities. The focus of public relations has often been on issues of management and managing publics, but Putnam's view of communities is broader, some say even communitarian; communities consist of their own historic developments, aims, and interests, and as such, can often not be controlled by organizational activities.

Putnam is beneficial for public relations because he concentrates on organizational forms of social capital, whereas other theorists of social capital often take an individual approach (e.g., Bourdieu, 1980; Burt, 2002; Coleman, 1988). This chapter argues that Putnam's theorizing on community and social capital can contribute to theory and practice of public relations. In fact, Putnam's thinking contributes to a metatheory of public relations, as it emphasizes the importance of creating social capital in the spirit of communitarism (Hallahan, 2004; Leeper, 2001; Wilson, 2001). Moreover, Putnam provides several practical ideas about the mechanisms of social capital creation, by describing the places and processes of building trust. What Putnam's studies are able to point out is the importance of social networks for the long-term organizational survival and prosperity (Putnam et al., 1993). For practitioners, Putnam offers a great metaphor on which to build the identity of the field: public relations practitioners should be seen as creators and maintainers of organizational social capital.

Establishing Community Through Public Relations

What Putnam was at pains to emphasize was the value of social networks, through which a sense of community is created (Putnam, 1993 , 2000). Networks may be personal or organizational, but their influences are always wider, even societal. It has been argued that through forming the necessary networks and connections for organizations and individuals, public relations plays a central role in maintaining a balanced society. Kruckeberg and Starck (1988; Kruckeberg, 2006; Starck & Kruckeberg, 2001) as well as Hallahan (2004) have argued that building a sense of community through communication is in fact the essence of modern public relations. Kruckeberg and Starck (1988) trace the formation and popularity of public relations to the development of society, and argue that "most of the concerns of public relations practitioners today simply did not exist before the loss of community…public relations came about to fill a social vacuum created by the disappearance of community" (p. 43). Putnam's thinking provides ideas of how this important task can be accomplished through creating social capital, whether on an organizational or national level.

Although Putnam does not apply the concept of public relations—nor define it precisely—in his work, he notes the importance of communication as an intermediary tool for the creation of community and social capital. Putnam does not, however, comment on the type of communication that would at best foster social capital, but marks all interaction as beneficial. It is communication that creates belongingness, whether it is a matter of joining a club or going bowling, and it is communication that keeps the relationship strong over time. However, Putnam does emphasize the importance of strategic community planning and the maintenance of reciprocal relationships for the survival of society at large (1993, 1995b; Putnam et al., 2003). Community does not happen by accident and neither does it prosper where it is not cultivated. In a similar manner, the cultivation of stakeholder relations ensures organizational survival.

The challenges public relations practitioners face today are not new. In fact, they resemble those faced by the early propagandists of the railroads in the 19th century: the need to "invite (a dispersed people) to act as a unified body" (Peters, 1995, pp. 17–18). As Dimock and Dimock noted in 1953, the aim of public relations "is to satisfy all parties of interest—public, employees, and management included" (p. 403). This building of common meanings and generating goodwill among publics can be aided by creation of social capital.

Another historical background is provided by the sociologists of the 20th century Chicago School. They theorized about possible ways of recreating and building the sense of community that had been lost in the formation of the big cities. Communication, they argued, was central for creating and maintaining a sense of community (i.e., Cooley, 1909, 1918; Damico, 1978; Dewey, 1916/1963a; McDermott, 1981; Mead, 1934). For example, Dewey believed that society existed purely through processes of communication, and saw the associated activity as a necessary condition for the creation of a sense of community. He believed that it was possible for "the Great Society" to reestablish its sense of community through communication and the media and become again what it had once been: "the Great Community" (Dewey, 1916/1963a; 1938/1963b).

These aims are clearly apparent in the recent trends of public relations development. Stakeholder thinking (Freeman, 1984; Mitchell, Agle, & Wood, 1997), relationship building (Grunig & Hon, 1999; Wilson, 2001), relationship management (Bruning, DeMiglio & Embry, 2006; Ledingham, 2003; Ledingham & Bruning, 2000), and social responsibility (Leeper, 2001; Wilson, 2001) all apply the ideas of community. They all deal with enabling different stakeholders and fostering collaboration with the communities and publics around the organization. The traditional management of publics and issues is turning towards ongoing interaction: building and maintaining a relationship between the stakeholders and the organization. This shift places more emphasis on those stakeholders with whom organizations have stable or frequent interaction, as they are the ones with whom a relationship can be built (Lahno, 1995; Luoma-aho, 2005). In fact, Putnam himself highlights the importance of frequent interaction. He concludes, "Again and again, we find that one key to creating social capital is to build in redundancy of contact" (Putnam et al., 2003, p. 291).

Public Relations or Community Relations?

The search for the great community continues as society becomes all the more fragmented. People are less willing to work together, and individual aims override common agendas (Putnam, 2000). One could argue that commitment is no longer the norm and that the concept of "the general public" has been replaced by diverse and fractured publics. As publics fracture, there is a loss of shared meaning that in turn affects cultural, moral, and political standards and participation (Leeper, 2001). The creation of shared meanings is a central function of public relations. In line with Putnam's views, public relations can be understood as a tool for maintaining a balanced society: Public relations contributes to society by making information available, by building relationships between possibly opposing views, and maintaining consensus (Burton, 1998; Cutlip, Center, & Broom, 1999; Hallahan, 2004). In fact, Hallahan (2004) even suggests that the field should be called community relations instead of public relations.

This is achieved in practice by making information available, building relationships between possibly opposing views, and aiming at harmony (Leeper, 2001). In fact, public relations can be understood as having the responsibility for creating, restoring, and maintaining the societal linkages between governments, civil society organizations, and corporations (Kruckeberg, 2006). Social capital is all about "making connections among people, establishing bonds of trust and understanding, building community" (Putnam et al., 2003, p. 9). The idea is related to what organizations were originally created for: reaching goals that for the individual alone would be difficult or impossible (Hatch, 1997). But achievement per se is not the point, as associations and groups provide the satisfaction of belonging, a sense of loyalty and community that motivates actions.

Social capital is associated with increased interaction and coordination of operations and can be said to boost achievement as cooperation becomes frequent and social ties enable the formation of trust (Putnam et al., 2003). Putnam's social capital refers to investments in social relations that create surplus value: relations between people and the various kinds of capital embedded in and mobilizable through those relations. If public relations aims at generating goodwill toward the organization, the amount of social capital could also be a measure of public relations efforts (Hazleton & Kennan, 2000). Public relations could profit from a redefinition: Public relations could be understood as the practice of creating organizational social capital.

Previous Studies that Apply Putnam's Theories

Community building and the ideas behind social capital creation are central for public relations (Burton, 1998; Hallahan, 2004; Kruckeberg, 2006; Kruckeberg & Starck, 2001; Leeper, 2001; Wilson, 2001). However, Putnam's theories on social capital and community have so far been only moderately applied to research and theory in the field. Some scholars have applied similar ideas with or without mentioning the concept of social capital. Among the most fruitful applications are the "Community Building Theory" by Kruckeberg and Starck (1988, 2001) and the writings on community as a foundation for public relations by Hallahan (2004). They focus on the role of public relations practitioners as restorers and maintainers of a sense of community. Like Putnam, they underline the social and historical elements behind the conceptualization of public relations, and note that the need for modern public relations is the result of a change in people and society: the inversion of public and private life. Kruckeberg and Starck (1988) define community relations as an "organization's planned, active, and continuing participation with and within a community to maintain and enhance its environment to the benefit of both the institution and the community" (p. 24). Public relations have often been accused of being too organization centered, and this definition is useful because it highlights the benefit of both the institution and community.

Others apply Putnam's ideas of social capital. Lehtonen (2002) writes of the arrival of a new era of intangibles, where social capital is the means through which more traditional forms of capital are materialized in corporations. Social capital acts as a catalyst for organizational functions, and because of this universal role its definition becomes difficult. Ihlen (2005) defines social capital and its organizational benefits through Bourdieu's view of social capital. For him, social capital, even in organizations, is individual; it is equal to the opportunities that accrue to an individual through membership. Bourdieu and Putnam share many aspects of theorizing, but only Putnam acknowledges the larger societal impact of social capital.

Many applications of Putnam's thinking for public relations are vague, and provide little concrete examples of the benefits. A more utilitarian application of social capital in public relations research comes from Hazelton and Kennan (2000). They note that organizations have two types of goals, instrumental and relational, and public relations is concerned with the latter. They apply the concept of social capital in arguing for the contribution of public relations to the organizational bottom line. Among the benefits of organizational social capital they list reduced transaction costs, improved productivity, efficiency, improved quality, and customer satisfaction. Hazleton and Kennan (2000) also note the central role of social capital as a link between and a way to acquire other forms of capital. They present three dimensions of social capital they see as important for public relations: the structural dimension, the content dimension, and the relational dimension. Communication, they argue, is not only the foundation for the emergence of social capital, but also the "mechanism whereby the available stock of social capital can be accessed and expended to further various organizational goals and objectives" (p. 83). To them, social capital is the property of a community.

Among public relations scholars, I have probably been the only one concentrating on Putnam's theorizing on social capital (Luoma-aho, 2005, 2006). For me, social capital is an organizational benefit. I have defined social capital as "the extent of the resources available to an organization through networks of trust and reciprocity among its stakeholders" (Luoma-aho, 2005, p. 150). Elsewhere I have argued that communication with stakeholders has both instrumental as well as eigenvalue: not only do stakeholder networks enable organizational survival, but having established channels of communication and being heard in today's communication entrenched society are of value by themselves (Luoma-aho, 2005).

What matters is not the network alone, but what is at the other end of it (Lin, 2001). Social networks are social capital if, and only if, they contain potential benefit and resources for the organization (such as organizational legitimacy or good reputation). Earlier (2005) I have built on Putnam's idea of long-term benefits of social relations, noting the importance of stakeholders with frequent interaction. Frequent stakeholders, if accompanied by high levels of trust toward the organization could be entitled faith-holders. Faith-holders are the organizational "regulars" that contribute to creating social capital (Luoma-aho, 2005).

Creating Social Capital

While all these applications of Putnam's theorizing for public relations are beneficial, they all fail to provide the mechanisms of how social capital could be produced. Public relations scholars and practitioners need to understand the processes of creating social capital. Putnam emphasizes the importance of past experiences for the creation and maintenance of social capital. In fact, networks of civil engagement work by fostering reciprocity, facilitating coordination, and amplifying information about the trustworthiness of other individuals; social networks embody past success at collaboration (Rothstein & Stolle, 2002). "Successful collaboration in one endeavor builds connections and trust—social assets that facilitate future collaboration in other, unrelated tasks" (Putnam, 1993, p. 3).

To fully understand community, the experiences of its members must be captured (Cohen, 1985). Elsewhere I have operationalized Putnam's views of social capital through the concepts of trust and reputation, both of which reflect the members' experiences (Luoma-aho, 2006). Stakeholder trust and a good reputation among stakeholders are important resources for organizations; even social capital (Luoma-aho, 2005; 2006). *Reputation* refers to the past history and the sum of the stories told about the organization among the stakeholders (Bromley, 1993; Fombrun & Van Riel, 2003; Sztompka, 2000), whereas *trust* refers to the future expected behavior of the organization, what is believed and expected of it (Rothstein, 2003; Seligman, 1997). Trust here is understood as faith in the interaction continuing (Seligman, 1997), yet also a prerequisite of a cohesive society (Putnam et al., 1993). Reputation and trust are both formed within the context of continuous meetings and interaction between an organization and its stakeholders. They are interrelated because "Trust turns into reputation as the present turns into history" (Luoma-aho, 2005, p. 142).

Drawing on Putnam's arguments presented in *Making Democracy Work* (1993), Figure 12.1 simplifies the process of social capital creation. Figure 12.1 demonstrates how at best, a good reputation and high levels of trust lead to social capital (Luoma-aho, 2005; Rothstein & Stolle, 2002). It is vital to note, however, that when there are no previous experiences, a reputation can be formed through others' experiences as well as mediated information, which in turn is subject to change should personal experiences become available.

Figure 12.1 is a simplified and polarized model and hence has its limitations. However, since it shows the importance of experiences and expectations, it is of value when considering Putnam's contributions to the study of public relations. The process is cyclic, and starts with experiences, whether of a person, group, or organization. These experiences (whether mediated or personal) of working together, either good or bad, form a reputation. In itself, reputation carries with it certain expectations and facilitates willingness to trust (Luoma-aho, 2006; Misztal,

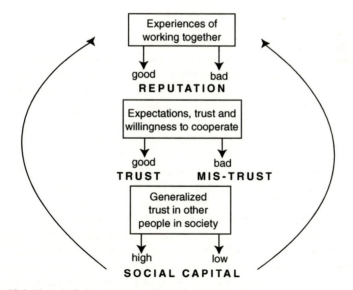

Figure 12.1 Model of the extremes of social capital creation.

1996; Putnam et al., 1993; Sztompka, 2000). The level of trust results in high or low amounts of social capital, which in turn shape experiences and expectations and thus the possibilities for working together (Putnam, 2000; Putnam et al., 1993, 2003).

Figure 12.1 describes the process of how social capital is created. The model has both instrumental and theoretical value, which demonstrates how experiences become expectations, which contribute to reality. Putnam et al. (1993) note: "Citizens in civic communities expect better government and (in part through their own efforts) they get it" (p. 182). However, for this prophecy to be fulfilled, it needs a society (e.g., a democratic societal system), in which various voices are enabled and allowed to be heard. Fostering such a society is one of the core responsibilities of public relations.

Once created, social capital feeds on itself. However, it is important to remember that reputation may be either positive or negative: a good reputation creates trust whereas a bad reputation may diminish trust. Trust on the other hand is unequivocal: it exists to some degree or it is lacking. Whatever the content, the mechanism seems to hold. The organization–stakeholder relationship develops over time and a good reputation is formed through trustworthy conduct. Untrustworthy conduct or a bad reputation can be amended and improved over time with positive experiences. Research has shown, however, that it is much harder to reverse a negative reputation and poor trust than to repair damage done to a hitherto good reputation and high levels of trust (Sjovall & Talk, 2004).

Putting Social Capital to Use

Putnam's theories on the importance of social connectedness and social cohesion provide a point of entry for public relations by highlighting the consequences of uncultivated relationships; not only are organizations and individuals affected, but also society at large. The building and maintaining of relationships is presumably close to what Putnam, given the emphasis he places on reciprocal relationships and trust, would see as "creating" new social capital. The key in creating social capital is getting people to work together and trust each other on a smaller scale (Putnam et al., 2003). Important public relations functions, such as maintaining harmony and creating a sense of community are achieved through communication, by building relationships among the stakeholders (Grunig & Hon, 1999; Ledingham & Bruning, 2000). Organizations that cultivate social capital aim at becoming the neighbors of choice for the communities around them. This process requires building relationships as well as establishing practices that enable exchange of expectations, concerns, and issues (Hallahan, 2004).

Social capital has to be established before it can be used, and this amplifies the need for strategic public relations. Public relations should be, above all, a proactive process of building and preserving social capital, not the often applied (and reactionary) reconciliation of organizations with the community (Hallahan, 2004). Many of the ideas concerning civic involvement are related to public relations functions. In fact, the creation and maintenance of organizational social capital can be seen as underlying the theory and practice of public relations, as behind all PR-theories is the assumption that organizations benefit from good relationships with stakeholders (Luoma-aho, 2005). Burton (1998) calls for public relations to once again assume a community-building role, as this role will otherwise be taken over by other sources, whether activist, bloggers, or journalists. He notes that two-way communication "can help make sense in the information flowing within a community and can help develop a healthier social structure. PR, with its firm grounding in communications approaches, is well positioned to take an active step in facilitating the two-way flow of communications within a community" (p. 39).

There are several aspects of Putnam's theorizing in addition to the model of social capital creation that could benefit the theory and practice of public relations. For example, Putnam's distinction between bridging and bonding social capital could be applied to better understand the value of communicating with both internal and external stakeholders. Bridging social capital describes the relationships an organization has toward its external publics, whereas bonding capital is needed for internal communication or the internal relations of the organization. Bonding social capital is good for the creation of a sense of community within an organization, as it promotes cohesion by "undergirding specific reciprocity and mobilizing solidarity" (Putnam, 2000, p. 22). Bridging social capital, or external stakeholder relations as looser networks are "better for linkage to external assets and for information diffusion" (p. 22).

A stable organization needs both types of capital, and public relations should aim at ensuring the formation and maintenance of both kinds of ties. The ties should first be formed inside the organization (bonding); for example, through a shared identity, as the organizational reputation among the external stakeholders is greatly influenced by the organization's internal reputation. Only after bonding capital is established, can organizations build bridging social capital. As well understood by network theorists, those with central roles in the social networks will be able to direct the crucial resource flows of information. Public relations practitioners should aim at becoming central in both bonding and bridging social networks related to the organization.

Public relations and Putnam's social capital have many features in common: they are long-term social functions that aim at goodwill and cooperation. They both aim to create a feeling of belonging, a "we-feeling." As intangibles and still in the process of development, both are concepts that can be overlooked and considered unnecessary during good times, but when crises arise they are critical for organizational or societal survival (Ledingham & Bruning, 2000; Putnam et al., 2003). In fact, it is the public relations professionals who bring the lone bowlers, the various stakeholders, into the club; into a joint discourse with the organizations. Public relations practitioners turn bowling alone into bowling together, and their value will increase in the future as they are equipped to build and cultivate long-term relationships with both external and internal organizational stakeholders (Ledingham & Bruning, 2000; Putnam et al., 2003). Despite these shared traits, applying Putnam's theories to the theory and practice of public relations does not occur without problems, and these problems are discussed next.

Problems with Putnam in Public Relations

Introducing new theories has its dangers; their application involves generalizations that may water down their original ideas. Moreover, when theories are applied and borrowed across disciplines and even across sciences, the original problems the theories addressed can be forgotten. In the context of public relations, Putnam's theories run the same risk, yet offer something very valuable in return: a macroview of social processes and a better understanding of societal consequences of cultivating relationships.

Putnam's theories have been developed for the fields of political science and sociology. They focus mostly on societal processes, which is both their strength and weakness. Many of the traditionally central issues of public relations research are not addressed. Putnam's thinking does not address how organizations could best build social capital, but rather the benefits and the importance of social capital. Neither can these theories be applied to describe the type of communication or its contents, but rather affirm that communication is beneficial in the long run. Putnam's theories provide no measure or proof for the benefit of public relations activities, but they give a name and value to the outcome, through the concept of social capital. The problem with all applications of Putnam's theories for public relations lies in the scope: while most scholars agree that social capital is an activator of other beneficial types of capital for organizations, almost all scholars apply Putnam's theories only in part.

Social capital, as understood by Putnam, is always positive to those possessing it, but it can be harmful to those outside the group (Ojala et al., 2006). In the case of bridging social capital, excess is seldom problem. However, in the case of excess bonding social capital, external stakeholders may be feel ignored and the organization even harmed through these feelings. In sum, social capital provides organizational efficiencies that provide for long-term existence and success. For public relations, social capital creation can be modeled through the creation of trust and reputation among organizational stakeholders (Hazelton & Kennan, 2000; Luoma-aho, 2005). As with all new theories, one should apply what is useful, and leave out what does not fit.

Conclusion

Public relations theory has long been organization-centered and lacking in metalevel theorizing. The thinking of Robert Putnam makes way for a deeper understanding of public relations through introducing the importance of maintaining a sense of community. Putnam has been able to prove the value of long-term benefits of social networks, a result which still remains unproved by public relations scholars. Moreover, as Putnam focuses on the larger societal benefits brought about by social relations, he reminds us that publics and communities also form without and despite organizational existence and action (Hallahan, 2004; Putnam et al., 2003). As the publics fracture, the process of creating a sense of community becomes of central importance. Despite these insights, so far Putnam's theories have been applied only moderately to the theory and practice of public relations. The model of social capital creation presented in this chapter derives from Putnam's theorizing, and marks a starting point for a more holistic development of public relations toward communitarism and social capital creation.

Putnam writes at the close of *Making Democracy Work* (1993): "Building social capital will not be easy, but it is the key to making democracy work" (p. 185). If, as suggested here, public relations builds organizational social capital, then it is a necessary force not only for organizational legitimacy, but for the prosperity of democratic society. This thinking is timely, as the democratization of many developing countries is still underway, and as society today shows no signs of becoming more predictable or less risky in the future. Public relations in modern society has the potential for much greater influence than has thus far been acknowledged. As the benefits of social capital become better known (relationships, interaction, and collaboration) the importance of social capital for the practice of public relations will increase. In fact, a new, more holistic definition of public relations could be *the creation and maintenance of organizational social capital.*

References

Bourdieu, P. (1995). *The logic of practice*. Cambridge, UK: Cambridge University Press. (Original work published 1980)

Bromley, D. B. (1993). *Reputation, image and impression management*. Chichester, UK: Wiley.

Bruning, S., DeMiglio, P., & Embry, K. (2006). Mutual benefit as outcome indicator: Factors influencing perceptions of benefit in organization-public relationships. *Public Relations Review, 32*, 33–40.

Burt, R. (2002). The social capital of structural holes. In M. Guillén, R. Collins, P. England, & M. Meyer (Eds.), *New dimensions of economic sociology* (pp. 148–190). New York: Russell Sage Foundation.

Burton, St. J. III (1998). Public relations as community-building: Then and now. *Public Relations Quarterly, 43*(19), 34–40.

Cohen, A. P. (1985) *The symbolic construction of community*. London: Routledge.

Coleman, J. S. (1988). Social capital in the creation of human capital. *American Journal of Sociology, 94*, 95–120.

Cooley, C. H. (1909). *Social organization*. New York: Scribner.

Cooley, C. H. (1918). *Social process*. New York: Scribner.

Cutlip, S., Center, A., & Broom, G. (1999). *Effective public relations*. (8th ed.). Upper Saddle River, NJ: Prentice-Hall.

Damico, A. J. (1978). *Individuality and community: The social and political thought of John Dewey*. Gainesville, FL: University Presses of Florida.

DeFilippis, J. (2001). The myth of social capital in community development. *Housing Policy Debate, 12*(4), 781–806.

Dewey, J. (1963a). *Democracy and education*. New York: Macmillan. (Original work published 1916)

Dewey, J. (1963b). *Experience and education*. New York: Collier Books. (Original work published 1938)

Dimock, M. E., & Dimock, G. O. (1953). *Public administration*. New York: Rinehart.

Fombrun, C., & van Riel, C. (2003). *Fame and fortune: How successful companies build winning reputations*. Upper Saddle River, NJ: Prentice-Hall.

Freeman, R. E. (1984). *Strategic management: A stakeholder approach*. Boston: Pitman.

Fukuyama, F. (1995). *Trust: The social virtues and the creation of prosperity*. New York: Free Press.

Granovetter, M. (1973). The strength of weak ties. *American Journal of Sociology, 78*(6), 1360–1379.

Grunig, J., & Hon, L. (1999). *Guidelines for measuring relationships in public relations*. The Institute for Public Relations Commission on PR Measurement and Evaluation. Retrieved January 1, 2007 from http://www.instituteforpr. com/index.phtml?article_id=pdf

Hallahan, K. (2004). "Community" as a foundation for public relations theory and practice. *Communication Yearbook, 28*(1), 233–279.

Hatch, M. (1997). *Organization theory: Modern symbolic and postmodern perspectives*. New York: Oxford University Press.

Hazleton, V., & Kennan, W. (2000). Social capital: Reconceptualizing the bottom line. *Corporate Communications: An International Journal, 5*(2), 81–86.

Ihlen, Ø. (2005). The power of social capital: Adapting Bourdieu to the study of public relations. *Public Relations Review, 31*(4), 492–496.

Kruckeberg, D. (2006, June–July). *An "organic model" of public relations: The role of public relations for governments, civil society organizations (CSOs) and corporations in developing and guiding social and cultural policy to build and maintain community in 21st Century civil society.* Paper presented at the International Conference on Municipal Social Policy and Publics: Realities and Perspectives, Ulan-Ude, Buryatia, Russia.

Kruckeberg, D., & Starck K. (1988). *Public relations and community: A reconstructed theory.* New York: Praeger.

Lahno, B. (1995). Trust, reputation, and exit in exchange relationships. *The Journal of Conflict Resolution, 39*(3), 495–510.

Ledingham J. (2003). Explicating relationship management as a general theory of public relations. *Journal of Public Relations Research, 15*(2), 181–198.

Ledingham, J., & Bruning, S. (Eds.) (2000). *Public relations as relationship management: A relational approach to the study and practice of public relations.* Mahwah, NJ: Erlbaum.

Leeper, R. (2001). In search of a metatheory for public relations: An argument for communitarianism. In R. L. Heath (Ed.), *Handbook of public relations* (pp. 93–104). Thousand Oaks, CA: Sage.

Lehtonen, J. (2002). *Samspel och kommunikation* [Cooperation and communication]. Jyväskylä, Finland: University of Jyväskylä Press.

Lin, N. (2001). *Social capital: A theory of social structure and action.* Cambridge: Cambridge University Press.

Luoma-aho, V. (2005). *Faith-holders as social capital of Finnish public organizations.* Jyväskylä, Finland: University of Jyväskylä Press.

Luoma-aho, V. (2006). Intangibles of public organizations: Trust and reputation. In V. Luoma-aho & S. Peltola (Eds.), *Public organizations in the communication society* (pp. 11–58). Jyväskylä, Finland: University of Jyväskylä Press.

McDermott, J. J. (1981). *The philosophy of John Dewey.* Chicago: University of Chicago Press.

Mead, G. H. (1934). *Mind, self, and society* (C. W. Morris, Ed). Chicago: University of Chicago Press.

Misztal, B. (1996). *Trust in modern societies.* Padstow, UK: Polity Press.

Mitchell R., Agle, B., & Wood D. (1997). Toward a theory of stakeholder identification and salience: Defining the principle of who and what really counts. *Academy of Management Review, 22*(4), 853–886.

Ojala, J., Hakoluoto, T., Hjorth, A., & Luoma-aho, V. (2006). Hyvä paha socialize pääoma [Good and bad social capital]. In P. Jokivuori, R. Latva-Karjanmaa, & A. Ropo (Eds.), *Työelämän taitekohtia* [Turning points of work life] (pp. 13–33). Helsinki, Finland: Työministeriö.

Patulny, R. (2003). Bonding, bridging and investment: important aspects of a national social capital policy strategy. *Melbourne Journal of Politic, 3*, 68–80.

Peters, J. (1995). Historical tensions in the concept of public opinion. In T. Glasser & C. Salmon (Eds.), *Public opinion and the communication of consent* (pp. 3–32). New York: Guilford Press.

Pizzorno, A. (2004, August). *Resources of social capital: Reputation and visibility.* Keynote speech, ECSR Summer School on Social Capital, Trento, Italy.

Platt, J. (1973). Social traps. *American Psychologist, 28,* 641–665.

Putnam, R. D. (1993). The prosperous community: Social capital and public life. *The American Prospect, 4*(13), 36–42.

Putnam, R. D. (1995a). Bowling alone: America's declining social capital. *Journal of Democracy, 6,* 65–78.

Putnam, R. D. (1995b). Tuning in, tuning out: The strange disappearance of social capital in America. *Political Science and Politics, 28,* 664–683.

Putnam, R.D. (1996). The strange disappearance of civic America. *The American Prospect, 7*(24), 34–48.

Putnam, R. D. (2000). *Bowling alone: The collapse and revival of American community.* New York: Simon & Schuster.

Putnam, R. D. (Ed.). (2002). *Democracies in flux: The evolution of social capital in contemporary society.* New York: Oxford University Press.

Putnam, R. D., Feldstein, L., & Cohen, D. (2003). *Better together: Restoring the American community.* New York: Simon & Schuster.

Putnam, R. D., Leonardi, R., & Nanetti, R. Y. (1993). *Making democracy work: Civic traditions in modern Italy.* Princeton, NJ: Princeton University Press.

Rothstein, B. (2003). *Sociala fällor och tillitens problem* [Social traps and the problem of trust]. Stockholm, Sweden: SNS Förlag.

Rothstein, B., & Stolle, D. (2002, August). *How political institutions create and destroy social capital: An institutional theory of generalized trust.* Paper presented at the Annual Meeting of the American Political Science Association, Boston.

Rousseau, D. M., Sitkin, S. B., Burt, R. S., & Camerer, C. (1998). Not so different after all: A cross-discipline view of trust. *Academy of Management Review, 23,* 393–404.

Seligman, A. B. (1997). *The problem of trust.* Princeton, NJ: Princeton University Press.

Sjovall, A., & Talk, A. (2004). From actions to impressions: Cognitive attribution theory and the formation of corporate reputation. *Corporate Reputation Review, 7*(3), 269–281.

Starck, K., & Kruckeberg, D. (2001). *Public relations and community: A reconstructed theory revisited.* In R. L. Heath (Ed.), *Handbook of public relations* (pp. 51–59). Thousand Oaks, CA: Sage.

Sztompka, P. (2000). *Trust: A sociological theory.* New York: Cambridge University Press.

Wilson, L. J. (2001). *Relationships within communities: Public relations for the new century.* In R. L. Heath (Ed.), *Handbook of public relations* (pp. 521–526). Thousand Oaks, CA: Sage.

Life and Work of Robert David Putnam

Robert David Putnam is a political scientist and the Peter and Isabel Malkin Professor of Public Policy at Harvard University. Putnam is best known for his famous arguments regarding loss of community in modern society, which, he claims, has had several negative consequences. His many books have been translated into 17 languages, including the best-selling *Bowling Alone.* Over the past several decades, Putnam's books and articles have been among the most cited publications in the social sciences.

Putnam was born in Rochester, New York on January 9, 1941 to a moderate Republican family living in a small community. He graduated from the liberal Swarthmore College in 1963, where he met his wife Rosemary. Putnam was a Fulbright scholar at Oxford University and earned his doctorate from Yale University in 1970. Putnam has held many posts at the University of Michigan and Harvard and served as chairman of Harvard's Department of Government, director of the Center for International Affairs, and dean of the John F. Kennedy School of Government. Putnam has received honorary degrees from Swarthmore and Stockholm University and served on the staff of the National Security Council. Putnam has worked with top political leaders and activists. He is also the principal investigator of The Saguaro Seminar and the 2006 winner of the Johan Skytte Prize in Political Science.

Major works with relevance for this text: Putnam (1993, 1995a, 1995b, 1996, 2000, 2002; Putnam et al., 1993, 2003).

Chapter 13

On Feminist Theory of Public Relations

An Example from Dorothy E. Smith

Lana F. Rakow and Diana Iulia Nastasia

Abstract

The need to develop a feminist theory *of* public relations rather than a feminist theory *for* public relations makes the work of Canadian sociologist Dorothy E. Smith useful. Her work should be considered in light of various feminist theoretical positions—liberal, radical, socialist, postmodernist, multicultural, and postcolonial—which contextualize the ways in which Smith discusses gender systems, women's identities, power relations, social injustice, and social change. Ultimately, a critical feminist theory of public relations would focus on the consequences rather than the efficacy of institutional discourses, and on structures of power and group relations rather than on relations between individual women and men.

What would public relations theory and research *for* women look like, and why do we need it? The question may seem to be covering old ground: there is nothing new in arguing in favor of a feminist theory in public relations. Influenced by women's movements for social change and by feminist scholarship across academic disciplines, feminist public relations researchers have been concerned about the status of women in public relations as a professional practice. They have been concerned about shifts in the numbers of women and men in public relations practice, disparate salaries and responsibilities between women and men, and "glass ceilings" that block women from moving into senior public relations positions. They have argued for incorporating feminine/feminist values into public relations practice. Despite over two decades of academic argument in favor of it, however, a feminist theory of public relations remains underdeveloped and uneven because the goal has been a feminist theory *for* public relations rather than *of* public relations. Current efforts have not taken into account various feminist theoretical positions that illuminate rather than take for granted gender systems, women's identities, power relations, social injustice, and social change. The work of Canadian sociologist Dorothy E. Smith incorporates most of these theoretical positions in order to problematize features of the social world, making her an important example of how feminist social theory can be used to develop a critical public relations theory with the goal of benefiting women and, ultimately, all people.

In order to proceed according to a basic tenet of feminist theorizing that rejects the canonization of "great men" (or alternatively "great women") theorists and proposes the encouragement of theory coming from collective yet diverse experiences of women (and men), and to gain the most value from Smith's contributions to a feminist social theory, we locate her work within multiple theoretical positions. Following categories used by feminist metatheorists, we present the ways in which six feminist theoretical positions—liberal feminism, radical feminism, socialist feminism, postmodernist feminism, multicultural feminism, and postcolonial feminism—have configured social theory, starting from sometimes converging and sometimes diverging assumptions about gender, woman/women, power, injustice, and change. With Dorothy Smith, we then provide an example of employing feminist theory not only in the understanding but also in the problematization of the social realm, by conceiving a sociology for women and ultimately for people, by identifying the "mothertongue" and the phenomenon of "bifurcated consciousness," by examining the "relations of ruling" and the "circle of men," and by developing "institutional ethnography" as a methodology for change. The analysis of feminist theoretical positions, and of Dorothy Smith's work at the intersection of such positions, enables us to see that concerns expressed to date about women and public relations have been concerns about the *lives of women in public relations* rather than concerns about *public relations in the lives of women.*

Feminist Theoretical Positions and Their Potential for Public Relations

Chris Weedon (1997) asserted that "*feminism is a politics*" (p. 1), acknowledging that existing power relations between men and women structure all areas of life, and that these power relations are unjust. Like all politics, feminism has its roots in political movements (Weedon, 1997), namely, the women's liberation movements in the United States and Western Europe in the late 19th century and the early 20th century. When considering the succession of women's movements, scholars have classified feminism into the first wave or the suffrage movement, from the 1850s to the 1950s; the second wave or the women's rights movement, between the 1960s and the 1980s; and a third wave or a micropolitics movement, from the 1990s on (Bailey, 1997; Rosen, 2001).

Judith Grant (1993) stated that although the history of feminist theories "is tangled up with this well-known narrative" of the feminist movements, feminism needs to turn from asking "What did we do and when did we do it?" toward inquiring "What did we know and when did we know it?" It has been affirmed that feminism is not only a politics but also a theory, or rather a range of theories (Butler & Scott, 1992; Garry & Pearsall, 1996), each constituting a particular project for understanding *gender, woman/women, power, injustice, and change* (Carby, 1987; Firestone, 1970). Considering the variety of feminist theorizing, scholars have divided feminism into classes including but not reduced to a liberal feminist position against gender inequality, a radical feminist position against women's oppression by men, a socialist feminist position against the exploitation of women's and men's labor, a postmodernist feminist position against the mystification of grand narratives such as gender, a multicultural feminist position against sexism–racism combinations, and a postcolonial feminist position against the colonization of third-world women (Donovan, 1985; Tong, 1989). Each feminist position has potential for understanding and critiquing public relations, although feminist discussions about public relations have been primarily from a liberal feminist position, with few radical feminist and multicultural feminist counterpoints (Aldoory, 2003, 2005). Socialist, postmodernist, and postcolonial feminist theoretical positions still need to be accounted for by feminist public relations scholarship. The key points of each feminist position are summarized in Table 13.1.

Liberal Feminism

Liberal feminism, the dominant paradigm of feminist theory in the Western world, has been much admired and critiqued. Evans (1995) suggested that there is more liberal feminist empirical scholarship than liberal feminist theoretical development, because it is broadly assumed that liberal feminism is respectable and does not need much proof. For liberal feminists from Harriet Taylor or Susan B. Anthony in the 19th century to Betty Friedan (1963) and Janet Radcliffe Richards (1980) in the 20th century, all women and men should be considered full individuals, capable of making rational decisions; a special focus should be placed upon opportunities for women to increase social and political participation only because women have not been treated as full individuals for a long time, and only until this disadvantage for women is overcome. Liberal feminist authors have been critiqued for reducing the feminist category "woman" to the liberal concept of individuality (Nash, 1997), as well as for reducing the dynamics of women of many races and ethnicities to one static typology (Coole, 2000) and for ignoring issues of class (Jaggar, 1983). Yet liberal feminism has been reclaimed: for example, Eisenstein (1981) considers that liberal feminism seems to support the liberal doctrine of individualism, yet it destabilizes this doctrine by theorizing the radical notion of women's groups; and Ken-

Table 13.1 A Classification of Feminist Theoretical Positions

Position	Liberal feminism	Radical feminism	Socialist feminism	Postmodernist feminism	Multicultural feminism	Postcolonial feminism
Gender systems	Gender systems should be minimized (androgyny)	Patriarchy, a pervasive gender system, should be critiqued	Gender and class systems, both expressions of dominance, should be exposed	"Gender," one grand narrative of humankind, should be demystified	Mixed gender–race systems, forms of oppression, should be challenged	Gendered systems, forms of colonialism, should be overthrown
Women's identities	Woman = rational, individualist, just like man	Woman = collective experiences, different from men's discourses	Woman = primarily unwaged labor; unlike men's mostly waged work	"Woman" = not what it is but what it means in the nexus of structures of and for men and women	Women = not unique unproblematic category, but plurality of colors and voices	"Women" = "Others," third-world women = ultimate Others
Power relations	Unequal distributions of gender roles, to be reformed	The oppression of women by men, to be combated	Inequitable distributions of forces and means of production, to be rebalanced	Tensions between structural centrality and marginality, to be reinterpreted	The reification of an unreflective standpoint of Whiteness, to be eradicated	Strategies for representing and exploiting third-world women, to be addressed
Social injustice	Women's discrimination throughout history	Continuing violence against and silencing of women	Exploitation of women and men from lower classes by those in a higher class, peaking during capitalism	Exploitation through knowledge structures, peaking in Western modernity	Combination of sexism, racism, and in/difference	Use of marginals, especially of third-world women, in the colonial patriarchies
Social change	Reparation within the existing social structures	Total makeover of existing social structures	Revolution of socio-economic structures	Transformations not through macro- but micropolitics	Social acceptance of difference, dissonance	Letting the subaltern speak

singer (1997) writes that liberal feminism cannot be accused of having ignored ethnicity since among those essential for its development were Sojourner Truth and Ida B. Wells.

In sum, liberal feminism asserts that (1) gender systems should be minimized; (2) woman's identity is rational and individualist, just like man's; (3) power relations, namely unequal distributions of roles between individual men and women, need to be reformed; (4) social injustice encompasses women's discrimination throughout history; and (5) social change should consist of reparation within existing social structures. Liberal feminist theorists in public relations studies have rejected treating women and men differently in this profession, and have advocated for ensuring that women be able to compete with men for comparable jobs with comparable salaries (Aldoory & Toth, 2002; Cline et al. 1986; Grunig, 1988; Toth & Grunig, 1993).

Radical Feminism

Radical feminism has been commended as a trend infused with emotional and intellectual energy, pointing at contradictions within liberal feminism and problematizing gender and patriarchy; however, it has been critiqued for failing to theorize the relationships between patriarchy and capitalism/imperialism, and to construct a pluralist category for "women" (Echols & Willis, 1990; Thompson, 2001). Radical feminists have made efforts to conceptualize oppression, patriarchy as a system of oppression, and woman as an oppressed category, and concomitantly have advocated for the need to begin an all-embracing change rather than envisaging a few superficial reforms (Firestone, 1970; Sarachild, 1978). However, radical feminists have been critiqued for proclaiming a total makeover without providing a clear platform for this. Moreover, although liberal feminists have argued for basic equality between women with men (Okin, 1989), whereas radical feminists have argued for significant differences between women and men while valuing women (Daly, 1973), both liberal and radical feminists promote a universal sisterhood not accounting for the diversity of women (see Bryson, 1992). With its pluses and minuses, radical feminism remains "among the most highly original, provocative, and politically charged bodies of work in feminism today" (Grant, 1993, p. 74); in addition, some radical feminists have problematized or abandoned universalist categorizations (Frye, 1983; Thompson, 2001).

In sum, radical feminists state that (1) patriarchy, a pervasive gender system, should be critiqued; (2) woman's identity is made of collective experiences, different from man's; (3) power relations, namely the oppression of women by men, need to be combated; (4) social injustice comprises the continuing violence against and silencing of women; and

(5) social change should comprise a makeover of existing social structures. Radical feminist theorists in public relations have tried to shift from women's assimilation into patriarchal structures such as public relations to the critique of a profession organized around masculine values, and have strived to envisage the possibility of organizing public relations around feminine values such as intuition and cooperation (Grunig et al., 2000; Hon, 1995).

Socialist Feminism

According to Shelton and Agger (1993), socialist feminism denotes "any intellectual and political perspective sympathetic to both Marxism and feminism" (p. 27). Socialist feminists have critiqued liberal feminists for seeking to improve "the situation of middle- and upper-middle class women by affording them somewhat greater opportunities for career mobility," and radical feminists for arguing that "women's subordination in the household is somehow prior to, and more important than, their subordination in the paid labor force" (Shelton & Agger, 1993, pp. 27–28). Unlike liberal and radical feminists, socialist feminists have expanded Marxist theories in order to include both waged and unwaged labor (Kuhn & Wolpe, 1978), thus "refusing to accept a separation of public and private spheres" (Shelton & Agger, 1993, p. 33). Socialist feminism has been critiqued primarily for discussing women only through relations of production and reproduction, thus essentializing "woman" as laborer and ignoring women's diverse profiles (Fraser, 1989; Weedon, 1997); however, some left feminists approach gender and class relations in conjunction with race and ethnicity (Carby, 1997; Joseph, 1997).

In sum, socialist feminism affirms that (1) gender and class systems, both expressions of dominance, should be exposed; (2) woman's identity springs from women's assignment primarily to unwaged labor unlike men's performance mostly of paid work; (3) power relations, that is, inequitable distributions of forces and means of production across genders and classes, need to be rebalanced; (4) social injustice represents the exploitation of women and men from lower classes by those in a higher class, present throughout history but peaking during capitalism; and (5) social change should involve the revolution of socioeconomic structures. Although the intersection of Marxism and feminism has not served as a theoretical foundation for feminist public relations scholarship, socialist feminism has the potential of illuminating the complex connections between gender and class for public relations, and even of calling into question the very existence of those capitalist patriarchal enterprises which employ public relations to carry out exploitative social relations.

Postmodernist Feminism

Seyla Benhabib (1995) suggested that feminists are no longer preoc-
cupied by the Marxism–feminism union, but have become interested
in the alliance between feminism and postmodernism, both contesting
grand narratives of humankind. Postmodernist feminism positions itself
in contradiction with liberal feminism that supports rationality and
individuality (Butler, 1990), and in partial agreement with radical feminism that denounces patriarchal mechanisms of oppression (Jardin,
1985), and socialist feminism that denounces capitalist mechanisms of
production/reproduction (Di Stefano, 1990). However, postmodernist
feminists suggest the disappearance of authenticity whereas radical feminists assert the value of women's authenticity (Creed, 1987), and postmodernist feminists approach multiple forms of exploitation whereas
socialist feminists concentrate on exploitation through labor (Fraser
& Nicholson, 1990). Postmodernist feminists are concerned not with
what woman *is* in economic, political, or cultural structures, but with
what "woman" means in such structures (Grant, 1993). Postmodernist
feminism is attractive because "it allows women to talk about gender,
oppression, freedom, and personal politics while avoiding essentialism"
(p. 135), yet it is frustrating because it robs us "of a way to conceptualize
women as subjects and agents of change" (p. 134).

In sum, postmodernist feminists contend that: (1) "gender," one
grand narrative of humankind, needs to be demystified; (2) "woman" is
a matter of meaning; (3) power relations need to be reinterpreted over
and over again; (4) social injustice refers to exploitation through language and knowledge structures, peaking in Western modernity; and
(5) social change should be brought about through micropolitics. Public relations theorists increasingly use postmodernism as a framework
for discussing power and centrality/marginality (Duffy, 2000; Mickey,
2003); however, feminist public relations scholars have not yet utilized
postmodernism to discuss gender and power in this profession. Turning
attention to postmodernist feminist theory could yield a more sophisticated understanding of how power discourses such as public relations
inscribe social relations of centrality and marginality that essentialize
gender and women.

Multicultural Feminism

Women of color in the United States and Western Europe critique a
feminism that assumes a universal category of woman and an unproblematic sisterhood among women, and that takes Whiteness for granted
throughout its theory and practice (Albrecht & Brewer, 1990). Categorized as multicultural feminists, multiracial feminists, pluralist

feminists, or womanist theorists, women of color in the Western world admonish White feminists for reproducing rather than critiquing systems of oppression; for example, in Bethel's "What Chou Mean *We*, White Girl?" (1979), and Moraga and Anzaldua's collection *This Bridge Called My Back* (1981). Women of color also draw attention to the discrepancy between White feminists' overreliance on Eurocentric systems of thought—including liberalism, Marxism, and postmodernism—and their declared independence from patriarchal thinking. Paula Gunn Allen (1986) chided White feminists for their lack of knowledge of their "red roots," asserting that matrifocal models sought by many feminists existed among Native Americans prior to White colonization. As bell hooks (1984) envisioned, under pressure from women of color, feminists from various trends have started to acknowledge that diversity means not only harmony but also dissonance.

In sum, multicultural feminism asserts that: (1) mixed gender-race systems, forms of oppression, should be challenged; (2) women's identities correspond to a plurality of colors, cultures, and voices rather than to a unique unproblematic category; (3) power relations, namely the reification of an unreflective standpoint of Whiteness, need to be eradicated; (4) social injustice is the combination of sexism, racism, and *in/difference*; and (5) social change should consist of the social acceptance of difference and dissonance. Although some women of color have critiqued the public relations profession for its racial practices (Kern-Foxworth, 1989a, 1989b; Kern-Foxworth et al., 1994; Pompper, 2004), they have done this primarily from within a liberal feminist perspective that accepts social structures and attempts to reform them. Therefore, a multicultural feminist public relations theory, to account for the inherence of Whiteness to and the consequences of racism for public relations, remains to be produced.

Postcolonial Feminism

Postcolonial feminists draw on Marxism in their analyses of hegemonic strategies utilized by imperialist forces to exploit "third world" women, and on postmodernism in their examinations of grand narratives employed by colonial powers to mystify the third world women (Spivak, 1988a). Postcolonial feminists have affirmed that most first world feminists fail to understand women from other cultural spaces, and to theorize the relations between gender, nationalism, and imperialism (Mohanty, 1991). Inspired by the works of Edward Said (1978), postcolonial feminists have asserted that third world women are the ultimate Other, conceived as weak and uncivilized both in first world colonial discourses and in third world nationalist ones (Lewis, 1995). Following the lead of Gayatri Chakravorty Spivak (1988b) (see chapter 14, this volume), who explored the differences between men and women able to negotiate with "structures of violence" and to gain "voice," and the "subaltern" (especially women) unable to access colonial discourses and thus remaining voiceless, postcolonial feminists have discussed the consequences of the third world women's marginalized relationships with colonial power (McClintock, 1995).

In sum, postcolonial feminists state that (1) gendered colonial systems, forms of hegemony, should be overthrown; (2) women's identities are shaped by women's positioning as "others," and of third world women as "ultimate others"; (3) power relations, namely strategies for representing and exploiting third world women, need to be addressed; (4) social injustice consists of the use of marginals, especially of third world women, in colonial patriarchies; and (5) social change should arise from subaltern speech. Postcolonial feminism has not been considered in public relations theory, yet it could bring a better understanding of the consequences of public relations practices in the lives of the marginalized from around the world, especially third world women. Postcolonial feminist approaches to public relations would critically examine the globalization of large Western industrial corporations and governmental organizations, and the use of public relations discourses to reproduce international relations of domination that affect women's lives.

Feminist Theoretical Positions in Public Relations Scholarship

The theoretical positions described above offer different views on how societies are explained and carried out by people, placing emphasis on different aspects of gender, women, power, injustice, and change. Most feminist public relations scholarship, however, begins with and argues only from liberal or radical feminist theoretical positions, but often without explicit identification of underlying assumptions. We will look at this work briefly before suggesting how Dorothy Smith's feminist sociology can be drawn on to reveal problematics that have originated in other feminist theoretical positions, and that have eluded feminist public relations scholarship.

Feminist ideas in public relations emerged in the United States in the 1980s, when "the field became over 50% female," and some feared that since the profession was populated by more women than men it was being "feminized" (Aldoory & Toth, 2002, p. 104). Since other occupations in which women predominate, such as nursing or teaching, are commonly viewed as less prestigious and less valuable than those in which men predominate, such as science or engineering, some authors of business and of academic analyses became concerned that the preponderance of women might signal or create a decline in the field of public relations (Lauzen, 1992; Lesly, 1988). Feminist public relations researchers started examining disparities faced by women in pay, work roles, and promotion, despite the number of women employed, and attempted to assert that the feminization of this career was not synonymous with its decay. The literature is considered to begin with the landmark *Velvet Ghetto* study (Cline et al., 1986), whose title echoes a statement from an 1978 article in *Business Week* that public relations was turning into "the velvet ghetto of affirmative action," meant to compensate for women's scarcity in managerial positions. The focus of the *Velvet Ghetto* report, to assess the impact of the increasing percentage of women in business communication, became the aim of following feminist approaches to public relations, such as the 1988 special issue of *Public Relations Review* entitled "Women in Public Relation," and the 1989 collection *Beyond the Velvet Ghetto.*

In spite of the growing sophistication of theoretical enterprises, and against some warning that the liberal feminist approach "has not worked in public relations" (Aldoory & Toth, 2002, p. 104), much feminist public relations scholarship since the mid-to-late 1980s has been modeled after the *Velvet Ghetto* study, reproducing a liberal feminist position against gender discrimination and for equal opportunities. Toth (1988) affirmed that practitioners in public relations should aim at "eventual parity in salaries" (p. 40), and at gradual abandonment of organizational myths that "men are groomed for the manager role" while women must earn "access to decision-making" (p. 42) as well as of gender stereotypes that women are too emotional or too unorganized (p. 42). Cline (1989) highlighted that progress toward removing salary differences and biases against women in public relations were slow, and asserted that under these circumstances women had to take action, namely "individual responsibility for one's personal and professional career" as well as "networking and cooperation of strong individuals" (p. 308).

Throughout the 1990s and at the beginning of this millennium, salaries, gender roles, and gender stereotypes have remained the main concerns of feminist public relations scholarships, and individualism has remained an overarching ideological frame. Toth and Grunig (1993) proposed the expansion of gender role theories from a two-factor construct, with managerial and technical dimensions, to a combination of roles construct, indicating that women managers as well as male technicians accomplish mixed technical and managerial functions, whereas male managers perform only managerial functions and women technicians carry out only technical activities. Aldoory and Toth (2002) reiterated that unequal and discriminatory practices in the public relations profession are linked to more advantageous types of hiring, salaries, and promotion for men than for women.

The dominant feminist trend in theorizing public relations still stems from liberalism, yet some feminist work about public relations "resonates with a radical feminist perspective in its focus on systemic problems" (Aldoory, 2003, p. 239). Some studies have combined liberal feminism with radical feminism in attempts to move from describing what is to envisioning what could be: Hon (1995) offered "a feminist theory of public relations" through a shift from "women's assimilation into patriarchal systems" to "a genuine commitment to social restructuring," and through a move from characterizing women's discrimination as male dominance at work, women's "balancing" between career and family, and gender stereotypes, to mapping women's values such as holism, inclusiveness, and complexity (p. 80). Wrigley (2002) attempted to present the factors contributing to glass ceilings and women's responses to glass ceilings, but she also tried to make recommendations for educators, students, and practitioners about strategies for change. Some feminist studies in public relations have been immersed in the ideas of radical feminism. Creedon (1993) conceived a feminist analysis of systems theory. Grunig et al. (2000) argued for "Feminist Values in Public Relations," juxtaposing cooperation, respect, caring, nurturance, interconnection, justice, equity, honesty, sensitivity, perceptiveness, intuition, altruism, fairness, morality. and commitment, with norms of public relations, and arguing for the incorporation of feminist values into professional practice. Others using a radical feminist approach avoided essentializing women, men, and the field of public relations as inherently possessing any values. Rakow (1989) asserted that gender is not merely "a property acquired by individuals" but "it is a principle around which social life is organized" (p. 290), and that organizations, including public relations structures, are not just promoting men but are structured hierarchically around masculine values of "efficiency, rationality, individualism, and competition" (p. 291).

In the main, then, with few exceptions, the feminist public relations literature has dealt with feminist theory *for* public relations, not feminist theory *of* public relations, and has used a liberal feminist social theory for advocating improvements in the position of women as public relations practitioners, with some interest in radical feminism because of the appeal of values associated with women and feminism for the practice of public relations. Theorizing race and ethnicity, and promoting social and cultural diversity, have also occurred within a primarily liberal social theory, concerned with the status of women of color in public relations practice, including the roles of women of color in public relations departments and firms, and the forms of discrimination against women of color in these public relations entities (Kern-Foxworth, 1989a, 1989b; Kern-Foxworth, Gandy, Hines, & Miller, 1994; Pompper, 2004). Recently, some arguments for bringing critical race theory into public relations theory and research have been made (Pompper, 2005).

Metatheoretical approaches to public relations have confirmed the primacy of liberal feminism, supplemented by aspects of radical feminism and elements of multiculturalism, yet have also envisioned more plural approaches. Aldoory (2003) argued that most feminist scholarship in public relations utilizes liberal feminism yet some scholarship recognizes radical feminism. Aldoory envisaged a feminist paradigm for public relations reconceiving its attention from roles, glass ceiling, salaries, and job satisfaction to being multimethodological, multifeminist, critical, collective, collaborative, and contextual focused on power relations, acknowledging the interdependence of researcher and researched, applicable to everyday communication (2003, p. 246), or reconceiving its attention from gender as female and power as property to gender as learned, power as discursive legitimacy, and diversity as situated meanings (Aldoory, 2005, pp. 674–677). Larissa Grunig (2006) described feminist public relations theory as having gone through five phases of research of reflection on gender: male scholarship (focusing on men), compensatory (profiling impressive women), bifocal (conceptualizing women and men as separate but equal), feminist (conceptualizing women on their own terms), and multifocal (conceptualizing human experience along a continuum). Grunig envisioned a sixth, integrative phase, providing a holistic perspective on communication professionals in the context of their work, family, and community. We suggest that Grunig's classification of feminist theories incorporates liberal feminism (phases 2 and 3), and radical feminism (phases 4 and 5), with the possibility of more inclusive ways of feminist theorizing in phase 6. We argue that our classification of feminist theoretical positions and our explanation of their importance for public relations are intended to complement and illuminate the new paradigms and phases envisgaed by Aldoory and Grunig.

Dorothy Smith's Insights at the Crossroads of Feminist Theoretical Positions

We have seen that different feminist theoretical positions propose specific ways of conceptualizing, critiquing, and changing knowledge forms and social structures that contribute to diverse interpretations of gender, woman/women, power, injustice, and change. We have also seen that some feminist theoretical positions have been extensively employed in public relations scholarship, whereas some others are missing from scholarly analyses of public relations, and we have tried to understand what the consequences of these omissions are. We are now turning to the work of feminist sociologist Dorothy Smith, because it is situated at the crossroads of numerous feminist approaches and problematics.

Some reasons for placing Dorothy Smith at the intersection of many trends are coming from *her life experience*. Being born in Britain, coming to the United States for graduate school, and settling in Canada as a professor, Smith had opportunities to reflect on the multiple facets of imperialism, from the perspective of a White educated woman. Through the experiences of being married and divorced, having children, and being a single mother, earning a living from secretarial work in her youth, and as a professor later in life, Dorothy Smith personally encountered patriarchal relations in many different situations, and thought of incorporating these personal encounters in her feminist writings (Smith, 2007). As a student and then a professor of sociology, Smith observed that women had not participated in the construction of knowledge in the social sciences, and that women's ways of constructing knowledge about the social world were different from those described and canonized by sociologists. As a participant in women's movements in academia and as one of the first instructors in women's studies in Canada, Smith noticed that many women were excited about the potential of feminist activism yet felt uneasy about the institutionalization of feminist discourses (Campbell, 2003).

Another reason for placing Dorothy Smith at the crossroads of many problematics is *her relationship to feminist standpoint theory*. Smith is often considered among the promoters of feminist standpoint theory (Alcoff & Potter, 1993; Kang, 2005), "an epistemological argument that tries to describe a distinctly 'female' or 'feminine' knowledge through recourse to the experiences of women" (Grant, 1993, p. 92). Smith agrees with standpoint theorists that "women's biology, women's intuition, what women say, or women's experiences" should be included among valid knowledge constructions (Harding, 1991, p. 167), and that these have "liberatory potential" (Hartsock, 1983, p. 232); however, she departs from standpoint theory because she remains concerned with practical politics whereas other standpoint feminists segregate epistemological from social issues (Smith, 1992, p. 89).

Another reason for placing Dorothy Smith at the intersection of many trends comes from *her refusal to be confined to only one feminist theoretical position*. According to Alcoff and Potter (1993), Dorothy Smith and other feminist standpoint theorists consider that liberal feminism starts from the lives of upper-middle-class women in Europe and the United States in the 18th and the 19th century; socialist feminism from the lives of working class women in Western countries in 19th and the 20th century; and postcolonial feminism from the lives of predominantly upper- and middle-class women in non-Western countries currently; yet feminist standpoint theory argues that "each of these groups of women's lives is a good place to start" for explaining certain aspects of the social order (p. 60). Smith's writings have been loosely associated with radical feminism because she "writes compellingly about the importance of feminism consciousness raising" (Grant, 1993, p. 103), and with socialist feminism because she uses elements of Marxism "to argue that knowledge is not abstract and neutral, but differentially available to different social actors and scholars" (Kang, 2005, p. 79). Although confronting postmodernist feminists for their disbelief in the authenticity of voice (Smith, 2004), Smith has integrated postmodernist concepts such as intertextuality and hyperreality in her examination of social practices. Although not directly associated with multiculturalism or postcolonialism, Smith has often appraised critically her Whiteness and first world status, and has theorized women as the "marginal" or "subordinate" who can offer valuable alternative views of the world if they gain opportunities to speak (Smith, 1987, 2005).

Criticism of Smith's Work

Smith's discourse in favor of women's experiences and against patriarchal relations, at the intersection of numerous trends, has many times been praised for its unsettling tones (Harding, 1991; Spender, 1982), yet has sometimes been critiqued as essentialist (Grant, 1993; Longino, 1999).

As Judith Grant (1993) asserts, Smith "wants to include everything as epistemologically important," without separating "the insignificant from the significant," and without providing a hierarchy of these in what concerns experiences (p. 105). Grant acknowledges that Smith "wants to make the notion of 'experience' more immediate and authentic," yet she doubts Smith's success in doing so: "I am not sure that all our experiences matter in equally important ways" (p. 105). Grant opposes Smith's employment of experience in such indiscriminate ways to Patricia Hill Collins's (1990) use of experience by focusing on the differences between experiences, the given hierarchies of experiences, and the possibility to subvert these hierarchies of experiences.

Other scholars (Heckmann, 1997; Longino, 1999) have asserted that Smith essentializes gender and woman not because she does not approach the hierarchization of our experiences, but because she unifies women's standpoint without recognizing differences of race, ethnicity, class, or education. These critics of Smith consider that by attempting to construct an overarching intersubjectivity or intertextuality as a collective rendering of individual voices and experiences, Smith fails to acknowledge that in these processes some voices and experiences either will be muted or will remain silent. Smith herself has responded to such accusations by affirming that a women's standpoint is not based on the sensibilities of particular groups of women, but rather coconstructed subjectively by women and men of diverse economic, social, educational, political, racial, and ethnic backgrounds (Smith, 2005).

The Relevance of Smith's Key Concepts for Public Relations Scholarship

Smith attempts to raise critical awareness about gender by turning a sociology for women into a broader sociology for people, about women by theorizing "bifurcated consciousness," about power by addressing the "relations of ruling," about injustice by critiquing the "circle of men," and about change by proposing "institutional ethnography." The key points of Smith's life and work are summarized in Box 13.1. By locating Smith's theoretical work in the context of multiple theoretical positions, we are able to uncover assumptions in feminist public relations theory in need of reflection if we are interested in creating a critical public relations theory and research agenda for women and other groups outside of dominant power structures. Among any number of trajectories that Smith's work might lead us down, we should consider these:

The Problematization of Gender

Sandra Harding (1995) stated that Dorothy Smith's feminist work has the potential of enabling us "to understand women's lives, men's lives, and the relations between the two" (p. 342). Harding (1995) asserts that although Smith's theories are generated by her observations of "women's experiences," and her advocacy for placing these among legitimate and important knowledges, her theories are made for women as well as men since "men, too, can learn to start their thought from women's lives" (p. 343). Smith considers that women's ways of being and knowing are different from those carried on by means of patriarchal relations; yet she considers both men and women responsible for current patriarchal hierarchies, as well as capable of grounding their views in women's lives (Grant, 1993). For example, Smith (1987) writes that because of "women's exclusion from the ruling apparatus and its processes of textual discourses and organization," a sociology beginning from the standpoint of women "takes up the relation to this ruling apparatus of those whose work has been both necessary to and unrecognized by it" (p. 153). However, this sociology is not exclusively for women but broadly "for people," aiming to become "a resource that can be translated into people's everyday work knowledge" (Smith, 2005, p. 1). Smith speaks against feminist theory and activism in which gender remains unproblematized, and for those that seek "critical awareness about gender" (Kang, 2005, p. 80).

Dorothy Smith's insights about gender might offer a more comprehensive yet more critical understanding of the relationships between women and men than those provided by current feminist theories in public relations. So far, feminist public relations theorizing has taken for granted the man/woman dichotomy, opposing women's status or values in public relations, predominantly thought of as lower, to men's status or values in this profession, prevalently credited as higher. By following Smith's example, feminist public relations scholarship will have a chance to acknowledge that there are women as well as men who willingly or unwillingly contribute to the reification of patriarchy, capitalism, Western racism, and colonialism, and there are women as well as men who do not support or accept these. Instead of contrasting women to men in public relations, and of advocating a shift from masculine dominance or values to feminine dominance or values in public relations, feminist public relations theorists might attempt to contrast women and men in positions of power to people outside of circles of power, to question the public/private dichotomy, and to advocate a shift from focusing on discourses of power to highlighting everyday experiences.

The Problematization of Woman/Women

Dorothy Smith opens her book *The Conceptual Practices of Power* (1990) with the following paragraph from Gail Scott's work *Spaces Like Stairs* (1989):

> We women have two ways of speaking. The first begins in our mother's womb as we listen to the rhythms of her body (likewise for our brothers).... But at the same time we are developing another relationship to the "fathertongue" of education, the media, the law—all patriarchal institutions. (p. 3)

Smith (1990) affirms that other theorists have understood "woman" as body, sensibility, or sphere of being, but she understands "woman" as the experience of the unnurtured voice outside "man's world" (p. 3), referring to something challenging rather than something taken for granted about women, yet still formulating something that women have in common and are able to share. Also, Smith agrees with the problematic expressed by Scott, but unlike authors such as Scott or Kristeva who look for the language prior to the "fathertongue" (1990, p. 3), she finds a "bifurcated consciousness" in women (p. 19) that enables them to "slide away sideways from the ruling institutions and find modes of speaking the 'mothertongue' into texts" (p. 6).

Dorothy Smith's thoughts about women's identities and language can be relevant for critical feminist approaches to public relations. To date, most feminist public relations scholarship has made its concern women who practice public relations activities, examining the climate of the workplace, disparities in salary and assignment, and contributions they make to good public relations practices; following Smith, we can say that most feminist public relations scholars have focused on women's use of and proficiency in speaking the "fathertongue," rather than concentrating on women's ways of sliding away sideways toward the "mothertongue," on stances of bifurcated consciousness. Instead of asking how women in public relations produce effective institutional discourses, feminist public relations theorists might want to address how institutional discourses including public relations have created a patriarchal way of speaking which has become "common sense" and ubiquitous, and how this way of speaking can eventually be disrupted through subtly subversive oral and written accounts of experience.

The Problematization of Power

As a sociologist and a feminist, Smith has elaborated repeatedly on power relations in both social life and mainstream sociology. According to Smith (1987), existing social structures are based on the "relations of ruling," a complex of practices and discourses providing direction and regulation (p. 3). Relations of ruling are "objectified, impersonal, claiming universality" (p. 4), and display "a specific interrelation" between "patriarchal forms of our contemporary experience" and "the distinctive forms of organizing and ruling contemporary capitalist society" (p. 3). For Smith, in the social system built from relations of ruling emerging from capitalism and from patriarchy women and other oppressed people do not have a place. In patriarchal capitalism, women are forbidden to contribute to the language and culture of men, yet are asked to learn these, and women are not allowed in the work sphere of men, that of administration and ideas, yet they are asked to support this by means of housekeeping and secretarial chores (Smith, 1987, 2004). As Smith affirms (1987, 1990, 2004, 2005), traditional sociology, male and capitalist, White and Western, strengthens instead of changing these power relations. As Smith (1987) states, "Sociologists, when they go to work, enter into the conceptually organized society they are investigating," and "observe, analyze, explain and examine" that world "as if there were no problem in how it becomes observable to them" (p. 16).

Dorothy Smith's insights about power relations in both the social and the theoretical realms have the potential to constitute yet another resource for a critical feminist public relations theory. So far, feminist public relations theorizing has occurred mostly as if institutions, publics, and public relations were given and observable; relying on Dorothy Smith, we assert that the public relations profession has rarely been theorized by feminists as if the relations of ruling were problematic and questionable. Men's and women's work in the profession of public relations has been an issue for numerous feminist public relations theorists, yet women's labor to maintain the language and culture of men at the intersection of patriarchy and capitalism, and at the intersection of multiple forms of racism and colonialism, have not been approached by feminist public relations scholars. Feminist public relations scholarship in a critical note will make the consequences not the efficacy of public relations practices its object of inquiry. A critical feminist public relations theory will challenge existing relations of ruling, and will make propositions to change them.

The Problematization of Injustice

In *Women of Ideas (and What Men Have Done to Them)*, Dale Spender (1982) writes:

> All human beings are constantly engaged in the process of describing and explaining, and ordering the world, but only a few have been, or are, in a position to have their version treated as serious, and accepted. These few Dorothy Smith aptly terms the "circle of men"—who are the philosophers, politicians, poets and policy makers—who have for centuries [been] writing and talking to each other about issues which are of significance to them.

Spender (1982) declares Smith's notion that "we are born into a society in which we come to our human-ness by making sense of the world through this inherited patriarchal tradition" (p. 10) as a "breakthrough" (p. 75), and employs this notion in her own analysis of "the invisibility of women" from the cultural heritage. As Spender pertinently observed, this understanding of patriarchal capitalist injustice as the "circle of men" is one of the most sophisticated contributions of Dorothy Smith to feminist theory. According to Dorothy Smith, the "circle of men" is an order to which women contribute yet from which they are excluded, to which women are confined yet in which they feel strangers (Smith, 1987, 2005). Unlike some dichotomist feminists viewing society as separated into a private sphere traditionally assigned to women and a public sphere traditionally assigned to men, Dorothy Smith sees society as a nexus of power in which patriarchal relations are at the center, and women's experiences and work are beyond marginal since they remain unaccounted for.

Smith's depiction of "the circle of man" is a breakthrough conceptualization for many areas of human study, and has much potential to be employed in critiques of public relations. To date, public relations scholarship has been effectuated by looking at organizations which make or use public relations, not by looking at women and men who are subjected to public relations; drawing from Smith, we suggest that most public relations scholarship, even most feminist public relations scholarship, has been written from within not from without the "circle of men," from within not from without spheres of patriarchal and capitalist power and influence. By reconceptualizing injustice as exclusion, theorists can generate questions about why women are assigned to caring for everyone's bodies and cleaning houses and workplaces, and what type of system assigns body and support activities to some people and "head" and leading work to other people (Altcoff & Potter, 1993, p. 55); theorists can generate new models for how institutions should respond to needs of publics comprised of outsiders as well as insiders, those at margins as well as those at centers, rather than working from models in which people respond to the needs of institutions, no matter how symmetric the intent of public relations practitioners.

The Problematization of Change

In her feminist work, Smith has attempted not only to unsettle society and social theory but also to propose a methodology for change. Among strategies outlined by Smith for challenging White, Western capitalist patriarchy and for providing a sociology for women or for people, some of the most useful are considering the everyday world as problematic rather than given (Smith, 1987, p. 106), and considering textual realities as relational, connected to specific standpoints, rather than universal, the same from all possible standpoints (Smith, 1990, p. 61). Since the ruling apparatus is the familiar complex of government, management, intelligentsia, professions, discourses, and mediations that form the fabric of everyday world as well as the texts of the ruling, thinking outside of this interconnected everydayness and textuality means challenging the system (Smith, 1987, p. 108; 1990, p. 63). The skeptical look at ready-made everyday/every night and textual realities is part of an intense effort to provide an instrument for subverting institutionalization, namely institutional ethnography (Smith, 1987, p. 151; 2005, p. 29). Inquiry of this kind begins in the actualities of lives involved in institutional processes, focuses "on how those actualities were embedded in social relations" (Smith, 2005, p. 31), discloses "a number of different viewpoints from which the workings of a whole (though 'open-ended') complex of relational processes come into view" (Smith, 1987, p. 177), and examines the experiences with the respective processes of as many marginal(ized) people as possible.

Dorothy Smith's attempt to envision a critique of institutions that would become a methodology for change has the potential to provide a model for a critical feminist public relations theory. So far, feminist public relations theorizing has been concerned with enhancing the presence of women in the public relations profession, either by arguing on liberal feminist grounds for the rights of women to have equal opportunities with men and to be treated fairly, or on radical feminist grounds for the positive impact on public relations practice that could result from valuing women and their contributions. Expanding Dorothy Smith's thought, we assert that most feminist public relations scholarship has devised methodologies to maintain rather than to change the ruling apparatus. By turning to institutional ethnography, feminist public relations scholarship will be able to consider how theory and research might identify "ideological seams" (Radway, 1986), disjunctures in meaning systems, where the arbitrariness of power language can be revealed and alternatives, such as a feminist analyses, can be provided. Thanks to the groundwork laid by Dorothy Smith and others, methodological tools are available and used in other areas of social and cultural studies.

Dorothy E. Smith and Public Relations

In sum, a critical feminist public relations theory that draws on Dorothy Smith's ideas would look to women's everyday lived experiences as a source of knowledge about the need for political, economic, and social change. In contrast to current public relations scholarship about women, the focus would not be on women who are public relations practitioners but on those women who are the object of public relations discourses, those women who are outside the "circle of men" whose knowledge is validated and replicated by public relations programs and campaigns, and those women who are subjugated by the "relations of ruling" that characterize patriarchal, racist, and colonial societies. The "bifurcated consciousness" that results from the discrepancies between official discourses (the "father tongue") about the social world and the experiences of everyday life (the "mothertongue") can be a source of great insight into how discourses must change to emancipate women and men from oppressive institutional meanings and social relations. In developing this new position, feminist public relations scholars must be careful not to resort to an essentialism that presupposes a universal womanhood and a universal victimization of all women by all men. Men, too, can experience the everyday world in similar ways, depending upon their social location. Women, too, can speak the "fathertongue" and be included in the "circle of men" that excludes and devalues the knowledge of others.

Conclusion

We began with the question "What would public relations theory and research for women look like and why do we need it?" and we have argued that the answer lies in a shift from a feminist theory *for* public relations to a feminist theory *of* public relations. Our review of major feminist theoretical positions and of each one's analysis of *gender systems*, *women's identities*, *power relations*, *social injustice*, and *social change* reveals gaps in feminist public relations theorizing. The current feminist public relations literature has utilized primarily a liberal feminist position that generally accepts the social order as it is, including capitalism, representative democracy, and interest group pluralism, but reject sexism within the social order, with some attention to a radical feminist position that rejects a male standard by which women are judged, instead critiquing the social theory of patriarchy which accords men power over women. To date, feminist public relations theories have integrated multicultural concerns into the liberal position, and have neglected insights from socialist, postmodernist, and postcolonial positions.

We utilize Dorothy Smith's work as an example of feminist theory that problematizes gender by conceiving a sociology for people, women by discussing the "bifurcated consciousness," power by addressing the "relations of ruling," injustice by critiquing the "circle of men," and change by developing "institutional ethnography." With the help of Dorothy Smith, viewed in the context of feminist theoretical positions and across a wide range of feminist assumptions, we can see the contours of a critical feminist public relations theory. It would be concerned with *public relations in the lives of women* rather than with *the lives of women in public relations*, and would be focused on the consequences of all institutional discourses, including public relations, on women and other outsiders, rather than on their proficiency using institutional discourses. It would see power not simply nor only in the relations between individual women and men within an organization, but in the structure of society in which powerful institutions produce and enforce meanings about the social order and the place of groups of people within it. Dorothy Smith made the everyday experiences of women her starting point and continuous return. A critical feminist public relations theory would benefit from doing the same.

References

Albrecht, L., & Brewer, R. (Eds.). (1990). *Bridges to power: Women's multicultural alliances*. Philadelphia, PA: New Society.

Alcoff, L., & Potter, E. (1993). *Feminist epistemologies*. New York: Routledge.

Aldoory, L. (2003). The empowerment of feminist scholarship in public relations and the building of a feminist paradigm. *Communication Yearbook, 27*, 221–255.

Aldoory, L. (2005). A (re)conceived feminist paradigm for public relations: A case for substantial improvement. *Journal of Communication, 55*(4), 668–684.

Aldoory, L., & Toth, E. L. (2002). Gender discrepancies in a gendered profession: A developing theory for public relations. *Journal of Public Relations Research, 14*(2), 103–126.

Allen, P. G. (1984). *The sacred hoop.* Boston: Beacon Press.

Bailey, C. (1997). Making waves and drawing lines: The politics of defining the vicissitudes of feminism. *Hypatia, 12*(3), 17–28.

Benhabib, S. (1995). Feminism and postmodernism: An uneasy alliance. In S. Benhabib, J. Butler, D. Cornell, & N. Fraser, *Feminist contentions: A philosophical exchange* (pp. 17–35). New York: Routledge.

Bethel, L. (1979). What chou mean we, white girl? *Conditions: Five, 11*(2), 86–92.

Bryson, V. (1992). *Feminist political theory: An introduction.* London: Macmillan.

Butler, J. (1990). *Gender trouble. Feminism and the subversion of identity.* New York: Routledge.

Butler, J., & Scott, J. W. (Eds.). (1992). *Feminists theorize the political.* New York: Routledge.

Campbell, M. (2003). Dorothy Smith and knowing the world we live in. *Journal of Sociology and Social Welfare.* Retrieved March 10, 2007 from http://www.findarticles.com/p/articles/mi_m0CYZ/is_1_30/ai_99018712

Carby, H. V. (1987). *Reconstructing womanhood.* Oxford, UK: Oxford University Press.

Carby, H. V. (1997). White woman listen! Black feminism and the boundaries of sisterhood. In R. Hennesy & C. Ingraham (Eds.), *Materialist feminism* (pp. 110–128). New York: Routledge.

Cline, C. G. (1989). What now? Conclusions and suggestions. In E. L. Toth & C. G. Cline (Eds.), *Beyond the velvet ghetto* (pp. 299–308). San Francisco, CA: International Association of Business Communicators.

Cline, C. G., Toth, E. L., Turk, J. V., Walters, L. M., Johnson, N., & Smith, H. (1986). *The velvet ghetto: The impact of the increasing percentage of women in public relations and business communication.* San Francisco, CA: International Association of Business Communicators.

Coole, D. (2000). Threads and plaids or an unfinished project? Feminism(s) through the twentieth century. *Journal of Political Ideologies, 5*(1), 35–54.

Creed, B. (1987). From here to modernity: Feminism and postmodernism. *Screen, 28*(2), 47–67.

Creedon, P. J. (1993). Acknowledging the infrastructure: A critical feminist analysis of systems theory. *Journal of the Public Relations Research, 19*(2), 157–166.

Daly, M. (1973). *Beyond god the father: Toward a philosophy of women's liberation.* Boston: Beacon Press.

Di Stefano, C. (1990). Dilemmas of difference: Feminism, modernity, and postmodernism. In L. Nicholson (Ed.), *Feminism/Postmodernism* (pp. 63–83). New York: Routledge.

Donovan, J. (1985). *Feminist theory.* New York: Unger.

Duffy, M. (2000). There's no two-way symmetric about it: A postmodern examination of public relations handbooks. *Critical Studies in Mass Communication, 17*(3), 294–315.

Echols, A., & Willis, E. (1990). *Daring to be bad: Radical feminism in American, 1967–1975*. Minneapolis: University of Minnesota Press.

Eisenstein, Z. (1981). *The radical future of liberal feminism*. Boston: Northeastern University Press.

Evans, J. (1995). *Feminism theory today: An introduction to second-wave feminism*. Thousand Oaks, CA: Sage.

Firestone, S. (1970). *The dialectic of sex: The case for feminist revolution*. New York: Morrow.

Fraser, N. (1989). *Unruly practices: Gender, discourse and power in social theory*. Minneapolis: University of Minnesota Press.

Fraser, N., & Nicholson, L. (1990). Social criticism without philosophy: An encounter between feminism and postmodernism. In L. Nicholson (Ed.), *Feminism/Postmodernism* (pp. 19–38). New York: Routledge.

Friedan, B. (1963). *The feminine mystique*. New York: Norton.

Frye, M. (1983). *The politics of reality: Essays in feminist theory*. New York: Crossing Press.

Garry, A., & Pearsall, M. (1996). *Women, knowledge, and reality: Explorations in feminist philosophy*. New York: Routledge.

Grant, J. (1993). *Fundamental feminism: Contesting the core concepts of feminist theory*. New York: Routledge.

Grunig, L. A. (2006). Feminist phase analysis in public relations: Where have we been? Where do we need to be? *Journal of Public Relations Research, 18*(2), 115–140.

Grunig L.A. (1988). Women in public relations [Special issue]. *Public Relations Review, 14*(3).

Grunig, L. A., Toth, E. L., & Hon, L. C. (2000). Feminist values in public relations. *Journal of Public Relations Research, 12*(1), 49–68

Harding, S. (1991). *Whose science? Whose knowledge? Thinking from women's lives*. Ithaca, NY: Cornell University Press.

Harding, S. (1995). Strong objectivity: A response to the new objectivity question. *Synthese, 104*, 331–349.

Hartsock, N. (1983). The feminist standpoint: Discovering the ground for a specifically feminist historical materialism. In S. Harding & M. B. Hintikka (Eds.), *Discovering reality: Feminist perspectives on epistemology, metaphysics, methodology, and philosophy of science* (pp. 283–310). Boston: Reidel.

Heckman, S. (1997). Truth and method: Feminist standpoint theory revisited. *Signs, 22*(2), 341–366.

Hill Collins, P. (1990). *Black feminist thought: Knowledge, consciousness, and the politics of empowerment*. New York: Routledge.

Hon, L. C. (1995). Toward a feminist theory of public relations. *Journal of Public Relations Research, 7*(1), 27–88.

hooks, b. (1984). *Feminist theory: From margin to center*. New York: South End Press.

Jaggar, A. (1983). *Feminist politics and human nature*. Totowa, NJ: Rowman & Allanheld.

Jardin, A. (1985). *Gynesis*. Ithaca, NY: Cornell University Press.

Joseph, G. (1997). The incompatible ménage a trios: Marxism, feminism and racism. In R. Hennesy & C. Ingraham (Eds.), *Materialist Feminism* (pp. 107–109). New York: Routledge.

Kang, L. H. Y. (2005). Epistemologies. In P. Essed, D. T. Goldberg, & A. Kobayashi (Eds.), *A companion to gender studies* (pp. 73–86). New York: Blackwell.

Kensinger, L. (1997). (In)quest of liberal feminism. *Hypanthia, A Journal of Feminist Philosophy, 12*(4), 178–195.

Kern-Foxworth, M. (1989a). The assessment of minority female role and status in public relations: Trying to unlock the acrylic vault and assimilate into the velvet ghetto. In E. L. Toth & C. G. Cline (Eds.), *Beyond the velvet ghetto* (pp. 287–298). San Francisco, CA: International Association of Business Communicators.

Kern-Foxworth, M. (1989b). Public relations books fail to show women in context. *Journalism Educator, 44*, 31–36.

Kern-Foxworth, M., Gandy, O., Hines, B., & Miller, D. A. (1994). Assessing the managerial roles of Black female public relations practitioners using individual and organizational discriminants. *Journal of Black Studies, 24*, 416–434.

Kuhn, A., & Wolpe, A. M. (1978). *Feminism and materialism: Women and modes of production*. Boston: Routledge.

Lauzen, M. (1992). Effects of gender on professional encroachment in public relations. *Journalism Quarterly, 69*, 173–180.

Lesly, P. (1988). Public relations numbers are up but stature down. *Public Relations Review, 14*, 3–7.

Lewis, R. (1995). *Gendering orientalism: Race, femininity and representation*. New York: Routledge.

Longino, H. (1999). Feminist epistemology. In J. Greco & E. Sosa (Eds.), *The Blackwell guide to epistemology* (pp. 327–353). Malden, MA: Blackwell.

McClintock, A. (1995). *Imperial leather: Race, gender and sexuality in the colonial contest*. New York: Routledge.

Mickey, T. J. (2003). Representation of woman. In T. J. Mickey, *Deconstructing public relations: Public relations criticism* (pp. 47–60). Mahwah, NJ: Erlbaum.

Mohanty, C. (1991). Under western eyes: Feminist scholarship and colonial discourses. In C. Mohanty, A. Russo, & L. Torres (Eds.), *Third world women and the politics of feminism* (pp. 51–80). Bloomington: Indiana University Press.

Moraga, C., & Anzaldua, G. (Eds.). (1981). *This bridge called my back: Writings by radical women of color*. New York: Kitchen Table Press.

Nash, K. (1997). The feminist critique of liberal individualism as masculinist. *Journal of Political Ideologies, 2*(1), 13–28.

Okin, S. M. (1989). *Justice, gender, and the family*. New York: Basic Books.

O'Neil, J. (2003). An analysis of the relationships among structure, influence, and gender: Helping to build a feminist theory of public relations. *Journal of Public Relations Research, 15*(2), 151–195.

Pompper, D. (2004). Linking ethnic diversity and two-way symmetry: Modeling female African American's roles. *Journal of Public Relations Research, 16*(3), 269–299.

Pompper, D. (2005). "Difference" in public relations research: A case for introducing critical race theory. *Journal of Public Relations Research, 17*(2), 139–169.

Radway, J. (1986). Identifying ideological seams: Mass culture, analytical method, and political practice. *Communication, 9*, 93–124.

Rakow, L. F. (1989). From the feminization of public relations to the promise of feminism. In E. L. Toth & C. G. Cline (Eds.), *Beyond the velvet ghetto* (pp. 287–298). San Francisco, CA: International Association of Business Communicators.

Rakow, L. F., & Wackwitz, L., (Eds.). (2004). *Feminist communication theory: Selections in context.* Thousand Oaks, CA: Sage.

Richards, J. R. (1980). *The sceptical feminist: A philosophical enquiry.* Boston: Routledge.

Rosen, R. (2001). *The world split open: How the modern women's movement changed America.* New York: Viking Press.

Said, E. (1978). *Orientalism.* New York: Vintage Press.

Sarachild, K. (1978). *Feminist revolution.* New York: Random House.

Shelton, B. A., & Agger, B. (1993). Shotgun wedding, unhappy marriage, no fault divorce? Rethinking the feminism-Marxism relationship. In P. England (Ed.), *Theory on gender/Feminism on theory* (pp. 25–42). New York: Aldine de Gruyter.

Smith, D. E. (1978). A peculiar eclipsing: Women's exclusion from man's culture. *Women's Studies International Quarterly, 1*(4), 281–296.

Smith, D. E. (1987). *The everyday world as problematic: A feminist sociology.* Boston: Northeastern University Press.

Smith, D. E. (1990). *The conceptual practices of power: A feminist sociology of knowledge.* Boston: Northeastern University Press

Smith, D. E. (1992). Sociology from women's experience: A reaffirmation. *Sociological Theory, 10*(1), 88–98.

Smith, D. E. (2004). *Writing the social: Critique, theory and investigations.* Toronto, Canada: University of Toronto Press.

Smith, D. E. (2005). *Institutional ethnography: A sociology for people.* New York: Altamira.

Smith, D. E. *Dorothy Smith.* Retrieved March 10, 2007, from http://faculty.maxwell.syr.edu/mdevault/dorothy_smith.htm

Spender, D. (1980). *Man made language.* Boston: Routledge.

Spender, D. (1982). *Women of ideas (and what men have done to them).* Boston: Ark.

Spivak, G. C. (1988a). *In other worlds: Essays in cultural politics.* New York: Methuen.

Spivak, G. C. (1988b). Can the subaltern speak? In C. Nelson & L. Grossberg (Eds.), *Marxism and the interpretation of culture* (pp. 271–313). New York: Routledge.

Thompson, D. (2001). *Radical feminism today.* Thousand Oaks, CA: Sage.

Tong, R. (1989). *Feminist thought: A comprehensive introduction.* Boulder, CO: Westview.

Toth, E. L. (1988). Making peace with gender issues in public relations. *Public Relations Review, 14*, 36–47.

Toth, E. L., & Cline, C. G. (Eds.). (1989). *Beyond the velvet ghetto.* San Francisco: International Association of Business Communicators.

Toth, E. L., & Grunig, L. (1993). The missing story of women in public relations. *Journal of Public Relations Research, 5*(3), 153–175.

Walby, S. (1986). *Patriarchy at work: Patriarchal and capitalist relations in employment*. Minneapolis: University of Minnesota Press.

Weedon, C. (1997). *Feminist practice and poststructuralist theory*. Oxford, UK: Blackwell.

Wrigley, B. J. (2002). Glass ceiling? What glass ceiling? A qualitative study of how women view the glass ceiling in public relations and communications management. *Journal of Public Relations Research, 14*(1), 27–55.

Life and Work of Dorothy E. Smith

Dorothy E. Smith was born in 1926 in England. She worked as a secretary in book publishing during her early youth. She completed a BA degree in sociology at the London School of Economics in 1955. She earned her doctorate in sociology from the University of California, Berkeley in 1963. She was a lecturer in sociology at Berkeley (1964–1966), and she then returned to Great Britain to teach at the University of Essex (1966–1968). She accepted a professorship at the University of British Columbia in Canada (1968), and was one of the first instructors of women's studies in Canada. She joined the Ontario Institute for Studies in Education in Toronto (1976), and is currently a professor emeritus there.

Smith's major works include *Feminism and Marxism: A Place to Begin, A Way to Go* (1977), *The Everyday World as Problematic: A Feminist Sociology* (1987), *Texts, Facts, and Femininity: Exploring the Relations of Ruling* (1990), *The Conceptual Practices of Power: A Feminist Sociology of Knowledge* (1990), *Writing the Social: Critique, Theory, and Investigations* (1999), *Institutional Ethnography: A Sociology for People* (2005). Smith's main theoretical contributions include a sociology for women and ultimately for people, mothertongue and the bifurcated consciousness, a critique of the relations of ruling, a critique of women's exclusion from the circle of men, questioning the everyday world as problematic, questioning textual realities as ideological practices, and institutional ethnography as a methodology for change.

Smith's work has been recognized with numerous awards, including the American Sociological Association's Career of Distinguished Scholarship Award (1999), the Jessie Bernard Award for Feminist Sociology (1993), and two awards from the Canadian Sociology and Anthropology Association: the Outstanding Contribution Award, 1990, and the John Porter Award for *The Everyday is Problematic: A Feminist Sociology*, 1990.

Chapter 14

On Spivak

Theorizing Resistance—Applying Gayatri Chakravorty Spivak in Public Relations

Mohan Jyoti Dutta

Abstract

This chapter discusses key insights from the works of Gayatri Spivak in order to suggest openings for conceptualizing postcolonial approaches to public relations scholarship and practice. The chapter suggests that public relations knowledge structures ought to be situated in the backdrop of the politics of representation, power, and materiality that constitute these structures. Furthermore, Spivak's work offers the foundations for locating public relations knowledge at the intersections of culture, structure, and agency, and for exploring the ways in which these intersections offer possibilities for both examining neocolonial practices and resisting such practices. The chapter closes with a call for resistive politics in postcolonial public relations scholarship that is continuously open to deconstructions and is committed to emancipatory goals.

The work of Gayatri Chakravorty Spivak is deeply insightful in connecting public relations theory to postcolonial studies. Postcolonial studies as a field of inquiry not only seeks to understand the processes underlying colonization, but also is committed to an emancipatory politics that attempts to undo these processes of colonization; it is fundamentally transformative in seeking to alter those knowledge structures that erase the stories of violence inherent in global neocolonial configurations and create spaces for listening to the voices of the subaltern sectors of the globe. Connecting the histories and geographies of colonialism with the project of modernity and modern knowledge structures, postcolonial scholarship[1] attempts to "redo such epistemic structures by writing against them, over them, and from below them by inviting reconnections to obliterated presents that never made their way into the history of knowledge" (Shome & Hegde, 2002, p. 250). With reference to theorizing and scholarship in public relations, a postcolonial approach draws attention to the unequal terrain of disciplinary knowledge in public relations that has been dominated by primarily U.S.-based and to some extent, Europe-based perspectives—see, for instance the two volumes on public relations theory edited by Botan and Hazleton (1989, 2006). Further, the deconstructive move in the postcolonial approach creates openings for disciplinary transformations through the interrogation of the taken-for-granted assumptions in Westcentric productions of knowledge (Broadfoot & Munshi, 2007 ; Dutta-Bergman, 2005; Pal & Dutta, 2008a,b).

This transformative impulse of postcolonial studies is reflected in Gayatri Spivak's interrogation of the colonial histories and geographies of disciplinary structures and institutional knowledge that constitute the Anglo-European academy. Her work helps locate public relations theory in the realm of the neocolonial politics of globalization processes, the formations of the new world order, dialogic opportunities with marginalized communities that are erased by the dominant economic logics of globalization, and the possibilities of transformative politics in the context of globalization processes (Spivak, 1993, 1996, 1999). Furthermore, her scholarship has charted an intellectual trajectory that covers feminist deconstruction, Marxist critiques of international divisions of labor and the global flow of capital, critiques of imperial and colonial discourses, and critiques of race in the context of the intersections among nationality, ethnicity, and the politics of representation in a neocolonial world (Landry & MacLean, 1996). In situating public relations scholarship in the realm of postcolonial studies, and more specifically with reference to the work of Gayatri Spivak, this essay responds to the call issued by Raka Shome and Radha Hegde (2002), who suggest the imminent need for communication theorizing that locates communication processes in the realm of the historical and geographical contexts of postcolonial politics, and explores the intersections between communication and postcoloniality in the realm of the relationships among nation-states in the geopolitical landscape. It demonstrates that public relations scholars are particularly well suited to interrogate the communicative practices that connect transnational corporations, nation-states, and global structures; and offer strategies and concepts for engaging postcolonial studies in public relations theorizing and practice.

Spivak and Postcolonial Theory

In an expansive and highly influential body of scholarship that spans almost four decades, Spivak (1993, 1999) has offered insights that offer entry points for entire bodies of work in communication. From these insights, I have selected a few conceptual markers for introducing postcolonial studies into public relations. Even as I introduce these key concepts, I will attempt to weave in recent articles in the public relations literature that demonstrate a welcome move toward engaging with the critical and transformative impulses of postcolonial studies (Dutta-

Bergman, 2005; Munshi & Kurian, 2005; Pal & Dutta, 2008b; Said, 1978), and particularly toward engaging the work of Gayatri Chakravorty Spivak in public relations scholarship.

Representation, Materiality, and Politics

The mobilization of representations is central to the circulation of discourses in the realm of the global geopolitical processes that sustain and reinforce the new world order. Representation, Gayatri Spivak (1999) suggests, is inherently political because it serves the basis for the politics of power and control in the realm of transnational corporations and neoimperialism, and also as the basis for resistive political action directed at emancipatory politics in the new world order. Even as representation draws upon a certain sense of materiality of the structures within which representation happens, these structures themselves are tied to their portrayals as we come to talk about them in the dominant discursive spaces, circulating and reifying certain forms of power and control in the global world order. Therefore, essential to the material shifts in neocolonial structures is a transformation in the representations that constitute, propagate, and reify these structures; ruptures in the modernist discourses of neoliberal politics open up opportunities for such transformation. Interrogating the central role of public relations in the circulation of representations that support neocolonial and transnational hegemonies provides an interpretive framework for understanding the ways in which communicative practices are mobilized to maintain international divisions of labor and disparities in access to resources (Curtin & Gaither, 2006; Dutta-Bergman, 2005). For instance, the representations of corporate social responsibility in the mainstream public relations literature (Pratt, 2006) as a harbinger of development and progress maintain and propagate inequities in global distributions of resources within and across nation-states by promoting the agendas of transnational corporations at the cost of policies that relate to the issues affecting those who live in poverty. Similarly, the dominant representations of democracy promotion efforts sponsored by the United States Agency for International Development (USAID) and carried out by public relations specialists (Taylor & Kent, 2006) manipulate the languages of democracy and participation to minimize the participatory opportunities for the underserved sectors and to create spaces of support for neoliberal policies (Dutta-Bergman, 2005). Representations of development are circulated in aid efforts supported by organizations such as USAID that actually seek to create pro-U.S. public opinion in the targeted communities in the name of development (Dutta, 2006). It is through such interrogations of the mainstream public relations practices that seek to maintain the global order that postcolonial theorists in public relations can begin to envision entry points for alternative representations that offer transformative possibilities (Dutta-Bergman, 2005; Pal & Dutta, 2008a,b). Note here that a postcolonial entry point into public relations calls for redefinition of the discipline as one that serves managerial and bureaucratic interests to one that seeks to disrupt the status quo and bring about change in the dominant structures that perpetuate global inequities (Pal & Dutta, 2008a). This redefinition of public relations offers openings for theorizing about, empirically studying, and working with activist movements with the goal of disrupting neoliberal politics that perpetuate global inequities rather than aiding mainstream organizations in co-opting or mainstreaming activist politics in order to serve the status quo.

For Spivak, representation is simultaneously aesthetic and political, both intertwined and predicated upon each other; the realization of the interconnectedness between the aesthetic and the political aspects of representation offers the substratum for political action (Landry & MacLean, 1996). Performances in the realm of the aesthetics (such as stories, plays, songs, art) through which subaltern subjects and texts are constituted and represented also politically participate with and challenge the status quo. Political projects in the mainstream are played out through cultural texts, and this is achieved through a variety of multimedia-based public relations practices; postcoloniality in public relations inverts this logic through the articulation of resistive politics in cultural forms. This interplay of the political and the aesthetic domains of representation is made visible in Spivak's interview with the poet Alfred Artega where she discusses the formation of the Indian People's Theater Association (IPTA; Boal, 1985, 1998) that took to performance as a medium of protest in response to the famine that was artificially created by the British military in Calcutta during the Second World War in order to feed the British soldiers (Spivak, 1996). It is through representation that the taken-for-granted assumptions about the natural occurrence of famines are brought to question, and the political and social processes constituting famines are contested. In this instance, it is in the realm of representations that opportunities for political action are constituted. Tying the idea of aesthetic politics with the context of neocolonialism then provides the impetus for performance-based activist politics that challenges dominant neoliberal agendas that promote new colonialisms by perpetuating dominant ideological configurations. Aesthetic representations such as graffiti, street theater, and culture jamming (activist anti-ads that utilize the slickness of advertising and music videos to communicate resistive messages) offer spaces for communicating resistive politics. In this sense, communicative processes and platforms that utilize art and performance as forms of protest to dominant social structures, offer invaluable entry points for public relations theorists and practitioners who work alongside and as activists to develop sophisticated public relations strategies and tactics directed at disrupting the status quo.

Beyond the political nature of representation, however, Spivak also draws our attention to the continuous flux within which representative politics gets situated. Representation and its politics, according to Spivak, are reflective of both treading in the shoes of those that one represents as well as the continuous portrayal of the represented. Drawing upon the original work of Marx in German, she suggests that representation has two meanings, which otherwise escape the English reader, as these two meanings collapse in the English usage of representation. In an interview with Sara Harasym, talking about representation, Spivak notes (1990a):

> Treading in your shoes, wearing your shoes, that's Vertretung. Representation in that sense: political representation. *Darstellung—Dar*, "there", some cognate. Stellen, is "to place," so "placing there." Representing: "proxy" and "portrait".... Now the thing to remember is that in the act of representing politically, you represent yourself and your constituency, in the portrait sense, as well...you do not ever "simply" *vertreten* anyone, in fact, not just politically in the sense of true parliamentary forms, but even in political practices outside of parliamentary form. (Spivak, 1990a, p. 108; see also Harasym, 1990)

Even as one draws upon the essence of a certain marginalized group as this group gets represented in the discursive space, Spivak suggests that this essence is always the *Darstellung*. For instance, the political representation of a subaltern group in an activist performance is built upon a portrayal of the group. For the public relations scholar engaging with postcolonial theory that seeks to create spaces for listening to subaltern voices, Spivak argues that these voices that we set out to listen to are always representations, not just of the subaltern voices but also of us as scholars. She suggests that "a deconstructive awareness would insistently be aware that the masterwords are catachreses...that there are no literal referents, there are no 'true' examples of the 'true worker,' the 'true woman,' the 'true proletarian' who would stand for the ideals in terms of which you've mobilized" (1990, p. 104). It is this recognition of the two meanings of representation that is essential to the understanding of and learning from political movements that seek liberation and yet end up in oppressive fundamentalisms, and to avoiding the mistakes of activism that might otherwise end up in fundamentalisms even as one engages in processes that seek to bring about social change through their representations of underserved constituencies. In other words,

Spivak's work suggests the importance of continual reflexivity in activist politics built on the awareness of the representational nature of such politics. She further draws our attention to the notion that even as one seeks to create spaces for listening to the other, this other is continually erased from the discursive spaces of mainstream social systems.

Knowledge and Imperialism

Much of Spivak's thinking follows the trajectory of deconstruction and Marxist theory as she discusses the interplay between colonialism and capitalism in the constitution of discursive spaces and knowledge structures (Spivak, 1999). It is in her suggestion that knowledge structures be examined in the backdrop of the imperialist desires that constitute them that Spivak is most relevant for public relations scholars studying public relations practices in the context of globalization politics. These structures of knowledge must erase as they pursue the desire to represent; furthermore, these representations serve as instruments of neocolonialism through their depictions of the colonized subject as the subject of intervention and through the erasures of the voices of the subaltern sectors. The colonized subject therefore becomes the focal point as she represents the object of desire, constituted within the discursive space as a marker of the colonial move; her erasure is written over in these representations.

For Spivak, deconstructing the structures of knowledge and locating knowledge at the intersections of power, colonization, and transnational hegemony creates possibilities for transformative politics. The postcolonial deconstruction that emerges from her work is not only embedded therefore in colonial historicity but also connects to the neocolonial present, demonstrating the relevance of contemporary criticisms of the common threads of modernist logics that have dominated the grand narratives of development:

> ...the great narrative of Development is not dead.... Many of the functionaries of the civilizing mission were well-meaning; but alas, you can do good with contempt or paternal-maternal-sororal benevolence in your heart. And today, you can knife the poor nation in the back and offer Band-aids for a photo opportunity...the phrase "sustainable development" has entered the discourse of all the bodies that manage globality.... The general ideology of global development is racist paternalism (and alas, increasingly, sororalism); its general economics capital-intensive investment; its broad politics the silencing of resistance and of the subaltern as the rhetoric of their protest is constantly appropriated. (Spivak, 1999, pp. 371–373)

Gayatri Spivak's work questions the very rhetoric of "sustainable development," "corporate social responsibility," "poverty reduction," and "democracy promotion" that have become buzz words and catch-phrases for couching the imperialist logic of transnational politics that seeks to open up spaces in the global South to the free market economy in order to serve the interests of transnational hegemony. Development and globalization therefore become rhetorical weapons that justify the violence over subaltern spaces and the co-optation of subaltern resistance. Our engagement with Spivak confronts us with the co-optive politics played out by academic structures and academics in supporting agendas of dominant social actors and in thwarting opportunities for subaltern resistance.

The Politicization of Dialogue

As Spivak (1987) notes in her interview with Rashmi Bhatnagar, Lola Chatterjee, and Rajeshwari Sunder Rajan, held during her visiting professorship at the Center for Historical Studies at Jawaharlal Nehru University, New Delhi, there is no such thing as a neutral communication situation that constitutes free dialogue. Communication is always political and is always embedded within relationships of power that constitute the terrains and contents of communication. In her articulation of the political nature of communication, Spivak directly critiques the Habermasian notion of dialogue without politics:

> It is not a situation that ever comes into being—there is no such thing. The desire for neutrality and dialogue, even as it should not be repressed, must always mark its own failure.... The idea of neutral dialogue is an idea which denies history, denies structure, denies the positioning of subjects. I would try to look, how, in fact the demand for a dialogue is articulated. (Spivak, 1990a, p. 72)

Beginning with the notion of impossibility of a neutral communication situation, Spivak suggests the relevance of exploring and understanding the underpinnings of one's own privilege that forecloses the possibilities of dialogue. She calls for situating discussions of communicative spheres within the realm of histories and social structures, and the positioning of the subjects with respect to these structures. She further interrogates the underlying structures within which the desires for dialogue are articulated, and brings forth the politics underlying such desires for neutrality.

Spivak suggests that the very notion of neutrality of communication hides the structures and historical contexts within which communication is constituted and is connected to imperial and capitalist agendas.

It ignores the material structures and linkages of capitalism and colonialism that constitute the modernist spaces within which possibilities of neutral dialogues are imagined, practiced, and evaluated. The very neutrality of dialogue assumes equal access to so-called dialogic spaces of mainstream public spheres where issues are articulated, debated, configured, and reconfigured. In the context of the new world order, calls for dialogue and participation often serve as maneuverings for closing the opportunities for "real" dialogues and instead serve the neocolonial and neoliberal agendas of the new world order. What then are the specific strategies through which so-called neutral dialogues are mobilized to erase stories of violence and oppression? The politicization of dialogue underscores the political purposes served by communication and situates communicative practices in the realm of modernist political configurations.

As noted earlier, important in Spivak's work is not only the discursive closures brought about by talks of neutral dialogues, but also the possibilities for countering these closures by presenting opportunities for listening to subaltern voices so they are no longer subaltern. What then are the openings for dialogue in the realm of transformative politics? What are the ways in which scholars might engage in emancipatory politics built on dialogue that seeks to undo the disciplinary structures that hide the colonial agendas of one-way communicative practices under the veneer of neutral dialogue? For instance, mainstream public relations tactics of media relations and community relations under the broader agenda of U.S.-sponsored democracy promotion in the Third World (Haiti, Nicaragua, Chile, Philippines) actually serve to create pro-U.S., pro-free market, protransnational spaces of support in the Third World, simultaneously co-opting or subverting democratic possibilities of subaltern participation in these spaces (see Dutta-Bergman, 2005). The very processes of democracy promotion that are supposedly mobilized to create participatory spaces end up minimizing the opportunities for subaltern participation by co-opting the participatory platforms.

For Spivak (1990b), the possibility of engaging in emancipatory politics begins with unlearning one's privilege through the deployment of similar kinds of strategies based upon which we learn our privileges. Unlearning one's privilege means critiquing and challenging the history that has closed the opportunities for alternative knowledge, other options, and other possibilities; therefore, unlearning one's privilege is coming face-to-face with one's loss. It is this notion of unlearning one's privilege as one's loss in Spivak's writing that is eloquently articulated by Landry and MacLean (1996):

> Unlearning one's privilege by considering it as one's loss constitutes a double recognition. Other privileges, whatever they may be

in terms of race, class, nationality, gender, and the like, may have prevented us from gaining a certain kind of Other knowledge; not simply information that we have not yet received, but the knowledge that we are not equipped to understand by reason of our social positions. To unlearn our privileges means, on the one hand, to do our homework, to work hard at gaining some knowledge of the others who occupy spaces most closed to our privileged view. On the other hand, it means attempting to speak to those others in such a way that they might take us seriously and, most important of all, be able to answer back. (p. 5)

Unlearning one's privilege as a scholar and practitioner is fundamental to the creation of communicative spaces that allow opportunities for dialogue with marginalized voices that have otherwise been erased. In this sense, power cannot be wished away, and yet it is the reflexive awareness of the power attached to one's positionality that creates opportunities for dialogue.

The Organic Intellectual

What is the role of the intellectual in the realm of the emancipatory politics of postcolonial studies? Spivak argues that the "complicity between cultural and economic value systems is acted out in almost every decision we make" (Landry & MacLean, 1996, p. 166), drawing our attention to the economic value of academic identity. Spivak at once notes the institutional embedding of knowledge production and the political and economic foundations of the knowledge structures within which academics engage in the teaching, production, and recirculation of knowledge. It is with this in mind that she suggests a role for the academic in offering a responsible criticism of these structures even as she participates in the processes and mechanisms that constitute these structures. For the intellectual, engaging in critique makes one aware of the very structures within which she is situated even as one seeks to critique these structures from within them. In this sense, continuous reflexivity creates openings for fracturing the dominant neocolonial structures within which knowledge is articulated, circulated, and utilized.

Beyond the reflexivity in the academic exercise that is brought to bear by such insistent structural critique, for Spivak, it is important for the academic to go public. In going public, the academic reflexively interrogates the structures of knowledge and the ways in which practices are constituted by such structures, and continually suggests entry points for a transformative politics that is deeply aware of the oppressive and fundamentalist tendencies that might surge within the political movements of liberation that seek social change. In a deconstructive sense, the role of the intellectual is essential to the critical impulse of liberation movements that seek to address inequities in divisions of labor across a variety of divides of race, class, gender, and nationality. Spivak (1996) further talks about a practical politics of the open kind, where opportunities for reflection are built into movements that seek to bring about emancipation. Even as scholars and activists imagine possibilities of emancipation brought about by their political involvement, they also ought to become increasingly sensitized to the opportunities for co-optation, and to the moments of becoming that which they seek to resist. In this sense, resistive impulses can feed into mechanisms of control, and a critical impulse keeps the activist-scholar continually vigilant of this moment of control.

Postcolonialism in Public Relations Scholarship

As a modernist enterprise, the practice of public relations is squarely located within the realm of modernity. Its ideals and values are embedded within the Eurocentric logics that constitute much of the practice, theorizing, and empirical observations carried out in public relations. It is this Eurocentric politics of public relations practice that is theorized by the application of postcolonialism in public relations.

Power, Materiality, and Representation

Spivak's work is particularly insightful for understanding the practice of public relations as much of what constitutes public relations is representation of various stakeholder groups. Who gets represented within discursive spaces and who is erased from such spaces? What are the dynamics of power within which discourses are circulated? What are the material structures underlying the discursive spaces and how are values articulated within these spaces even as public relations activities assign and negotiate exchange values to commodities and organizations that are (re)presented and exchanged? What are the roles of representations in global politics, and what are the limits on the contours of representation imposed by public relations practices of global organizations? What are the ways in which transnational hegemony operates through the discursive manipulation of images? What are the possibilities for countering such representations and creating opportunities for transformative politics in the context of the international division of labor?

Spivak's writing on representation draws our attention to the ways in which neocolonial interests get discursively framed and constituted through public relations activities. It is this neocolonial impulse underlying seemingly benevolent "do-good" efforts of global corporations that is of interest to the postcolonial public relations scholar. The discursive constructions of modernity in the backdrop of the portrayals of the primitiveness of so-called Third World spaces provide the impetus and justification for neocolonial efforts. Public relations efforts frame modernist solutions as reasons for penetrating Third World spaces; it is after all the "burden of the soul" that needs to be lifted by the emancipatory message of transnational hegemony. In other words, representations lie at the core of the materiality of the practices of neocolonialism; it is through the questioning of these very representations that opportunities can be opened up for interrogating neocolonial structures.

For instance, in his postcolonial critique of U.S. civil society efforts in the Third World, Dutta-Bergman (2005) interrogates the seemingly benevolent public relations activities centered on democracy promotion and nation building. Based on his analysis of documents published by USAID, Dutta-Bergman demonstrates that such democracy promotion efforts that seem on the surface to be directed toward creating participatory spaces in the global South are actually directed toward creating and fostering hegemonic spaces of support for the U.S. agenda, and for nurturing transnational hegemony. The examples of U.S. democracy promotion efforts in Chile, Haiti, Philippines, and Nicaragua demonstrate that so-called efforts of democracy promotion actually worked toward subverting populist participatory movements and instead promoted the interests of the national elite and pro-free market policies that would create open spaces for transnational corporations, most of which were based in the global West. A postcolonial approach to public relations demonstrates that colonialisms are not simply matters of the past, but rather colonial representations circulate in the current transnational hegemonic corporations that maintain dominance of certain nation-states coupled with the transnational corporations and local elites in the global South. Similarly, media relations activities directed at building free media are often efforts to create spaces of support for pro-U.S. media that support the agendas of transnational hegemony (Dutta-Bergman, 2005, 2006).

The imperialist tendencies underlying seemingly benevolent nation building efforts are marked by the portrayal of colonized spaces as "primitive" and hence, in need of interventions. The imperialist intervention and subsequent nation building efforts are seen then as necessities, as efforts of altruism directed at the colonized spaces. This logic is well articulated in the following excerpt on nation building:

> Charges of three decades of misrule—the antithesis of good governance—resulted in the removal of Saddam Hussein's government and its key supporters: the Republican Guard, the Baath Party and the Fedayeen Saddam. The resulting political vacuum and the dire need for reconstruction echo those that preceded the Marshall

> Plan. At this writing, the international community, led by the United States, is funding programs and projects to stabilize and rebuild Afghanistan and Iraq—perhaps on a scale comparable to that of the Marshall Plan. (Pratt, 2006, p. 253)

Note here the representation of an imperialist invasion as a necessity to bring about good governance. Implicit in this assumption is the superiority of the colonizer as a messiah of modernity in a primitive society. Imperialism gets justified as a necessity that responds to the plight of ordinary citizens of the colonized spaces (Pratt, 2006); as a solution to the needs of spaces whose "economies and infrastructures damaged by decades of misrule and neglect by dictatorial regimes, whose political systems are in shambles, and whose citizens are deprived of the essentials of normal living" (Pratt, 2006, p. 253). The economic logics of imperialism such as profits from oil and profits for global corporations involved in the restructuring efforts are framed under the logic of providing support in order to stabilize and rebuild the region. Corporations enter this neoimperialist logic of nation building as catalysts for human rights protections, contributors to local economies, and harbingers of sustainable development even as they profit from the contracts, funding support, raw materials, labor, and new markets opened up to them through the imperialist interventions (Pratt, 2006). Spivak's work is particularly relevant in the light of the contemporary politics of public relations as the rhetoric of globalization and development obscure the exploitative and co-optive facets of seemingly benevolent representations of public relations efforts in forms such as corporate social responsibility, democracy promotion, and nation building.

The co-optive tendency in dominant knowledge structures of public relations is also evident in the recent spurt in theoretical and empirical scholarship on the community building function of public relations that suggests that public relations practitioners have an important role to play in building communities, and connecting the communities to corporations. As channels for promoting corporate interests then, public relations practices directed at serving corporate interests get framed within the appearance of accountability (Kruckeberg & Starck, 1988). The seemingly benevolent task of promoting communities is framed within the broader desire to control local communities to serve organizational interests. Similarly, citing examples such as toxic dumping and oil drilling in marginalized communities, Munshi and Kurian (2005) point out that "the phrase 'sustainable development,' an example of PR-speak, centers not only on the 'silencing of resistance'" (Spivak, 1999, p. 373), but also on appropriating the voice of the subaltern" by simultaneously promoting the rhetoric of sustainable development and the green image and threatening, through a variety of corporate practices, the health and well-being of marginalized communities that typically don't have access to the discursive spaces where the policies are debated and articulated. They thus argue that neocolonial practices subsume those on the periphery (Munshi & Kurian, 2005).

In recent years, scholars have drawn attention to the nature of public diplomacy as an international public relations activity. Historically, such public diplomacy efforts carried out by the West have demonstrated similar colonial agendas as the colonized have been constituted and constructed in the discursive spaces of public diplomacy (Dutta-Bergman, 2006). Postcolonial analyses of public diplomacy efforts reveal the neocolonial agendas that are often couched under the chador of public diplomacy. For instance, U.S. public diplomacy efforts in the Middle East utilize the rhetoric of listening and open communication in order to push U.S. agendas. The benevolent framing of building democratic spaces is utilized in order to support neocolonial interventions often carried out through grossly undemocratic means. For instance, the penetration of spaces such as Afghanistan and Iraq are couched under the frameworks of bringing about peace, building democracy, and liberating the people of oppressed nation-states. In such instances, the manufacturing and marketing of the images of benevolence serve as the basis for global expansionism of transnational corporations.

It is also in the realm of representations that public relations knowledge continues to support hegemonic configurations. Spivak's scholarship further directs us toward the continual displacements that happen in representations. The West and the Third World constituted in discourses are continually displaced as they represent and narrate continually shifting and changing points of reference. This dynamic nature of representation suggests that representations are always constituted in relationship to something else; that which gives meaning to the representations. Therefore, meanings of terms such as *democracy, modernity,* and *civil society* are constituted with reference to their opposites such as *totalitarianism, primitiveness,* and *uncivilized societies.* The existence of civil societies, for example, is dependent upon the representations of uncivil societies; a postcolonial lens draws our attention to these relationships that constitute the dynamic fields of representations within neocolonial configurations.

Worth emphasizing here is the impetus toward criticism that connects images and representations with the materiality of such representations in the global distributions of power. Even as Spivak's work directs us toward the continual displacements that happen in representations and the continually displaced fields of representations, it also draws our attention toward the politics of representations, the material consequences of representations, and the global configurations of colonialisms within which representations happen. Even as postcolonial critics interrogate and rupture the constructions of the Third World's spaces and peoples, their interrogations also make us keenly aware of the global politics of West-Third, North-South, developed-undeveloped within which the logics of neocolonialism operate. Representations carried out through public relations activities are closely intertwined with material structures. It is after all in the domain of the structures that material constructions are constituted, contested, and circulated, and it is also through these representations that structures are created, challenged, and metamorphosed.

Culture-Structure-Agency

What are the relationships among culture, structure, and agency, and how do these relationships influence the representations that circulate in public relations practice? Structures constitute cultural logics and in turn are constituted in the realm of cultures (Dutta, 2007). It is in the realm of structurally situated cultural practices that subaltern participants enact their agency, participating in and challenging the structures through culturally situated practices. Postcolonial analysis points out that knowledge is constituted in the realm of social structures, and serves dominant power structures through a variety of disciplinary moves and representations. A postcolonial analysis of public relations scholarship for instance demonstrates the dominant logics of capitalism that are built into public relations exercises (e.g., Munshi & Kurian, 2005). Even scholars suggesting critical stances in public relations operate within this logic of capitalism and offer their critiques within capitalist frameworks (Toth, 2002). What then are the possibilities of conceptualizing the possibilities of public relations when the taken-for-granted assumptions that drive it are procapitalist and are fundamentally driven by inherent managerial biases dictated toward serving dominant power structures?

Furthermore, knowledge networks in public relations circulate certain cultural assumptions that reflect the propensities of these dominant structures; this is where we come to see the intersections between culture and structure in public relations scholarship. For instance, much of the dominant public relations scholarship treats culture as a static entity. The categories utilized for measuring, systematizing, and evaluating cultures have originated in the Anglo-European academy and continue to circulate the dominant configurations of knowledge networks. For instance, much of the scholarship on global public relations utilizes categories such as power distance, uncertainty avoidance, individualism/collectivism, and masculinity/femininity that reify Eurocentric Cartesian dualism and a categorical view of culture as a static entity (e.g., Sriramesh & Verčič, 2003). Culture gets fixed into a box and offers a schema for categorizing nation-states, national cultures, and national practices; it becomes an object of study elsewhere that can be measured under a categorical lens to offer a point of comparison to normative practices that are typically based on dominant Eurocentric understandings of public relations.

Similarly, frameworks for categorizing nation-states based on their media systems reflect dominant Eurocentric biases in their privileging of certain media systems and implicit assumptions about the inherent value of modernist categorization schemes such as free media systems (Sriramesh & Verčič, 2003). Such concepts as free media are then mobilized in order to justify neocolonial interventions (Dutta-Bergman, 2005). Also, the normative models that dictate much of the knowledge structures in public relations are predominantly Anglo-European. As articulated earlier in this section then, these models offer the basis for cross-cultural comparisons. In other words, the points of reference for culture-based public relations scholarship originate from the Westcentric models of public relations, and use the normative values of the West to categorize public relations practices in other spaces.

Gayatri Spivak's work also suggests that we interrogate the neutrality of dialogue that is celebrated in much of the public relations literature and offers the basis for some of the dominant models in public relations (Kent & Taylor, 2002). Neutrality of dialogue obscures the politics within which it gets situated, and in doing so, serves the dominant power structures that seek to utilize seemingly dialogic platforms in order to push dominant agendas; see Dutta-Bergman (2005) for a postcolonial critique of civil society efforts that seemingly promote dialogue and yet in substance, close off opportunities for dialogue. Therefore, the very desire for neutral dialogue serves as a façade that masks the neocolonial impulses of dominant public relations activities. Interrogating the neutrality of dialogue confronts us with the politics of dialogue. Munshi (1999) draws our attention to this very notion of neutrality in dialogue when he critiques the symmetrical model in public relations and suggests that the model obscures the power relationships within which organizations communicate with their stakeholders. Similarly, Taylor's call for dialogue and public relations obscures the power relationships within which such possibilities of dialogue are created or constrained. Interrogating this very politics of public relations, Dutta-Bergman (2005) calls for a culture-centered approach to public relations that is sensitized to the inequities of power in the realm of dialogue, and suggests the necessity for engaging with a resistive stance that seeks to open up discursive spaces for listening to the voices of subaltern groups by attending to the inequities that constitute the discursive spaces.

Resistance in Public Relations

What then are the praxeological implications of Spivak's work for public relations scholars? By interrogating the power structures within which knowledge is constituted and by questioning the neocolonial impulses of knowledge configurations, postcolonial scholarship resists the dominant structures and suggests openings for transforming the transnational hegemony. More specifically in public relations scholarship, the capitalist basis of public relations activities is no longer taken for granted but rather is interrogated and made explicit (Berger, 2005; Dutta-Bergman, 2005). This making explicit of the taken-for-granted capitalist basis of dominant public relations scholarship and the questioning of its managerial biases are themselves resistive acts because they open up possibilities for alternative epistemological foundations of public relations knowledge, what constitutes this knowledge, and subsequently, the ways in which such knowledge might be deployed by practitioners of public relations. Along these lines, Dutta-Bergman (2005) questions the seemingly altruistic civil society building efforts espoused by public relations scholars (Taylor & Kent, 2006) and examines the underlying capitalist pro-free market logics of such efforts. The modernist benevolence embodied in the rhetoric of such efforts is questioned in the backdrop of the intentions and the practice of the projects (see Dutta-Bergman, 2005). This postcolonial stance supplies the substratum for reconceptualizing public relations practice as activist practice that resists the power and control of the dominant coalition by fundamentally bringing to fore the hypocrisies of the interventions carried out by the dominant coalition.

Ultimately, the postcolonial stance is concerned with the erasures achieved by the deployment of mainstream knowledge: what then has been erased from the dominant Eurocentric narrativizing of public relations? These erasures become the bases for questioning the dominant logics of public relations scholarship that seek to serve as a strategic managerial tool. It is through this questioning of accepted practices that other possibilities are opened up. As articulated earlier, the questioning of the ways in which activism is constructed in the dominant public relations literature allows postcolonial scholars to reconceptualize the field. Asking the question, "Where are the voices of activists in the public relations literature?" draws our attention to the dominant interests served by mainstream public relations work and the ways in which these interests have erased alternatives. Instead of conceptualizing activist publics as a stakeholder group to be managed by public relations practitioners in order to serve the agendas of the organization, conceptualizing activists as practitioners of public relations activities that seek to represent images and issues in contested terrains open up new possibilities for knowledge production (Dutta-Bergman, 2004). Locating agency within activist movements opens up possibilities for listening to voices that challenge the dominant configurations and suggest alternatives to dominant articulations. For instance, although much has been written in the dominant literature about the Union Carbide poisonings in Bhopal, India, public relations scholarship has systematically obliterated the voices of the people of Bhopal who have participated in movements of change, seeking justice. A postcolonial stance opens up the discursive space to journeys of solidarity with the people of Bhopal and to dialogues with subaltern classes who have often been categorized as the victims of the tragedy and subsequently erased from the discursive space. This resistive stance simultaneously ruptures the silences in the dominant literature through the presence of hitherto erased voices, and disrupts the dominant hegemony through the presence of alternative interpretations, meaning frames, and communicative processes articulated through the dialogues with subaltern groups.

Note, however, that the dialogue articulated in resistive politics is markedly different from the notion of apolitical and neutral dialogue in the dominant coalition as such form of resistive dialogue is imbued with its politics of seeking to challenge and alter the status quo. As opposed to the co-optive stance of neutral dialogue that seeks to serve the managerial bias (Kent & Taylor, 2002), dialogue in a postcolonial sense seeks to undo the dominant structures through journeys of solidarity with subaltern classes and in resistance to dominant structures. Dialogue in a postcolonial sense is resistive in its very desire to listen to subaltern voices even as it grapples with the impossibility of listening as the subaltern is continually displaced from the discursive space. In this sense, a move toward dialogue is fundamentally confronted with its impossibility, based on the knowledge that dialogue displaces and erases even as it seeks to represent. This notion of impossibilities of dialogue in subaltern contexts contradicts the mainstream notion of dialogue that assumes mutuality, collaboration, and mutual equality in dialogue (Kent & Taylor, 2002). As opposed to the taken-for-granted notions of equality of the participants in dialogue (Kent & Taylor, 2002), a postcolonial reading of dialogue foregrounds the unequal terrain of relationships that constitutes dialogue. Whereas the dominant articulation of dialogue writes away the interplays of power and control, a postcolonial approach situates dialogue in the reality of the power and inequities that constitute it. Dialogue in a postcolonial sense begins with unlearning one's privilege by doing the homework about the subject position as the investigating subject. Unlearning one's privilege by seeing privilege as a loss, as a discursive closure to alternative possibilities and imaginations, the postcolonial scholar can seek out entry points into dialogue.

The subject position of activism as a position of desire in the dominant public relations scholarship is contested as postcolonial scholarship directs us toward the agency of subaltern groups that typically are constituted outside the arenas of mainstream discourse. An activist stance in public relations treats activism as being subject to a journey of solidarity that challenges the neocolonial agendas of transnational hegemony. In this sense then, the postcolonial scholar is both a scholar and an activist, performing her activism through various avenues of expression that connect her subjectivity to the politics of resistance through performance. A performative stance in public relations then explores the intersections of the aesthetic and the political and explores the ways in which aesthetic representations intersect with political representations (Conquergood, 1982a, 1982b, 1988, 1989, 1991). It is in this sense of aesthetic and political representations that the postcolonial scholar might chart out a vision for organic involvement with the communities that she walks with. An activist stance is keenly aware of the social and economic structures that constitute academia even as it seeks to offer its criticisms from within these structures. Relationships built with local communities reflect this activist stance in their fundamental interrogation of the privilege inherent in dominant knowledge structures and the ways in which knowledge politics might undermine the very structures within which knowledge gets constituted. For instance, the interrogation of the dominant knowledge structures that produce public relations activities for development programs creates vistas for activist politics that entertain other possibilities beyond the taken-for-granted modernist logics of development. In the crisis communication literature, critical interrogation of the dominant knowledge structures that produce the knowledge about effective maintenance and management of crises opens up other possibilities for envisioning the ways in which crises might be approached (see for instance, Kim & Dutta, in press). Even as we engage with such alternative possibilities, however, Gayatri Spivak's work draws our attention to the continually displaced representations, the interplays of aesthetic and political representations, the vulnerabilities inherent in representations, and suggests the relevance of deconstructive vigilance.

Deconstructive Vigilance

Finally, for public relations practitioners and theorists who seek to participate in the resistive politics that interrogates the dominant power structures, Gayatri Spivak writes a note of caution, pointing out the relevance of constant vigilance through a deconstructive stance. This reflexivity built into postcolonial praxis foregrounds the vulnerability of representations, and draws on the idea that political representations are always intertwined with aesthetic representations. Representation in a political sense therefore becomes grounded in the knowledge that it is always a representation, and is situated within contested terrains of power and control. For the public relations scholar, this continuously critical stance makes her aware of the ways in which she participates in propagating the power and control of dominant social structures even as she seeks to resist them. This continual awareness builds reflexivity into the academic structures and connects the critical impulse of postcolonial scholarship with the politics of social change in the face of neoliberal politics. For the public relations practitioner working on projects of activism in subaltern contexts, the vigilant stance opens up spaces for exploring the co-optive moments in practice, as well as for engaging with the interplays of power and control in activist politics. The deconstructive vigilance in activist work brings home the point that even when the subaltern is represented in mainstream public spheres through activist politics, these representations are also representations as articulated by activist practitioners who have access to mainstream public spheres.

The role of the public relations scholar as an organic intellectual then is imbued with the displacements within which representations occur. Any form of representation exists in relationship with other representations, and gains meaning within these discursive chains of representations. These discursive chains of representations are situated within continuously shifting relationships of power and control. A critical stance in activist practice that is reflexive about the relationships of power and moments of control in emancipatory politics creates openings for revisiting the goals of the movement and its emancipatory politics, and offers avenues for a "practical politics of an open end." Such a practical politics of an open end is always open to criticisms, reevaluations, renegotiations, and reinterpretations.

It is through this critical stance that the public relations scholar-activist can become aware of her or his privilege, and engage with this privilege rather than writing it off. Even in imagining possibilities of emancipation brought about by their political involvement, scholar-activists ought to become increasingly sensitized to the moments of co-optation in emancipatory politics. These are the critical moments where emancipatory political movements risk the chance of becoming that which they seek to resist. In this sense, resistive impulses can feed into mechanisms of control, and a critical impulse keeps the activist-scholar continuously vigilant of these moments of control. The contributions of the postcolonial scholar working with activist movements are in creating openings for emancipation through continual reflections and critique; this deconstructive stance contributes to the movement through its sustained evaluation of the rhetoric and practice of emancipatory politics, and the juxtaposition of practice in the backdrop of the rhetoric of the movement.

Conclusion

In conclusion, the work of Gayatri Spivak provides a fertile ground for an entire generation of public relations scholarship, especially in the context of the current global transnational politics within which the scholarship and practice of public relations are situated. This work is particularly relevant in locating public relations practices with reference to neoimperial agendas of globalization politics, and particularly, in drawing attention to the congruities and discrepancies between the rhetoric and practice of public relations efforts. By approaching public relations through lenses of continually displaced reflections, Spivak's scholarship suggests avenues for exploring the ways in which representations serve dominant agendas, continue to recirculate dominant configurations, and minimize opportunities for resistance. Simultaneously, Spivak's scholarship opens up the field to new possibilities for activist politics that offer opportunities for resisting the neoliberal agendas of dominant public relations scholarship and practice. Furthermore, this work creates a space for additional scholarship that explores the intersections between scholarship and practice as we envision the role of organic intellectuals in neocolonial and neoimperial politics. Also, this is a starting point for further exploring the reflexive role of the public relations scholar as she engages with activist politics and critically engages with the tensions between emancipatory politics and politics of a co-optive nature that continuously threatens the emancipatory goals of activist politics.

Note

1. This essay on postcolonialism particularly builds on the work of Spivak. Other key figures in postcolonial theory such as Bhabha, Chaturvedi, Chatterjee, and Mohanty provide us with additional entry points for engaging with public relations theory. However, given the emphasis of this project on drawing out the main works of Spivak, we will not be engaging with these very important theorists in this essay.

References

Berger, B. K. (2005). Power over, power with, and power to relations: Critical reflections of public relations, the dominant coalition, and activism. *Journal of Public Relations Research, 17,* 5–28.

Boal, A. (1985). *Theater of the oppressed* (C. A. & M. L. McBride, Trans.). New York: Theater Communications Group.

Boal, A. (1998). *Legislative theatre* (A. Jackson, Trans.). London and New York: Routledge.

Botan, C., & Hazleton, V. (1989). *Public relations theory.* Mahwah, NJ: Erlbaum.

Botan, C., & Hazleton, V. (2006). *Public relations theory II.* New York: Routledge.

Broadfoot, K., & Munshi, D. (2007). Diverse voices and alternative rationalities: Imagining forms of postcolonial organizational communication. *Management Communication Quarterly, 21,* 249–267.

Conquergood, D. (1982a). Communication as performance: Dramaturgical dimensions of everyday life. In J. I. Sisco (Ed.), *The Jensin lectures: Contemporary communication studies* (pp. 24–43). Tampa: University of South Florida Press.

Conquergood, D. (1982b). Performing as a moral act: Ethical dimensions of the ethnography of performance. *Literature in Performance, 5,* 1–13.

Conquergood, D. (1988). Health theater in a Hmong refugee camp. *The Drama Review, 32,* 174–208.

Conquergood, D. (1989). Poetics, play, process, and power: The performative turn in anthropology. *Text and Performance Quarterly, 9,* 82–88.

Conquergood, D. (1991). Rethinking ethnography: Towards a critical cultural politics. *Communication Monographs, 58,* 179–194.

Curtin, P. A., & Gaither, T. K. (2006). Contested notions of issue identity in international public relations: A case study. *Journal of Public Relations Research, 18,* 67–89.

Dutta, M. (2006). Theoretical approaches to entertainment education: A subaltern critique. *Health Communication, 20,* 221–231.

Dutta-Bergman, M. (2005). Civil society and public relations: Not so civil after all. *Journal of Public Relations Research, 17,* 267–289.

Dutta-Bergman, M. (2006). U.S. public diplomacy in the Middle East: A critical approach. *Journal of Communication Inquiry, 30,* 102–124.

Harasym, S. (Ed.). (1990). *The postcolonial critic: Interviews, strategies, dialogues.* New York: Routledge.

Kent, M. L., & Taylor, M. (2002). Toward a dialogic theory of public relations. *Public Relations Review, 28,* 21–37.

Kim, I., & Dutta, M. (in press). A subaltern studies approach to crisis communication. *Journal of Public Relations Research.*

Kruckeberg, D., & Starck, K. (1988). *Public relations and community: A reconstructed story.* New York: Praeger.

Landry, D., & MacLean, G. (1996). *The Spivak reader.* New York: Routledge.

Munshi, D. (1999). Requisitioning variety: Photographic metaphors, ethnocentric lenses, and the divided colours of public relations. *Asia Pacific Public Relations Journal, 1,* 39–51.

Munshi, D., & Kurian, P. (2005). Imperializing spin cycles: A postcolonial look at public relations, greenwashing and the separation of publics. *Public Relations Review, 31,* 513–520.

Pal, M., & Dutta, M. (2008a). Public relations in a global context: The relevance of critical modernism as a theoretical lens. *Journal of Public Relations Research, 20,* 159–179.

Pal, M., & Dutta, M. (2008b). Theorizing resistance in a global context: Processes, strategies, and tactics in communication scholarship. *Communication Yearbook, 32,* 41–87.

Pratt, C. (2006). Reformulating the emerging theory of corporate social responsibility as good governance. In C. Botan & V. Hazleton (Eds.), *Public relations theory* (pp. 249–277). Mahwah, NJ: Erlbaum.

Said, E. (1988). Foreword. In R. Guha & G. C. Spivak (Eds.), *Selected subaltern studies* (pp. v–xii). New York: Oxford University Press.

Said, E. W. (1978). *Orientation.* Harmondsworth, UK: Penguin.

Shome, R., & Hegde, S. R. (2002). Postcolonial approaches to communication: Charting the terrain, engaging the intersections. *Communication Theory, 12,* 249–270.

Spivak, G. C. (1987). *In other worlds: Essays in cultural politics* (R. Guha, Ed.). London: Methuen.

Spivak, G. C. (1990a). The post-colonial critic. *The postcolonial critic: Interviews, strategies, dialogues* (S. Harasym, Ed., pp. 67–74). New York: Routledge.

Spivak, G. C. (1990b). Questions of multi-culturalism. *The postcolonial critic: Interviews, strategies, dialogues* (S. Harasym, Ed., pp. 59–66). New York: Routledge.

Spivak, G. C. (1993). *Outside in the teaching machine: Toward a history of the vanishing present.* London: Routledge.

Spivak, G. C. (1996). Bonding in difference: Interview with Alfred Arteaga. In D. Landry & G. MacLean (Eds.), *The Spivak reader: Selected works of Gayatri Chakravorty Spivak* (pp. 15–28). New York: Routledge.

Spivak, G. C. (1999). *A critique of postcolonial reason: Toward a history of the vanishing present.* Cambridge, MA: Harvard University Press.

Spivak, G. C. (2003). *Death of a discipline.* New York: Columbia University Press.

Sriramesh, K., & Verčič, D. (2003). A theoretical framework for global public relations research and practice. In K. Sriramesh & D. Verčič (Eds.), *The global public relations handbook* (pp. 1–21). Mahwah, NJ: Erlbaum.

Taylor, M., & Kent, M. (2006). Public relations theory and practice in nation building. In C. Botan & V. Hazleton (Eds.), *Public relations theory* (pp. 341–359). Mahwah, NJ: Erlbaum.

Taylor, M., Kent, M. L., & White, W. J. (2001). How activist organizations are using the Internet to build relationships. *Public Relations Review, 27,* 263–284.

Toth, E. (2002). Postmodernism for modernist public relations: The cash value and application of critical research in public relations. *Public Relations Review, 28,* 243–250.

The Life and Work of Gayatri Chakravorty Spivak

Gayatri Chakravorty Spivak was born in Calcutta, West Bengal, February 24, 1942. She received her bachelor's degree in English from the University of Calcutta, her master's in English from Cornell University, and her doctorate from the University of Iowa. Spivak translated Derrida's *Of Grammatology*, the preface to which set new standards in self-reflexivity for prefaces. Subsequent work focused on historical studies, poststructuralist literary criticism, deconstruction of Marxism, literary critiques of imperialism and international feminism, and translations of the Bengali writer Mahasweta Devi. Spivak has taught at Columbia University since 1991 and was appointed University Professor, the institution's highest faculty rank, in 2007. Her major works include: *In other worlds: Essays in cultural politics, Selected subaltern studies* (1987), *The postcolonial critic: Interviews, strategies, dialogues* (1990a), *Outside in the teaching machine, A critique of postcolonial reason: Toward a history of the vanishing present* (1993), and *Death of a discipline* (2003).

Chapter 15

On Weber

Legitimacy and Legitimation in Public Relations[1]

Arild Wæraas

Abstract

This chapter discusses insights from Max Weber's sociology in order to expand our understanding of the field of public relations. More specifically, the chapter argues that (1) his concepts of legitimacy and legitimation are relevant for understanding the purpose as well as the practice of public relations; (2) efforts to justify organizational existence and cultivate beliefs in an organization's right to exist can be seen as central elements of public relations; and (3) the concept of charismatic legitimation sheds light on the current tendencies in public relations practice to endow organizations with attractive personality characteristics. Both practical and theoretical implications of these ideas for the field of public relations are discussed.

Max Weber's theories on legitimacy and legitimation go to the core of what the public relations discipline is about: acquiring and preserving support from the general public. Defining legitimacy as the justified right to exist, Weber observed that any formal system of organization or "domination" needs legitimacy. He also noted that any such system must base its existence on a principle of legitimation, either the legal-rational, traditional, or the charismatic. Since public relations discipline is concerned with the need for support from the general public as well as how to retain it, Weber's ideas may provide a more complete understanding of the role and purpose of public relations. In this chapter, it is argued that a central purpose of public relations is to acquire and preserve organizational legitimacy.

The chapter first reviews the sociology of Weber and outlines his concepts of domination, authority, and legitimacy. The concept of legitimation is subsequently emphasized, particularly his idea of charismatic legitimation. Because of the emergence of a rational order in society, Weber predicted that a legal-rational principle of legitimation would prevail in the future. However, as a result of a growing emotional order in society, this chapter argues that his notion of charismatic legitimation is valuable to understand the basis for organizational legitimacy and legitimation today, and hence for public relations. The relevance of these ideas for public relations is discussed. Finally, some implications for practitioners and suggestions for further research are offered.

The Sociology of Max Weber

Max Weber is considered to be one of the most influential social scientists of all time. His works span a wide range of social theory and have inspired a tremendous amount of research and debate in several fields including political science, philosophy of science, sociology, and history. One of his classic texts, *Economy and Society* (1922/1968), published posthumously, serves as a hallmark for all social science by clarifying central concepts like power, legitimacy, authority, and rationality. It has also made him one of the most important social theorists for the emergence and development of organization studies. Textbooks in organizational theory (e.g., Hall, 1991; Scott, 1998) typically use Weber's theories as a background for describing the emergence of rational forms of production and organizing, as well as the legitimate basis for existing as a formal organization.

Weber's production is so vast that it is virtually impossible to give an account of his sociology without compromising it. In this chapter, some of his ideas are presented on the basis of their assumed relevance for the field of public relations.

A central ambition for Max Weber was to understand contemporary Western society in its totality. He saw a shift in human motivation as an important distinguishing feature from societies of the past, which led humans to be dominated by goal-oriented rationality instead of acting on the basis of traditions, values, or emotions. The result would be an increasingly rationalized, rule-oriented, and ultimately less human society. In this context his view had some similarities to Karl Marx's concept of alienation, as they both agreed that rational organizing threatened individual freedom and deprived humans of the ability to make decisions about their own lives. However, Weber did not agree with Marx's claim that alienation is a phenomenon that would occur only in capitalist systems. He believed that alienation is a consequence of the rationalization of society and an inescapable result of *any* system of rationally coordinated production (Coser, 1977). It follows that a socialist system would be even more bureaucratic and rule-oriented than a capitalist system because of its centralized economic system.

However, Weber was not an advocate for capitalism. He viewed capitalism as a major force paralleling the increasing tendencies in society to regulate, standardize, and rationalize. In *The Protestant Ethic and the Spirit of Capitalism* (1904/1991), he discussed the connection between Protestantism and the capitalist spirit, suggesting that this constellation would lead to an iron cage of rationality that in turn would undermine the importance of emotions and individually differentiated behavior. Modern governments and organizations would not be legitimate unless they displayed sufficiently rational and goal-oriented behavior. This brings us to Weber's most important concepts: power, domination, and authority, as well as legitimacy and legitimation, which will be discussed in more depth in this chapter.

Power, Domination, Authority, and Legitimacy

In *Economy and Society*, Max Weber (1922/1968) elaborated on the concepts of power, domination, and authority. Focusing on the right to rule and the principles on which this right could be exercised, Weber was less interested in power, which he saw as an actor's "position to carry out his own will despite resistance" (1922/1968, p. 53). Instead, he focused on *Herrschaft*, which "constitutes a special case of power" (p. 941), and which is similar to the English term *domination*:

> To be more specific, domination will thus mean the situation in which the manifested will (command) of the ruler or rulers is meant to influence the conduct of one or more others (*the ruled*) and actually does influence it in such a way that their conduct...occurs as if the ruled had made the content of the command the maxim of their conduct. (Weber 1968, p. 946, italics in original)

Thus, for Weber every form of domination implies some sort of voluntary compliance. The will of the ruler is obeyed because there is an interest in obedience, or at a minimum, a sense of duty to obey, due to the ruler's acknowledged right to rule. Weber referred to this phenomenon as domination "by virtue of authority" (1922/1968, p. 943), which is fundamentally different from ruling on the basis of power. Examples could include parent–child relationships, religious leaders and their followers, kings and subjects, and the relationship between a formal organization and its environments. The latter is usually not based on giving and receiving orders, yet it is characterized by some elements of domination. Often, organizations seek to "influence the conduct of one or more others" (Weber, 1922/1968, p. 946); for example, through marketing and public relations campaigns, but are usually in no position to impose demands on them. Therefore, to be successful, organizations depend on voluntary compliance from their environments. Weber referred to such compliance as legitimacy: Once organizations have an acknowledged right to rule, they are seen as legitimate. As a result, legitimacy implies that the organization enjoys sufficient voluntary external support to continue to exist.

Principles of Legitimation

Domination by virtue of authority is not likely to have long-term success unless there is a strong belief in the system's legitimacy. The survival of the system must be ensured by continuously enabling the support and endorsement of the subjects, ensuring that they perceive the system as "worthy" of voluntary compliance. In other words, existing and acting as a ruling government, or as any organization, is a sort of a privilege that must be justified. Anyone who is more favored feels "the never ceasing need" to see his or her position as legitimate and deserved (Weber, 1922/1968, p. 953). Consequently, to survive, every system develops some sort of myth that "cultivates the belief in its legitimacy," functioning as a justification of the system's existence (p. 213). Thus for Weber, a myth is a story that successfully justifies the system's privilege of existing and conducting operations.

Weber not only implied that legitimacy is socially constructed, but also that the potential for acquiring legitimacy lies in the citizens' perceptions of the system; in other words, in their beliefs. The myths that are created and cultivated are not necessarily facts and cannot have a legitimizing impact unless people believe in them. Similarly, a system is legitimate only as long as people have faith in its justified right to exist. Acquiring legitimacy, according to Weber, is thus a matter of influencing beliefs by gaining acceptance for a particular "myth," making legitimation a strategic process that entails justifications as well as attempts to influence public opinion.

Weber did not go much further in clarifying the myths of a system and how they are developed and used in practice to create and cultivate favorable beliefs. Instead, he directed his focus on ideal-typical principles on which a system's legitimacy may be based, arguing that the basis for a system's legitimacy varies according to the kind of beliefs that support it. Specifically, the validity of the claims to legitimacy may be based on:

1. Rational grounds—resting on a belief in the legality of enacted rules and the right of those elevated to authority under such rules to issue commands;
2. Traditional grounds—resting on an established belief in the sanctity of immemorial traditions and the legitimacy of those exercising authority under them;
3. Charismatic grounds—resting on devotion to the exceptional sanctity, heroism, or exemplary character of an individual person. (Weber, 1922/1968, p. 215)

It follows that Weber's understanding of "claims to legitimacy" is rather abstract and theoretical. He did not demonstrate explicitly the connection between such claims and the subsequent beliefs; rather we must infer from his ideal-typical descriptions that legitimation is an inherent element of successful domination. Furthermore, the type of legitimation will differ fundamentally, depending on what basis legitimacy is claimed.

Legal–rational legitimation is based on laws and rules that assure that rationality is implemented in every aspect of the system and at every level. Assuming that society's belief in rationality is strong—which indeed Weber did—people will look favorably upon a system that works according to a principle that they embrace themselves. Thus, legal-rationality is the very source of legitimacy. In particular, the bureaucratic form of organization adheres to this principle—it is a "pure" type of legal–rational domination. As a system capable of "attaining the highest degree of efficiency," it is "the most rational known means of exercising authority over human beings" (1922/1968, p. 223). Any organization that conducts its operations on the basis of bureaucratic structures will derive legitimacy from its environments.

Traditional legitimation rests on the continuous cultivation of a belief in the sanctity of old tradition and habit. The system is regulated by a set of traditional rules and norms that gives the ruler authority and his or her government the right to exercise domination. As long as the tradition is shared and the ruler acts in accordance with it, the members of the system will perceive the system as justified and legitimate. New rules can be legitimized only by the claim that they have "always" been there.

Charismatic legitimation rests on devotion to the exceptional character of the leader. The system is legitimate because its leader is:

> considered extraordinary and treated as endowed with supernatural, superhuman, or at least specifically exceptional powers or qualities. These are such as are not accessible to the ordinary person, but are regarded as of divine origin or as exemplary, and on the basis of them the individual concerned is treated as a "leader." (Weber, 1922/1968, p. 241)

Because charisma cannot exist unless it is believed in, the emergence of charisma is determined by how the individual is perceived by the followers. A person *is* a charismatic leader, if that person is socially defined as charismatic, irrespective of whether he or she actually possesses exceptional traits. This means that charisma, like legitimacy, is a social construction that to some extent can be manipulated. Weber did not fully elaborate on this phenomenon, but he did contrast charisma, which is inherited "by virtue of natural endowment" (i.e., pure charisma) with charisma which is "produced artificially in an object or person through some extraordinary means" (Weber, 1922/1968, p. 400). This distinction has inspired neocharismatic theorists to suggest that charisma is first and foremost an attribution (Conger & Kanungo, 1994) and that, given the right circumstances, any leader could be perceived as charismatic. In this perspective, the legitimacy of charismatic leadership is an attribute of the belief of the followers and not of the quality of the leader (Bensman & Givant, 1975). Consequently, charismatic legitimation becomes a matter of using the best techniques of persuasion.

Charismatic Legitimation of Institutions

Weber recognized the constructivist nature of charisma in his descriptions of the ways in which charisma could be "depersonalized." In his book *Economy and Society* (1922/1968, p. 1135) he argued that charisma could be transformed from a unique gift of grace into a quality that is either transferable, personally acquirable, or attached to an institutional structure regardless of the people involved. It could be transferred from one person to another through ceremonies, for example through a priest's ordination or a king's coronation. Or, charisma could simply be learned through a process of charismatic education (p. 1143). Finally, even institutions could be endowed with charisma:

> Here we find that peculiar transformation of charisma into an institution: as permanent structures and traditions replace the belief in the revelation and heroism of charismatic personalities, charisma becomes part of an established social structure. (Weber, 1922/1968, p. 1139)

Although Weber primarily identified charisma as a characteristic related to individuals, he made reference to the institutionalization of charisma in organizations, describing it in terms of "charismatic legitimation of institutions" (1922/1968, p. 1141) or "the charisma of office" (p. 1140). In this sense, charisma could be seen as an attribute of the organization. It is depersonalized and rests on "the belief in the specific state of grace of a social institution" (p. 1140), in other words, on the perceived extraordinary qualities of an organization. Thus, according to Weber, an organization may base its legitimacy on the belief that it is endowed with exceptional qualities as an entity. By allowing for this possibility, Weber not only regarded individual charisma as a source of organizational legitimacy, he also suggested that *organizational* charisma may become a source from which legitimacy can be derived (Wæraas, 2004). In theory, any organization that succeeds in conveying the impression of itself as exceptional and extraordinary and in cultivating the belief that it is so, could acquire a status as legitimate.

The Iron Cage of Rationality

Weber predicted that charisma would be a significantly less important phenomenon in the future because of the prevalence of the rationalist order. He elaborated on the causes for this development in *The Protestant Ethic and the Spirit of Capitalism* (1904/1991). Claiming that Western societies had become heavily influenced by a new ethic that promoted the values of discipline and rationality, Protestantism—especially in its puritan form—had generated a particular frame of mind encouraging rationally pursued economic activity. It had formed the spirit of capitalism, which in turn had transformed not only forms of domination and authority but also forms of administration. Weber was very skeptical of these trends and feared that the rationalist order would become an iron cage in which humanity would be imprisoned "perhaps until the last ton of fossilized coal is burnt" (Weber, 1904/1991, p. 181). His conclusion was: "The fate of our times is characterized by rationalization and intellectualization" (1948, p. 155). The only way of escaping the iron cage would be to establish democratic social institutions with charismatic leaders and great emphasis on emotions and value-oriented behavior.

It could be argued that Weber's skepticism toward rationalization, and more positive attitude toward charisma, demonstrate that he was a "product" of his time. The emerging tendencies of rationalization and bureaucratization in society led him to a somewhat deterministic view of the future. On the other hand, there can be no doubt that the rationalist order does not exert the same influence today and has become a less significant phenomenon than Weber predicted. It is still true that modern institutions are law and rule oriented, and that goal-rational behavior has had a major importance in the development of management systems. However, legal–rational values and characteristics play a less prominent role in legitimation. For example, the tendencies to use public relations and corporate communication to promote unique and exceptional features of organizations are one of many signs indicating that an emotional and value-oriented order has been brought into play and partly replaced, partly supplemented the rational order.

Criticism

Because of his vast production, theory-heavy arguments and many controversial thoughts, a number of scholars have criticized Weber. One particularly controversial theory is his assertion that the Protestant ethic formed the capitalist spirit and therefore was the cause of the rationalist order (Green, 1959; Tawney, 1926). Another common criticism is that Weber gave an oversimplified and one-dimensional account of the rational order. By using ideal–typical models emphasizing only selected aspects, it is claimed that Weber overestimated the significance of rationality and underestimated many important aspects of society, especially irrational ones.

Weber has also been reproached for distorting the essential meaning of legitimacy (Habermas, 1976). His concept of legitimacy does not refer to criteria that are commonly used to assess the validity of a system, the correctness of its procedures, and the justifications for its decisions (Grafstein, 1981). For Weber, legitimacy refers to characteristics of the citizens' beliefs, not to characteristics of the system directly. In fact, Weber did not really offer a consistent definition of legitimacy, and his way of using the term is circular and tautological: Legitimacy is the belief of citizens that the system is legitimate (Grafstein, 1981). This is why legitimation, for Weber, is a matter of cultivating beliefs, while it for Habermas may be "without an immanent relation to truth" (1976, p. 97). If the belief in legitimacy is not really associated with what is true, he claims that "the grounds upon which [legitimacy] is explicitly based has only psychological significance" (Habermas, 1976, p. 97).

On the one hand, the problems with Weber's use of the concept restrict its potential for using it as an analytical lens through which to study legitimation efforts. On the other hand, the ambiguity allows for a variety of interpretations and uses. For example, the psychological significance referred to by Habermas, in other words, Weber's emphasis on the importance of cultivating beliefs, will here serve as a starting point for discussing the relevance of legitimacy and legitimation for understanding the practice of public relations.

Relevance for Public Relations

In this section of this chapter, three points are discussed. First, Weber's concept of legitimacy is relevant in itself for understanding public relations practice. The next section of the chapter will be devoted to outlining this argument. Second, Weber demonstrated the dependence on legitimacy and the need to cultivate beliefs in order to justify and preserve a legitimate status in society. A Weberian focus on public relations thus contributes to a better understanding of legitimacy as the purpose of public relations. Third, an interesting match between charismatic legitimation and public relations practice deserves more attention. A closer examination of this match may prove helpful for a more complete view of the nature of public relations and the type of legitimation involved.

Public Relations and Legitimacy

Although the concept of legitimacy is rarely used in the public relations literature, the idea of gaining and preserving external support is central and well known in public relations theory and practice. As observed in 1939 by one of the early public relations pioneers, Arthur Page, "All business in a democratic country begins with public permission and exists by public approval" (cited in Griswold Jr., 1967, p. 13). This way of conceptualizing the relation between organizations and their environments is also found in the literature on corporate social responsibility, where an implicit social contract is assumed to hold organizations accountable to society's expectations and demands (Wartick & Cochran, 1985). If organizations are approved, they are awarded a "license to operate" (Howard-Grenville, Nash, & Coglianese, 2008; Zinkin, 2004).

Despite the obvious similarities to the concept of legitimacy, only a handful of scholars have demonstrated its relevance for the public relations discipline (Christen, 2005; Coombs, 1992; Holmström, 2005; Jensen, 1997; Metzler, 2001a, 2001b; Munk Nielsen, 1998; Yoon, 2005). Several reasons may account for this absence. First, public relations literature tends to focus more on practices and techniques rather than on the actual objective of the efforts. The purpose is usually seen as obtaining "good relations" with the public, but this objective is not always defined more specifically as one precise construct that sums up the relationship between the organization and its environments. To the extent that this is done, it more often involves obtaining and maintaining goodwill, a good image or a good reputation, rather than acquiring legitimacy. Another reason could be that public relations theory is relatively little inspired by organization theory, where legitimacy is a central concept (Meyer & Rowan, 1977; Scott, 1998). Public relations and corporate communication have more in common with marketing as a scholarly discipline than organization theory, although all embrace a focus on the relationship between organizations and their environments. This suggests that there is much to gain from combining these perspectives. Third, the concept may be absent from public relations theory due to its somewhat theoretical and abstract content. Unlike image or reputation, which are constructs that give meaning intuitively in an everyday setting and some sense of direction for action, the notion of legitimacy is harder to grasp. It is usually only when legitimacy is questioned that it becomes an issue (Habermas, 1976). Metzler (2001b) argues these situations are the issues that public relations scholars and practitioners need to investigate.

Expanding on Weber, we may assert that public relations is involved not only in acquiring legitimacy and making sure the organization has the voluntary support of its stakeholders, but also in protecting the organization's legitimacy when questioned. If one accepts the idea that public relations involves establishing good relations with the public and that those relations secure the organization's survival, then we may easily argue that public relations is all about obtaining and preserving legitimacy. As observed by Metzler (2001b): "establishing and maintaining organizational legitimacy is at the core of most, if not all, public relations activities." Inspired by Weber, she defines legitimacy as the "right to exist and conduct operations" (p. 321). Thus, the purpose of public relations, seen from the perspective of Weber, is to acquire and preserve organizational legitimacy.

Justifications and the Cultivation of Beliefs

One of the reasons why there is such a function as public relations at all rests on the Weberian argument that existing as an organization and conducting business is a sort of privilege that must be justified. As discussed previously, the relationship between an organization and its environments is usually not based on giving and obeying orders. Nevertheless, as organizations often seek to influence the conduct of others to acquire a larger share of society's resources, the relationship is characterized by some elements of domination. As observed by Weber, the privilege to influence creates a "never ceasing need" to justify the organization's existence. Furthermore, because successful domination depends on the continuous voluntary support and endorsement from the public, justifications of the right to continue operations will be *demanded*. Responding to such demands is a central function of public relations. When valid justifications are presented, the environments comply voluntarily with the organization's goals and raison d'être. Without them, the organization may lose its privileges and the right to exercise domination. This is why organizations—formulated in Weberian terms—create and cultivate a myth revolving around their right to exist and conduct business.

Although expressed in different terms, public relations often involves making justifications and cultivating beliefs, and in many cases the creation and cultivation of myths. Justifications may apply to the organization's existence in general as well as to particular actions. For example, the area of strategic public relations involves making decisions about goals and objectives (Cutlip, Broom, & Center, 1999). Most organizations have a written statement of goals and objectives, corporate visions, or a mission statement, where the main purpose is to convey concisely *why* an organization exists. Such statements serve as justifications of the right to exist, as well as a means of cultivating the belief in this right. If no such statement exists, it is considered a central task of the public relations unit to suggest one (Cutlip et al., 1999). In addition, public relations employees monitor public opinion, cultural and social change, and political movements, to help the organization adjust and adapt their goals and objectives to their environments. They then work with management to develop strategic plans of responsiveness, making sure that the organization's mission and values are understood and accepted by the public opinion.

The need to justify the existence of an organization becomes particularly apparent in situations in which the organization is faced with criticism, in other words, when it is under attack from important stakeholder groups or from the general public. Such instances usually occur when the organization has done or said something that is not in accordance with what is expected on the basis of general social norms and values. Pressure groups and stakeholders in the organization's environments may question the very existence of the organization. In this case, public relations personnel have a particular responsibility to respond strategically to these groups by providing a justification or an apology of criticized actions or statements. These efforts are often referred to in terms of crisis communication strategies (Coombs, 1999) or image repair strategies (Benoit, 1995).

Weber used the term *myths* when he referred to the beliefs that are created and cultivated. According to Weber, the interesting aspect of myths is not really whether the myths are true or not, but rather that they are believed in. As long as the public believes in the organization's right to exist, the organization *is* legitimate. This phenomenon illustrates the constructivist nature of legitimacy (Ashforth & Gibbs, 1990; Suchman, 1995). Valid justifications and successful cultivation of perceptions will ultimately produce legitimacy. Using Weber's line of reasoning we may argue that a central function in public relations is to provide valid strategic justifications in situations where positive beliefs need to be propagated about the organization.

Beliefs, Myths, and Ethics

Weber's understanding of legitimation as the cultivation of beliefs and myths calls ethics into question. A consequence of relying on beliefs and myths in public relations may be what Habermas (1976, p. 97) referred to as being "without an immanent relation to truth": the temptation to present more positive images of an organization than really is the case. In fact, some public relations practitioners have relied on using myths to such an extent that they have been labeled "spin doctors." The "dark" side of the public relations discipline includes a history of propaganda, cover-up campaigns, the promulgation of false myths, and the manipulation of public opinion (Ewen, 1996).

Although it could be argued that spin is in accordance both with Weber's notion of cultivating beliefs and with the concept of domination in the sense that a certain will is meant to influence the conduct of others (Weber, 1922/1968), it is difficult to find support in his works for the idea that legitimation could or should involve spin. For Weber, whose definition of legitimacy is largely functional, spin would be too easy to uncover, and, therefore, not give sufficient stability for continued existence. Weber's interest in legitimacy was not related to ethics per se; he was more interested in legitimacy from a functional standpoint. Thus, spin is wrong, not from a moral standpoint, but simply because it does not work. The most important way in which favorable beliefs are created and preserved is by proving oneself in practice. The evidence for this may come in different forms, but primarily from the way in which the organization exercises domination. Beliefs are cultivated, and the organization's domination is justified, by performing organizational actions, communicating, and making decisions that are in accordance with the environments' norms for acceptable conduct. This means that an organization can exist only as long as it receives recognition and approval from its environments and could lose its "privileged position" if it fails to respect the limits of its domination. If an organization's way of operating is not in accordance with what is expected from this particular type of domination, resistance will arise.

However, in charismatic legitimation, a certain degree of manipulation of perceptions will inevitably play an essential part. Organizations do not have charisma of the pure type that allows them to perform revelations or otherwise prove their "divine mission" through actions. Therefore, if charismatic legitimation is to be successful, organizations must rely on verbal communication to construct and sustain images of themselves as endowed with a humanlike charismatic character. Perceptions of performance and qualities, more or less induced by the organization, will serve as the means by which the organization succeeds in creating emotional support. Thus, organizational charisma exists only to the extent that the environments believe in the organization's extraordinary qualities. Understanding the nature of these qualities is a question that deserves more attention. It leads us to an examination of a central parallel between public relations and Max Weber's notion of charismatic legitimation.

Public Relations as Charismatic Legitimation of Organizations

Charismatic legitimation of organizations presupposes that it is possible to perceive an organization as an entity or "super-person" (Sevón, 1996) whose qualities and personality are similar to that of a charismatic individual. As organizational charisma rests on an affectionate devotion to the perceived character of an organization, it is a social construction that can be manipulated and resides fully "in the eyes of the beholder." At the same time, it may represent an important basis for the environments' support and endorsement. The question is; can the public relations discipline contribute to promoting a charismatic organizational personality that could constitute the basis for legitimacy, and if so, under what conditions? The remaining sections of this chapter will discuss this question by expanding on Max Weber's theory. As a starting point for the discussion, a brief attention will first be given to the background for which charismatic legitimation of organizations has emerged as a significant phenomenon today.

Background for Charismatic Legitimation

As previously referred to in this chapter, several phenomena indicate that an emotional order or spirit has partly supplemented and partly replaced the rational order. Although there are still many laws and rules in society, they do not seem to represent the powerful source of legitimacy that Weber envisaged. Currently, it is commonly assumed that we have too many rules and laws. Bureaucracy has become a word of abuse. It is claimed that we live in a "dream society" (Jensen, 1999) or "experience economy" (Pine & Gilmore, 1999) instead of a rational society. To obtain support and endorsement, organizations must appeal to the environments' dreams and aspirations and connect with them on an emotional rather than rational level. Customers demand emotional satisfaction and rely increasingly on their senses and emotions when acting and making purchase decisions (Hill, 2003). Building emotional appeal has become crucial for organizational survival and success (Aaker, 2004; Fombrun & van Riel, 2004; Hill, 2003; Jensen, 1999; Keller, 2000).

Because individuals will support an organization to the extent that they like, trust, and identify with it, it could be argued that charisma emerges as an important element in this relationship. A customer may develop a deep sense of affection or devotion to a company and its products. Brands seem to have "spiritual power" today in the sense that they "have become some kind of replacement or supplement for religious belief" (Olins, 2000, p. 63). There is a clear parallel between this line of reasoning and Weber's notion of charisma as a property of objects. Because of the decline of the rational order, organizations do not want to be perceived as rational machine bureaucracies, but rather as entities with exceptional and attractive corporate personalities. An organization is "born" with neither charisma nor a specific personality, but as it grows, engages in relationships with its stakeholders and becomes admired and even worshiped, it may be perceived with traits of a charismatic individual. Some companies have customers who are so dedicated and committed that they follow the company almost blindly, as in the case of Harley Davidson or Apple Computer. Some Harley Davidson bikers are so devoted that they have the brand name tattooed on their arm, and some Apple users are so intense in their dedication that they sometimes refer to themselves as "Apple evangelists" or "Apple zealots."

Simply stated, today it is expected that organizations express their personalities and their values. If they fail to do it—particularly with regards to building emotional appeal—their legitimacy may be threatened. This concern drives organizations to invest more and more of their efforts into building an attractive organizational identity or personality and managing people's perceptions of themselves (Schultz, Hatch, & Larsen, 2000). Activities that aim to express such a charismatic "self" are here seen as linked to the management of legitimacy.

Expressing a Charismatic Organizational Character through Public Relations

As an essentially expressive and extroverted discipline, public relations is ideal for building relationships with its constituents in a strategic manner by communicating "who" and "what" it is in terms of values and characteristics. Developing personal relationships with stakeholders and presenting the organization's "self" in order to win general support now seems to be an important part of strategic public relations. Typically, organizations claim to be "honest," "change oriented," "reliable," "visionary," "responsible," and so on. Furthermore, they engage in activities revolving around corporate social responsibility and seek to ensure that they, in Weber's terms, bring "well-being to [their] faithful followers" (Weber, 1922/1968, p. 1114). It seems to be a widely shared current belief that relationships based on trust and devotion to an attractive humanlike character are essential for organizational success and survival (Davies, Chun, Roper, & Silva, 2003).

However, although public relations serves to develop strategic relationships of this kind, it is preferable to discuss in more depths the conditions under which such efforts may be seen as charismatic legitimation. The question is: How do we separate public relations activities that involve charismatic legitimation from those that do not? More precisely, is it possible to identify attempts at charismatic legitimation based on observation of the content of an organization's communication and actions? Max Weber's description of charisma (1922/1968) is of some help in answering these questions. Charisma is related to heroism, oratory, vision, spiritual gifts, and the capacity to perform revelations. A leader who is believed to be blessed with such qualities is a charismatic leader. Thus, displaying such qualities in behavior and communication in order to create and sustain the belief that the organization possesses them could be regarded as efforts of charismatic legitimation.

It should be noted that Weber's ideas regarding charismatic legitimation of organizations are somewhat general. The lack of specificity limits our understanding of their nature. Therefore, in the following discussion, a more specific theory presented by Conger and Kanungo (1987, 1994, 1998) will be used to clarify Weber's ideas. Adopting an instrumental approach to the study of individual charisma, they claim that charismatic leadership should be considered as an observable behavioral process "that can be described and analyzed in terms of a formal model" (1987, p. 639). Treating charisma essentially as an attribution, the authors assume that certain characteristics are causally responsible for the attribution of charisma, while other characteristics are not. In their refined model (1998, pp. 114–115), they propose that being visionary, articulate, sensitive to the environments, sensitive to member needs, unconventional, and taking personal risks, are the central characteristics that may to lead to such attributions.

Using this attribution theory, we may assert that strategic self-presentation that promotes *any* character or personality as visionary, articulate, sensitive to the environments and to member needs, unconventional, and risk-taking, are attempts at charismatic legitimation. By substituting "leader" with "organization," and "member needs" with "stakeholder needs," the theory could be adapted to the organizational level and used to clarify the conditions under which public relations may involve charismatic legitimation. Still, in this context it is important to note that not all characteristics that define charisma on the individual level may apply to the organizational level. For example, while an individual may be perceived as a hero when taking personal risks and therefore be perceived as charismatic, there is nothing heroic in jeopardizing the existence of an organization or the safety of its employees. Taking personal risk does not seem to add meaningfully to our understanding of organizational legitimation and will therefore be excluded from the following discussion.

As for the other characteristics, public relations may involve presenting the organization to stakeholders and the general public as visionary, articulate, sensitive to the environments, and to stakeholders' needs, and as unconventional. If the attribution of charisma is likely to be made when an individual person displays such characteristics, then the same kind of attributions should occur when a corporate "persona" appears to possess these characteristics. Thus, to the extent that public relations is involved in presenting the organizational character in this way, charismatic legitimation represents a valuable Weberian concept on the basis of which to understand this phenomenon.

Vision

As previously noted, a public relations strategy will often be based on a vision. The vision would not only be used internally as a means of improving efficiency in goal attainment. It seems to be taken for granted today that it is important to communicate the vision to external stakeholder groups and the general public. Thus, the vision has a symbolic external effect that goes beyond the instrumental internal effects related to goal attainment, namely that the organization is perceived as *visionary*. Since most organizations today present their visions on their Internet homepages, as well as in documents that are visible to stakeholders and the public, including annual reports and letters to shareholders, being visionary seems to be one of the most attractive corporate characteristics with which an organization currently can be associated. Organizations that are thought of as visionary stand out as model examples for other organizations (Collins & Porras, 1994).

Articulation

Similarly, it could be argued that the practice of public relations contributes to promoting organizations as *articulate*. Visions and mission statements, press releases and newsletters, as well as various messages about the organization are formulated with style and elegance, and are tailored for different stakeholder groups. External public relations consultants are hired to assist in making the statements as eloquent as possible, in the private as well as in the public sector (Wæraas, 2004). In addition, public relations executives and consultants often train top managers or other organizational spokespersons prior to media interviews, with the purpose of representing the organization in the most articulate way. Some public relations firms specialize in this service. The importance of being viewed as an articulate and expressive organization is further confirmed by the concept of storytelling used currently by many organizations, and offered by many public relations firms. Corporate stories contribute to creating an aura of magic around the organization, thus reinforcing—in the Weberian sense—the organization's myth about itself.

Sensitivity

In several ways organizations signal sensitivity *to the environment* and to *stakeholder needs*. A basic task in public relations is to monitor public opinion so that the organization can adapt its behavior and communication more effectively to changes in preferences. Just as a charismatic leader wins support from his or her followers by furthering their well-being, organizations may display the same kind of sensitivity to win a similar type of support. In this context a public relations strategy may consist of making the organization's sensitivity known to the public. For example, while corporate social responsibility (CSR) initiatives are primarily about sensitivity to the environment, not all organizations that are CSR-actors trust actions to be enough, in other words, to communicate sufficient sensitivity. In addition, they want CSR initiatives to be communicated verbally, a task which is often handled by public relations personnel. Furthermore, service mindedness and the organization's willingness to comply with customer needs and demands are often conveyed through slogans, visions, missions, and corporate values.

Unconventional

Finally, today the field of public relations plays an important role in presenting an organization as *unconventional*. Because the rapid spread of technology has resulted in products that are more and more similar, and thus caused greater problems for customers of making purchase decisions, the ability to create differentiation on the organizational level has become a necessity (Ind, 1997; Olins, 2000). It seems to be increasingly important to do things that others do not, and to do them in ways that are perceived as unique. In this respect, promoting the organization as unconventional is one way of standing out. Studies have shown that organizations with the strongest reputations are perceived to be unique (Fombrun & van Riel, 2004). Therefore, building on the most unique and unconventional characteristics of the organization is assumed to be essential when developing a communication strategy (van Riel, 1995).

The perceived characteristics are interrelated and form a constellation of components (Conger & Kanungo, 1987). A charismatic organization is one that is believed to be visionary, articulate, sensitive to the environments and to stakeholder needs, and unconventional. Theoretically speaking, charismatic legitimation consists of cultivating the belief that the organization possesses *all* these characteristics. This may happen through verbal and visual communication as well as through CSR-actions serving the well-being of the public. Even if the devotions to charismatic organizations such as Apple Computer or Harley Davidson also are the result of influences other than public relations efforts, there should be no doubt that public relations play an essential part in *producing* and *reinforcing* them. If establishing and maintaining legitimacy is at the core of public relations, and organizational legitimacy today depends on presenting charismatic characteristics, then charismatic legitimation becomes an important part of public relations. By promoting emotional and affectionate devotions, public relations may play an essential part in revitalizing organizations, making sure attractive humanlike characteristics are promoted in order to acquire legitimacy which in Weber's terms is based on affectionate devotion.

Relevance for Practitioners

Although Weber's notions primarily have theoretical interest, some practical implications can be retained. His way of conceptualizing legitimacy and legitimation confirms that the basis for legitimacy is found in the beliefs of the public and that successful legitimation comes from the strategic influencing of those beliefs. The role of public relations personnel is to develop and communicate a successful strategy (or "myth") that ensures the organization's support. On the other hand, Weber also highlighted the notion that organizational success and survival depend on enduring voluntary support from the environments and that public relations is not only about short-term but also long-term existence. "Cultivating beliefs" in this respect requires organizational actions and communication that respect the limits of what the constituents find acceptable. As such, domination by virtue of authority or voluntary support, as Weber pointed out, depends not on "spin" but on legitimation efforts whose content is in accordance with the actual nature of the organization. In other words, creating myths and cultivating beliefs should not be seen as the manipulation of public opinion in the negative sense described by Ewen (1996). Rather, it is a way of justifying an organization's existence through a principle of legitimation. Unethical public relations (spin), or legitimation efforts that fail to adhere to such principles, will not lead to legitimacy.

Furthermore, Weber's emphasis on organizational justification serves as a reminder that public relations practitioners have a responsibility for communicating the reason for an organization's existence and for protecting its legitimacy. His principles of legitimation demonstrate that justifications can be given on different grounds. The implication of charismatic legitimation for public relations is to emphasize the organization's attractive qualities and to develop emotional attachments. Projecting an image of the organization as visionary, articulate, sensitive to the environment, and to stakeholder needs, and unconventional, helps produce emotional attachments. By doing so, the practice of public relations may challenge the rational order and contribute to the emerging emotional order.

Conclusion

This chapter has argued that Weber's concepts of legitimacy and legitimation have relevance for understanding public relations theory and practice. Weber's theory that any successful system of domination needs legitimacy is in accordance with the underlying public relations logic of creating external support. Engaging in public relations activities whose purpose is to acquire such support is, in Weber's terminology, a way of justifying the system's existence by cultivating the belief in its legitimacy. Thus, the purpose of public relations is to acquire and maintain organizational legitimacy. Activities that contribute to achieving this purpose are seen as legitimation efforts.

The chapter has also argued that Weber's concept of charismatic legitimation expands our understanding of public relations practice. Contrary to Weber's predictions, but in accordance with his hopes, acquiring and preserving legitimacy depends on emotional support. As a result, organizations do not want to be perceived as rational machine bureaucracies. Displaying attractive and charismatic characteristics through public relations is seen as central for legitimacy.

Future public relations research may benefit from a clearer focus on legitimacy as the ultimate purpose of public relations and on legitimation as the means of achieving this purpose. Studying the theoretical basis for organizational existence as well as the formation of beliefs based on emotional attachments may enrich both practical and theoretical knowledge of public relations. In addition, attention should be given to the long-term effects of charismatic legitimation and their implications for public relations. Weber viewed the concept of charismatic domination positively, but warned that it could be more fragile and have a shorter life cycle than other forms of domination. In line with this argument, future research should seek to determine whether charismatic legitimation is more appropriate in some situations than in others, for example, if it is more relevant when confronted with legitimacy threats, that is, when preserving legitimacy, or if it is more relevant when trying to acquire legitimacy.

Note

1. A previous version of this chapter was published as: The re-enchantment of social institutions: Max Weber and public relations, in *Public Relations Review, 33*(3), 2007.

References

Aaker, D. A. (2004). Leveraging the corporate brand. *California Management Review, 46*(3), 6–19.

Ashforth, B. E., & Gibbs, B. W. (1990). The double-edge of organizational legitimation. *Organization Science: A Journal of the Institute of Management Sciences, 1*(2), 177–194.

Benoit, W. L. (1995). *Accounts, excuses, and apologies: A theory of image restoration strategies.* Albany, NY: SUNY Press.

Bensman, J., & Givant, M. (1975). Charisma and modernity: The use and abuse of a concept. *Social Research, 42*(4), 570–614.

Christen, C. (2005). The restructuring and reengineering of AT&T: Analysis of a public relations crisis using organizational theory. *Public Relations Review, 31*(2), 239–251.

Collins, J. C., & Porras, J. I. (1994). *Built to last. Successful habits of visionary companies.* New York: HarperBusiness.

Conger, J. A., & Kanungo, R. N. (1987). Toward a behavioral theory of charismatic leadership in organizational settings. *Academy of Management Review, 12*(4), 637–647.

Conger, J. A., & Kanungo, R. N. (1994). Charismatic leadership in organizations. Perceived behavioral attributes and their measurement. *Journal of Organizational Behavior, 15*(5), 439–452.

Conger, J. A., & Kanungo, R. N. (1998). *Charismatic leadership in organizations.* Thousand Oaks, CA: Sage.

Coombs, T. (1992). The failure of the task force on food assistance: A case study of the role of legitimacy in issue management. *Journal of Public Relations Research, 4*(2), 101–122.

Coombs, T. (1999). *Ongoing crisis communication: Planning, managing, and responding.* Thousand Oaks, CA: Sage.

Coser, L. A. (1977). *Masters of sociological thought: Ideas in historical and social context* (2nd ed.). New York: Harcourt Brace Jovanovich.

Cutlip, S. M., Broom, G. M., & Center, A. H. (1999). *Effective public relations* (8th ed.). Upper Saddle River, NJ: Prentice-Hall.

Davies, G., Chun, R., Roper, S., & Silva, R. M. V. D. (2003). *Corporate reputation and competitiveness.* London: Routledge.

Ewen, S. (1996). *PR! A social history of spin.* New York: Basic Books.

Fombrun, C., & van Riel, C., B. M. (2004). *Fame and fortune: How successful companies build winning reputations.* Upper Saddle River, NJ: Prentice-Hall.

Grafstein, R. (1981). The failure of Weber's conception of legitimacy: Its causes and implications. *Journal of Politics, 43*(2), 456–472.

Green, R. W. (Ed.). (1959). *Protestantism and capitalism: The Weber thesis and its critics.* Boston: Heath.

Griswold Jr., G. (1967, Fall). How AT&T public relations policies developed. *Public Relations Quarterly, 12,* 7–16.

Habermas, J. (1976). *Legitimation crisis.* London: Heinemann.

Hall, R. H. (1991). *Organizations: Structures, processes, and outcomes* (5th ed.). Englewood Cliffs, NJ: Prentice-Hall.

Hill, D. (2003). *Body of truth: Leveraging what consumers can't or won't say.* Hoboken, NJ: Wiley.

Holmström, S. (2005). Reframing public relations: The evolution of a reflective paradigm for organizational legitimization. *Public Relations Review, 31*(4), 498–504.

Howard-Grenville, J., Nash, J., & Coglianese, C. (2008). Constructing the license to operate: Internal factors and their influence on corporate environmental decisions. *Law & Policy, 30*(1), 73–107.

Ind, N. (1997). *The corporate brand.* Basingstoke, UK: Macmillan.

Jensen, I. (1997). Legitimacy and strategy of different companies: A perspective of external and internal public relations. In D. Moss, D. Verčič, & T. MacManus (Eds.), *Public relations research: An international perspective* (pp. 225–246). London: International Thomson Business Press.

Jensen, R. (1999). *The dream society: How the coming shift from information to imagination will transform your business.* New York: McGraw-Hill.

Keller, K. L. (2000). Building and managing corporate brand equity. In M. J. Hatch, M. Schultz, & M. H. Larsen (Eds.), *The expressive organization: Linking identity, reputation and the corporate brand* (pp. 115–137). Oxford, UK: Oxford University Press.

Metzler, M. S. (2001a). Responding to the legitimacy problems of Big Tobacco: An analysis of the "People of Philip Morris" image advertising campaign. *Communication Quarterly, 49*(4), 366–382.

Metzler, M. S. (2001b). The centrality of organizational legitimacy to public relations practice. In R. L. Heath & G. Vasquez (Eds.), *Handbook of public relations* (pp. 321–333). Thousand Oaks, CA: Sage.

Meyer, J. W., & Rowan, B. (1977). Institutionalized organizations: Formal structure as myth and ceremony. *American Journal of Sociology, 26*(1), 340–363.

Nielsen, J. Munk (1998). *Legitimitetsbegrebets muligheter: En teoretisk rekonstruksjon med relevans for public relations* [The possibilities of the concept of legitimacy: A theoretical reconstruction with relevance for the field of public relations]. Unpublished master's thesis, Roskilde University Center, Roskilde, Denmark.

Olins, W. (2000). How brands are taking over the corporation. In M. Schultz, M. J. Hatch, & M. H. Larsen (Eds.), *The expressive organization: Linking identity, reputation and the corporate brand* (pp. 51–65). Oxford, UK: Oxford University Press.

Pine, B. J., & Gilmore, J. H. (1999). *The experience economy: Work is theatre & every business a stage*. Boston: Harvard Business School Press.

Schultz, M., Hatch, M. J., & Larsen, M. H. (Eds.). (2000). *The expressive organization: Linking identity, reputation, and the corporate brand*. Oxford, UK: Oxford University Press.

Scott, W. R. (1998). *Organizations: Rational, natural, and open systems* (4th ed.). Upper Saddle River, NJ: Prentice-Hall.

Sevón, G. (1996). Organizational imitation in identity transformation. In B. Czarniawska & G. Sevón (Eds.), *Translating organizational change* (pp. 49–67). New York: Walter de Gruyter.

Suchman, M. C. (1995). Managing legitimacy: Strategic and institutional approaches. *The Academy of Management Review, 20*(3), 571–610.

Tawney, R. H. (1926). *Religion and the rise of capitalism: A historical study*. New York: Penguin.

van Riel, C., B. M. (1995). *Principles of corporate communication*. London: Prentice-Hall.

Wæraas, A. (2004). *Den karismatiske offentlige organisasjon: Konstruksjonen av organisasjonslegitimitet ved hjelp av private kommunikasjonsrådgivere* [The charismatic public organization: Constructing organizational legitimacy through communication consultants]. Unpublished doctoral dissertation, University of Tromsø, Tromsø, Norway.

Wartick, S. L., & Cochran, P. L. (1985). The evolution of the corporate social performance model. *Academy of Management Review, 10*(4), 758–769.

Weber, M. (1948). *From Max Weber: Essays in sociology*. London: Routledge & Kegan Paul.

Weber, M. (1968). *Economy and society*. New York: Bedminster. (Original work published 1922)

Weber, M. (1991). *The Protestant ethic and the spirit of capitalism*. London: Harper-Collins. (Original work published 1904)

Yoon, Y. (2005). Legitimacy, public relations, and media access: Proposing and testing a media access model. *Communication Research, 32*(6), 762–793.

Zinkin, J. (2004). Maximising the "License to Operate": CSR from an Asian perspective. *Journal of Corporate Citizenship, 14*(Summer), 67–80.

Life and Work of Max Weber

Maximillian Weber (1864–1920) was born in Erfurt, in Thuringia, Germany. Weber enrolled at the University of Heidelberg in 1882 as a law student and received his doctorate in 1889. His dissertation was on legal history, *Zur Geschichte der Handelsgesellschaft im Mittelalter* (*The History of Medieval Business Organizations*). He then worked as a lecturer at the University of Berlin where he pursued studies in history. In 1894 he was appointed professor of economics at the University of Freiburg and three years later moved to Heidelberg where he occupied the same position. After his father's death in 1897, he suffered from a nervous breakdown that made it impossible for him to work. Weber resigned as a professor in 1903, and became an associate editor of the *Archives for Social Science and Social Welfare*, and wrote one of his major works while working there, *Die Protestantische Ethik und der Geist des Kapitalismus* (1904) (*The Protestant Ethic and the Spirit of Capitalism,*1930). In 1918 Weber decided to return to teaching and headed the first department of sociology in Germany, at the University of Munich. Two years later he died of pneumonia.

Many of Weber's most important works were collected and published posthumously by his students and other sociologists. English translations include *From Max Weber: Essays in Sociology* (1948), *The Methodology of the Social Sciences* (1949), *The Sociology of Religion* (1964), *Economy and Society: An Outline of Interpretive Sociology* ([1922] 1968), *The Agrarian Sociology of Ancient Civilizations* (1976). Major works interpreting Weber include Randall Collins' *Weberian Sociological Theory* (1986) and Stephen Kalberg's *Max Weber's Comparative-Historical Sociology* (1994). The *Max Weber Studies* is a journal dedicated to the application and interpretation of Weber's ideas.

Chapter 16

Conclusions on the Domain, Context, Concepts, Issues, and Empirical Avenues of Public Relations

Øyvind Ihlen and Piet Verhoeven

Abstract

At least five conclusions can be drawn from the collective output of the essays in this book: public relations can be studied as a social activity in its own right; it must be understood in relation to its societal context; the crucial concepts of public relations are trust, legitimacy, understanding, and reflection; issues of power, behavior, and language are at the forefront of public relations study; and social theory is necessary to understand the practice of public relations and to raise important empirical questions about it. This chapter elaborates on these points, while at the same time acknowledging the richness and diversity of the theories discussed by the contributors, which do not lend themselves easily to the tasks of summarizing and drawing parallels.

What should readers take away from the collective output of the essays in this book? It would be quite foolhardy to lump together the wide array of theoretical directions that have been presented here, and we are rather in awe of the sheer intellectual breadth that has been displayed by the theorists presented. A further caveat is that the task of summarizing and drawing parallels can hardly do justice to the sophisticated philosophical systems that underpin the different approaches. We also do not expect all of the contributors to agree with our views in this respect. Nonetheless, we would like to suggest that five major conclusions may be drawn for public relations from the work of the social theorists presented here. These conclusions relate to (1) what the *domain* of public relations as an academic field should be; (2) the importance of seeing public relations in its societal *context*; (3) what the central *concepts* for public relations are; (4) what important social *issues* are brought to the fore by applying social theory to public relations activity; and (5) the possibilities the presented approaches present for raising *empirical questions* about public relations. In the following, we elaborate on these five themes.

Domain: Warts and All

The public relations literature often describes public relations as having evolved to today's ethical practice of communication management from more or less unethical publicity activities (Duffy, 2000; Moloney, 2000). The picture painted of the history of public relations is often one of five consecutive phases which are based on the way the public was treated in each time frame: the public is damned or ignored (1865–1900); the public is informed or served (1900–1918); the public is educated or respected (1918–1945); the public is known (1945–1968); and the public is involved (1968–today) (van der Meiden & Fauconnier, 1994). Some of the literature seems to conflate the normative ideals of public relations with its observed day-to-day practice. However, if the existence of front groups is any measure, unethical public relations practices seem to thrive. Public relations practitioners, including such pioneers as Edward L. Bernays and Ivy Lee (Cutlip, 1994; Ewen, 1996; Tye, 1998/2002), also have a legacy of working for rather dubious clients. More recently, public relations agencies have taken assignments from such clients as the former Romanian dictator Nicolae Ceausescu, Haiti's Jean-Claude "Baby Doc" Duvalier, the Nigerian military regime during the 1990s, and the Chinese regime after the Tiananmen Square massacre (Stauber & Rampton, 1995). When the Chinese government cracked down on Tibetan protests before the 2008 Olympics, they also went shopping for public relations services in an effort to control the damage to their reputation (Pickard & McGregor, 2008). Public relations agencies in Western countries are also confronted with or reminded of ethical dilemmas; for example, Hill & Knowlton's well-known cases in the United States in the 1990s: the pro-life account for Catholic bishops and the account for the lobby group Citizens for a Free Kuwait in the run-up to the 1991 Gulf War (Pratt, 1994). There seem to be plenty of such examples to go around, as is documented on these websites: http://www.prwatch.org, http://www.corporateeurope.org/, and others.

Indeed, the history of the profession can be portrayed as the business answer to the muckraking journalism of the first decades of the 20th century, and during the 1970s, to the upsurge of public interest groups. Corporations have sought to defend their interests by promoting certain issues and by courting public opinion through, for instance, nonproduct advertisements. The aim of these activities is often described as counteracting "media bias" or "misleading information" or overcoming public hostility to corporate activities "because of ignorance or misinformation." Public relations has frequently jumped to the rescue of capitalism and free-enterprise democracy, and during the 1970s this work took on a more systematic and proactive character (Cheney, 1991; Crable & Vibbert, 1995; Ewen, 1996; Heath, 1980; Marchand, 1998). In a sense, the starting point for the practice of public relations has been the advocacy of *particular* interests rather than the public interest. No matter how the latter concept is defined, public relations has for the most part been looking out for the interests of powerful major corporations.

This legacy and the unethical practices that have been observed have led some observers to portray *all* public relations activities as sinister activities that work against the public interest (i.e., Beder, 1998; Stauber & Rampton, 1995). The flipside of the coin is that public relations can also be put to work for public causes and issues such as justice, the environment, and health. In terms of media relations, two conflicting tendencies can be noted: powerful sources have been able to consolidate their access, but alternative sources have also been able to gain access (Davis, 2000). The clever use of public relations has also yielded political results for groups not normally associated with public relations (see chapter 4 on Bourdieu). The almost classic example of this development is the 1995 battle between Shell and Greenpeace over the Brent Spar oil drilling platform. Greenpeace succeeded in gaining the support of international public opinion to force Shell (and the British government) to hold off on plans for the deep sea disposal of the Brent Spar (e.g., Anderson, 1997; Jensen, 2003; Zyglidopoulos, 2002).

In this sense, the all-out and sometimes unthinking criticism of public relations is similar to the attacks on rhetoric in ancient times. Those condemning rhetoric tended to forget that their criticism was in itself a form of rhetoric, just as those condemning public relations often use public relations techniques to gain publicity for their views. One question for the critics might be: Can an organization *not* use public relations? Can it *not* communicate with its publics? The obvious answer that arises from the social theories dealt with in this book is "no": just as individuals cannot *not* communicate (Watzlawick, 1976), organizations and social systems cannot *not* communicate because one of their basic elements is subjectless communication (see Holmström, chapter 10, this volume).

Luckily, not all of the literature paints either an idyllic or a demonizing picture. Much of it instead takes a sobering look at what public relations means in society (e.g., Coombs & Holladay, 2007). This edited volume is meant to be a further contribution in this direction. Our hope is that the book will give readers the ideas, tools, and perspectives necessary to study and understand public relations just like any other social activity; that is, as a social activity that is neither inherently good nor bad, but as one that lies at the heart of society and therefore constitutes one of the foundations of social communication (Avenarius, 2000). To paraphrase Rakow and Nastasia (chapter 13, this volume), the prime object of inquiry should be the *consequences* of public relations practice, not its efficacy. In an age of negotiation, when fundamental consensus is absent, communication has become fundamental (Deetz, 1997). Deliberation and research from different social theory perspectives will lead to a better understanding of public relations practices and the consequences those practices have for society.

Context: Description of Society

Social theory in general is supposed to help us make sense of our lives by questioning the value and meaning of what we see around us. Most of the theorists in this book present diagnoses of contemporary society and use different labels to describe social change. The earliest analysis presented is that of Weber, who predicted that society would be dominated by a rational order that would come into being through modernization processes. As Wæraas writes in chapter 15, a shift has taken place that has led "humans to be dominated by goal-oriented rationality instead of acting on the basis of traditions, values, or emotions" (p. 302). Myth and faith are replaced by rationality; that is, individuals, organizations, and societies make decisions based on rational grounds. This rational decision-making process is at the heart of the narrative of modernity and has taken a central position, which is guarded by legal systems, in almost all spheres of modern societies. Wæraas, and many others, however, argue that Weber's "iron cage of rationality" today thrives alongside an emotional and value-oriented order. This duality is part of what Lyotard (1979) called the postmodern condition, which is characterized by pluralism (e.g., Berger, Foucault), polycontextuality (Luhmann), and situated knowledge (e.g., Foucault, Smith, Spivak). Many theorists agree that conflict and dissensus are the central features of contemporary societies and that they are accompanied by all kinds of activism (Spivak). On the one hand, this postmodern situation is welcomed by some as a way of overcoming hegemony and dominance both locally and globally. Others, on the other hand, point to the different crises that have arisen in the past few decades. Several of these are encountered in this book: the crisis of knowledge and experts (Foucault, Smith, Spivak, Beck), the crisis of meaning (Berger), and the crisis of social cohesion (Putnam). The central issue that summarizes these crises is whether today's atomized individual who is bowling alone is able to make sense of his or her surroundings based on situated knowledge.

The theorists who point to these different crises do not usually label contemporary society as postmodern, but rather as a new phase of modern society. They use such phrases as "late modernity" (Giddens), "reflexive modernity" (Beck), and "postsecular" society (Habermas). The different methods that are proposed to handle the crises in society range from accepting dissensus and conflict as the norm and studying them reflectively from a systemic point of view (Luhmann) to accommodating and solving conflicts through communicative action (Habermas) or through the "third way" of social instruments (Giddens) such as public relations. Still others state that we have never been modern at all (Latour) and that we should study the way in which our current nonmodern condition is being constructed from scratch by all kinds of different actors and actants (see chapter 9 on Latour).

The (social) constructivist perspective seems to dominate the way in which social theorists have described the process by which late modern society has come into being. For example, in the work of Berger, modern society is seen as a subjective construct shaped by individuals' conceptions and their interaction with social structures. Language is central in his social constructivist theory. Bourdieu focused on how the social world is structured, constituted, and reproduced through individual and collective struggle, particularly in relation to how reality can be legitimately defined (Bourdieu, 1990). Relations are the dominant factor here, and, with the three concepts of habitus, field, and capital, he constructed a type of sociology that he argued made the opposition between subjectivism and objectivism obsolete. At the core of human existence, however, conflicts and the relational production of difference remain. In Foucault's critical analysis of social institutions, power, knowledge, and discourse (understood as language and institutions together) are intimately intertwined. He considered that certain discourse coalitions produced modern knowledge and that these discourses express power at the individual and societal levels. This is made manifest in, for example, what Smith called the macrostructure of gender and patriarchy and in Beck's concept of a risk society in which the production of knowledge about risks and the distribution of these risks are central.

Within this constructivist perspective, communication has acquired a central position at all levels of analysis (micro, meso, and macro). Communication is seen as central to the lives of individuals, groups, organizations, social systems, and societies. Using a dramaturgical perspective, Goffman looked to face-to-face interaction and interpersonal relationships and the way in which these reflect and add meaning and structure to social life. Through such concepts as impression management, framing, and front- and backstage behavior, Goffman showed how we act differently in different settings, thus demonstrating that society is neither static nor homogeneous. From this perspective, face-to-face interaction and interpersonal communication are the basis of social communication. Interpersonal communication also lies at the heart of the public sphere, as Habermas conceived of it in his history of the development and transformation of that sphere in Britain, France, and Germany. Citizens engaging in critical and rational discussions about political matters, either face-to-face or through communication media, constitute the public sphere. This public sphere functioned at first as a mediator between society and the state and facilitated ideals of equality, justice, and human rights. In the course of time, however, it developed in the direction of serving the special private interests of political and commercial actors (Burkart, chapter 8). Mayhew, largely building on the work of Habermas and, to a lesser degree, Talcott Parsons, explicitly researched the way in which professional communicators influence society or the public sphere, which he saw as threatened by this group of public relations practitioners, advertisers, and political communicators. These professionals now dominate public communication and have replaced an open public sphere with a "new public" that is subject to mass persuasion by all kinds of private actors (Stanton, chapter 11).

Mediated and nonmediated communication has become, implicitly or explicitly, a central characteristic of social theory about contemporary society. Communicative issues in the democratic context are crucial in all of the theories presented: from dialogue and communicative action to the formation of discourse coalitions and narratives and communication processes without people on the level of social systems.

Reading between the lines in many of the chapters provides leads for the further development of a critical perspective on society and the role of public relations and professional communicators in society. For example, from her Marxist-feminist-deconstructivist perspective, Spivak sees society as basically unjust: there are fundamental inequities bred by international divisions of labor and fed by the neoliberal projects of transnational capitalism (Dutta, chapter 14). These inequities not only play a role on a global scale, but also on national scales and in the communication between organizations and their publics. Hamelink (2006) raised a similar issue by pointing out the striking consistency between the results of a dialogue process and the position of the most powerful party in that dialogue. Questions about inequity and power connect to broader questions about society and the role of communication today.

For public relations scholars, these broader questions about society and public relations can be clustered around four main social science themes, which are the same themes that Golding (2006) proposed for mass communications scholars: questions of power and the distribution of power in society; questions of equality and inequality in relation to communication; questions of identity-building through communication; and questions about social change and the role of communication in it. These four themes can also be derived from the social theories presented in this book. The different understandings of society, social order, and social change described above create the context for public relations and for research into it. These analyses have consequences for what can be seen as the crucial concepts of public relations and for what kind of social issues can be highlighted as important for public relations studies on different levels of analysis.

Concepts: Trust, Legitimacy, Understanding, Reflection

Trust and *legitimacy* are key words in several of the chapters, as society has changed in a way that often causes people to question authority. Organizations now have to legitimize their decisions on a continuous basis. Such issues have indeed been the focal point of public relations for a long time, as illustrated by a statement Arthur Page made in 1939: "All business in a democratic country begins with public permission and exists by public approval" (cited in Griswold Jr., 1967, p. 13; see also Wæraas, chapter 15). Even earlier public relations pioneers such as Ivy Lee would probably argue along similar lines: you have to take into consideration what the public thinks of you if you are to secure your continued existence (i.e., Hiebert, 1966). Various public relations scholars have touched upon the concept explicitly or implicitly since the scholarly field was established. The so-called excellence or symmetrical theory, for instance, sees public relations as a legitimate practice when it is built on the principles of symmetry and dialogue. Organizations and publics should adjust to others, rather than trying to control how others think and behave (Grunig, 2006). The rhetorical approach to public relations advocated by Heath (2000, 2001) sees organizations as gaining legitimacy by putting their ideas to the test in a public marketplace in which those ideas that are narrowly self-interested will not withstand public scrutiny.

In this book, we have gone to the roots of the concept of legitimacy, that is, to the original thinkers, to see what they have to say about it and whether we can adapt some of their thinking to public relations. Critics have faulted public relations theory for not having a developed ontology (e.g., Cheney & Christensen, 2001), a fault we believe can be rectified using social theory. Although the use of the theoretical lenses presented in the previous chapters does not necessarily represent a paradigm shift, we would emphasize that the book offers valuable new theoretical insights that are grounded in social theory. Some of these theoretical points can be found in other publications by the contributors to this book, but we would also argue that their treatment in this collection enhances their overall theoretical value. Furthermore, we urge readers to look closely at the nuances on offer that make it difficult to conflate or subsume many of the theoretical points with current theories of public relations.

We are offered several definitions of legitimacy in this book, spanning from the classic Weberian take of "the justified right to exist" to Luhmann's "generalized preparedness to accept decisions within certain boundaries of tolerance; decisions which are still undecided as regards contents" (Luhmann, 1969/1993, p. 28). Legitimacy in the work of Weber, however, is not the same concept as it is in, say, Habermas' work. Whereas the latter would tie legitimacy to truth, Weber focused on the *beliefs* of the audience. As Aristotle argued about the ethos of a rhetor in *On Rhetoric* (1991), it is sufficient that the audience *believes* the rhetor possesses certain qualities such as loyalty and honesty. This, of course, is not to condone the absence of sincerity or truth, but rather it is a sobering analytical perspective on what works. Wæraas argues that organizations are bound by what the environment finds acceptable. To paraphracs Holmström: To an organization, legitimacy defines the boundaries for decisions, which are perceived as socially acceptable within a given time, context and perspective (chapter 10).

Wæraas uses Weber to write about how practitioners can build charismatic legitimacy for their organizations by emphasizing specific, admired qualities, such as being a visionary or being sensitive to stakeholder needs. Wæraas calls for further studies of the construction of charismatic legitimation and its long-term effects and implications for public relations. Is charismatic legitimation more appropriate in some situations than others?

Burkart uses the work of Habermas to suggest a model that can be applied by practitioners to help further the understanding between organizations and their publics. This in turn might be a basis for legitimacy. He calls for more studies of how trustworthiness in particular is created and for explorations of the way in which the different validity claims put forward by organizations are interrelated.

Burkart also focuses on the creation of understanding and places the public relations practitioner in the midst of the process. Falkheimer too gives public relations a central role. Using Giddens, he argues that public relations is one of the main strategies that organizations implement when they try to handle development in a fast-changing society. Public relations is a reflexive social expert system.

Holmström presents a somewhat similar view, but distinguishes between a reflexive system (a rather self-obsessed, nonproblematizing perspective) and *reflection*. Using Luhmann, she writes about how public relations is a functional system that has turned into a reflective practice that helps organizations to become more sensitive and to realize that their perspective is just one of many. This reflective turn is necessitated by the increased need for organizations to legitimate their existence and their conduct. Holmström poses reflection as the core demand on organizational legitimacy, and she sees it as a consequence of organizations acting out of enlightened self-interest. The crucial tasks of public relations are to increase reflection (the sensor function), integrate reflection (the leadership function), and communicate reflection (the communicative function) (Holmström, 2004a, 2004b, 2005). Nonetheless, some commentators have challenged the duality of reflexiveness and reflection, arguing that it leaves out the gray areas in between (Bentele & Wehmeier, 2007).

Despite the insistence on trust as a focus for public relations, research on the public's level of trust in the public relations industry tends to show rather abysmal results (i.e., Larsson, 2007). This negative public sentiment toward public relations, coupled with a descriptive perspective of its everyday practice, has led some commentators to argue *against* the close relationship between trust and public relations. Instead, public relations "should be redefined as the communicative expression of competing organizations and groups in pluralist states" (Moloney, 2005, p. 554).

A similar view is put forward by Ihlen in his adaptation of the work of Bourdieu, who sees struggle as being at the center of society. Ihlen argues that public relations should thus be seen as a practice that assists organizational actors in pursuing their interests. To be trusted and to be seen as a legitimate enterprise, that is, to have symbolic capital, can have a double function in this sense because it can be both a means and an end. Similarly, the development of social capital can also be seen as a means and an end for public relations. For the most part, however, the main goal of organizations is to position themselves in what Bourdieu calls "fields."

Precisely this development of social capital is the focus of Luoma-aho's chapter on Putnam. She sees public relations as having a positive role to play as a vehicle to create social capital. Indeed, she would like to redefine public relations as "the practice of creating organizational social capital" (p. 240). She operationalizes Putnam's social capital concept by using the concepts of reputation (centered on past history) and trust (focused on the future).

To sum up, many of the contributors to this volume see the purpose of public relations as the building of trust and legitimacy, either as an end in itself or as a means for organizational goals such as survival or expansion. It may be worth noting, however, that the ontological perspectives of the theories presented imply that communication, legitimacy, and trust are not necessarily something that can be *managed*. Many scholars would like to see public relations become a management discipline, and various definitions exist that describe public relations as the management of communication or the management of relationships. Other scholars point out the futility of this ideal. Wehmeier, for instance, points out that legitimacy is conferred upon an organization by different publics, and hence it cannot be managed (Wehmeier, 2006). Taking contemporary social theory on board means that the picture becomes more complicated, sometimes frustratingly so, but it still provides a more realistic grip. Public relations has to do with the negotiation of knowledge, meaning, and behavior, and, in this sense, it also involves issues of power, as discussed in the following section.

Issues: Power, Behavior, and Language

In one way or another, several of the chapters in this book deal with the issues of power and language. Public relations has to do with the negotiation of meaning, but also with the negotiation of behavior (J. E. Grunig, personal communication, December 19, 2007). Public relations obviously aims to influence how an organization acts, not only how these acts are interpreted. It is, however, very difficult to separate these domains: "Symbolic and behavioral relationships are 'intertwined like the strands of a rope'" (Grunig, 1993, p. 121). How can one's act not be interpreted in one way or another? How can the public be given a voice in management decisions without meaning being created? How can a dialogue be created with publics without communicating why this is beneficial for the publics and the organization? A call for studies of how meaning is created in such instances is not a call for public relations to abandon studies of other types of organizational acts or indeed the aspiration to influence such acts. The so-called behavioral approach and the interpretive approach are not mutually exclusive, although they are sometimes treated as if they were. Indeed, several of the theories presented in this book explicitly or implicitly talk about speech acts.

Referring to Goffman, Johansson writes about face-to-face interaction and the impressions that public relations practitioners and individual managers consciously and unconsciously create and communicate in different organizational settings. How are these impressions managed at the front and back stage? What impressions are apprehended and perceived by different audiences or publics? Using a distinctly interpersonal approach, Johansson argues that, at the core, public relations is about relationships with individuals who, in turn, make up publics. She demonstrates the way in which the interpersonal relationships in a meeting are expressions of power that can be usefully analyzed via the concepts of framing, face, and footing.

One of the resounding insights originally presented by Berger and Luckmann (1966) posits that reality is a social construction. Truth is seen as inseparable from discourse, that is, it is inseparable from the way in which we use language and interact with one another. This view is seen as opposing that of realists who think that objective knowledge is obtainable. Looking at the field of environmental sociology, it has been argued that because most scholars acknowledge elements of the others' positions, *weak realism* and *weak constructionism* might better describe their positions (Nørbech, 1997).

Exceptions do exist, but such epistemological concerns seem to have gained scant attention in public relations. It is often implied, for example, that information about the environment is something that the public relations practitioner collects when he or she engages in boundary-spanning on behalf of an organization. The belief seems to be that there exists an objective world out there that remains to be discovered and that the more information the practitioner makes available, the clearer the picture of that world becomes. Human existence and the sense-making process are thus oversimplified (Pieczka, 1996, 2006).

As discussed by Heide in chapter 3, Berger asks that, to gain a better understanding of public relations as an institution, we look behind the façade and inquire into how public relations functions as the producer of certain dominating realities in society. These constructed realities also have a cognitive dimension, just as the public sphere has. Public relations, therefore, also plays an important role in the construction of knowledge and in the "tribunals of reason" (Latour, 1987) that take place before data become established knowledge or facts in society. Public relations *produces*, rather than reveals knowledge about the products and services organizations offer or the issues they deal with. One area in which this cognitive dimension of public relations' contribution to the construction of reality can easily be studied is that of risk and crisis communication. Risk and safety have, in Beck's risk society, become largely communicative constructions. Risks are decided upon, produced by industry, and calculated by industry. Some risks have become predictable and are statistically safe, whereas others are too big and too difficult to calculate. Risk has thus become a knowledge problem, and communication plays an important role in the establishment of that knowledge. Taking the subdiscipline of crisis communication as an example, Heide also shows us the importance of a social constructionist perspective. He questions the separation between risk and crisis communication and draws attention to the sense-making process of individuals. He faults the literature on crisis communication for assuming that a crisis is an "objective" phenomenon that hits an organization. In reality, crises are much more complex phenomena, and studying them from a social constructionist perspective provides better insight into their origin, progress, and decline.

Verhoeven suggests that the way public relations practitioners construct reality can be fruitfully studied with the help of Latour's actor-network-theory; for instance, by looking at the associations they form. Public relations plays a part in dealing with the uncertainties surrounding the nature of groups, actions, objects, facts, and the study or production of the text itself.

The way meaning is created and the type of meaning that is created have huge implications for issues of power. With the help of Foucault, Motion and Leitch help us to see that public relations is not solely found in the discourse domain of business, but also in the discourse domain of politics. Public relations is seen as "a discursive meaning creation process" (p. 94). It establishes or reinforces particular truths, hence its link to power. Why is something accepted as truth? As Berger (1999) points out, public relations can be seen as "a process intended to construct [an] ideological world view" (p. 200).

The work of Foucault alerts us to the importance of discourse, and Ihlen quotes Bourdieu in this sense: "linguistic relations [are] always relations of symbolic power" (Bourdieu & Wacquant, 1992, p. 142). Language similarly structures our perspectives on the world, and it is the medium by which these understandings are communicated. Language is a form of symbolic power; it is a weapon, but at the same time a battlefield.

Public relations research has often taken the position of the corporation, as witnessed by such a title as *Managing Activism: A Guide to Dealing With Activists and Pressure Groups* (Deegan, 2001). Ihlen argues that it is obvious that activist groups also use public relations, and he would like to see studies of this practice also become a "natural" part of public relations.

Rakow and Nastasia in chapter 13 point to a different type of exclusion from public relations, namely that based on gender, and they discuss this exclusion in relation to power. Using the work of Smith, they point out that public relations has mostly been "working from models in which people respond to the needs of the institutions" and that there is a need to develop theory that "contrast[s] women and men in positions of power to people outside of circles of power" (p. 267). Power is typically held by "the circle of men," and, as Smith has pointed out, "women have not participated [in] the construction of knowledge in the social sciences, and...women's ways of constructing knowledge about the social world [are] different from those described and canonized by sociologists" (p. 265). This is also a call for the study of power in individual relations, as well as in the macrostructure in which certain powerful institutions produce meanings and hierarchies.

Dutta points to yet another type of exclusion. Taking up the postcolonial theory put forward by Spivak, he argues that public relations often helps to strengthen the neoimperial agendas of globalization politics by recirculating "dominant configurations, and minimiz[ing] opportunities for resistance" (p. 297). Again, attention is directed toward representations and how, for instance, the third world is portrayed as a primitive space that needs to be opened up for such "ultimate goods" as the market economy and democracy. With the help of Spivak, Dutta also helps us to see that dialogue is not necessarily a neutral tool, but rather that it is something that may obscure politics and thus something that either props up the status quo or furthers dominant interests.

In the preceding sections and in our discussion of the domain, context, concepts, and issues of public relations, we have also established a basic framework for the empirical investigation of public relations. In the following section, we elaborate on this framework.

Empirical Avenues: A Research Program for Public Relations

The essays on social theory and public relations presented in this book give new theoretical perspectives on public relations. They also produce a wide range of analytical-level insights into public relations and individuals, organizations, and the broader society. These analyses show clearly that we need social theory to understand what is happening in the professional field of public relations and how it influences other areas of society. They also open up the possibility of formulating empirical questions and hypotheses within the framework of the social theories presented here. This empirical research can lead to further theory building about public relations.

Empirical research into public relations from these different theoretical perspectives will have a common footing that accounts for the "communicative," "linguistic," or "discursive" turn that has been dominant in social theory and the philosophy of science for some decades. This linguistic turn means that "one can evaluate the truth of a statement only when an idea is formulated in language" and that reality is "constructed culturally by being expressed discursively" (Leydesdorff, 2003, p. 310). For the study of public relations, this means a fundamental constructivist starting point, a starting point that is present in most of the theoretical perspectives in this book, ranging from Goffman's microperspective of framing to Luhmann's constructivist system theory. Conducting research from this joint starting point could lead to the development of an empirical research program within what Holmström (2004a) has called a reflective paradigm of public relations research. Such a research program would be complementary and feed into the reflective communication management view of public relations practice (van Ruler & Verčič, 2005). Public relations research based on social theory will be a useful counterpart to the research carried out within the managerial or behavioral paradigms that have dominated the field for the past few decades (Botan & Taylor, 2004; Ihlen & van Ruler, 2007). A social theoretical perspective will also broaden the horizon from the mesolevel of an organization's reputation and relations with its stakeholders to the micro- and macrolevels of analysis.

A reflective paradigm provides the opportunity to build public relations theory using social theoretical terms, as described in this book. Analytically speaking, public relations research that is informed by social theory is able to focus on agency on the one hand and structure on the other, or it can attempt to overcome this agency/structure problem by working from theoretical perspectives that have moved beyond this traditional dualism (see Falkheimer, chapter 6, for an explanation of the agency/structure problem). Research that focuses on the human agency side of public relations fits in with the work of such theorists as Goffman, Berger, Putnam, and Latour. Research that focuses on social structural dimensions can be carried out within the framework of the theories of Luhmann, Foucault, and Mayhew. Studies that attempt to combine agency and structure can be conducted from the perspectives of Habermas, Bourdieu, Giddens, and Beck. Observing public relations on different levels of analysis can lead to a better understanding of the effect of public relations actions (the microlevel) on structure (the macrolevel) and vice versa. After all, the construction of meaning on the microlevel can produce unintended consequences for the macrolevel of society. For example, an organization's claims about social responsibility on the microlevel (such as "we are a socially responsible company") may conflict with the health and environmental effects of its production methods on the macrolevel, and this may produce controversy on the societal level.

A reflective paradigm also moves communication theory to the center of public relations research on all levels of analysis. First, it is seen as an abstraction of the interaction that takes place between individual subjects, between groups, and between discourses or social systems. This provides an opportunity to conceptualize public relations as different forms of communication, ranging from symbolic interpersonal and social communication to the nonpersonal communication function in system theory (e.g., Fauconnier, 1986; Holmström, chapter 10). Second, such a paradigm is able to distinguish between mediated and nonmediated communication on the micro-, meso-, and macrolevels and to acknowledge the increasing importance of mediated communication for public relations in societies that are connected by a global media system. Third, it opens up the possibility of explicitly connecting public relations theory to mass communication theory, thereby acknowledging the roots of the discipline in mass media use in the 20th century and in the increasing mediatization of culture (Thompson, 1995). In this extended mediatization, media logic has become an important point of reference for individuals, organizations (Verhoeven, 2008), and the mass media themselves. Mass communication and mediated interpersonal communication are at the heart of late modernity or the postmodern condition.

In the empirical avenue of social theory and public relations, questions can be raised and hypotheses formulated about the four first conclusions presented in this chapter: the domain of public relations as an academic field, the societal context of public relations, the central concepts of public relations, and the social issues that surround public relations activities. The issues to be studied with the instrumentation of social theorists leads to a whole new range of situated knowledge about public relations.

Final Words

To summarize, we argue that (1) public relations has great influence in society and that it can be used for purposes that are at the same time good and bad, public and private. Although it is not inherently ethical or unethical, we believe it can and should be studied like any other social activity. In other words, the academic discipline of public relations should not be limited by an insistence on its applied nature. (2) The contributors to this book suggest that society is characterized by such traits as increased complexity and large-scale social change and that the practice of public relations must be understood in its societal context. (3) The latter point has implications for what are seen as the crucial concepts of public relations, and many of the contributions in this book single out trust, legitimacy, and reflection as the most important. (4) A societal perspective on the practice brings issues of power, behavior, and language to the center and invites investigation into the ways in which public relations creates meaning. (5) Using social theory in the practice of public relations invites a particular research program that opens up to macrolevel empirical questions. The assumed common starting points would be a constructivist perspective that involves theories of communication and an interest in agency and structure.

As stated in the introductory chapter: "The core questions for every public relations researcher are how does public relations work and what does it do in, to, and for organizations, publics, or the public arena, in other words, society as a whole." As we also pointed out, however, we are not looking to argue for one general theory of public relations. Instead, we are celebrating the diversity of methodologies in the widest sense. It is also worth repeating that although the contributors to this volume have mined the works of "their" social theorists thoroughly, there is more to be had from these theorists, as well as from others who are not included in the book. Social theory can indeed be said to provide a rich source of material for research endeavors into the consequences of public relations in society.

References

Anderson, A. (1997). *Media, culture and the environment*. London: University College London Press.

Aristotle. (1991). *On rhetoric: A theory of civic discourse* (G. A. Kennedy, Trans.). New York: Oxford University Press.

Avenarius, H. (2000). *Public relations*. Darmstadt, Germany: Darmstadt.

Beder, S. (1998). *Global spin: The corporate assault on environmentalism*. London: Chelsea Green.

Bentele, G., & Wehmeier, S. (2007). Applying sociology to public relations: A commentary. *Public Relations Review, 33*(3), 294–300.

Berger, B. K. (1999). The Halicon affair: Public relations and the construction of ideological world view. *Journal of Public Relations Research, 11*(3), 187–203.

Berger, P., & Luckmann, T. (1966). *The social construction of reality: A treatise in the sociology of knowledge.* London: Penguin Books.

Botan, C. H., & Taylor, M. (2004). Public relations: State of the field. *Journal of Communication, 54*(4), 645–661.

Bourdieu, P. (1990). *The logic of practice* (R. Nice, Trans.). Cambridge, UK: Polity Press.

Bourdieu, P., & Wacquant, L. J. D. (1992). *An invitation to reflexive sociology.* Cambridge, UK: Polity Press.

Cheney, G. (1991). *Rhetoric in an organizational society: Managing multiple identities.* Columbia, SC: University of South Carolina Press.

Cheney, G., & Christensen, L. T. (2001). Public relations as contested terrain: A critical response. In R. L. Heath (Ed.), *Handbook of public relations* (pp. 167–182). Thousand Oaks, CA: Sage.

Coombs, W. T., & Holladay, S. J. (2007). *It's not just PR: Public relations in society.* Malden, MA: Blackwell.

Crable, R. E., & Vibbert, S. L. (1995). Mobil's epideictic advocacy: "Observations" of Prometheus bound. In W. N. Elwood (Ed.), *Public relations inquiry as rhetorical criticism: Case studies of corporate discourse and social influence* (pp. 27–46). Westport, CT: Praeger.

Cutlip, S. M. (1994). *The unseen power: Public relations: A history.* Hillsdale, NJ: Erlbaum.

Davis, A. (2000). Public relations, news production and changing patterns of source access in the British national media. *Media, Culture & Society, 22*(1), 39–59.

Deegan, D. (2001). *Managing activism: A guide to dealing with activists and pressure groups.* London: Kogan Page.

Deetz, S. (1997). Communication in the age of negotiation. *Journal of Communication, 47*(4), 118–134.

Duffy, M. E. (2000). There's no two-way symmetrical about it: A postmodern examination of public relations textbooks. *Critical Studies in Mass Communication, 17*(3), 294–315.

Ewen, S. (1996). *PR! A social history of spin.* New York: Basic Books.

Fauconnier, G. (1986). *Algemene communicatietheorie* [General communication theory]. Leiden, the Netherlands: Martinus Nijhof.

Golding, P. (2006, June). *Mass communication theory: Do we need it?* Paper presented at the 56th annual ICA conference, Dresden, Germany.

Griswold Jr, G. (1967). How AT&T public relations policies developed. *Public Relations Quarterly* (Fall), 7–16.

Grunig, J. E. (1993). Image and substance: From symbolic to behavioral relationships. *Public Relations Review, 19*(2), 121–139.

Grunig, J. E. (2006). Furnishing the edifice: Ongoing research on public relations as a strategic management function. *Journal of Public Relations Research, 18*, 151–176.

Hamelink, C. (2006, July). *Communicating about Europe.* Paper presented at BledCom, Lake Bled, Slovenia.

Heath, R. L. (1980). Corporate advocacy: An application of speech communication perspectives and skills—and more. *Communication Education, 29*, 370–377.

Heath, R. L. (2000). A rhetorical perspective on the values of public relations: Crossroads and pathways toward concurrence. *Journal of Public Relations Research, 12*(1), 69–92.

Heath, R. L. (2001). A rhetorical enactment rationale for public relations: The good organization communicating well. In R. L. Heath (Ed.), *Handbook of public relations* (pp. 31–50). Thousand Oaks, CA: Sage.

Hiebert, R. E. (1966). *Courtier to the crowd: The story of Ivy Lee and the development of public relations.* Ames: Iowa State University Press.

Holmström, S. (2004a). *Grænser for ansvar: Den sensitive virksomhet i det refleksive samfund* [Limits for responsibility: The sensitive business in the reflective society]. Doctoral dissertation no. 41/2003, Roskilde Universitetscenter.

Holmström, S. (2004b). The reflective paradigm of public relations. In B. v. Ruler & D. Verčič (Eds.), *Public relations and communication management in Europe: A nation-by-nation introduction to public relations theory and practice* (pp. 121–134). Berlin: Walter de Gruyter.

Holmström, S. (2005). Reframing public relations: The evolution of a reflective paradigm for organizational legitimization. *Public Relations Review, 31*(4), 497–504.

Ihlen, Ø., & van Ruler, B. (2007). How public relations works: Theoretical roots and public relations perspectives. *Public Relations Review, 33*(3), 243–248.

Jensen, H. R. (2003). Staging political consumption: A discourse analysis of the Brent Spar conflict as recast in the Danish media. *Journal of Retailing and Consumer Services, 10*(2), 71–80.

Larsson, L. (2007). Public trust in the PR industry and its actors. *Journal of Communication Management, 11*(3), 222–234.

Latour, B. (1987). *Science in action: How to follow scientists and engineers through society.* Cambridge, MA: Harvard University Press.

Leydesdorff, L. (2003). *A sociological theory of communication: The self-organization of the knowledge-based society.* Boca Raton, FL: Universal.

Luhmann, N. (1993). *Legitimation durch Verfahren.* Frankfurt, Germany: Suhrkamp. (Original work published 1969)

Lyotard, J. F. (1979). *La condition postmoderne* [The postmodern condition]. Paris: Editions de Minuit.

Marchand, R. (1998). *Creating the corporate soul: The rise of public relations and corporate imagery in American big business.* Berkeley, CA: University of California Press.

Moloney, K. (2000). *Rethinking public relations: The spin and the substance.* London: Routledge.

Moloney, K. (2005). Trust and public relations: Center and edge. *Public Relations Review, 31*(4), 550–555.

Nørbech, T. (1997). Et nytt sosiologisk paradigme? [A new sociological paradigm?]. In A. Nilsen (Ed.), *Miljøsosiologi: Samfunn, miljø og natur* [Environmental sociology: Society, environment and nature] (pp. 212–227). Oslo, Norway: Pax Forlag.

Pickard, J., & McGregor, R. (2008, April 3). Beijing seeks PR advisers on Tibet. *Financial Times*. Retrieved April 10, 2008 from http://ft.com

Pieczka, M. (1996). Paradigms, systems theory and public relations. In J. L'Etang & M. Pieczka (Eds.), *Critical perspectives in public relations* (pp. 124–156). London: International Thomson Business Press.

Pieczka, M. (2006). Paradigms, systems theory, and public relations. In J. L'Etang & M. Pieczka (Eds.), *Public relations: Critical debates and contemporary practice* (pp. 333–357). Mahwah, NJ: Erlbaum.

Pratt, C. B. (1994). Hill & Knowlton's two ethical dilemmas. *Public Relations Review, 20*(3), 277–294.

Stauber, J., & Rampton, S. (1995). *Toxic sludge is good for you! Lies, damn lies, and the public relations industry.* Monroe, ME: Common Courage.

Thompson, J. B. (1995). *The media and modernity.* Stanford, CA: Stanford University Press.

Tye, L. (2002). *The father of spin: Edward L. Bernays and the birth of public relations.* New York: Henry Holt. (Original work published 1998)

van der Meiden, A., & Fauconnier, G. (1994). *Profiel en professie, inleiding in de theorievorming van public relations* [Profile and profession, introduction in the formulation of public relations theory]. Leiden, the Netherlands: Martinus Nijhoff.

van Ruler, B., & Verčič, D. (2005). Reflective communication management: Future ways for public relations research. In P. J. Kalbfleisch (Ed.), *Communication Yearbook* (Vol. 29, pp. 239–274). Mahwah, NJ: Erlbaum.

Verhoeven, P. (2008). The mediatization of organization theory. In W. Donsbach (Ed.), *The international encyclopedia of communication* (pp. 3044–3047). Oxford, UK: Wiley-Blackwell.

Watzlawick, P. (1976). *How real is "real"? Confusion, disinformation, communication.* New York: Random House.

Wehmeier, S. (2006). Dancers in the dark: The myth of rationality in public relations. *Public Relations Review, 32*(3), 213–220.

Zyglidopoulos, S. C. (2002). The social and environmental responsibilities of multinationals: Evidence from the Brent Spar Case. *Journal of Business Ethics, 36*, 141–151.

Chapter 17

Commentary
Linking Sociology with Public Relations— Some Critical Reflections in Reflexive Times[1]

Günter Bentele and Stefan Wehmeier

Abstract

The chapters in this book look more at the effects of public relations communication than at how public relations takes place, and they look at reflexivity and reflective modes rather than emphasizing effectiveness or efficiency. The texts are neither easy to read nor do they address practical public relations issues, but they do offer the open minded reader new insights into the realm of public relations. We believe that it will be both necessary and fruitful to think further along these lines, in order to compare the different approaches and to analyze where they do in fact have commonalities and incommensurabilities. The potential of these sociological approaches seems to be even broader than has been shown so far.

This book, edited by Øyvind Ihlen, Betteke van Ruler, and Magnus Fredriksson, challenges the knowledge that is produced by most public relations scholars. When one looks at public relations textbooks it seems clear what public relations is about: it is a management oriented communication practice that can be strategically planned, tactically executed, and empirically evaluated. It has roots in rhetoric, is organization based, and well established in Western democracies (Cutlip, Center, & Broom, 2006). It is not that this book denies those elements, but it questions the role public relations plays in society (Heath, 2006). To make it short: The chapters look more at *effects* of public relations communication than how it is done and it looks at reflexivity and reflective modes rather than emphasizing effectivity or efficiency. The chapters are neither easy-to-read nor practical but they do offer the open minded reader new insights into the realm of public relations The sociological perspectives range from macro- to mesotheory and from postmodernity to postcolonialism. Consequently, while this edited volume has an inherent diversity, there are many connections, such as those between the concepts of trust and legitimacy, which are central to most of the papers.

Ulrich Beck

The paper on Ulrich Beck, one of the most productive German sociologists in the 1980s and 1990s, and one whose work is known to a wider public, tries to apply the concept of reflexive modernity to public relations. While using Beck's differentiation between modernity and late modernity, Fredriksson tries to draw a sociohistoric picture of the development and genuine function of public relations. But the picture is not dense enough to make it completely convincing. In contrast to Holmström's sociohistoric sketch of public relations based on Luhmann, the role public relations plays in the development of reflexive modernity is less elaborately worked out. It is noted that public relations has become a managerial tool while society is confronted with the pitfalls of modernity, and that public relations can be seen as a means by which corporate bodies gain legitimacy and trust. But the question is not asked, and it is not spelled out, how public relations itself plays a vital role in transforming modernity to a reflexive modernity. We agree that public relations is interested in gaining "discursive control over our perceptions on risks and their consequences" (p. 92). However, the examples given to demonstrate this process are examples taken from Beck and not from public relations research that is linked by the author to the theory of reflexive modernity. The opposite happens when it comes to the term *mediatization*. Fredriksson clarifies that this concept is not used by Beck but states that it can be understood as an example of how mass media and other symbolic means are integrated in reflexive modernity. That might be true but in our view the concept of mediatization is too loosely coupled with Beck's theory that focuses mainly on the consequences of a modernization of modernity and less on the purely symbolic character of politics, an aspect that has been analyzed in depth by other scholars (Sarcinelli, 1987). More convincing is the part about public relations as a tool for subpolitics. Here, Fredriksson claims that to fully apply the theory of Beck to public relations a perspective that turns away from formal organizations and formal strategies would be useful. In social networks public relations techniques are often used with a sense of irony and creativity. Especially on the Internet, counterpublics or loosely coupled social communities reinterpret public relations messages in order to criticize the official message or in order to give it a new meaning (Malchow & Schulz, 2008).

Peter L. Berger

Peter L. Berger, one of the most distinguished living sociologists, has dealt with many general questions of social analysis and he especially has got an international profile with his works on the sociology of religion and the sociology of knowledge and culture. Probably he would be astonished to read that his work is seen as a theoretical basis for public relations, crisis communication in particular. It is not possible, of course, to deduce concrete rules of crisis management and crisis communication from his writings. But Berger's social constructionist perspective—like similar perspectives of other sociologists—can give insights into the fact that social reality and especially crisis never is a phenomenon "out there," a phenomenon only in the "outer world," but that social reality has to be seen more realistically as constructed by human beings, and that language and interpretation plays an important role in this process. We doubt that there are scholars nowadays who don't see and realize this social construction of the social world, of social reality, which leads to social structures, organizations, and institutions; society in itself predefines for us that "fundamental symbolic apparatus with which we grasp the world, order our experience and interpret our own existence" (Berger, 1963, p. 117).

Of course, a crisis cannot be seen as an independent entity in the "outer world." Crises should and must always be seen as social processes in which different social actors play decisive roles. Even if we look at crises that result from natural events like earthquakes, floods, and volcanic eruptions, the particular crisis itself can be analyzed only as a social and communicative process in which the crisis itself and its component parts are defined and therefore "constructed" socially. An example from Germany can demonstrate the decisive role that language, interpretation, and sense making play in crises and crisis communication.

In 1993, when the chemical company Hoechst was faced with the effects of a chemical accident in which tons of poison were released, and moreover could be seen in neighborhood gardens as a yellow colored slime, the company used the phrase *less toxic*, a term that was common on an often used chemistry scale. But when workers in white hazmat suits arrived to clean up the gardens, the media and those in the neighborhood of the Hoechst facility realized that *less toxic* was the same term used to designate insect repellents. Then a certain discrepancy became apparent between the lay interpretation of "less toxic" and the chemists' use of the term. This "misunderstanding" clearly amplified the crisis. If the communication managers responsible had been aware of sense-making processes and different interpretations of a given term by different constituencies, this crisis could have been avoided (Kepplinger & Hartung, 1995). The writings of Peter L. Berger cannot give concrete instructions for crisis communication, but they can help us to become more sensitive to the issue that every crisis, whatever its nature, is always also a social process, in which language and interpretation play decisive roles.

Pierre Bourdieu

As noted by Øyvind Ihlen, Pierre Bourdieu has to date rarely influenced public relations theory building. One reason for this situation might lie in the fact that Bourdieu is discussed to a greater degree in Europe and known better in rather "soft" social sciences—parts of sociology, cultural anthropology, or cultural science—rather than in "harder" parts of sociology, which primarily work by and with empirical studies and which use middle range rather than grand theories. On the other hand, Bourdieu himself was not only the author of many new or newly interpreted concepts and theories; he also conducted a lot of empirical fieldwork, using qualitative and also mathematical methods for his studies.

Øyvind Ihlen focuses his chapter primarily on three of Bourdieu's basic concepts: habitus, field, and capital and on the importance of the five concepts of institutionalization as well as four types of capital: economic capital, knowledge capital, social capital, and symbolic capital. Ihlen shows that these concepts can open new perspectives for questioning and analyzing public relations phenomena. To give an example: The degree of institutionalization of any organization influences the forms of communication or public relations of that organization; the amount of economic capital also influences or determines the possibilities of organizational communication, and the personal or corporate reputation is narrowly connected with the *symbolic capital* in the meaning. These are all concepts used by Bourdieu. We do not deny here that many of Bourdieu's concepts can inspire a new perspective on public relations phenomena and the questions Ihlen puts in this context may lead to further insights. It should, however, be mentioned that the conceptual framework offered by Bourdieu seems to be less concrete than that offered by other theoretical approaches. Ihlen states that Bourdieu's sociology offers a "perspective on public relations...that is more realistic than the prevailing theories of the discipline" (p. 62). If this statement can be understood in the sense that a conflict based model can be seen as more realistic than a consensus based model, we would agree with such a position.

Michel Foucault

In their chapter about the French sociologist and philosopher Michel Foucault, Judy Motion and Shirley Leitch apply three central dimensions of Foucault's work to public relations: discourse, power/knowledge, and subjectivity. Given the functional and positivist dominance in PR research, Foucault is rarely used in public relations theory building. However, Leitch and Motion highlight that his central concerns—the production of meanings, the strategies of power, and the propagation of knowledge—belong to the core of public relations communication processes. By focusing on these concerns the authors broaden academic public relations in two ways. First, the organizational mesoperspective is broadened to a meso–macro perspective in which the role of public relations in society is highlighted. Second, not only the actions and reactions of the organization are analyzed but also the communicative interplay between organizations and stakeholders. Discourse is manifest in "systems of thought that determine what could be said and who could speak" (p. 86). A similar concept is known in the sociology of science as "styles of thought" (Fleck, 1980), which have an impact on both research topics and methods. Motion and Leitch argue that PR practitioners influence, create, or transform the systems of thought that shape how we think about things. "Discourse may be contested, resisted, or transformed by any discourse actor but this work often falls to public relations practitioners" (p. 94).

The questions at hand are: How is discourse transformed and who is able to transform it? This point is highlighted in the next dimension: power/knowledge: When public relations practitioners deploy successful discourse strategies, the resulting discursive change "may achieve hegemonic status" (p. 88), an outcome the authors describe as "common sense." The example they give is the shift from the Keynesian to the neoliberal economic hegemony, which, according to the authors, was accompanied by powerful public relations activity. More recent examples can be found; for instance, the neoliberal campaign "new social market economy" in Germany: Since 2000, there has been an attempt by mostly conservative managers, politicians, and scholars to change the German mindset, which remains strongly related to the social market economy introduced in Western Germany after 1945. This social market economy represents a moderate form of capitalism, buffered by a large social net. The initiative tries to change this stance by claiming the "social is, what accomplishes jobs." In so doing, the term *social* is transformed into a capitalist meaning that is freed from welfare connotations. While systems theory inspired authors like Ronneberger and Rühl (1992) to highlight the welfare-oriented function of public relations, Motion and Leitch argue that public relations practitioners establish a common sense of particular truths by virtue of power.

At the organizational level, the work of Foucault can be taken to describe a different form of corporate identity that is not functional and not top-down. Instead, it is subject to the discursive practices of an organization's members. This concept goes beyond business oriented philosophy and connects corporate identity with ethnomethodology. In Germany, this method is used by historians to describe culture and identity in firms (Götz, 2000).

In sum, this perspective brings fresh ideas to public relations theory building. However, we disagree with the authors' conclusion that "public relations shifts from the discourse domain of business…,to the discourse domain of politics, where it is understood as a power effect that produces and circulates certain kinds of truths" (p. 98–99). We think that it shifts to the domain of sociology where it can be understood as a power effect that produces and circulates certain kinds of truths in certain fields of society.

Anthony Giddens

The work of Anthony Giddens is rarely used in public relations theory building. However, attempts have recently been made to apply structuration theory to public relations (Jarren & Röttger, 2004; Zerfaß, 2004) and related fields such as environmental reporting (Buhr, 2000). Regarding this issue, Jesper Falkheimer focuses mainly on three areas:

- the importance of storytelling, shared meanings, and sense making in the entire organizational communication process;
- the idea of public relations as a communication system that is constructed by all organization members—in contrast to the view of public relations as a functional subsystem of organizations;
- the view of public relations as an ideological communication force that leads to mere replication of social structures as well as to change and transformation.

The good thing about these perspectives is that they could broaden, if not shift, the research in public relations from a functional and positivist perspective to a qualitative and ethnomethodologist one, which would be very welcome. Less welcome is the fact that the social constructionist perspective of this approach seems to be more grounded in the work of Karl Weick than in the work of Anthony Giddens. A combination of Weick and Giddens might be more fruitful because Giddens's work relates more to the forming and changing of social structure at the macrolevel while Weick focuses more on the micro- and mesolevels of individuals and organizations (Weick, 1979).

Falkheimer challenges the open systems perspective of public relations that is used by Cutlip et al. (2006) and others. He argues that structuration theory focuses more on describing than prescribing the role of public relations, which in open systems theory is identified as a response system, "especially used towards conflicting publics" (p. 8). Falkheimer criticizes systems theory for modeling organizations as stable entities, trying only to maintain their structures. Instead, structuration theory underlines both the reproduction and the transformation of structures. Public relations is seen as a force that serves to maintain or to change the organization's dominant ideology. We agree with this position. However, it should be noted that the open systems model is not state of the art systems theory. In more advanced approaches social systems are not perceived as stable but as complex and changing (Busch & Busch, 1992; Holmström, chapter 10, this volume; Luhmann, 1984).

When it comes to Giddens's concept of late modernity, Falkheimer, like Holmstrøm, uses the term *reflexivity*. However, the meaning they give to the term differs: By focusing on social context, ethics, and social responsibility, Falkheimer's reflexivity is more comparable to Holmström's reflection. Due to the fact that in late modernity people are disembedded from many social realities, they have to trust expert systems like the medical and legal professions. Falkheimer suggests that public relations might be such a profession too. Its function is to create trust and legitimacy. To sum up, the work of Giddens (like the work of Luhmann) provides us with a sociohistorical explanation of why public relations evolved. Furthermore it challenges (as does the work of Luhmann) the functional understanding of systems theory and its application in public relations theory. However, in the end, we agree with Falkheimer's opinion: "A skeptic, and I would not totally disagree, would say that the structuration theory describes something simple in a very complicated way" (p. 112–113).

Jürgen Habermas

Jürgen Habermas's theories have already been used in some approaches to develop different public relations theories. It seems to be obvious that Habermas's theory of society, his approach to the structural transformation of the public sphere (Calhoun, 1992; Habermas, 1991), or his theory of communicative action, can serve as a profound theoretical basis from which to reflect on the historical development of public relations, different functions of public relations in society, or different communicative styles of public relations. Pearson (1989), for example, developed some fundamental thoughts about the ethics of public relations, going back to Habermas's idea of the "ideal speech situation" and his theory of communicative action, and, in particular, his concept of "discourse," which is connected with the concept of the "ideal speech situation" (Bowen, 2005). This ideal is a "contrafactual" expectation and requirement for factual discussions and dialogues.

Habermas (1984) argues that we need this requirement to a certain degree in order to communicate in reality, although we know that every dialogue and discussion is limited in respect of time and space, although we know the ideal of the ideal speech situation. Burkart (1993, 2005) takes these theoretical elements of Habermas's theory of communicative action and develops a normative theory of "consensus oriented public relations" (COPR), which is an interesting approach and one that can guide the work of practitioners. With Burkart's approach—which we see as a type of practical oriented, normative, middle range theory—it seems to be possible to reflect different dimensions and different phases of a practical communication process between organizations and specific publics, and through reflection of this process to try to develop more awareness about the process itself. By making the participants conscious of these different dimensions and phases in an organization's communication process it seems to be possible to improve the control of such processes, not by one-way communication, but through dialogue between the participants in such a process. Unfortunately, only one case study has been connected so far with Burkart's model—the case of a planned landfill in Austria (Burkart, 1993)—as Burkart mentions (chapter 8, this volume). This model should be applied in other cases, and in other countries, to test its practical value.

As mentioned before, there are also other aspects of Jürgen Habermas's writings which could be applied to public relations theory, especially his early thoughts on the functioning of the public sphere (Habermas, 1991), ideas which he has now developed further (Habermas, 2006) and which seem to be very useful for developing PR theory in a macrosocietal context. As far as we can see, Habermas revised his original highly critical point of view concerning public relations and, to mention one example, understands lobbyists in their societal function as being parallel to politicians or actors of the civil society.

Niklas Luhmann

The distinction between reflexivity and reflection and its impact on public relations is the central topic of Susanne Holmström's paper. Holmstrøm gives some insights into the complex systems theory of Niklas Luhmann. Like Parsons, Luhmann prefers nonnormative grand theory. His sociological reasoning focuses on the differentiation of self-creating (autopoietic) social systems. Self-creating social systems have specific communicative filters through which the world is recognized and the overwhelming environmental complexity is reduced. As a result of the self-creating process being regulated by internal communicative filters, external control and regulation of social systems are almost impossible to achieve.

By highlighting Luhmann's distinction between reflexivity and reflection Holmström sketches the emergence of public relations in modernity and builds a framework for analyzing PR practices. According to Holmstrøm, in the age of reflexivity organizations take their own worldview for a given. Public relations activities spread the organizational truth as the only truth that is relevant. Organizational decisions and organizational communication underlie a functional primate. Organizations see themselves as possessing natural social responsibility—a perspective, Ganesh termed "organizational narcissism" (2003, p. 558). On reflection, however, organizations recognize that their environment is polycontextual.

Each individual system has a different worldview and no one system is superior to another, a view that produces both uncertainty and a new form of public relations, one in which it is the task of PR to constantly legitimate organizational actions to diverse stakeholders. Gaining trust turns out to be one of the central aims of public relations activities, because trust is a mechanism to reduce uncertainty and complexity. The functional concept of direct control is detached by concepts of context regulation and polycontextualism.

This theoretical approach to public relations provides us with a sociological frame for seeing the stages of PR development in a broader societal context. Further, it matches with some theories of the middle range that already exist; for example, the theory of public trust (Bentele, 1994). It also has connections to other papers in this volume; for instance, the paper on Weber (legitimacy and legitimation) and the paper on Giddens (trust in expert systems).

However, we do have some critical comments: Some of the ideas presented in this paper can be traced back to scholars other than Niklas Luhmann: The notion of the reflective organization that is able to realize polycontextuality goes back to Heinz von Foerster and his concept of second order cybernetics (Foerster, 1993). The concept of context regulation originates in sociocybernetics (Bühl, 1989; Busch & Busch, 1992). Furthermore we challenge the duality of reflexivity and reflection as a distinction that is able to identify the empirical reality. In reflexivity, selfishness prevails while in reflection, social responsibility is an inherent part of public relations. Organizations question their own identity, role, and responsibility. This duality is not able to describe modes that are in between. There is evidence that many organizations merely try to appear reflective. They see very clearly that society expects them to be responsible. But by knowing this they try to do both—be responsible in some areas yet remain 19th-century capitalists in other areas. The case of British Petroleum (BP) might exemplify this strategy. BP was very successful in creating the slogan "beyond petroleum." In a simple way stakeholders got the idea of a refined global player, which nowadays cares for the environment and for the people. But this image was recently deconstructed as a half-truth when due to poor safety standards BP workers died in an accident. Consequently "beyond petroleum" was transformed in public communication to "beyond safety" (Pitzke, 2007). While BP's external communication and inventions in clean technologies showed the mode of reflection, its internal security measures have been on the level of reflexivity. To sum up, we believe that the distinction between the reflexive and the reflective stage is an appropriate tool to describe processes analytically, but that it fails to describe reality, which is neither white nor black, but grey.

Erving Goffman

Like Jürgen Habermas, Erving Goffman is seen by most sociologists and many other scientists as a classic scholar in sociology. Many of his concepts—for example, the concepts of impression management and framing—have turned out to be very fruitful and capable of inspiring many analyses not just in sociology, but also in social psychology, communication, and media research. The concept of frame and the approach(es) of frame analyses (Scheufele, 2003) have, in particular, proved to be fruitful for analyzing communicative situations in interpersonal and in mass media communication. Goffman's (1959) "dramaturgical approach"—originally developed in and primarily for the interpersonal context—seems to have been a rich source of inspiration for the analysis of several phenomena on public relations practice and it must be seen, therefore, as an important theoretical approach for public relations research.

Catrin Johansson (chapter 7) focuses on four key concepts of Goffman's theory: impression management, framing, footing, and face. She demonstrates that these concepts can be very useful when analyzing interaction and communication in organizational contexts. As regards the concept of impression management, Johansson argues that this concept "has so far only been studied in relation to organizational crises" (p. 129). While this assertion may be valid for the English literature, the concept of "impression management" has been applied to public relations in the German context (Piwinger & Ebert, 1999). Rosumek (2003) analyzed portrayal photography as an instrument of organizational impression management. In another example, Biel (2003) analyzed the presentation of the CEO at the annual general shareholders' meeting, his verbal and nonverbal performance, the staging of the stage itself and the general auditorium setting, and the similarities with real stage performances. The differentiation between frontstage and backstage and the entire metaphorical dramaturgical approach seem to be very well suited to analyzing situations and contexts which involve organizational, but at the same time public, communication with interpersonal aspects. Deekeling and Arndt (2006) have looked at CEO communication and the staging of the CEO in public or organizational settings. In conclusion, it can be said that Goffman's conceptual framework has already demonstrated its fruitfulness for analyses of public relations practice, especially on a microlevel. It should be applied to more cases, instruments, and communicative situations during the coming years as many other instruments could be analyzed in a similar way.

Bruno Latour

Piet Verhoeven concentrates on the actor-network theory (ANT) that was launched by Bruno Latour and Michel Callon approximately 30 years ago. Most of Latour's work is grounded in the sociology of science. Latour focuses on the construction or the fabricating of scientific knowledge. Verhoeven tries to connect this concept of construction to public relations. And this is quite inspiring.

However, the claim that a constructivist perspective is not frequently used in public relations research is not entirely true. German public relations research in particular includes constructivist perspectives of public relations (Jarchow, 1992; Merten & Westerbarkey, 1994; Kückelhaus, 1998). While these approaches mainly concentrate on constructivism as a theory of cognition, Latour's constructivism focuses on the world that is not given but made by the interaction of actors (humans) and objects (nonhumans). For Verhoeven, ANT can be used to study the role public relations plays in constructing a reality through discursive interaction. If we look at the field of science and science communication this becomes obvious: Wine makers, for instance, are interested in the impact of red wine on health. Results of studies that are done in this field have to be communicated not only in order to communicate the results, but also to demonstrate responsibility. Public relations practitioners are at the core of this communication process; they frame and translate science into communication for wider publics. By doing this they construct a reality, they frame facts in specific ways.

By using Latour's five types of controversies (nature of groups, nature of actions, nature of objects, nature of facts, nature of study) Verhoeven sketches how reality is fabricated in a situational and contextual perspective. But in contrast to Burkart's consensus oriented public relations, ANT cannot be understood as explaining how public relations should be practiced. Instead of a practical and normative orientation, ANT offers scholars a way to study public relations. "A network," Verhoeven says, "is not a thing out there but a concept, a tool to help describe something" (p. 178). The use of the five types of controversies leads Verhoeven to the claim that "concepts like nature, society, the social, but also facts, truth, being right or being wrong are the result and not the cause of the settlement of controversies" (p. 179). We agree, but we would add that communication is a process in which facts, truths, and so on are the result *and* the cause of the settlement of controversies.

Although the constructivist perspective is not a new concept, the

ANT-version of constructivism has so far not been linked with public relations. This perspective seems to be promising due to the fact that it can be used to locate the public relations practitioner in a network of different dimensions and to describe and analyze how he or she is involved in the process of reality construction. The ANT perspective can be linked to neoinstitutional analysis of organizational fields (DiMaggio & Powell, 1983) as well, and it can be combined with processes of sense making. Verhoeven's approach places public relations communication not in a strategic but in an interpretive setting: he does not speak of diffusion processes when talking about public relations but of translation processes like Czarniawska and Joerges (1996) would do.

Leon Mayhew

Politics are at the center of Mayhew's theory. His final work *The New Public* was published in 1997, and he died three years later after a long illness. The motivation to write this book came in 1988, during a several month period of bed rest (Mayhew, 1997, p. ix), while he watched and read about the American television election campaign that year. The fact that sociologists are regularly watching television and building theories on the basis of such a media use, probably is a very rare occurrence and therefore such approaches should be taken seriously. The New Public is understood as a situation in which communication specialists dominate the public sphere. This perspective of course is directly linked and combined with a perspective and analyses of public relations. Public relations is a part of Mayhew's approach.

To mention some critical arguments: Mayhew doesn't see public relations up close, but has a distant perspective. In comparison to the realistic picture of political communication and consulting in particular, including the analysis of U.S. presidential campaigns, public relations is not reconstructed very precisely, neither its origins or its structures. Although the theory is based on valuable observations and evaluations, it is not empirically tested so far, and the historic–empirical depth is lacking to a certain degree.

Moreover, the theory is also built primarily from a U.S. perspective, although it is integrated with Habermas's historically founded theory (structural change of the public sphere), which was built primarily in an European context. Mayhew's sociological approach seems to be valid primarily in a U.S. context. So in European contexts the communication techniques, employed by these communication specialists of the New Public cannot be seen as "historically rooted in commercial promotion" (Mayhew, 1997, p. 4). It seems that the historical development of public relations in general in Europe had not been influenced by advertising (as Habermas also states), but much more by the development of the media system and, connected with this, by the development of certain styles of press information, released by press departments.

Many of Mayhew's statements would have been validated empirically and historically. His approach is inspiring, but many statements have to be proved and also elaborated in historical and systematic public relations research.

Robert Putnam

The concept and the theory of social capital developed by Harvard scholar Robert D. Putnam, not much older than 10 years, has become popular not only in the United States and not only in political science, but also in some European countries and in other social sciences. Although the term *social capital* has been used at least since 1916, by Lydia Judson Hanifan, many social theorists like Norbert Elias, Theodor W. Adorno, Pierre Bourdieu, and James S. Coleman used this term in their approaches to analyzing social resources which can be linked to social relationships and social networks.

Of course, and this is shown by Vilma Luoma Aho's chapter on Putnam, his approach can be interesting for public relations scholars, because he concentrates on organizational forms of social capital and because his thinking contributes to a kind of metatheory of public relations. Yet some critical arguments concerning the general approach of Putnam, and also concerning the applicability of this approach to public relations theories should be mentioned. First of all, it has to be stated that the basic term *social capital* has limitations and only makes sense in a theoretical framework and in societal analyses which use the term *capital* and therefore distinguish between different forms of "capital." This kind of analysis is fundamentally based in economics rather than communication. There are some arguments that the exchange of goods and the building of economic capital might be seen as being important to communication between human beings. The term *social capital*, although not very precisely defined by Putnam, generally makes sense. But it is doubtful that social capital can be understood as a derivative of economic capital.

Social trust, especially the erosion of social trust, plays a very important role in this approach. Trust is a key category for public relations theories because organizations of all kinds are forced to maintain, build, and rebuild trust. But the phenomenon of trust in Putnam's approach is understood (and reduced) to social trust; that is, interpersonal trust which is built in social networks. In media societies, however, trust in publicly perceivable persons (e.g., politicians, CEOs), organizations (e.g., political parties, companies), and systems (e.g., the health system of a society, its political or economic system) is built publicly;

that is, in a complex process of public communication which can and should be analyzed by communication scholars. Trust processes in this perspective are processes of building and losing "public trust." Trust factors which can be analyzed theoretically and empirically, which have to be constructed and communicated by PR practitioners, and which are interpreted by journalists, play a decisive role. So public relations and journalism can be seen as "trust intermediates" (Bentele, 2008) that are working together (and sometimes against each other) and who are bound to each other in an inescapable way. The processes of building, gaining, maintaining, and losing public trust are a very important part of establishing trust and have to be kept in mind when the erosion of trust is analyzed.

Dorothy E. Smith

While the postcolonialism of Gayatri Spivak can be read as a feminist approach, too, Lana F. Rakow and Diana Iulia Nastasia present remarks about a feminist theory of public relations. In their chapter about the feminist sociology of Dorothy E. Smith, Rakow and Nastasia draw six different lines of feminist theory with postcolonial feminism as one of it. Lana Rakow and Diana Nastasia want to emphasize that, by working with Smith's concept, it is the aim to develop a feminist theory *of* public relations rather than a feminist theory *for* public relations. What does that mean? The authors argue that it is one thing to take gender systems, women's identities, power relations, and social injustice for granted, as is the case in existing feminist theories for public relations, but it is another thing to illuminate, analyze, and criticize these concepts "with the goal of benefiting women and ultimately, all people" (p. 253). The first critique we have is that the general section about different lines of feminist theory and the current use of feminist theory in public relations research is too long. It takes up more than half of the text. As a consequence, the potential of Smith's feminist approach seems to be underdeveloped. The authors claim that the benefit of Smith's position is the combination of epistemological and social issues in feminist thought. Further on they say that core concepts like the differentiation between "mothertongue" and "fathertongue" as well as "bifurcated consciousness" would be very important for a feminist theory of public relations. However, these concepts remain kind of vague and they are more used to criticize dominant feminist discourses in public relations than to build a new feminist theory of public relations. On the other hand, the authors give some answers to the question of how a feminist theory of public relations could look or at least what questions should be asked:

> Men's and women's work in the profession of public relations has
> been an issue for numerous feminist public relations theorists, yet

women's labor to maintain the language and culture of men at the intersection of patriarchy and capitalism, and at the intersection of multiple forms of racism and colonialism, have not been approached by feminist public relations scholars. (p. 269)

By citing Smith the authors say that public relations scholarship should break the "circle of men" and write (feminist) theories from outside this circle. However, one question arises: If all people are born into and socialized within the circle of men, how to break out? There is one statement we definitely agree with: "Feminist public relations scholarship in a critical note will make the consequences not the efficacy of public relations practices its object of inquiry" (p. 269). We believe that public relations scholars rarely look at public relations from a critical perspective and we hope that this chapter and this entire book will be a starting point to do that more often. Finally, we agree with Rakow and Nastasia's idea that by relying on Smith's feminist theory, scholars can try to generate models for mapping how institutions should respond to the needs of publics rather than working with models in which people respond to the needs of institutions, "no matter how symmetric the intent of public relations practitioners" (p. 270).

Gayatri Chakravorty Spivak

Let us begin this part of the commentary with a brief story: We wanted to update our knowledge by rereading some of the works of Gayatri Chakravorty Spivak. We found six of her books in the Saxon Library in Dresden and we thought: ok, let's get them all. So we went into this huge building, having the shelf marks listed and set out to collect her books. We expected the books would be on one shelf, but we were totally wrong. It took almost an hour to track them down because one was located in literary studies, one in sociology, one in English studies, one in philosophy, and so on. The story demonstrates that Gayatri Spivak publishes in many disciplines; she not only speaks many languages but also many disciplinary languages. Mohan Jyoti Dutta, who has written this chapter, is an expert in Spivak's work. His chapter is well structured as he tries to combine the main topics that Spivak promotes with public relations. Dutta's main focus is to describe the promotion of U.S. democracy and the public relations of global corporations within the critical framework of postcolonialism. Spivak's work, Dutta emphasizes, offers entry points for questioning the very rhetoric of "sustainable development," "corporate social responsibility"... and democracy promotion. According to Dutta these terms become rhetorical weapons because they are framed by Western or colonial thought. For example, by citing Spivak he argues that democracy promotion does not mean that the U.S. government is really interested in activist movements in so called third world countries. Following Dutta, the U.S. government is only interested in rebuilding these countries in a Western style.

Also the claim that stakeholder communication would represent stakeholders is challenged by Dutta using Spivak's postcolonial and Marxist theory. For Dutta, stakeholder communication models are lacking power dynamics; international corporations, he argues, only serve the neoliberal model. Neocolonial interests are transported through public relations. Sure, especially in Old Europe we sometimes have a feeling that something of this is true. But what about the evidence—or is evidence only a rhetorical tool of a Western science model? Dutta cites his own works as providing some evidence, but nothing else. As inspiring as the framework is, it could and should be better empirically grounded.

Some more problems are manifested in the use of central terms such as *dominant coalition*. Each time Dutta uses the term ("The dominant public relations coalition"; "the dominant economic logics"; "the dominant discursive spaces"; "the dominant public relations literature") it is not explicated. Another example is Dutta's critique of the term *sustainable development*. He claims that sustainable development is an example of "PR-speak," used to silence resistance (a core concept in the work of Spivak). But is this critique really appropriate when it is not clarified that the origins of the term are in forestry and the ecological protest movement? It looks as though Dutta on the one hand criticizes mainstream public relations practice and research for being blind and only serving neoliberal ideas and on the other hand he is blindly promoting activist strategies against this "hegemonic" frame.

Further on we are not totally convinced that the postcolonial scholar should work with activist movements in creating openings for emancipation through continual reflections and critique, as Dutta demands. Does that mean public relations scholars should work together with Attac or Greenpeace and other movements that have communication specialists acting no differently from neoliberal public relations managers? We don't think so. The main role of the scholar should still be: observing, describing, analyzing, criticizing, but not being part of a movement. That would only diminish his or her trustworthiness. Although, however, we have criticized some aspects of this framework, Dutta's chapter is definitely worth reading; it maybe oversimplifies reality, but it makes the reader look at core concepts of public relations from a different standpoint.

Max Weber

Arild Wæraas makes one very obvious connection to classic public relations thinking and practice by focusing on the concept of legitimacy and legitimation. Some scholars see this concept as the core function of public relations practice (Ronneberger, 1977). By stating legitimacy as the core function of PR these scholars use systems theory and neoinstitutionalism as theoretical frames. However, Wæraas reminds us that it was Max Weber who introduced the concept. The author argues: For Weber, any organization must gain support for a particular myth about itself and cultivate the belief in its own right to exist. If you look at public relations today, practitioners as well as theorists believe that it is very important to have a story to tell and to create myths (Posner-Landsch, 2006). Margot Wallstrøm, EU-commissary for communication, points out that its failure to have such a story was one main reason why support for the European Convention was lacking (Volkery, 2007).

Of course, Weber's theories are more related to the realm of politics, administration, and formal bureaucracy, but it is legitimate to broaden this perspective. All organizations, Wæraas argues, even corporations, depend on voluntary compliance to be successful. The author focuses primarily on the concept of charismatic legitimation. He argues that public relations plays an important role in creating brands like Apple and Harley Davidson that have not only mere customers but also true fans or believers. Myths and stories are socially constructed. People want to see something behind the mere corporation; they want to let brands guide their life, and so they believe in what they are told about a brand and tell others what they believe. But social construction also implies the possibility of deconstruction: The "greening" of British Petroleum (see above) is one such example and the "greening" of Ford and its deconstruction is another (Luke, 2001). Consequently, to become myths, stories have to have a true core. There is one criticism we have to make: The rise of charismatic organizational legitimation in our times is based on Wæraas's assumption that the rational order has declined. We only partially agree with this. This assumption might be true in many parts of society, but in public relations it is not. The rise of the myth and story-driven charismatic organization that is based on emotional intelligence is only one side of the coin.

Look, for example, at initial public offerings: The equity story has to be unique; it needs emotion and charisma. But when it comes down to day-to-day business, stockholders do not want to see vision alone; they want to see cash and rational business plans, strategies and tactics. And to give them what they need the organization has to create another myth: the myth of rationality (Wehmeier, 2006). This myth consists of, for instance, showing stockholders that the organization uses the latest control inventions such as balanced scorecards. The objective is to convince stockholders to believe in the rationality and efficiency of the organization.

Concluding Remarks

In 2001, David McKie complained about the "insularity" of public relations research (p. 76). This book can help to build bridges between the island called public relations and the mainland that is called society. There are bridges to many sociological key concepts, such as symbolic interactionism, structuration theory, critical theory, feminism, post-colonialism, and actor-network-theory. It is especially the link from organizational public relations studies to the full range of macro- and microapproaches of sociology that is illuminating. In sociology itself this micro–macro link was buried for a long time. Robert King Merton's (1968) statement that we should look for theories of the middle range instead of searching for a catch-all sociological grand theory had the effect on U.S. sociology of diminishing interest in general theories. Not long ago this changed, as Turner and Boyns (2006) point out. There seems to be a need to look at society as a whole and by thinking about what role public relations plays in producing, changing, and reproducing societal structure (Heath, 2006) sociological questions and public relations theory building can be brought together.

It is enlightening and useful to look at the different theoretical approaches that are collected here. We believe that it will be as necessary as it is fruitful to think further along these lines, in order to compare the different approaches and to analyze where they do in fact have commonalities and incommensurabilities. The potential of these sociological approaches seems to be even broader than shown so far, and other aspects of these theories, which are not mentioned in the chapters, could further inspire public relations theory building. Further on, most of these approaches can inspire theory building at a macrolevel. Public relations always takes place on an organizational level, in other words a mesolevel, but public relations does have a function for society in general. Habermas, Luhmann, and other authors dealt with in this volume have developed theories of society, theories in which certain functional subsystems (the economic system, the political system, but also the media) have certain societal roles or functions. For this reason, it might be worth trying to model public relations as a social system in society. Public relations can be seen as a functional social system that provides organizations as well as individuals with legitimacy and trust if—to use Holmstrøm's analytical distinction—it is done in a reflective way. But it might be a source of distrust as well, if it is framed in the mode of reflexivity—then it will be part of a risk producing reflexive modernity.

Note

1. A previous version of this chapter was published as: Applying sociology to public relations: A commentary, in *Public Relations Review 33*(3), 2007.

References

Bentele, G. (1994). Öffentliches Vertrauen: Normative und soziale Grundlage für Public Relations. [Public trust. A normative and social basis for public relations] In W. Armbrecht & U. Zabel (Eds.), *Normative Aspekte der Public Relations* [Normative aspects of public relations] (pp. 131–158). Opladen, Germany: Westdeutscher Verlag.

Bentele, G. (2008). *Trust of publics.* In W. Donsbach (Ed.), *The international encyclopedia of communication* (pp. 5180–5184). Malden, MA: Blackwell-Wiley.

Berger, P. L. (1963). *Invitation to sociology. A humanistic perspective.* Garden City, NY: Anchor Books.

Biel, B. (2003). Die Jahreshauptversammlung als Inszenierung [The sociologic systems theory: Lines of development]. In G. Bentele, M. Piwinger, & G. Schönborn (Eds.), *Kommunikationsmanagement: Strategien, Wissen, Lösungen* [Communication management: Strategies, knowledge, solutions]. Neuwied, Germany: Luchterhand.

Bowen, S. (2005). Ethics of public relations. In R. Heath (Ed.), *Encyclopedia of public relations* (pp. 294–297). Thousand Oaks, CA: Sage.

Bühl, W. L. (1989). Entwicklungslinien einer soziologischen Systemtheorie [The sociologic systems theory: Lines of development]. *Annali di Sociologia,* 5(2), 13–46.

Buhr, N. (2000). A structuration view of the initiation of environmental reports. *Critical Perspectives on Accounting, 13,* 17–38.

Burkart, R. (1993). *Public Relations als Konfliktmanagement: Ein Konzept für verständigungsorientierte Öffentlichkeitsarbeit.*[Public relations as conflict management: A concept for a consensus oriented public relations practice]. Vienna, Austria: Braumüller.

Burkart, R. (2005). Verständigungsorientierte Öffentlichkeitsarbeit [Consensus public relations]. In G. Bentele, R. Fröhlich, & P. Syszka (Eds.), *Handbuch der Public Relations* [Handbook of public relations] (pp. 223–240). Wiesbaden, Germany: VS.

Busch, J. A., & Busch, G. A. (1992). *Sociocybernetics. A perspective for living in complexity.* Jeffersonville, IN: Social Systems Press.

Calhoun, C. (Ed.). (1992). *Habermas and the public sphere.* Cambridge, MA: MIT Press.

Cutlip, S. M., Center, A. H., & Broom, G. M. (2006). *Effective public relations* (9th ed.). Upper Saddle River, NJ: Prentice-Hall.

Czarniawska, B., & Joerges, B. (1996). The travel of ideas. In B. Czarniawska-Joerges & G. Sevon (Eds.), *Translating organizational change* (pp. 13–48). Berlin, Germany: de Gruyter.

Deekeling, E., & Arndt, O. (2006). *CEO-Kommunikation: Strategien für Spitzenmanager* [CEO-Communication: Strategies for top managers]. Frankfurt, Germany: Campus.

DiMaggio, P. J., & Powell, W. W. (1983). The iron cage revisited: Institutional isomorphism and collective rationality in organizational fields. *American Sociological Review, 48,* 147–160.

Fleck, L. (1980). *Entstehung und Entwicklung einer wissenschaftlichen Tatsache* [The genesis and development of a scientific fact]. Frankfurt, Germany: Suhrkamp. (Original work published 1935)

Foerster, H. v. (1993). *Wissen und Gewissen* [Knowledge and conscience]. Frankfurt, Germany: Suhrkamp.

Ganesh, S. (2003). Organizational narcissism: Technology, legitimacy, and identity in an Indian NGO. *Management Communication Quarterly, 16*(4), 558–594.

Goffman, E. (1959). *The presentation of self in everyday life.* Garden City, NY: Doubleday.

Götz, I. (2000). Erzählungen als Indikatoren für Unternehmenskultur [Stories as indicators for corporate culture]. In C. Wischermann, P. Borscheid, & K.-P. Ellerbrock (Eds.), *Unternehmenskommunikation im 19. und 20. Jahrhundert* [Corporate communication in the 19th and 20th century] (pp. 227–244). Dortmund, Germany: Gesellschaft für Westfälische Wirtschaftsgeschichte.

Habermas, J. (1984). *The theory of communicative action: Vol. 1. Reason and the rationalization of society.* Boston: Beacon Press.

Habermas, J. (1991). *The structural transformation of the public sphere: An inquiry into a category of bourgeois society.* Cambridge, MA: MIT Press.

Habermas, J. (2006). *Political communication in media societies—Does democracy still enjoy an epistemic dimension?* Paper presented at ICA Annual Convention.

Heath, R. L. (2006). Onward into more fog: Thoughts on public relations research directions. *Journal of Public Relations Research, 18*(2), 93–114.

Jarchow, K (1992). *Wirklichkeiten, Wahrheiten, Wahrnehmungen* [Realities, truths, perceptions]. Bremen, Germany: WMIT.

Jarren, O., & Röttger, U. (2004). Steuerung, Reflexierung und Interpretation: Kernelemente einer strukturationstheoretisch begründeten PR-Theorie [Control, reflexivity and interpretation. Core elements of a structuarlist PR theory]. In U. Röttger (Ed.), *Theorien der Public Relations* [Theories of public relations] (pp. 25–45). Wiesbaden, Germany: VS.

Kepplinger, H. M., & Hartung, U. (1995). *Störfallfieber: Wie ein Unfall zum Schlüsselereignis einer Unfallserie wird* [The heat of breakdowns: How a breakdown becomes a key event for a series of technical breakdowns]. Freiburg, German: Alber.

Kückelhaus, A. (1998). *Die Konstruktion von Wirklichkeit* [The construction of reality]. Wiesbaden, Germany: Westdeutscher Verlag.

Luhmann, N. (1984). *Soziale Systeme* [Social systems]. Frankfurt, Germany: Suhrkamp.

Luke, T. (2001). SUVs and the greening of Ford. *Organization & Environment, 14*(3), 311–335.

Malchow, T., & Schulz, J. (2008). Emergenz im Internet. Protest, Konflikt und andere Formen verständigungsloser Kommunikation im Internet [Emergence on the internet. Protest, conflict and other forms of non-understanding communication on the internet]. In C. Thimm & S. Wehmeier (Eds.), *Organisationskommunikation online. Grundlagen, Praxis, Empirie* [Organizational communication online. Foundations, practice, empiricism] (pp. 61–81). Frankfurt, Germany: Peter Lang.

Mayhew, L. H. (1997). *The new public: Professional communication and the means of social influence.* Cambridge, UK: Cambridge University Press.

McKie, D. (2001). Updating public relations: "New Science," research paradigms and uneven developments. In R. L. Heath (Ed.), *Handbook of public relations* (pp. 75–92). Thousand Oaks, CA: Sage.

Merten, K., & Westerbarkey, J. (1994). Public Opinion und Public Relations [Public opinion and public relations]. In K. Merten, S. J. Schmidt, & S. Weischenberg, (Eds.), *Die Wirklichkeit der Medien. Eine Einführung in die Kommunikationswissenschaft* [The reality of mass media. An introduction to communication science] (pp. 188–211). Wiesbaden, Germany: Westdeutscher Verlag.

Merton, R. K. (1968). *Social theory and social structure.* New York: Free Press.

Pearson, R. (1989). *A theory of public relations ethics.* Unpublished doctoral dissertation, Ohio University, Athens, Ohio.

Pitzke, M. (2007). Das BP-Inferno [The BP inferno]. *Spiegel* online. Retrieved January 17, 2007, from http://www.spiegel.de/wirtschaft/0,1518,460234,00.html.

Piwinger, M., & Ebert, H. (1999). Impression Management: Zur Selbstdarstellung von Personen und Institutionen [Impression management: Self presentation of people and institutions]. *PR Forum, 5*(1), 15–19.

Posner-Landsch, M. (2006). *Story telling—story selling.* Cologne, Germany: Herbert von Halem Verlag.

Ronneberger, F. (1977). *Legitimation durch Information* [Legitimation through information]. Germany: Nürnberg.

Ronneberger, F., & Rühl, M. (1992). *Theorie der PR* [Theory of public relations. A sketch]. Wiesbaden, Germany: Westdeutscher Verlag.

Rosumek, L. (2003). Auffallend gut: Portraitfotos als Instrument des Impression Management [Striking good: Mugshots as an instrument of impression management]. In G. Bentele, M. Piwinger, & G. Schönborn (Eds.), *Kommunikationsmanagement* [Communication management. Strategies, knowledge, solutions]. Neuwied, Germany: Luchterhand.

Sarcinelli, U. (1987). *Symbolische Politik. Zur Bedeutung symbolischen Handelns in der Wahlkampfkommunikation der Bundesrepublik Deutschland* [Symbolic poilitics. The meaning of symbolic action in German election campaigns]. Opladen, Germany: Westdeutscher Verlag.

Scheufele, B. (2003). *Frames–Framing–Framing-Effekte* [Frames, framing, framing-effects]. Wiesbaden, Germany: Westdeutscher Verlag.

Turner, J. H., & Boyns, D. E. (2006). The return of grand theory. In J. H. Turner (Ed.), *Handbook of sociological theory* (pp. 353–378). New York: Springer.

Volkery, C. (2007). Der EU fehlt die Story [EU communication without a story]. *Spiegel* online. Retrieved January 17, 2007, from http://www.spiegel.de/politik/ausland/0,1518,459792,00.html

Wehmeier, S. (2006). Dancers in the dark: The myth of rationality in public relations. *Public Relations Review, 32*(3), 213–220.

Weick, K. (1979). *The social psychology of organizing.* Reading, MA: Addison-Wesley.

Zerfaß, A. (2004). *Theorie der Unternehmenskommunikation* [A theory of corporate communication] (2nd ed.). Wiesbaden, Germany: VS.

Contributors

Dr. Günter Bentele is full professor for Public Relations at the University of Leipzig, Germany. Previously he has held positions at University of Bamberg and the Free University of Berlin. He has also served as the president of the German Association for Communication and Media Studies and of EUPRERA. He is author and co-author of 16 books, has edited and co-edited 21 additional books, and authored more than 280 scientific articles. In 2004 he was named the "PR personality 2004" by the German Association for Public Relations, and in 2007 he was honored, out of more than 700 nominees, with the German award "Professor of the Year."

Dr. Roland Burkart is associate professor at the Department of Communication, University of Vienna, Austria. He has a postdoctoral lecture qualification, holds an honorary doctorate from the University of Sofia (Bulgaria), and he served as a guest-professor at several universities. His main research interests and teaching activities are communication theory, mass media effects, audience research, and public relations. He has published several articles and books, one of which is *Kommunikationswissenschaft: Grundlagen und Problemfelder* (*Communications: Basics and fields of problems;* Wien, Köln, Böhlau/UTB).

Dr. Mohan Jyoti Dutta is associate professor of health communication, public relations and mass media in the Department of Communication at Purdue University. Currently, he serves as the Director of Graduate Studies in the Department of Communication. He has published *Communicating Health: A Culture-centered Approach* (Polity Press), and has edited *Emerging Perspectives in Health Communication: Meaning, Culture, and Power* (Routledge) with Dr. Heather Zoller. Dutta has published over 80 articles in scholarly journals and book chapters and was selected as the 2006 Lewis Donohew Outstanding Scholar in Health Communication.

Dr. Jesper Falkheimer is Head and Associate Professor at the Department of Communication Studies, Campus Helsingborg, Lund University in Sweden. Among other topics, he has done research in crisis communication, place branding and communication strategy. He has published in journals such as *Public Relations Review, Journal of Contingencies and Crisis Management,* and *Event Management* and published several books.

Dr. Magnus Fredriksson is a lecturer at University or Gothenburg and former director of the program in Communication Management at the University West, both in Sweden. He has published in Swedish public relations anthologies, written for two government commission reports, and been chronicler for the Swedish Public Relations Association. Fredriksson is co-founder of the Nordic research network LOKE and a board member of the Swedish Association for Media and Communication Research. His current research focus is on corporate identity, social responsibility, and rhetoric.

Dr. Mats Heide is Associate Professor at the Department of Communication Studies at the Lund University in Sweden. Mats is director of the department's master program in strategic communication. His research is focused on crisis communication in change processes, organizational learning and strategic communication in a broad sense. He has published several books and articles in journals such as *Journal of Contingencies and Crisis Management, Corporate Communications: An International Journal,* and *Noridom Review.*

Dr. Susanne Holmström is Adjunct Professor, Institute for Communication and Business Studies at Roskilde University, Denmark. She initiated the research program of "the reflective paradigm," is co-initiator of the public relations study at Roskilde University, co-founder of the Nordic research network LOKE, and has served on the boards of EUPRERA, and The Danish Public Relations Association, among others.

Dr. Øyvind Ihlen is a Post Doctoral Research Fellow at the Department of Media and Communication, University of Oslo; and Associate Professor at Hedmark College, both in Norway. He has published in several anthologies as well as journals such as *Public Relations Review, Journal of Public Relations Research, Journal of Communication Management, International Journal of Strategic Communication, Corporate Communications: An International Journal, Journal of Public Affairs,* and *Business Strategy and the Environment.* His current research focuses on communication and corporate social responsibility.

Dr. Catrin Johansson is an Associate Professor in the Department of Media and Communication at Mid Sweden University. She has published in journals such as *Corporate Communications: An International Journal, Nordicom Review,* and *Public Relations Review.* Her research belongs to organizational communication and public relations, focusing communication between managers and employees; communication on change; and roles, status and legitimacy of PR practitioners. She has co-authored the first Swedish book on Organizational Communication and initiated and arranged Communiqué—a Swedish research conference on organizational communication.

Dr. Vilma Luoma-aho is a lecturer and researcher of Organizational Communication and PR at the Department of Communication, University of Jyväskylä, Finland, and Adjunct Professor at the University of Vaasa, Finland. Lately, she has been a visiting scholar at the Innovation Journalism program at Stanford University, California. She has lectured at Annenberg School for Communication, University of Southern California, as well as at the University of Leipzig, Germany. Luoma-aho is the author of several book chapters and articles on the topics of reputation, social capital, and stakeholder relations, and has published in journals such as *Corporate Reputation Review, The International Journal of Public Sector Management,* and *Tiedotustutkimus.* Her current research focuses on organizational legitimacy and innovations.

Dr. Judy Motion is Professor and Research Director of the School of Management and Marketing in the Faculty of Commerce at the University of Wollongong, Australia. Judy is a New Zealander who has held positions at the University of Auckland and the University of Waikato. Her research adopts a discourse perspective to investigate communication, public relations, marketing, and public policy issues. Her research has been published in *Public Relations Review, Journal of Public Relations Research, Discourse Studies, the Journal of Communication Management, Media Culture and Society,* and *Management Communication Quarterly.*

Diana Iulia Nastasia worked as an assistant professor at the Romanian-American University and at the National School of Political Studies and Public Administration in Bucharest, Romania. She was an associate editor of the *Romanian Review of Communication and Public Relations.* Diana came to the United States as a Fulbright visiting researcher at the University of North Dakota, Grand Forks, in 2002, and since 2003 she has been a PhD student in Communication and a Graduate Teaching and Research Assistant at UND. She focuses her scholarship and service on building international understanding in various aspects of socio-cultural life, and across theoretical frameworks.

Dr. Shirley Leitch is Professor and Dean of Commerce at the University of Wollongong in Australia. Her research focus on corporate and societal discourses is interdisciplinary in character and has led to publications in the public relations, marketing, and management literatures including articles in the *Public Relations Review, European Journal of Marketing, Journal of Brand Management, Organization Studies, International Studies of Management and Organization, Science and Public Policy,* and *Human Relations.*

Dr. Lana F. Rakow is a professor in the School of Communication at the University of North Dakota and director of the university's Center for Community Engagement. She has professional public relations experience and has authored or edited numerous articles and four books on gender and communication, including *Feminist Communication Theory: Selections in Context* (with Laura Wackwitz, Sage, 2004). Lana serves on the editorial board of *Journal of Public Relations Research, Feminist Media Studies, Communication, Cultural and Critique, Journalism and Mass Communication Quarterly,* and others.

Dr. Betteke van Ruler is a professor at the Department of Communication Science at the University of Amsterdam, the Netherlands. van Ruler is a member of a number of editorial boards, among them *Public Relations Review* and *Corporate Communications: An International Journal.* In 2004–2006 she was Chair of the Department of Communication Sciences of the University of Amsterdam. She has also served as the President of the European Public Relations Education and Research Association (Euprera) and Chair of the Public Relations Division of the International Communication Association.

Dr. Richard C. Stanton teaches graduate public relations and political communication at The University of Sydney, Australia. He is the author of *Media Relations* (Oxford University Press), and *All News Is Local: The Failure of the Media to Understand World Events in a Globalized Age* (McFarland). His present research is titled *Global Shift: the Transformation of Power From Journalism to Public Relations.*

Dr. Piet Verhoeven is an associate professor at the Department of Communication Science/Amsterdam School of Communications Research (ASCoR) of the University of Amsterdam, the Netherlands. His research interests lie in organizations and strategic communication/PR and in science in the mass media. He teaches courses at undergraduate and graduate levels on corporate communications and mass media.

Dr. Stefan Wehmeier is Adjunct Professor at the Institute for Marketing & Management at the University of Southern Denmark in Odense. Before he represented the chair of communication studies at the University of Greifswald, Germany. His research interests include the development of mass media, public relations, and the application of sociological and managerial theories to communication studies. He has published in journals such as *Public Relations Review* and *International Journal of Strategic Management.*

Dr. Arild Wæraas is Associate Professor of Organization Theory at the Department of Political Science at the University of Tromsø, Norway. His research interests focus on changes in organizational identity and the expression of identity symbols. His latest research and publications relate to corporate branding and reputation management in the Norwegian hospital sector and education market.

Index

A

Accountability, 29, 34, 36, 289
Actant, 168
Activism, 57, 264, 293–297, 326, 334
Actor, 5, 9, 13
Actor/agency, 9
Actor-network-theory, 166, 358
Adbusters, 34
Adorno, T.W., 141–142, 165, 353
Aesthetics ,100, 281
Agency, 233, 291–295
    agency of objects, 177
    agency vs structure, 64, 103–115,
        335–337
    agency vs subjectivity, 89–90
Agent/system, 9
Agger, B., 257
Alcoff, L., 264, 272
Aldoory, L., 8, 254, 256, 260, 261,
        262, 263, 272
Alienation, 302
Allen, M.W., 129, 130, 136–138–227,
        259
Allen, P.G., 273
Alvesson, M., 53, 58, 64, 120, 130
Animator, 124–125, 135
Anthony, S.B., 254
Anzaldua, G., 275
Apple, 313, 317, 357
Applied communication, 4
Archaeology, 84–85, 99, 102
Archer, M.S., 107, 117
Aristotle, 214, 330
Articulation, 33, 181, 281, 284, 394,
        316
Associational life, 233
Attac, 356
Austin, J.L., 143, 160

Autopoietic, 188, 211, 348

B

Backstage, 114, 122–123, 131, 327, 350
Banks, S., 8
Baudrillard, J., 23, 218
Beck, U., 12, 21–42, 44, 58, 69, 110,
        117, 144, 145, 160, 326, 336,
        342
Benhabib, S., 258
Bennet, L., 26, 35–37
Benson, R., 9, 68
Bentele, G., 7, 11, 14, 161–159, 331,
        341–342, 344, 346, 348–350,
        352, 354, 356, 358–358
Berger, B.K., 58, 99
Berger, P.L., 43–61, 327, 332–333,
        342–343
Bernays, E.L., 6, 181, 259, 324
Bifurcated consciousness, 253,
        266–277, 354
Boorstin, D.J., 6–7
Botan, C.H., 2, 4, 127, 279–297, 335
Bourdieu, P., 6, 12, 62–82, 105, 233,
        237, 241, 325, 327, 331, 334,
        336, 344, 353
Bowen, H.R., 145, 161, 347
Branding, 97
Brands, 26, 31, 36–37, 109, 313, 357
Brante, T. ,107, 117
British petroleum / BP, 349, 357
Brown, P., 57, 125–126, 136–137
Bureaucracy, 28, 64, 313, 357
Burkart, R., 9, 13, 141–160, 328, 330,
        347–348
Burt, R., 234, 235, 237
Burton, St. J. I., 240, 245
Busch, G.A., 347, 349

Busch, J.A., 347, 349
Bush, G.H.W., 214

C
Caillouet, R.H., 129–130, 136–138
Calhoun, C., 63, 161–159, 165, 347
Callon, M., 166, 351
Carey, J., 10, 54, 112, 117
Carroll, A.B., 145, 161
Castells, M., 26
Charisma, 305–307, 312–315, 357
Charismatic Legitimation of
    Organizations, 312–314
Chatterjee, L., 284
Cheney, G., 36, 53, 77, 127, 324, 329
Chicago school, 239
Chomsky, N., 216
Christensen, L.T., 53, 77, 127, 329
Church of Jesus Christ of Latter Day
    Saints, 214
Circle of men, 253, 266, 269–272,
    277, 334, 355,
Civic engagement, 231, 233, 237
Civic virtue, 233
Civil society, 240, 288, 290, 292–293,
    348
Class, 24, 254–255, 264–265, 286–287
    system, 255, 257
    middle, 46–47
    subaltern, 294
Cline, C.G., 256, 261
Cohen, A.P., 236, 242
Coleman, J.S., 233, 237, 353
Colonialism, 255, 267, 269, 278, 283,
    285, 355
Communication technology
    (technologies), 113, 126
Communicative action, 9, 151–165,
    221, 327–328
    theory of, 143, 146–148, 151, 162,
    165, 347–348
Communitarianism, 8
Community, 56–57, 215, 231–242,
    244–245, 247
    building, 231, 237, 238, 240–241,
    285, 289
    business, 196, 200, 203–204
    relations/relationship, 56–57, 69,
    239–241, 285
Complexity, 187–192, 194, 199–200,
    207, 337, 348–349
Conger, J.A., 306, 314, 317
Consensus, 7, 62, 122, 133, 325, 344

building theory, 5
consensus oriented public
    relations, 141, 144, 147–148,
    150–156, 348, 351
Constructionism, 11, 61, 332
    social, 12, 43, 45–48, 51, 61, 106,
    109
Constructivism, 3, 8, 167, 172,
    351–352
Controversy / controversies, 166,
    168–181, 186, 232, 336, 351
Coombs, W.T., 55, 71, 104, 117, 120,
    127, 129, 309, 311, 325
Coordinated dissent, 146
Cooren, F., 173–183
Corporate communication, 4, 307,
    309
Corporate interests, 141, 289
Cosmopolitan motif, 47
Cottle, S., 6, 8, 69, 174
Cozier, Z., 104, 111–112, 117
Crable, R.E., 324
Creedon, P.J., 262
Crisis, 43–45, 50, 52–53, 55–61, 333,
    343
    communication, 43–61, 129,
    136–137, 295, 311, 333, 343
    of knowledge, 326
    of meaning, 50, 58, 6, 326
    of the public sphere, 218
    of social cohesion, 326
Critical theory, 8, 58, 83, 115, 141,
    358
Cultivating beliefs, 308, 310–311, 318
Cultivation, 89, 238, 305, 310, 311
Cultural literacy, 62, 77
Cultural theory, 8, 63, 104
Curtain, P.A., 95
Cutlip, S., 27, 240, 310, 324, 341, 346

D
Davenport, S., 88, 99
Davis, A., 2, 6, 69, 71, 73, 216, 325
Deconstruction, 1, 172, 279, 283, 300,
    357
Deconstructive vigilance, 295–296
Deetz, S.A., 5, 36, 50, 53, 57–58, 64,
    326
Democracy, 142–159, 166, 168, 171,
    225–227, 232–233, 247
    promotion, 280, 284–285, 288–290,
    355
Deontological, 2, 6

Determinism, 107, 170
Dewey, J., 11, 239–247
Dialogue, 56, 216, 284–286, 292, 294,
    347–348
  ideal type, 144
  symmetry and dialogue, 329
Diffusion, 170–171, 180, 245
Disciplinary structures, 279, 285
Discourse, 83–103, 129–130, 146–159,
    327–328, 332–334, 344–347
  analysis, 86, 91, 133, 135
  feminist, 264
  formation, 85
  colonial, 259–250, 279
  discourse of responsibility, 21, 24
  institutional, 252, 268, 272
  production, 86, 96
  ethics, 144
  theory, 9, 122
  transformation, 87, 94
Discursive control, 29, 342
Disembedding, 109–110, 113–114
Dissensus, 5, 326
Divisions of Labor, 279–280, 287, 328
Dominance, 62, 255, 257
  positions of, 64, 66
  male/masculine, 262, 267
Dominant coalition, 99, 293, 294, 356
Domination, 301, 303–305, 307,
    310–312, 318
Dozier, D.M., 5, 44, 62
Dramaturgical approach, 350
Dreyfus, H.L., 84–85, 99
Duffy, M.E., 5, 258, 324
Dukakis, M., 214
Durham, E., 8
Durkheim, E., 46, 65, 107
Dutta, M. ,8, 14, 278–282, 284–286,
    288, 290–296, 300, 328, 334,
    355–356

E
Economic capital, 66, 70–71, 76, 344,
    353
Elving, W., 174
Emancipatory politics, 278, 280, 285,
    296–297
Enron, 44
Epistemology / epistemological,
    44–46, 51, 91, 109, 168, 216
  Giddens, 105–106
  epistemology and feminism,
    264–265

Luhmann, 187, 189, 194
Essentialism, 45, 258, 271
Ethics, 9, 144, 311–312, 347
Ethnicity, 65, 256, 257, 262, 265, 279
Ethos, 89, 219, 330
European parliament, 221
Evans, J., 254
Ewen, S., 27, 44, 93, 99, 104, 117, 181,
    311, 318, 324
Exclusion, 91, 235, 266, 270–277,
    334,
Expert system, 111, 114–115, 330
Externalization, 48, 58, 106

F
Face, 119–121, 125–126, 131–132
Facebook, 226
Fairclough, N., 94–96, 99
Fairhurst, G., 120, 131
Falkheimer, J., 12, 103–106, 108–110,
    112, 114, 116–118, 330, 336,
    346–347
Farrell, D., 219–220
Fathertongue, 267–268, 271, 354
Fauconnier, G., 175, 324, 336
Fearn–Banks, K., 45
Feminism/feminist theory, 218,
    253–272, 354, 358
Ferguson, M.A., 4
Field, 62, 65, 69, 73, 82
Footing, 124–125, 131–134, 136
Foucault, M., 12, 83–102, 326,
    333–334, 336, 344, 345
Framing, 119–121, 123–124, 130–131,
    133–134, 136–137, 350
Frankfurt school, 141
Fredriksson, M., 12, 341
Friedan, B., 254
Friedman, M., 36
Frontstage, 114, 122, 350
Functionalism, 3, 105, 104, 107
Functionalist, 4, 53, 108, 115, 188
Fundamentalism, 115

G
Gaither, T.K., 95, 99, 280
Gandy, O.H., 71, 262
Geist, U., 9, 322
Gender, 252–266, 272, 327, 334
Genealogy, 84–85, 99
Giddens, A., 12, 21, 26, 34, 42, 44,
    48, 68, 103–118, 326, 327, 330,
    336, 346–347, 349

Glass ceiling, 263, 277
Goffman, E., 12, 13, 114, 119–140, 327, 332, 335–336, 350
Golding, P., 175, 324, 336
Governmentality, 86, 88–90
Gramsci, A., 88
Grant, J., 95, 99, 218, 253, 256, 258, 264–266
Greenpeace, 174, 325, 356
Grunig, J.E., 4, 9–10, 44, 57, 62, 111, 117, 145–146, 239, 244, 329, 332
Grunig, L.A., 8, 44, 62, 132, 162–163, 256–257, 261–263

H
Habermas, J., 5–7, 9, 13, 64, 105, 120, 141–165, 190, 212–213, 216–220, 224–226–227, 308, 309, 311, 326–328, 330, 336, 347–348, 350, 352, 358–358
Habits, 49, 57, 126, 224
Habitus, 65, 67–69, 327, 344
Hallahan, K., 8, 120–131, 136, 237–238, 240–241, 244–245, 247–247
Hamelink, C., 328
Harding, S., 264–266
Harley Davidson, 313, 317, 357
Hazelton, Jr., V., 4, 74, 241, 247
Heath, R.L., 8, 44, 55–56, 62, 96, 117–318, 324, 329–338, 341, 358–358
Hegde, R., 278–279
Hegemony, 88, 96, 326, 283–284, 287–288, 293–295
Heide, M., 12, 43, 109, 117, 333
Hermeneutic approach, 106
Herrschaft, 303
Hiebert, R., 329
Hill & Knowlton, 324
Hoechst, 343
Holladay, S., 104, 117, 325
Holmström, S., 9, 13, 144, 187–211, 309, 325, 330–331, 335–336, 347–348
Holtzhausen, D., 8, 95
Hon, L., 8, 132, 239, 244, 257, 262
Horkheimer, M., 141–142
Human capital, 70, 233
Human motivation, 302
Hunt, T., 9, 111, 117, 146
Hyperreality, 265

I
Ideology, 22, 46, 64, 111, 196, 283, 347
Ihlen, Ø., 1–15, 62–82, 216, 241, 323–341, 344, 364
Imperialism, 256, 259, 264, 283, 289–300
Impression management, 97, 119–123, 128–130, 136–137, 327, 350
Individual freedom, 302
Individualism, 104, 114, 193, 237, 254, 261–262, 291
Inequality, 9, 254, 328
Information processing theory, 5
Information technology, 35, 37
Informationalization, 114
Institutional ethnography, 253, 266, 270–272–277
Institutionalization, 49, 70–71, 75
International Communication Association, 228–227, 366
Internet, 36–37, 153–154, 316, 342
Interpersonal communication, 119, 122, 127–129, 137, 327, 336
Intersubjectivity, 265

J
Jahansoozi, J., 128, 132
Jenkins, R., 63, 67, 69
Jensen, I., 9–10, 143, 309, 313, 325
Johansson, C., 12, 119–120, 122, 124, 126, 128, 130, 132–136, 140
Journal of Public Relations Research, 3, 99–137–277–297–338, 364–366

K
Kant, E., 84
Kanungo, R.N., 306, 314, 317
Kavanagh, D., 219
Kent, M.L., 56, 280, 292–294–297
Knowledge capital, 70, 72, 75–76, 344
Knowledge structures, 278, 283, 286, 289, 292
Krippendorf, K., 11
Kruckeberg, D., 8, 238, 240–241–247, 289
Kückelhaus, A., 9, 11, 351

L
L'Etang, J., 8, 56, 93, 213
Landry, D., 279, 281, 285–286–297

Language, 126, 258, 332, 334–335, 343, 355
and reality, 45–46, 49–50, 53–54
and power, 63–65
of men, 268–269
Latour, B., 13, 27, 166–186, 327, 333, 336, 351
Lauzen, M., 5, 261
Ledingham, J.A., 3, 127–137, 239, 244, 246
Leeper, R., 8–9, 144, 238–240
Legal-rational, 301, 305, 307
Legitimacy, 6, 25–36, 146–160, 191–209, 301–319, 329–331, 341–358
Leicthy, G., 8, 55
Leitch, S., 12, 83–102, 128, 132, 333, 344, 345
Levinson, S.C., 125–126, 136–137
Liberalism, 259, 262
Lin, N., 73, 74
Lippman, W., 216, 218, 224
Livesey, S.M., 9, 95
Lobbying, 69, 75, 220
Luckmann, T., 12, 43, 48, 50, 58, 61, 332
Luhmann, N., 9, 13, 34, 77, 105, 167, 187–211, 326, 329, 330, 335–336, 339, 342, 347–349, 358
Lundy, L.K., 131
Luoma-aho, V., 13, 231–247
Lyotard, J.F., 23, 109, 117, 326

M
MacLean, G., 279, 281, 285–286–297
Marchand, R., 324
Marcuse, H., 141
Marx, K., 65, 107, 141, 282
Mass communication, 5, 128, 173, 214, 336
Mass opinion, 213, 217
Mass public, 212–214, 217
Material resources, 62
Materiality, 14, 278, 280, 287–288, 290
Mayhew, L., 6, 8, 9, 13, 27, 212–230, 328, 336, 352
McCombs, M.E., 70
McKie, D., 4, 8, 93, 358
McNair, B., 218
Mead, G.H., 239
Meaning, 10–11, 45–57, 124–131, 168–180, 188–197, 326–327, 332–337

production of, 83–84, 93–94
Media relations, 6, 69, 71, 128, 285, 288, 325
Media sociology, 63, 69–70, 72
Media studies, 13, 68, 117
Mediators, 32, 177, 178, 180
Meisenbach, R., 9, 144
Merten, K., 8, 9, 149, 161, 351
Merton, R.K., 358
Metrology, 170
Metzler, M.S., 309, 310
Micheletti, M., 34–36
Mickey, T.J., 8, 258
Mission statement, 132, 310
Modernism, 193
Modernity, 21–42, 50, 103–116, 194–207, 287–290, 326, 342–348
Moffitt, A., 8, 129
Moloney, K., 9, 221, 324, 331–338
Montreal school, 173
Moraga, C., 259
Motion, J., 8–9, 12, 83–102, 333, 344–345
Multiculturalism, 57, 109, 263, 265
Mumby, D., 132
Munshi, D., 8, 93, 279–280, 289–292
Murphy, P., 45, 52
MySpace, 226
Myth, 96, 304, 310, 316, 318, 326, 357

N
Nastasia, D.I., 13, 252, 325, 334, 354
Nation-state, 22, 31
Neilson, D., 95, 128, 132
Neoliberal, 96, 280–281, 285, 296–297, 328, 345, 356
New media, 218, 232
New public, 212–215, 217–220, 222, 225–227, 328, 352
New world order, 279, 280, 285
Nimmo, D., 222–224
Norris, P., 217–218

O
O'Neil, A., 8
Objectivism, 51, 64, 65, 67, 104, 327
Öffentlichkeit, 10, 142–207
Olasky, M., 5, 9
Olins, W., 36, 313, 317
Orchard, L., 216, 218
Organizational discourse, 95, 99
Organizational structure, 35, 37
Organizational subsystem, 103, 111

P

Packard, V., 218
Page, A., 309, 329
Paradigms, 3, 4, 263, 335
Parsons, T., 138, 192, 212, 328, 348
Pathos, 219
Patriarchy, 255, 256, 267–270, 272,
    327, 355
Pearson, R., 9, 144, 175, 347
Persuasive leadership, 222
Phenomenology, 48
Pieczka, M., 8, 213, 333
Pitzke, M., 349
Plasser, F., 220
Plowman, K., 8
Political advertising, 220
Political consumption, 35, 37
Political movements, 253, 282, 286,
    296, 310
Political participation, 21, 22, 25–26,
    35, 254
Political system, 30, 190, 193, 199–
    200, 206, 358
Polycontextuality, 326, 349
Postcolonial theory, 8, 279, 282, 334
Postcolonialism, 265, 287, 341,
    354–355, 358
Postmodern, 95, 97, 109, 252, 326,
    336
Postmodernism, 8, 58, 109,
    258–259–272
Postmodernity, 23, 109, 341
Potter, E., 264, 270, 272
Power, 83–99, 216–224, 252–272,
    278–296, 302–303, 323–337,
    344–346
  and language, 63–64
  symbolic, 63–64, 82, 334
  in relationships, 125–135
  and knowledge, 83–89, 93, 95–99,
    344–345
Principles of legitimation, 304, 318
Private sphere, 215, 269
Problematization, 85–86, 92–96, 253,
    266–270
Professionalization, 213
Prolocutor, 223–224
Protestantism, 302, 307
Public interest, 7, 9, 32, 94, 324, 325
Public policy, 70, 212, 215–217,
    219–227, 251, 365
Public sphere, 6–10, 142–143, 202–206,
    212–229,   327–328,   347–348

Putnam, L.L., 53, 95, 99,120–137
Putnam, R., 13, 25, 73, 231–251, 326,
    331, 336, 353

R

Rabinow, P., 84–85, 97, 99–102
Racism, 254–255, 259, 267, 269, 355
Rajeshwari, S.R., 284
Rakow, L., 13, 71, 252–272, 325, 334,
    354–355
Rampton, S., 96, 104, 117, 324–325
Raplex, 50
Raupp, J., 10, 161
Realists, 51, 332
Reciprocity, 233–234, 242, 245
Redemption of Tokens, 212–213,
    219–220, 225
Reflective paradigm/perspective, 191,
    195, 199–207
Reflexive/reflexivity, 187, 191, 196,
    197, 200–207
Relationship management, 3, 83, 93,
    97–137, 231, 239
Resistance, 87, 89, 278–297
Resources, 34–37, 62–80, 242, 280
Rhetoric of presentation, 212–213,
    217–218, 225
Rhetorical tokens 13, 214–215, 217,
    220, 226
Richards, J.R., 254
Ritual model of communication, 112
Rogers, E., 180
Röglin, C., 145, 157
Ronneberger, F., 195, 347, 357
Roper, J., 8, 95, 314
Rothstein, B., 234, 236, 242–243
Rühl, M., 9, 10, 11, 195, 345

S

Sallot, L., 2, 4
Sarr, R., 131
Scheufele, B., 130, 350
Schlesinger, P., 6, 69, 72, 221
Schumpeter, J., 219
Schütz, A., 46
Scott, G., 70, 254, 267, 302, 309
Searle, J.R., 143
Seeger, M.W., 45
Sellnow, T.L., 45, 55
Sense-making, 43, 106, 115, 333
Shell, 100, 174, 325
Shelton, B.A., 257
Shome, R., 278–279

Situated knowledge, 326, 337
Smith, D.E., 13, 99–100, 121–140,
        252–277, 326–327, 334,
        354–355
Social capital, 73–76, 231–247, 331,
        344, 353
Social constructionism, 43–61,106,
        109
Social injustice, 252, 255–260, 272,
        354
Social movements, 21, 22, 26, 34, 37,
        197, 203
Social norms, 112, 155, 201, 206, 236,
        311
Social responsibility, 198, 336, 347,
        349
    corporate; 22, 56, 280, 284, 289,
        309, 314, 316, 322, 355
    defined, 145, 203–204
Social system, 14, 46, 189–190, 211,
        268, 358
Socialization, 46–47, 50, 58, 106, 198
Sociodrama, 128
Sociology for women, 253, 266, 270,
        277
Sociology of associations, 166–168,
        171–172, 178, 180–182
Sociology of science, 168, 345, 351
Sommerville, I., 173
Spectacle, 216, 218
Spender, D., 265, 269
Spin doctors, 229, 311
Spivak, A.G.C., 14, 259, 278–300, 326,
        328, 334, 354–356
Sriramesh, K., 57, 104, 117, 291–292
Stacks, D., 4
Stanton, R., 13, 212–227, 328, 366
Stauber, J., 96, 104, 117, 324–325
Stolle, D., 34–35, 234, 242–243
Storytelling, 112, 316, 346
Strategic action, 103, 148, 190
Stretton, H., 216, 218
Structural holes, 235
Structuralism, 99, 105, 107
Structuration theory, 103–109, 111–
        113, 115–116, 346–347, 358
Subalterness, 9
Subjectivism, 64–65, 104, 327
Subjectivity, 83–86, 89–91, 295, 344
Sustainable development, 100, 204,
        283–284, 289, 355–356
Symbolic reality, 10
Symbolic spaces, 113, 114

Symbolic violence, 64
Symbols, 31, 33, 36, 90, 121, 218, 367
Symmetrical communication, 57, 196
System of Oppression, 256
Systems theory, 107, 113, 191, 262,
        345–348, 357

T
Taylor, J.R., 2, 4, 5, 173–183
Taylor, M., 56, 119, 126–128, 280, 292,
        293, 294–297, 335
Technologies of power, 90–91, 102
Technologies of the Self 89–91
Technoscience, 174, 182
Temporal dimension, 108, 111, 197
The iron cage of rationality, 307
The organic intellectual, 286
Theory of practice, 64, 67–69, 82
Thompson, J.B., 32, 256, 336
Toth, E.L., 4, 8, 96, 119, 127, 256,
        260–261,262–272, 291
Transmission view, 54
Transnationality, 109
Transparency, 36–37, 132, 157, 198
Trust, 113–114, 195–209, 232–247,
        329–331, 342–354
Truthfulness, 141, 146–147, 150–151,
        154, 156, 158–159

U
Ulmer, R.R., 45
Union carbide, 294
Unrespectability motif, 46–47

V
van der Meiden, A., 175, 324
van Ruler, B., 1–15, 104, 111, 117–118,
        161, 167, 174–175, 182, 216,
        335–341
Vasquez, G., 5, 119, 126, 128
Velvet ghetto study, 261
Verčič, D., 5, 11, 104, 111, 117–118,
        161, 167, 175, 182, 335–338
Verhoeven, P., 13–14, 166, 177, 178,
        323, 333, 336, 351, 352
Vibbert, S.L., 324
Volker Nickel, 145

W
Wacquant, L.J.D. , 62–68, 72, 75, 334
Wæraas, A., 14, 301–322, 326,
        329–330, 356–357
Weaver, C.K., 8, 9, 95

Weber, M., 14, 65, 107, 301–322, 326,
    330, 349, 356–357
Weedon, C., 253, 257, 277
Wehmeier, S., 7, 14, 331, 341–358
Weick, K.E., 52, 54, 346
Welfare state, 22, 25, 28, 30, 142, 199
Whiteness, 255, 258–259, 265

Williams, S., 56, 129
Witmer, D., 104, 111–112, 117
Women's movements 252–253, 264
YouTube, 126

Z
Zoch. L.M., 45, 55